ISBN: 9781290736916

Published by:
HardPress Publishing
8345 NW 66TH ST #2561
MIAMI FL 33166-2626

Email: info@hardpress.net
Web: http://www.hardpress.net

STANDARD

NOVELS.

N° CX.

"No kind of literature is so generally attractive as Fiction. Pictures of life and manners, and Stories of adventure, are more eagerly received by the many than graver productions, however important these latter may be. APULEIUS is better remembered by his fable of Cupid and Psyche than by his abstruser Platonic writings ; and the Decameron of BOCCACCIO has outlived the Latin Treatises, and other learned works of that author."

THE IMPROVISATORE.

COMPLETE IN ONE VOLUME.

LONDON:

RICHARD BENTLEY, NEW BURLINGTON STREET
AND BELL & BRADFUTE, EDINBURGH.

1847.

THE

IMPROVISATORE:

OR,

LIFE IN ITALY.

From the Danish

OF

HANS CHRISTIAN ANDERSEN.

BY MARY HOWITT.

LONDON:

RICHARD BENTLEY, NEW BURLINGTON STREET;

AND BELL & BRADFUTE, EDINBURGH.

1847.

THE LIFE

OF

HANS CHRISTIAN ANDERSEN.

HANS CHRISTIAN ANDERSEN is one of those men who, from their earliest youth, have had to keep up a warfare with circumstances; a man, like Burns and Hogg, who seemed destined by Fate to end their lives unnoticed in a village, and yet through an instinctive sense of their destined pre-eminence in the beautiful regions of art and literature, and sustained by an irrepressible will, have made themselves a part of the great world.

During my residence in Copenhagen, says Marmier, in the year 1837, one day a tall young man entered my room. His timid, and embarrassed, and somewhat awkward manner, might, perhaps, have displeased a fine lady, yet at the same time his friendly behaviour, and his open, honest countenance, at the first meeting, must have awakened sympathy and confidence. This was Andersen. At that very moment a volume of his works was lying on my table; an acquaintance was thus soon made. Poetry is a sort of freemasonry; they who render homage to it are related, although they may come from the opposite ends of the world; they speak a word, make a sign, and immediately they know that they are brethren. They who live together impart to each other mutually the emotions of their hearts; they who meet on foreign ground relate to each other, like pious pilgrims, by what paths they have wandered thither, and through what cities they have come. Thus, then, it happened that Andersen, after we had passed a few hours together in conversation on poetry, which, more than any thing else, has the peculiarity of unlocking the heart and calling forth mutual confidence, told me of the adverse circumstances through which he had passed, and, at my request that he would make me acquainted with the history of his life, communicated to me the following details : —

Andersen's grand-parents were, at one time, well to do in the world, and even possessed of a farm in the country. All kind of misfortunes, however, befell them; the worst of which was, that the husband lost his mind. The poor wife then removed to Odensee, and placed there her only son as apprentice with a shoemaker. The boy, full of activity, found the beginning of his life happier than his later years; he employed his hours of leisure in reading Holberg, in making toys, and in composing music.

When he was scarcely twenty, in the spring of 1804, he married a young girl who was quite as poor as himself; and so great, indeed, was their poverty, that, in going to housekeeping, the young bridegroom could not afford to buy a bedstead, and contrived to obtain one in this manner. A count was dead somewhere in their neighbourhood, and while he lay in state his coffin was supported on a wooden frame made for the purpose, and this, after the funeral, being sold, was purchased by the husband-elect, who prepared it for future family use; and yet he could not have made very great alteration in it, for many years afterwards it might still be seen covered with its black cloth.

Upon this frame, on which had rested the corpse of

the noble count, in his last splendour, lay, on the 2d of April, 1805, poor, but living, the first-born of his humble parents, Hans Christian Andersen.

When the new-born child was taken to the church to be baptised, it cried resoundingly, which greatly displeased the ill-tempered pastor, who declared, in his passion, that " the thing cried like a cat;" at which his mother was bitterly annoyed. One of the god-parents, however, consoled her by the assurance, that the louder the child cried, the sweeter he would sing some day, and that pacified her.

The father of Andersen was not without education ; the mother was all heart. The married couple lived on the best terms with each other, and yet the husband did not feel himself happy ; he had no intercourse with his neighbours, but preferred keeping himself at home, where he read Holberg's " Comedies," " The Thousand-and-One Tales of the Arabian Nights," and worked at a puppet-theatre for his little son, whom on Sundays he often took with him to the neighbouring woods, where the two commonly spent the whole day in quiet solitude with each other.

The grandmother also, who was an amiable old lady, and who bore the misfortunes of her family with Christian patience, had great influence on the mind of the boy. She had been very handsome, was kind to every body, and, besides that, was scrupulously clean in her poor clothing. With a feeling of deep melancholy, she would often tell how her grandmother had been the daughter of a rich gentleman of family in Germany, who lived in the city of Cassel ; that the daughter had fallen in love with a comic-actor, had left her parents secretly to marry him, and after that had sunk into poverty.

" And now all her posterity must do penance for her sin !" sighed she.

Young Andersen was extremely attached to this good grandmother. She had to take care of a garden at the lunatic hospital, and here, among its sunny flowers, he spent most of the afternoons of his early childhood. The annual festival in the garden, when the fallen leaves were burnt, had for him an especial charm, although the presence of the insane ladies, a few of whom were allowed to wander about, terrified him greatly. Frequently one of the old nurses would fetch him into the house, and take him into the spinning-room, where all the old ladies would praise him for his eloquence, and would recompense him for it with tales and ghost-stories, which they related with wondrous effect, so that certainly no child of his years ever heard more of suchlike histories, neither could any child be more superstitious than he was.

Among the earliest recollections of Andersen, is that of the residence of the Spaniards in Fyen, in the years 1808 and 1809. A soldier of an Asturian regiment one day took him in his arms, and danced with him amid tears of joy, which no doubt were called forth by the remembrance of a child left behind him at home, along the street, and pressed the image of the Madonna to his lips, which occasioned great trouble to his pious mother.

In Odensee, at that time, many old festivities were still in use, which made a deep impression upon the excitable temper of the boy; the corporation went in procession, with their escutcheons, through the city; the sailors also marched round in Lent, and the people made pilgrimages to the miracle-performing well of the holy Regisse.

So passed on the first years of the youth of our poet. His father, in the mean time, read industriously in his Bible, but one day shut it with the words, " Christ became a man like to us, but a very uncommon man !" Upon which his wife burst into tears, at what she called the blasphemy of her husband," which made such a deep impression upon the son, that he prayed in solitude for the soul of his father. "There is no other devil," said he, afterwards, "but that which a man bears in his own breast!" After which, finding his arm scratched one morning when he awoke, probably by a nail, his wife told him that this was a punishment of the devil, who, at least, would show him of his real existence.

The unhappy temper of the father, however, increased from day to day: he longed to go forth into the world. At that time war was raging in Germany; Napoleon was his hero; and, as Denmark had now allied itself to France, he entered himself as a private soldier in a recruiting regiment, hoping that some time or other he should return as a lieutenant. The neighbours, however, thought that it was folly to let himself be shot to death for nothing at all. The corps, however, in which he served went no further than Holstein; the peace succeeded, and before long the voluntary soldier sat down again in the concealment of his citizen-dwelling in Odensee. But his health had suffered. He awoke one morning delirious, and talked about campaigns and Napoleon.

Young Andersen was at that time nine years old, and his mother sent him to the next village to ask counsel from a wise woman.

"Will my poor father die?" inquired he, anxiously.

"If thy father will die," replied the sibyl, "thou wilt meet his ghost on thy way home."

It is easy to imagine what an impression this oracle would make upon the boy, who was timid enough without that; it was, in fact, his only consolation, on his homeward way, that his father certainly knew how such an apparition would terrify his little son, and therefore he would not show himself.   He reached home without any unfortunate adventure, without seeing the ghost of his father; and on the third day after that the sick man died.

From this time young Andersen was left to himself; the whole instruction which he received was in a charity-school, and consisted of reading, writing, and arithmetic, the two last very imperfectly.

The poor boy, at this time, gained an entrance into the house of the widow of the Pastor Bunkeflod, of Oden-see, who died in the year 1805, and whose name, on account of some lyrical productions, is known in Danish literature.   He was engaged to read aloud to the widow and her sister-in-law; and here, for the first time, he heard the appellation poet, and saw with what love the faculty which made the dead a poet was regarded.   This sunk deeply into his mind.   He read some tragedies, and then determined to write a comedy, and to become also a poet, as the deceased pastor had been.

And now, actually, he wrote a true tragedy, for all the characters lost their lives in it; and the dialogue was inter-larded with many passages of Scripture.   His two first auditors received this first work of the young poet with unmingled applause; and, before long, the report of it ran through the whole street, and every body wished to hear the tragedy of the witty Hans Christian.   But here the applause was by no means unmingled; most people laughed right heartily at it, whilst others ridiculed him.   This wounded the poor boy so much that he passed the whole night in weeping, and was only silenced by his mother's serious admonition, that if he did not leave off such folly she would give him a good beating into the bargain. Spite of the ill success of his first attempt, however, he now, unknown to any one, set about a new piece, in which a prince and a princess were introduced.   But these lofty characters threw him into great perplexity, for he did not at all know how such noble people as these conversed, imagining, of course, that it must be impossible for them to talk as other people did. At length it occurred to him to interweave German and French words into their conversation, so that the dignified language of these princely personages became a perfect gibberish, which, however, according to the opinion of the young author, had in it a something very uncommon and sublime.

This masterpiece also was introduced to the knowledge of the neighbourhood, the result of which was, that not many days elapsed before he was derided by the wild boys in the streets, who shouted, as he went by, " Look ! look ! there goes the comedy-writer ! "

But it was not alone the rude boys, but the schoolmaster also, who entirely mistook the genius which clearly betrayed itself, even in suchlike productions ; for, one day, when young Andersen presented to him, as a birth-day present, a garland, with which he had twisted up a little poem of his own writing, he blamed him for it ; and the only reward which the poor poet had for his first poetical attempt consisted of trouble and tears.

In the meantime the worldly affairs of the mother grew worse and worse ; and as the son of a neighhour earned money in some kind of manufactory, it was determined also that the good Hans Christian should be sent there. The old grandmother conducted him to the master of the manufactory, and wept right bitter tears, that the lot of her grandson should be so early that of care and sorrow.

German workmen were principally employed in the manufactory, and to them the children used often to sing their Danish songs. The new-comer, Andersen, was desired to do so, and that he did willingly, because he knew that he could produce great effect with his singing : the

neighbours had always listened when at home he sung in
the garden; and once, indeed, a whole party, who were
assembled in the garden of the rich neighbour, had admired his beautiful voice, and loudly applauded him.
Similar applause fell to his share in the manufactory.

" I can also act comedy!" said poor Andersen one day,
encouraged by their approbation, and forthwith recited
whole scenes from Holberg's comedies.   All went well for
a time, and the other boys were compelled to do his work
whilst he amused the workmen; but presently persecutions
began, and he found himself so roughly handled, even by
his former admirers, that he left the place, and flew back
weeping to his mother, praying that he might never be
sent there again.

His prayer was granted, because, said his mother, he was
not sent there for the sake of what he would get, but that
he might be well cared for while she went out to work.

" The boy must go to the theatre!" many of her
neighbours had said to her; but, as she knew of no other
theatre than that of strolling players, she shook her head
thoughtfully, and determined rather to put her son apprentice to a tailor.

Andersen was now twelve years old, was altogether
quite at a loose end at home, and devoured the contents of
every book which fell in his way.   His favourite reading
was, however, an old prose translation of Shakspeare. From
this, with little figures which he made out of pasteboard,
he performed the whole of " King Lear" and " The
Merchant of Venice."   He very rarely went to the play-
house, but as he was in favour with the man who carried
out the bills, he obtained a copy of each of these from him,
and then, seating himself in the evening before the stove,
studied the names of the various actors, and thus supplied
to every piece which was performed an imaginary text.

Andersen's passion for reading, and his beautiful voice, had, in the meantime, drawn upon him the attention of several of the higher families of the city, who introduced him to their houses. The simple, childlike behaviour of the boy, his wonderful memory, and his sweet voice, gave to him, in fact, a something quite peculiar; people spoke of it, and several houses were very soon open to him. But still the first family which had noticed him and had received him with so much sympathy, nay, indeed, who had even introduced him to Prince Christian, remained his favourites. This family was that of Colonel Höegh Guldborg, a man whose great accomplishments equalled his goodness of heart, and the brother of the well-known poet of the same name.

About this time his mother married a second time, and, as the step-father would not at all interest himself about the education of the son, our young Andersen had still more liberty than hitherto. He had no playfellows, and often wandered by himself to the neighbouring woods, or, seating himself at home, in a corner of the house, dressed up little dolls for his theatre, his mother, thinking the while that, as he was destined to be a tailor, it was a good thing that he should practise sewing; and the poor lad consoled himself by thinking that, if he really must be a tailor, he should find many beautiful pieces of cloth from which he could, on Sundays, make new dresses for his theatrical wardrobe.

At length the time for his confirmation drew nigh, for which occasion he obtained the first pair of boots he ever had in his life; and, in order that people might see them, he pulled them up over his trousers. Nor was this all his finery; an old sempstress was employed to make him a confirmation dress out of his deceased father's great coat; and with this his festal attire was complete. Never before had Andersen been possessed of such beautiful clothes; his joy over which was so great, that the thoughts of them even disturbed his devotion on the day of consecration, and caused him afterwards such reproaches of conscience, that he besought of God to forgive him such worldly thoughts; and yet, at that very moment, he could not help thinking about the beautiful creaking boots.

After the conclusion of the confirmation festival, it had been determined that Andersen was to begin his tailor-apprenticeship; but he continually besought of his mother that she would permit him to go to Copenhagen, and visit the royal theatre there. He read to her the lives of celebrated men who had been quite as poor as himself, and assured her that he also would some day be a celebrated man. Already for several years had he hoarded up in a little save-all his spare money, and this had now grown into what seemed to him the inexhaustible sum of about thirty shillings of English money. The sight of this unexpectedly large sum of money softened also the maternal heart, and she began to incline towards the wishes of her son; but yet, before she fully consented, she thought it best to consult a wise woman on his future prospects. The sibyl was accordingly fetched to the house, and after she had read the cards, and studied the coffee-grounds, the oracle spoke these memorable words: —

"*Your son will become a great man. The city of Odensee will be illuminated in his honour!*"

So good a prophecy of course removed the last impediment out of the way.

"Go, then, in God's name!" said his mother.

When, however, her neighbours represented to her how foolish it was to let the boy of fourteen years old set off to the great city in which he did not know a single soul, she replied that he let her have no rest, and that she was convinced he would soon come back again when he saw the great water which he would have to cross.

Some one had mentioned to young Andersen a certain female dancer at the royal theatre, as being a person of very great influence : he obtained, therefore, from a man universally esteemed in Odensee a letter of recommendation to this lady; and provided with this important paper, and his thirteen rix-dollars, he commenced the journey on which depended his whole fate. His mother accompanied him to the gate of the city, and here he found waiting for him the good old grandmother, whose still beautiful hair had become grey within a few weeks. She kissed, with many tears, her beloved grandson ; her grief had no words; and within a very short time the cold grave covered all her troubles.

Andersen travelled as gratis passenger by the mail as far as Nyborg, and not until he was sailing across the Great Belt did he feel how forlorn he was in the world. The discomfort of a sea-voyage, even though short, would make him feel this if nothing else did. As soon as he came on shore in Zealand, he stepped to a spot that lay apart, and, falling on his knees, besought of God for help in his forlorn condition.

He rose up comforted, and went on now uninterruptedly for a day and a night through cities and villages until on Monday morning, the 5th of September, 1819, he saw the towers of Copenhagen. He had travelled, as before, free of cost, through the good-nature or compassion of the drivers of the mail, and now before he reached the gate of the city was obliged, of course, to dismount, and, with his little bundle under his arm, entered the great city.

The well-known Jews' quarrel, which at that time ex- tended from the south to the north of Europe, had broken

out here the very evening before, and all was in commotion.

His journey had cost him three rix-dollars, and, with
the remaining ten in his pocket, the young adventurer took
up his lodgings in a public-house. His first ramble into
the city was to the theatre, and with astonishment he surveyed the magnificent building, walked round it, and
prayed fervently that it might soon open itself to him, and
that he might become a skilful actor therein. At that time
certainly he had no presentiment that ten years afterwards
his dramatic work would be received with applause, and
that he would address the public for the first time.

On the following day, dressed in his confirmation suit,
he betook himself, with his letter of introduction in his
hand, to the house of the all-potential dancer. The lady
let him wait a long time on the steps; and when at length
he was permitted to enter her presence, his awkward and
naïve behaviour displeased her so much, that she regarded
him as insane, more especially as she knew nothing of the
gentleman who had addressed the letter to her.

After this unsatisfactory attempt, Andersen turned his
steps towards the director of the theatre, requesting from
him some appointment; but here also his efforts were
unsuccessful.

"You are too thin for the theatre," was the answer
which he obtained.

"Oh," replied Andersen, "if you will ensure me one
hundred dollars, I will soon become fat!"

But the director would not enter into arrangements on
these terms, and dismissed the poor supplicant, with the
information that they were not in the habit of engaging any
but people of education.

The poor lad went his way truly dejected in spirits: he
knew no creature who could give him counsel or comfort,

no human being on whose breast he could weep. He thought on death, and the terror of this thought drove him back to God.

"When every thing," said he, "goes quite unfortunately, then God will help me ; it is written so in every book that I ever read,—and in God I will put my trust !"

He then went out and bought a ticket for the gallery for "Paul and Virginia." The scene in the second act, where the lovers part, affected him so much that he burst into loud sobs, which drew upon him the attention of those who sat near to him. They spoke kindly to him, and inquired who he was. Their friendly sympathy unlocked his whole heart, and he told all that related to himself — who he was, and whence he came, and that his love to the theatre was not less than Paul's love to Virginia, and that he certainly should become as unhappy as Paul if he did not obtain some little post in the theatre. They all looked at him in amazement.

The next day brought no more cheering prospects, and his money had before long all melted away to one single dollar. What was he to do ? Either he must work back his passage in a vessel to his native city, and be laughed at there for his pains when he arrived, or else he must put himself here to some handicraft trade, which would be his fate if he returned to Odensee.

A joiner at that moment wanted an apprentice, and to him Andersen introduced himself, but here again it did not succeed : after a short time poor Andersen was persecuted by the journeymen, who found him an object of sport, and the end was like the working in the manufactory at Odensee ; and, with tears in his eyes, he parted from his master.

As now with a heavy heart he was walking through the streets crowded by his fellow-beings, yet without the consciousness of having one friend among them, it occurred to him that nobody as yet had heard his fine voice. Full of this thought, he hastened to the house of Professor Siboni, the director of the Royal Conservatorium, where a large party was that day at dinner, among whom were Baggesen the poet, and the celebrated composer, Professor Weyse. He knocked at the door, which was opened by a very lively young housemaid, and to her he related quite open-heartedly how forlorn and friendless he was, and how great was his desire to be engaged at the theatre, which the good-natured young serving-woman immediately retailed again to the company, who became curious to see the little adventurer, as Baggesen called him. He was now ordered in, and was desired to sing before the company, and to declaim scenes from Holberg. Whilst he was so doing, he came to a passage which brought to his remembrance his own melancholy circumstances, and he burst into tears. The company applauded him.

" I prophesy," said Baggesen, " that he will turn out something some day ; only don't become vain when the public applauds thee !" said he to him.

On this, Professor Siboni promised that he would cultivate Andersen's voice, in order that he might make his *début* at the Theatre Royal, and, highly delighted, the poor lad left that happy house.

The next day he was ordered to go to Professor Weyse's, who entered with the kindest sympathy into the forlorn condition of the poor youth, and who most nobly made a collection for him, which amounted to seventy dollars. After this Professor Siboni took him to his house, and half a year was spent in elementary instruction. But Andersen's voice was in its transition state ; and, by the end of this time, seemed entirely gone. Siboni, therefore, counselled him to return home and put himself to some handicraft trade. And once more poor Andersen stood again in the world as hopeless as at first. Yet, even in his apparent misfortune, there lay the seed of a better progress. He recalled to his memory, at this dark moment of need, that there lived in Copenhagen a poet named Guldborg, the brother of the kind colonel in Odensee. To him Andersen bent his steps, and was kindly received by him. When Guldborg saw that the young native of Odensee could scarcely write a word correctly, he offered to give him instruction in the Danish and German tongues, and made him a present of the profits arising from a little work which he had just published. The noble-minded Weyse, Kuhlau, and other respectable men, also extended to him a helping hand.

Andersen now hired a lodging for himself in the city : he lived with a widow, who seemed reasonable in her charges ; and yet, after all, she was a hard, unfeeling woman, who was not ashamed to fleece the poor lad of twenty dollars for his month's charges, although she allotted to him only a disused store-closet for his accommodation. He gave her, however, the required sum, and received from her now and then a few half-pence when he did errands for her in the city. Yet nobody could feel themselves happier than the young Andersen in his present condition, for Professor Guldborg had engaged the actor Lindgren to instruct him, whilst one of the solo-dancers had taken it into his head to make a dancer out of him. Thus he went daily to the dancing-school, made his appearance in one or two ballets, and, as his voice also was beginning to recover itself, he had to sing in chorus too.

Thus then actually he had become one of the theatrical corps, and nothing was now wanting but his *début* and the acquisition of the fixed salary belonging to it. Always, however, the slave of superstition, he determined with

himself that, if now, on this new-year's day, when he
came to the theatre, he were able there to declaim a piece,
he would hold it to be a certain token that, in the course
of the following year, he should be advanced to the dignity of an actor.   But, alas ! when he reached the house,
he found that, on this day, it was closed, and only by accident a small side-door was open. Through this he crept,
trembling as if he had something evil in his mind; onward he went to the dark stage, where not a creature was
to be seen, and, falling down upon his knees on the lamp-
stage, uttered the Lord's Prayer, the only thing, and the
best thing, which then offered itself to his mind, and,
after that, returned home comforted.

He always kept hoping that, by degrees, his fine voice
would wholly again return to him; yet that was scarcely
to be expected, because the poor youth, through want of
money, was almost always obliged to go with torn boots
and wet feet; neither had he any warm winter clothing.
He was now already sixteen years old, yet he was quite a
child; so much so, that he spent the whole evening alone
in his chamber, busied in making dolls for his little
theatre, which he dressed from the patterns which he was
in the habit of begging from the shops.

In this manner wore away his best years for learning;
and many a sorrowful day had he yet to spend before a
milder period arrived.   Guldborg practised him in the
Danish style, and, before long, he produced a rhymed
tragedy, which, from the facility and freedom of its language, won the attention of Ohlenschläger, Ingemann, and
others. But no *début* was permitted to him in the theatre;
they excused him from any further attendance at the
dancing-school, or from singing in chorus, as it was
wished, they said, that he should dedicate his time to
scientific studies; yet nobody did any thing for him in

this respect, and it was as much as the poor lad could do to obtain enough to keep body and soul together. In his great need he wrote a new dramatic piece, in the hope that it would be accepted; but the hope was disappointed, and, notwithstanding that, he persevered in a second and a third attempt.

Just at this time the distinguished Conference-councillor Collin, no less distinguished as an officer than universally esteemed for the goodness of his heart, became director of the theatre, and this wise and clear-sighted man soon perceived what slumbered in the young poet. It is true that he thought but little of his dramatic works; but he went immediately to the king, and obtained permission from him that young Andersen should be sent at government charges to one of the learned schools in the provinces, and became from this moment a father to him in the noblest sense of the word.

Andersen now went from dancing-lessons, romances, and dolls, to mathematics, Latin, and Greek; and the youth of seventeen had to place himself among boys of ten years old to learn the first elements of these things. The school-rector in the meantime treated him with great severity, pronounced him to be devoid of all intellectual ability, and so greatly forgot himself, and mistook so entirely the duty of a public instructor, as to make the poor youth the object of ridicule among his schoolfellows, which produced in him such a state of mental suffering as within a short time must have been the death of him, had he not been rescued from this misery. Two years had thus been spent here, when one of the teachers went to Copenhagen, and informed the Conference-councillor Collin how unkindly and negligently poor Andersen was treated by the rector. No sooner was the good man made acquainted with this than he took Andersen immediately from the school, and placed him in the hands of a private tutor. A year after this, in 1828, Andersen was academical citizen of Copenhagen.

Within a few months from this time appeared his first literary work in print, under the title of "A Journey on Foot to Amack" (a small island on which a part of Copenhagen is built), a humorous piece, which met with such great success, that within a very few days a second edition was called for, and after that a third. The young poet was now received every where with the most flattering attention. The Danish translator of Shakspeare, Commander Wulff; the celebrated naturalist, Orsted, received him at once as the friend of their house; whilst he found quite a paternal home with the Collin family.

" The Journey to Amack " was succeeded by a dramatic work, an heroic vaudeville, entitled, " Love on the Nicholas Tower," which was brought on the stage and reviewed by Professor David. After this, Andersen passed his second academical examination, in which he obtained the highest honours.

In a short time afterwards he published his first collection of grave and humorous poems, which met with great favour from the public. At school, Andersen had been so often accused of weakness, that afterwards he was frequently ashamed of his best feelings; and not seldom, when he had written a poem from the full, noble emotions of his soul, he would, as a sort of excuse for himself, write a parody upon it; hence, in this volume, there are frequent instances of this kind, which displeased many, who saw that a mind thus directed would be injurious to itself as well as others.

In the summer of 1830, Andersen made a journey through the Danish provinces, and, after his return, published a new collection of lyrical poems, under the title of

" Fancies and Sketches," which showed that a great change had taken place in him ; and, as if he would avenge himself for his former self-ridicule, these poems all bore the impression of a quiet melancholy. Many poems in this volume were translated into German ; and one poem in particular, " The Dying Child," is said to be possessed of such extraordinary pathos and beauty that it has been translated into German, French, English, Swedish, and Greenlandish. The poor Greenlanders, indeed, sing it when out on their desolate seas in their fishing excursions ; and it is to be found printed in their song-books.

This poem I have never met with ; indeed, I regret not being possessed of this volume of Andersen's poems ; however, I will subjoin here a translation of one which Chamisso has rendered into German, and which is so full of tenderness and beauty, that I am sure the reader will thank me for it : —

" THE MILLER'S JOURNEYMAN.

" In this mill I was a servant, even when I was a boy ;
And here have fled for ever my days of youthful joy.
The miller's gentle daughter was kind and full of grace,
One seem'd to read her gentle heart whilst looking in her face.

" In the evening oft so trustfully she sat down by my side ;
We talk'd so much together, I could nothing from her hide:
She shared with me my trouble, in my pleasure she had part ;
One only thing conceal'd I — the love within my heart.

" I think she might have seen it ; if she had loved she would ;
For there needs no word, no word at all, to make love understood !
I spoke unto my foolish heart — ' Forego it, and be still !
For thee, poor youth, such joy comes not — comes not, and never will ! '

" And whilst I thus was grieving, she said, with tenderest tone,
' Ah, why art thou so alter'd, and why so pale hast grown ?
Thou must again be joyful ; thy sorrow gives me pain ! '
And thus, because I loved so much, did I my love restrain.

" One day, beside the rocky wall, she took by me her stand,
Her eyes flash'd clearer light, and she laid on mine her hand,
' Now must thou wish me joy,' she said, ' must greet me as a bride,
And thou, thou art the first to whom I would my joy confide ! '

" The while I kiss'd her hand I conceal'd from her my face ;
I could not speak a single word, my tears flow'd down apace ;
It seem'd as if had perish'd, in that same hour of woe,
My thoughts and all my hopes in the deepest depths below !

" That eve was the betrothal, and even I was there ;
They set me in the chiefest place, beside the happy pair ;
They clink'd their merry glasses, they sung their songs of glee ;
I made myself seem happy, lest all the truth should see.

" Upon the following morning, my head spun round and round ;
How stupid and perplex'd was I where all were happy found !
What wanted I ? one only thing ! 'Twas wonderful, yet true,
And they all loved me — she herself, and he, the lover, too !

" They were so kind unto me, but my woe they could not guess !
And as I saw them love and talk, so full of happiness,
The wish to wander far and wide took hold upon my heart ;
So I made my bundle ready — 'twas right I should depart !

" Said I, ' Now let me see the world, and by its joy be bless'd ! '
But I only meant, forget the world that lies within my breast.
She look'd at me, and said, ' Oh, Heavens ! what's come to thee !
We love thee here so kindly, where canst thou better be ? '

" Then flow'd forth fast my tears, this time it was but right,
' One always weeps at parting ! ' said she, that parting night.
They went with me for company some distance on my track —
Now sick — sick unto death — they again have brought me back.

" With gentlest love and kindest care they tend me in the mill,
And she with her beloved comes to me when she will.
In July is the wedding ; and ever doth she say,
That I shall have a home with them, and soon again be gay.

" How dreamily I listen to the frothing waterwheel,
And think beneath it I might find the peace I cannot feel !
There know no longer sorrow, from every pain be free ! —
They wish me to be happy, and thus then let it be ! "

This is a beautiful poem ! And in the spring, when the
seas are open, and we can again have intercourse with the
north, I hope to receive Andersen's poems, from which, if
it be the pleasure of the public, I hope to give them other
specimens.   But let us now return to his life.

Andersen's health was not strong, and, in 1831, he made
a journey into the Saxon Switzerland, of which he published an account the same year.   Neither were his pecu-
niary circumstances flourishing : like most authors, he had

many anxieties; and, at this time, to add to his other perplexities, he furnished opera-text to the music of Bredahl, from Sir Walter Scott's "Bride of Lammermoor;" and for his old benefactor, Professor Weyse, "Kenilworth," from the same author. For these works the critics handled him severely. Yet, in the meantime, Andersen proved how true a lyrical poet he was, by his "Vignettes to the Danish poets," and his "Twelve Months of the Year." About this time, however, there appeared "Letters of a Wandering Ghost," a satirical work, in which Andersen was held up to ridicule, among other things, for his imperfect orthography. The poet's heart was wounded, his health was indifferent, his circumstances unprosperous, and the public laugh was against him, rather on account of his misfortunes than his faults; but, as had always been the case through his life, light broke in when the darkness seemed deepest, and at the very moment when he was smarting under the lash of these jeering letters, he received a royal stipend to enable him to travel through Germany, France, and Italy. This stipend was granted to him on the recommendation of Ohlenschläger, Ingemann, Heiberg, Orsted, and Thiele; and it is very remarkable that all these gentlemen had recommended the poet, each for a peculiar qualification; the one for his deep feeling, another for his wit, and a third for his humour. This mark of favour excited still more the envy of the baser class of minds, and many anonymous attacks were made upon him, which wounded him so deeply, that, despairing of himself and his own powers, he set out on the journey, which was to be to him the noblest school.

He went immediately to Paris; and it is singular that the first letter which he received from his native land was merely a blank envelope containing a newspaper, in which was a satirical poem on himself. Andersen made the ac-

quaintance of the first literary men in Paris; thence he
went to Switzerland, where he was invited by a family
with whom he was acquainted, and who were living in the
valley of the Jura Mountains, to pay them a visit. This
invitation he accepted, and under their roof, amid the deep
solitudes of nature, he completed a dramatic poem, entitled
"Agnes and the Waterman," which he had begun in Paris.
In this poem he poured out his whole soul, and hoped that
his fellow-countrymen would not begrudge him the favour
of his king, when through it they became better acquainted
with him.

On the anniversary of the day on which Andersen, fourteen years before, a stranger and friendless, had entered
the gate of Copenhagen, he wandered over the Simplon
into that beautiful land which was to open to him a new
spiritual world, and call forth the noblest characteristics of
his soul. He went though Milan, Genoa, and Florence, on
to Rome, where Thorwaldsen and all his countrymen there
received him with the greatest affection.

His residence in Rome began like a sunshiny summer
day; but while it yet was morning, clouds arose; the poem
which he had sent to Copenhagen, and which he hoped
would warm the hearts of his countrymen towards him, was
quite overlooked — a new young poet had just arisen, who
was the star of the moment. His friends wrote to him of all
these things, and candidly told him that they, like every one
else, thought that he was past his best. Another letter brought
him the sad intelligence of the death of his mother, the last
of his family connections. Andersen felt her death severely,
and many poems which he wrote at that time express the
dejection of his mind. Spite, however, of sadness and
untoward events, the glorious treasures of art around him,
and the fine country within which he was a sojourner,
with its bright southern life, operated beneficially on his

spirit. With that intense love for Italy, which is peculiar to the most spiritual-minded inhabitants of the cold north, and, in some cases, has amounted to a passion like the attachment of the Swiss to their mountains, Andersen entered into the spirit of the life of the people, and has reflected all back to us with the most beautiful colouring in his "Improvisatore."

Thorwaldsen gratified the poet by the warmest admiration of his last unfortunate production, "Agnes and the Waterman," and from the great sculptor he received the utmost kindness. Thorwaldsen told him how poor he also had been, and how, in his early artist-career, he had had to contend against envy, and how he also had been misunderstood.

At this moment Andersen's bitterest enemy, Herz, the author of the "Letters of the Wandering Ghost," arrived in Rome; and, as might often be the case would literary enemies only condescend to a personal knowledge of each other, no sooner did these two men meet than they became fast friends. This was a bright event to the warm heart of Andersen. They travelled together to Naples, and ascended Vesuvius during a splendid eruption. They visited Pæstum and the Grotto Azurra together; of all of which we have such an exquisite reflex in the following work.

The greatest harmony existed between these two Danish sons of the Muses, and exists still, we believe, to the present time.

In the following year Andersen returned home through Venice, Vienna, and Munich, making in the two last cities the acquaintance of the first German poets and artists. Immediately after his return he published his novel, "The Improvisatore," which was received with universal applause — which was read and re-read, and which the public never tired of reading. That a work of such singular originality and beauty was universally admired was not at all remarkable; but an extraordinary effect was produced which, it seems to me, tells greatly to the honour of the Danish heart. Not only did Andersen's friends, and the public generally, acknowledge the merit of his work, but they who had treated the poet with severity came now forward and offered him the hand of congratulation; and among them was the rector of the school, the hard-hearted teacher of the poor youth, who had taken all possible means to crush into the dust the talent which God had given him. He now came forward, acknowledged his fault, and deplored it, which touched the good heart of Andersen not a little. And this is but one of the many instances of generous enthusiasm which was excited by this beautiful work towards its author.

It does one's heart good to hear of noble actions, and I have written of these with pleasure. And now, dear reader, who hast gone with me thus far through the life of our author, to thee I commend the following story, which may be called a sermon preached from the text of his own life, and which seems to me to be full of great and good lessons. May it afford thee as much pleasure as it has afforded me!

The Elms, Clapton, January 15. 1845.

TO THE

CONFERENCE - COUNCILLOR COLLIN

AND

HIS EXCELLENT WIFE,

IN WHOM I FOUND PARENTS;

AND

TO THEIR CHILDREN,

IN WHOM I FOUND BROTHERS AND SISTERS;

IN WHOSE HOME, A HOME;

.

I BRING, WITH A FILIAL AND A FRATERNAL HEART,

THIS THE BEST WHICH I POSSESS.

THE AUTHOR.

IMPROVISATORE.

CHAPTER I.

THE CIRCUMSTANCES OF MY CHILDHOOD.

WHOEVER has been in Rome is well acquainted with the Piazza Barberina, in the great square, with the beautiful fountain, where the Tritons empty the spouting conch-shell, from which the water springs upwards many feet. Whoever has not been there, knows it, at all events, from copperplate engravings; only it is a pity, that in these the house at the corner of the Via Felice is not given, that tall corner-house, where the water pours through three pipes out of the wall down into a stone basin. That house has a peculiar interest for me; it was there that I was born. If I look back to my tender youth, such a crowd of bright remembrances meet me, that I scarcely know where to begin; when I contemplate the whole drama of my life, still less do I know what I should bring forward, what I should pass over as unessential, and what points may suffice to represent the whole picture. That which appears attractive to me may not be so to a stranger. I will relate truly and naturally the great story, but then vanity must come into play — the wicked vanity, the desire to please. Already, in my childhood, it sprung up like a plant, and, like the mustard-seed of the Gospel, shot forth

B

its branches towards heaven, and became a mighty tree, in which my passions builded themselves nests.

One of my earliest recollections points thereto. I was turned six years old, and was playing in the neighbourhood of the church of the Capuchins, with some other children, who were all younger than myself. There was fastened on the church-door a little cross of metal ; it was fastened about the middle of the door, and I could just reach it with my hand. Always when our mothers had passed by with us they had lifted us up that we might kiss the holy sign. One day, when we children were playing, one of the youngest of them inquired, " Why the child Jesus did not come down and play with us ? " I assumed an air of wisdom, and replied, that he was really bound upon the cross. We went to the church-door, and, although we found no one, we wished, as our mothers had taught us, to kiss him, but we could not reach up to it ; one therefore lifted up the other, but just as the lips were pointed for the kiss, that one who lifted the other lost his strength, and the kissing one fell down just when his lips were about to touch the invisible child Jesus. At that moment my mother came by, and, when she saw our child's play, she folded her hands, and said, " You are actually some of God's angels ! And thou art mine own angel ! " added she, and kissed me.

I heard her repeat to a neighbour what an innocent angel I was, and it pleased me greatly, but it lessened my innocence—the mustard-seed of vanity drank in therefrom the first sunbeams. Nature had given to me a gentle, pious character, but my good mother made me aware of it ; she showed me my real and my imaginary endowments, and never thought that it is with the innocence of the child as with the basilisk, which dies when it sees itself.

The Capuchin monk, Fra Martino, was my mother's confessor, and she related to him what a pious child I was. I also knew several prayers very nicely by heart, although I did not understand one of them. He made very much of me, and gave me a picture of the Virgin weeping great tears, which fell, like rain-drops, down into the burning flames of hell, where the damned caught this draught of refreshment. He took me over with him into the convent, where the open colonnade, which enclosed within a square the little potato-garden, with the two cyprus and orange-trees, made a very deep impression upon me. Side by side, in the open passages, hung old portraits of deceased monks, and on the door of each cell were pasted pictures from the history of the martyrs, which I contemplated with the same holy emotion as afterwards the masterpieces of Raphael and Andrew del Sarto.

" Thou art really a bright youth," said he ; " thou shalt now see the dead."

Upon this, he opened a little door of a gallery which lay a few steps below the colonnade. We descended, and now I saw round about me skulls upon skulls, so placed one upon another that they formed walls, and therewith several chapels. In these were regular niches, in which were seated perfect skeletons of the most distinguished of the monks, enveloped in their brown cowls, their cords round their waists, and with a breviary or a withered bunch of flowers in their hands. Altars, chandeliers, and ornaments, were made of shoulder-bones and vertebræ, with bas-reliefs of human joints, horrible and tasteless as the whole idea.

I clung fast to the monk, who whispered a prayer, and then said to me, —

" Here also I shall some time sleep ; wilt thou thus visit me ? "

I answered not a word, but looked horrified at him, and then round about me upon the strange grisly assembly. It was foolish to take me, a child, into this place. I was singularly impressed by the whole thing, and did not feel myself again easy until I came into his little cell, where the beautiful yellow oranges almost hung in at the window, and I saw the brightly-coloured picture of the Madonna, who was borne upwards by angels into the clear sunshine, while a thousand flowers filled the grave in which she had rested.

This, my first visit to the convent, occupied my imagination for a long time, and stands yet with extraordinary vividness before me. The monk seemed to me quite a different being to any other person whom I knew ; his abode in the neighbourhood of the dead, who, in their brown cloaks, looked almost like himself, the many histories which he knew and could relate of holy men and wonderful miracles, together with my mother's great reverence for his sanctity, caused me to begin thinking whether I, too, could not be such a man.

My mother was a widow, and had no other means of subsistence than what she obtained by sewing, and by the rent of a large room which we ourselves had formerly inhabited. We lived now in a little chamber in the roof, and a young painter, Federigo, had the saloon, as we called it. He was a life-enjoying, brisk young man, who came from a far, far country, where they knew nothing about the Madonna and the child Jesus, my mother said. He was from Denmark. I had at that time no idea that there existed more languages than one, and I believed, therefore, that he was deaf when he did not understand me, and, for that reason, I spoke to him as loud as I could ; he laughed at me, often brought me fruit, and drew for me soldiers, horses, and houses. We soon became acquainted ; I loved him much, and my mother said many a time that he was a very upright person.

In the mean time I heard a conversation one evening between my mother and the monk Fra Martino, which excited in me a sorrowful emotion for the young artist. My mother inquired if this foreigner would actually be eternally condemned to hell.

" He and many other foreigners also," she said, " are, indeed, very honest people, who never do any thing wicked. They are good to the poor, pay exactly, and at the fixed time ; nay, it actually often seems to me that they are not such great sinners as many of us."

" Yes," replied Fra Martino, " that is very true — they are often very good people ; but do you know how that happens ? You see, the devil, who goes about the world, knows that the heretics will some time belong to him, and so he never tempts them ; and, therefore, they can easily be honest, easily give up sin ; on the contrary, a good Catholic Christian is a child of God, and, therefore, the devil sets his temptations in array against him, and we weak creatures are subjected. But a heretic, as one may say, is tempted neither of the flesh nor the devil!"

To this my mother could make no reply, and sighed deeply over the poor young man; I began to cry, for it seemed to me that it was a cruel sin that he should be burned eternally — he who was so good, and who drew me such beautiful pictures.

A third person who played a great part in my childhood's life was Uncle Peppo, commonly called "Wicked Peppo," or "the King of the Spanish Steps*," where he had his daily residence. Born with two withered legs, which lay crossed under him, he had had from his earliest childhood an extraordinary facility in moving himself forwards with his hands. These he stuck under a frame which was fastened at both ends to a board, and by the help of this he could move himself forward almost as easily as any other person with healthy and strong feet. He sat daily, as has been said, upon the Spanish Steps, never indeed begging, but exclaiming, with a crafty smile, to every passer-by, "*bon giorno!*" and that even after the sun was gone down.

My mother did not like him much, nay, indeed, she was ashamed of the relationship; but, for my sake, as she often told me, she kept up a friendship with him. He had that in his chest which we others must look after, and if I kept good friends with him I should be his only heir, if he did not give it to the church. He had, also, after his own way, a sort of liking for me, yet I never felt myself quite happy in his neighbourhood. Once I was the witness of a scene which awoke in me fear of him, and also exhibited his own disposition. Upon one of the lowest flights of stairs sat an old blind beggar, and rattled with his little leaden box that people might drop a bajocco therein. Many people passed by my uncle without noticing his crafty smile and the wavings of his hat; the blind man gained more by his silence — they gave to him. Three had gone by, and now came the fourth, and threw him a small

* These lead from the Spanish Place up to Monte Pincio, a broad flight of stone steps. These, which consist of four flights, are an especial resort of the beggars of Rome, and, from their locality, bear the name of the Spanish Steps. — *Author's note.*

coin.   Peppo could no longer contain himself; I saw how
he crept down like a snake, and struck the blind man in
his face, so that he lost both money and stick.

" Thou thief !" cried my uncle, " wilt thou steal money
from me — thou who art not even a regular cripple ? Cannot see ! — that is all his infirmity ! — and so he will take
my bread from my mouth !"

I neither heard nor saw more, but hastened home with
a flask of wine which I had been sent to purchase.   On
the great festival days I was always obliged to go with
my mother to visit him at his own house ; we took with
us one kind of present or other, either fine grapes or preserved golden pippins, which were his greatest luxury.   I
was then obliged to kiss his hand and call him uncle ;
then he smiled so strangely, and gave me a half-bajocco,
always adding the exhortation that I should keep it to look
at, not spend it in cakes, for when these were eaten I had
nothing left, but that if I kept my coin I should always
have something.

His dwelling was dark and dirty : in one little room
there was no window at all, and in the other it was almost
up to the ceiling with broken and patched-up panes.   Of
furniture there was not one article, except a great wide
chest, which served him for a bed, and two tubs, in which
he kept his clothes.   I always cried when I had to go
there ; and true it is, however much my mother persuaded
me to be very affectionate towards him, yet she always
made use of him as a bugbear when she would punish me;
she said then that she would send me to my dirty uncle,
that I should sit and sing beside him upon the stairs, and
thus do something useful and earn a bajocco.   But I knew
that she never meant so ill by me ; I was the apple of her
eye.

On the house of our opposite neighbour there was an
image of the Virgin, before which a lamp was always burning.   Every evening when the bell rang the Ave Maria,
I and the neighbours' children knelt before it, and sang in
honour of the mother of God, and the pretty child Jesus,
which they had adorned with ribands, beads, and silver
hearts.   By the wavering lamp-light it often seemed to me

as if both mother and child moved and smiled upon us. I sang with a high clear voice; and people said that I sang beautifully. Once there stood an English family and listened to us; and, when we rose up from our knees, the gentleman gave me a silver piece; "it was," my mother said, "because of my fine voice." But how much distraction did this afterwards cause me! I thought no longer alone on the Madonna when I sung before her image; no! I thought, did any one listen to my beautiful singing; but always when I thought so there succeeded a burning remorse; I was afraid that she would be angry with me; and I prayed right innocently that she would look down upon me, poor child!

The evening-song was, in the mean time, the only point of union between me and the other neighbours' children. I lived quietly, entirely in my own self-created dream-world; I lay for hours upon my back, with my face to the open window, looking out into the wonderful, gloriously blue, Italian heaven, into the play of colours at the going down of the sun, when the clouds hung with their violet-hued edges upon a golden ground. Often I wished that I could fly far beyond the Quirinal and the houses, to the great pine-trees, which stood like black shadow-figures against the fire-red horizon. I had quite another scene on the other side of our room: there lay our own and our neighbours' yards, each a small, narrow space, enclosed by tall houses, and almost shut in from above by the great wooden balconies. In the middle of each yard there was a well enclosed with masonry, and the space between this and the walls of the houses was not greater than to admit of one person moving round. Thus, from above I looked properly only into two deep wells; they were entirely overgrown with that fine plant which we call Venus' hair, and which, hanging down, lost itself in the darkness. It was to me as if I could see deep down into the earth, where my fancy then created for herself the strangest pictures. In the mean time, my mother adorned that window with a great rod, to show me what fruit grew for me there, that I might not fall down and get drowned.

But I will now mention an occurrence which might easily have put an end to my life's history before it had come into any entanglement.

CHAPTER II.

THE VISIT TO THE CATACOMBS. —— I BECOME A CHORISTER. —— THE LOVELY ANGEL-CHILD. —— THE IMPROVISATORE.

OUR lodger, the young painter, took me with him sometimes on his little rambles beyond the gates. I did not disturb him whilst he was making now and then a sketch; and when he had finished he amused himself with my prattle, for he now understood the language.

Once before, I had been with him to the *curia hostilia*, deep down into the dark caves where, in ancient days, wild beasts were kept for the games, and where innocent captives were thrown to ferocious hyænas and lions. The dark passages; the monk who conducted us in, and continually struck the red torch against the walls; the deep cistern in which the water stood as clear as a mirror — yes, so clear, that one was obliged to move it with the torch to convince one's self that it was up to the brim, and that there was no empty space, as by its clearness there seemed to be; — all this excited my imagination. Fear, I felt none, for I was unconscious of danger.

" Are we going to the caverns?" I inquired from him, as I saw at the end of the street the higher part of the Colosseum.

" No, to something much greater," replied he; " where thou shalt see something! And I will paint thee, also, my fine fellow!"

Thus wandered we farther, and ever farther, between the white walls, the enclosed vineyards, and the old ruins of the baths, till we were out of Rome. The sun burned hotly, and the peasants had made for their wagons roofs of green branches, under which they slept, while the horses, left to themselves, went at a foot's pace, and ate from the

bundle of hay which hung beside them for this purpose.
At length we reached the grotto of Egeria, in which we
took our breakfast, and mixed our wine with the fresh
water that streamed out from between the blocks of stone.
The walls and vault of the whole grotto were inside covered
over with the finest green, as of tapestry, woven of silks
and velvet, and round about the great entrance hung the
thickest ivy, fresh and luxuriant as the vine foliage in the
valleys of Calabria.

Not many paces from the grotto stands, or rather stood,
for there are now only a few remains of it left, a little, and
wholly desolate house, built above one of the descents to
the catacombs. These were, as is well known, in ancient
times, connecting links between Rome and the surrounding
cities ; in later times, however, they have in part fallen in,
and in part been built up, because they served as concealment
for robbers and smugglers. The entrance through the
burial-vaults in St. Sebastian's church, and this one through
the desolate house, were then the only two in existence ;
and I almost think that we were the last who descended
by this, for, shortly after our adventure, it also was shut
up ; and only the one through the church, under the conduct of a monk, remains now open to strangers.

Deep below, hollowed out of the soft puzzolan earth, the
one passage crosses another. Their multitude, their similarity
one to another, are sufficient to bewilder even him who knows
the principal direction. I had formed no idea of the whole,
and the painter felt so confident, that he had no hesitation
in taking me, the little boy, down with him. He lighted
his candle, and took another with him in his pocket, fastened a ball of twine to the opening where we descended,
and our wandering commenced. Anon the passages were
so low that I could not go upright ; anon they elevated
themselves to lofty vaults, and, where the one crossed the
other, expanded themselves into great quadrangles. We
passed through the Rotunda with the small stone altar in
the middle, where the early Christians, persecuted by the
Pagans, secretly performed their worship. Federigo told
me of the fourteen popes, and the many thousand martyrs,
who here lie buried : we held the light against the great

cracks in the tombs, and saw the yellow bones within.*
We advanced yet some steps onward, and then came to a
stand, because we were at the end of the twine.   The end
of this Federigo fastened to his button-hole, stuck the
candle among some stones, and then began to sketch the
deep passage.   I sat close beside him upon one of the
stones ; he had desired me to fold my hands and to look
upwards.   The light was nearly burnt out, but a whole
one lay hard by ; besides which he had brought a tinder-
box, by the aid of which he could light the other in case
this suddenly went out.

My imagination fashioned to itself a thousand wonderful
objects in the infinite passages which opened themselves,
and revealed to us an impenetrable darkness.   All was
quite still, the falling waterdrops alone sent forth a monotonous sound.   As I thus sat, wrapped in my own thoughts,
I was suddenly terrified by my friend the painter, who
heaved a strange sigh, and sprang about, but always in the
same spot.   Every moment he stooped down to the ground,
as if he would snatch up something, then he lighted the
larger candle and sought about.   I became so terrified at
his singular behaviour, that I got up and began to cry.

"For God's sake, sit still, child!" said he — "for God
in heaven's sake!" and again he began staring on the
ground.

"I will go up again!" I exclaimed — "I will not stop
down here!"   I then took him by the hand and strove to
draw him with me.

"Child! child! thou art a noble fellow!" said he;
"I will give thee pictures and cakes — there, thou hast
money!"   And he took his purse out of his pocket, and
gave me all that was in it: but I felt that his hand was
ice-cold and that he trembled.   On this I grew more
uneasy, and called my mother; but now he seized me
firmly by the shoulder, and, shaking me violently, said,

---

* The monumental stones here are without any ornament; on the contrary,
one finds in the catacombs of St. Januarius, at Naples, the images of saints
and inscriptions, but all very indifferently done.   On the graves of th Christians a fish is figured, in the Greek name of which occur the initial letters of
('Ιησους Χριστος, Θεου υιος, σωτηρ) Jesus Christ, the Son of God, the Redeemer.—*Author's note.*

"I will beat thee if thou art not quiet!" Then he bound his pocket-handkerchief round my arm, and held me fast, but bent himself down to me the next moment, kissed me vehemently, called me his dear little Antonio, and whispered, "Do thou also pray to the Madonna!"

"Is the string lost?" I asked.

"We will find it—we will find it!" he replied, and began searching again. In the mean time the lesser light was quite burnt out, and the larger one, from its continual agitation, melted and burnt his hand, which only increased his distress. It would have been quite impossible to have found our way back without the string, every step would only have led us deeper down where no one could save us.

After vainly searching, he threw himself upon the ground, cast his arm around my neck, and sighed, "Thou poor child!" I then wept bitterly, for it seemed to me that I never more should reach my home. He clasped me so closely to him as he lay on the ground that my hand slid under him. I involuntarily grasped the sand, and found the string between my fingers.

"Here it is!" I exclaimed.

He seized my hand, and became, as it were, frantic for joy, for our life actually hung upon this single thread. We were saved.

Oh, how warmly beamed the sun, how blue was the heaven, how deliciously green the trees and bushes, as we came forth into the free air! Poor Federigo kissed me yet again, drew his handsome silver watch out of his pocket, and said, "This thou shalt have!"

I was so heartily glad about this, that I quite forgot all that had happened; but my mother could not forget it, when she had heard it, and would not again consent that Federigo should take me out with him. Fra Martino said also that it was only on my account that we were saved, that it was to me to whom the Madonna had given the thread—to me, and not to the heretic Federigo; that I was a good, pious child, and must never forget her kindness and mercy. This, and the jesting assertion of some of our acquaintance, that I was born to be of the priesthood, because, with the exception of my mother, I could not endure women, instilled into her the determination that I should become a servant of the church. I do not myself know why, but I had an antipathy to all women, and, as I expressed this unhesitatingly, I was bantered by every girl and woman who came to my mother's. They all would kiss me: in particular was there a peasant girl, Mariuccia, who by this jest always brought tears to my eyes. She was very lively and waggish, and maintained herself by serving as a model, and always appeared, therefore, in handsome, gay dresses, with a large white cloth over her hair. She often sat for Federigo, and visited my mother also, and then always told me that she was my bride, and that I was her little bridegroom, who must and should give her a kiss; I never would do so, and then she took it by force.

Once when she said that I cried childishly, and behaved myself exactly like a child that still sucked, and that I should be suckled like any other baby, I flew out, down the steps, but she pursued and caught me, held me between her knees, and pressed my head, which I turned away with disgust, ever closer and closer to her breast. I tore the silver arrow out of her hair, which fell down in rich abundance over me and over her naked shoulders. My mother stood on the hearth, laughed, and encouraged Mariuccia, whilst Federigo, unobservedly, stood at the door, and painted the whole group.

" I will have no bride, no wife!" I exclaimed to my mother; " I will be a priest, or a Capuchin, like Fra Martino!"

The extraordinary meditations into which I was wrapt for whole evenings also were regarded by my mother as tokens of my spiritual calling. I sat and thought then what castles and churches I would build, if I should become great and rich; how I then would drive like the cardinals in red carriages, with many gold-liveried servants behind; or else I framed a new martyr-story out of the many which Fra Martino had related to me. I was, of course, the hero of these, and, through the help of the Madonna, never felt the pangs which were inflicted upon me. But, especially, had I a great desire to journey to Federigo's home, to convert the people there, that they also might know something of grace.

Whether it was through the management of my mother or Fra Martino I know not, but it is enough that my mother, early one morning, arrayed me in a little kirtle, and drew over it an embroidered shirt, which only reached to the knees, and then led me to the glass that I might see myself. I was now a chorister in the Capuchin church, must carry the great censer of incense, and sing with the others before the altar. Fra Martino instructed me in the whole duty. Oh, how happy all this made me! I was soon quite at home in that little but comfortable church, knew every angel's head in the altar-piece, every ornamental scroll upon the pillars, could see even with my eyes shut the beautiful St. Michael fighting with the dragon*, just as the painter had represented him, and thought many wonderful things about the death's heads carved in the pavement, with the green ivy wreaths around the brow.

On the festival of All Saints, I was down in the Chapel of the Dead, where Fra Martino had led me when I was with him for the first time in the convent. All the monks sang masses for the dead, and I, with two other boys of my own age, swung the incense-breathing censer before the great altar of skulls. They had placed lights in the chandeliers made of bones, new garlands were placed around the brows of the skeleton-monks, and fresh *bouquets* in their hands. Many people, as usual, thronged in ; they all knelt, and the singers intoned the solemn *Miserere.* I gazed for a long time on the pale, yellow skulls, and the fumes of the incense which wavered in strange shapes between them and me, and every thing began to spin round before my eyes; it was as if I saw every-thing through a large rainbow ; as if a thousand prayer-bells rung in my ear; it seemed as if I was borne along a stream ; it was unspeakably delicious — more, I know not ; consciousness left me — I was in a swoon.

---

* The celebrated picture of St. Michael, the archangel, who, with the beauty of youth, and with great wings, sets his foot upon and pierces the head of the devil.—*Author's note.*

The atmosphere, made oppressive by crowds of people, and my excited imagination, occasioned this fainting-fit. When I came to myself again, I was lying in Fra Martino's lap, under the orange-tree in the convent garden.

The confused story which I told of what I seemed to have seen, he and all the brethren explained as a revelation: the holy spirits had floated over me, but I had not been able to bear the sight of their glory and their majesty. This occasioned me before long to have many extraordinary dreams; I also imagined some which I related to my mother, and she again communicated to her friends, so that I became daily more and more to be regarded as a child of God.

In the mean time, the happy Christmas approached. Pifferari, shepherds from the mountains, came in their short cloaks, with ribands around their pointed hats, and announced with the bagpipe, before every house where there stood an image of the Virgin, that the time was at hand in which the Saviour was born. I was awoke every morning by these monotonous, melancholy tones, and my first occupation then was to read over my lesson, for I was one of the children selected, " boys and girls," who, between Christmas and New-year, were to preach in the church *ara cœli*, before the image of Jesus.

It was not I alone, my mother, and Mariuccia, who rejoiced that I, the boy of nine, should make a speech, but also the painter Federigo, before whom I, without their knowledge, had had a rehearsal, standing upon a table; it would be upon such a one, only that a carpet would be laid over it, that we children should be placed in the church, where we, before the assembled multitudes, must repeat the speech, which we had learned by rote, about the bleeding heart of the Madonna, and the beauty of the child Jesus.

I knew nothing of fear; it was only with joy that my heart beat so violently as I stepped forward, and saw all eyes directed to me. That I, of all the children, gave most delight, seemed decided; but now there was lifted up a little girl, who was of so exquisitely delicate a form, and who had, at the same time, so wonderfully bright a countenance, and such a melodious voice, that all exclaimed aloud that she was a little angelic child. Even my mother, who would gladly have awarded to me the palm, declared aloud that she was just like one of the angels in the great altar-piece. The wonderfully dark eyes, the raven-black hair, the childlike, and yet so wise expression of countenance, the exquisitely small hands — nay, it seemed to me that my mother said too much of all these, although she added that I also was an angel of God.

There is a song about the nightingale, which, when it was quite young, sat in the nest and picked the green leaves of the rose, without being aware of the buds which were just beginning to form ; months afterwards, the rose unfolded itself, the nightingale sang only of it, flew among the thorns, and wounded itself. The song often occurred to me when I became older, but in the church, *ara cœli*, I knew it not, neither my ears nor my heart knew it !

At home, I had to repeat before my mother, Mariuccia, and many friends, the speech which I had made, and this flattered my vanity not a little ; but they lost, in the mean time, their interest in hearing it earlier than I mine in repeating it. In order, now, to keep my public in good humour, I undertook, out of my own head, to make a new speech. But this was rather a description of the festival in the church than a regular Christmas speech. Federigo was the first who heard it ; and, although he laughed, it flattered me still, when he said that my speech was in every way as good as that which Fra Martino had taught me, and that a poet lay hidden in me. This last remark gave me much to think about, because I could not understand it ; yet, thought I to myself, it must be a good angel which dwelt in me, perhaps the same which shows to me the charming dreams, and so many beautiful things when I sleep. For the first time during the summer, chance gave me a clear notion of a poet, and awoke new ideas in my own soul-world.

It but very rarely happened that my mother left the quarter of the city in which we lived ; therefore, it seemed to me like a festival when she said to me, one afternoon, that we would go and pay a visit to a friend of hers in

Trastevere.*   I was dressed in my holyday suit, and the gay piece of silk which I usually wore instead of a waist-coat was fastened with pins over the breast, and under my little jacket; my neckerchief was tied in a great bow, and an embroidered cap was on my head.   I was particularly elegant.

When, after the visit, were turned home, it was some-what late, but the moon shone gloriously, the air was fresh and blue, and the cypresses and pines stood with wonder-fully sharp outlines upon the neighbouring heights.   It was one of those evenings which occur but once in a person's life, which, without signalising itself by any great life-adventure, yet stamps itself in its whole colouring upon the Psyche-wings.   Since that moment, whenever my mind goes back to the Tiber, I see it ever before me as upon this evening; — the thick yellow water lit up by the moonbeams, the black stone pillars of the old ruinous bridge, which, with strong shadow, lifted itself out of the stream where the great mill-wheel rushed round, nay, even the merry girls who skipped past with the tambourine and danced the saltarello.†

In the streets around Santa Maria della Rotunda all was yet life and motion; butchers and fruit-women sat before their tables, on which lay their wares among garlands of laurel, and with lights burning in the open air.   The fire flickered under the chestnut-pans, and the conversation was carried on with so much screaming and noise, that a stranger who did not understand a word might have imagined it to be some contention of life and death.   An old friend whom my mother met in the fish-market kept us talking so long, that people were beginning to put out their lights before we set off again, and as my mother

* That part of Rome which lies on the higher banks of the Tiber.—*Author's note.*

† A popular Roman dance to a most monotonous tune.   It is danced by one or two persons, yet without these coming in contact with each other; most frequently by two men or two women, who, with a quick, hopping step, and with increasing rapidity, move themselves in a half-circle.   The arms are as violently agitated as the legs, and change their position incessantly, with all that natural grace peculiar to the Roman people.   Women are accustomed in this dance to lift up the petticoats a little, or else to beat time themselves upon the tambourine: this, otherwise, is done by a third person on the mono-tonous drum — the changes in the time alone consisting in the greater or less rapidity with which the strokes follow one another.—*Author's note.*

accompanied her friend to her door it had now become as silent as death in the street, even in the Corso; but when we came into the square di Trevi, where there is the beautiful cascade, it seemed, on the contrary, quite cheerful again.

The moonlight fell exactly upon the old palace, where the water streams out between the masses of foundation-rock which seem loosely thrown together. Neptune's heavy stone-mantle floated in the wind, as he looked out above the great waterfall, on each side of which Tritons, with puffed-out cheeks, guided sea-horses. Beneath these the great basin spread itself out, and upon the turf around it rested a crowd of peasants, stretching themselves in the moonlight. Large, quartered melons, from which streamed the red juice, lay around them. A little square-built fellow, whose whole dress consisted of a shirt, and short leather breeches, which hung loose and unbuttoned at the knees, sat with a guitar, and twanged the strings merrily. Now he sang a song, now he played, and all the peasants clapped their hands. My mother remained standing; and I now listened to a song which seized upon me quite in an extraordinary way, for it was not a song like any other which I had heard. No! he sang to us of what we saw and heard, we were ourselves in the song, and that in verse, and with melody. He sang, "How gloriously one can sleep with a stone under the head, and the blue heaven for a coverlet, whilst the two Pifferari blow their bagpipes!" and with that he pointed to the Tritons who were blowing their horns, "how the whole company of peasants who have shed the blood of the melon will drink a health to their sweethearts, who now are asleep, but see in dreams the dome of St. Peter's, and their beloved, who go wandering about in the Papal city." "Yes, we will drink, and that to the health of all girls whose arrow has not an open hand.* Yes," added he, giving my mother a little push in the side, "and to mothers who have for their sweethearts lads on whose chins the black down is growing.

* The arrow which the peasant women wear in their hair has a closed hand, if they are free; but if betrothed or married, it has an open one.—*Author's note.*

" Bravo !" said my mother, and all the peasants clapped
their hands and shouted, " Bravo, Giacomo ! bravo !"

Upon the steps of the little church we discovered, in the
mean time, an acquaintance — our Federigo, who stood
with a pencil and sketched the whole merry moonlight
piece.   As we went home, he and my mother joked about
the brisk Improvisatore, for so I heard them call the
peasant who sung so charmingly.

" Antonio," said Federigo to me, " thou, also, shouldst
improvise ; thou art truly, also, a little poet ! Thou must
learn to put thy pieces into verse."

I now understood what a poet was ; namely, one who
could sing beautifully that which he saw and felt.   That
must, indeed, be charming, thought I, and easy, if I had
but a guitar.

The first subject of my song was neither more nor less
than the shop of the bacon-dealer over the way.   Long
ago, my fancy had already busied itself with the curious
collection of his wares, which attracted in particular the
eyes of strangers.   Amid beautiful garlands of laurel hung
the white buffalo-cheeses, like great ostrich eggs ; candles,
wrapped round with gold paper, represented an organ ; and
sausages, which were reared up like columns, sustained a
Parmesan cheese, shining like yellow amber.   When in an
evening the whole was lighted up, and the red glass lamps
burned before the image of the Madonna in the wall among
sausages and ham, it seemed to me as if I looked into an
entirely magical world.   The cat upon the shop table, and
the young Capuchins, who always stood so long cheapening
their purchases with the signora, came also into the poem,
which I pondered upon so long, that I could repeat it
aloud and perfectly to Federigo, and which, having won
his applause, quickly spread itself over the whole house,
nay, even to the bacon dealer's signora, who laughed and
clapped her hands, and called it a wonderful poem — a
Divina Comedia di Dante !

From this time forth every thing was sung.   I lived
entirely in fancies and dreams.   In the church, when I
swung the censer, in the streets amid the rolling carriages
and screaming traders, as well as in my little bed beneath

the image of the Virgin and the holy-water vessel. In the winter-time, I could sit for whole hours before our house, and look into the great fire in the street, where the smith heated his iron, and the peasants warmed themselves. I saw in the red fire a world glowing as my own imagination. I shouted for joy, when in winter the snow of the mountains sent down to us such severe cold, that icicles hung from the Triton in the square ; pity that it was so seldom. Then, also, were the peasants glad, for it was to them a sign of a fertile year ; they took hold of each other's hands, and danced in their great woollen cloaks round about the Triton, whilst a rainbow played in the high-springing water.

But I loiter too long over the simple recollections of my childhood, which cannot have for a stranger the deep meaning, the extraordinary attraction, which they have for me. Whilst I recall, whilst I hold fast every single occurrence, it seems as if I again lived in the whole.

> " My childhood's heart was to my dreams a sea
> Of music, whereon floated picture-boats ! "

I will now hasten on to the circumstance which placed the first hedge of thorns between me and the paradise of home — which led me among strangers, and which contained the germ of my whole future.

CHAPTER III.

THE FLOWER-FEAST AT GENZANO.*

It was in the month of June, and the day of the famous flower-feast which was annually celebrated at Genzano approached. My mother and Mariuccia had a mutual friend there, who, with her husband, kept a public-house.† They had for many years determined to go to this festival,

* A little city in the mountains of Albano, which lies upon the high road between Rome and the Marshes —*Note by the Author*.

† " *Osteria e cucina*," the customary sign for the lower order of hotels and public-houses in Italy.—*Ibid.*

but there was always something or other to prevent it;
this time there was nothing.   We were to set off the day
before the flower-feast, because it was a long way; I could
not sleep for joy through the whole night preceding.

Before the sun had risen, the vitturino drove up to the
door, and we rolled away.   Never before had I been among
the mountains.   Expectation, and joy of the approaching
festival, set my whole soul in motion.   If in my maturer
years I could have seen nature and life around me with the
same vivid feeling as then, and could have expressed it in
words, it would have been an immortal poem.   The great
stillness of the streets, the iron-studded city gate, the
Campagna stretching out for miles, with the lonely monuments, the thick mist which covered the feet of the distant
mountains — all these seemed to me mysterious preparations for the magnificence which I should behold.   Even
the wooden cross erected by the way-side, upon which
hung the whitened bones of the murderer, which told us
that here an innocent person had perished, and the perpe-
trator of his death had been punished, had for me an
uncommon charm.   First of all, I attempted to count the
innumerably many stone arches which conduct the water
from the mountains to Rome, but of this I was soon
weary; so I then began to torment the others with a thousand questions about the great fires which the peasants had
made around the piled-up grave-stones, and would have an
exact explanation of the vast flocks of sheep, which the
wandering drivers kept together in one place by stretching
a fishing-net, like a fence, around the whole herd.

From Albano we were to go on foot for the short and
beautiful remainder cf the way through Arriccia.   Resida
and golden cistus grew wild by the roadside, the thick,
juicy olive-trees cast a delicious shade; I caught a glimpse
of the distant sea, and upon the mountain-slopes by the
wayside, where a cross stood, merry girls skipped dancing
past us, but yet never forgetting piously to kiss the holy
cross.   The lofty dome of the church of Arriccia I imagined to be that of St. Peter, which the angels had hung
up in the blue air among the dark olive-trees.   In the
street, the people had collected around a bear which danced

upon his hind-legs, while the peasant who held the rope blew upon his bagpipe the selfsame air which he had played at Christmas, as Pifferari, before the Madonna. A handsome ape in a military uniform, and which he called the corporal, made somersets upon the bear's head and neck. I was quite willing to stop there instead of going on to Genzano. The flower-festival was really not till to-morrow, but my mother was resolute that we should go and help her friend, Angeline, to make garlands and flower-tapestry.

We soon went the short remainder of the way and arrived at Angeline's house; it stood in that part of the neighbourhood of Genzano which looks on Lake Nemi; it was a pretty house, and out of the wall flowed a fresh fountain into a stone basin, where the asses thronged to drink.

We entered the hostel; there was a noise and a stir. The dinner was boiling and frizzling on the hearth. A crowd of peasants and town-folk sat at the long wooden tables drinking their wine and eating their presciutto. The most beautiful roses were stuck in a blue jug before the image of the Madonna, where the lamp would not burn well, because the smoke drew towards it. The cat ran over the cheese which lay upon the table, and we were near stumbling over the hens, which, terrified, hopped along the floor. Angeline was delighted to see us, and we were sent up the steep stairs near the chimney, where we had a little room to ourselves, and a kingly banquet, according to my notions. Every thing was magnificent; even the bottle of wine was ornamented; instead of a cork, a full-blown rose was stuck in it. Angeline kissed us all three; I also received a kiss whether I would or not. Angeline said I was a pretty boy, and my mother patted me on the cheek with one hand, whilst with the other she put my things to rights; and now she pulled my jacket, which was too little for me, down to my hands, then again up to my shoulders and breast, just as it ought to have been.

After dinner, a perfect feast awaited us; we were to go out to gather flowers and leaves for garlands. We went through a low door out into the garden; this was only a few ells in circumference, and was, so to say, one single bower. The light railing which enclosed it was strengthened with the broad, firm leaves of the aloe, which grew wild here, and formed a natural fence.

The lake slept calmly in the great, round crater, from which at one time fire spouted up to heaven. We went down the amphitheatre-like, rocky slope, through the great beech and the thick plantain wood, where the vines wreathed themselves among the tree-branches. On the opposite descent before us lay the city of Nemi, and mirrored itself in the blue lake. As we went along we bound garlands; the dark green olive and fresh vine leaves we entwined with the wild golden cistus. Now the deep-lying, blue lake, and the bright heavens above us, were hidden by the thick branches and the vine leaves; now they gleamed forth again as if they both were only one single, infinite blue. Every thing was to me new and glorious; my soul trembled for quiet joy. There are even yet moments in which the remembrance of these feelings come forth again like the beautiful mosaic fragment of a buried city.

The sun burned hotly, and it was not until we were by the lake-side, where the plantains shoot forth their ancient trunks from the water, and bend down their branches, heavy with enwreathing vines, to the watery mirror, that we found it cool enough to continue our work. Beautiful water-plants nodded here as if they dreamed under the deep shadow, and they, too, made a part of our garlands. Presently, however, the sunbeams no longer reached the lake, but played only upon the roofs of Nemi and Genzano; and now the gloom descended to where we sat. I went a little distance from the others, yet only a few paces, for my mother was afraid that I should fall into the lake where it was deep and the banks were sudden. Not far from the small stone ruins of an old temple of Diana there lay a huge fig-tree which the ivy had already begun to bind fast to the earth; I had climbed upon this, and was weaving a garland whilst I sang from a canzonet, —

> " Ah ! rossi, rossi fiori,
> Un mazzo di violi !
> Un gelsomin d' amore,"

when I was suddenly interrupted by a strangely whistling voice,—

"Per dar al mio bene !"

and as suddenly there stood before me a tall, aged woman, of an unusually slender frame, and in the costume which the peasant women of Frascati are so fond of wearing. The long white veil which hung down from her head over her shoulders contributed to give the countenance and neck a more Mulatto tint than they probably had naturally. Wrinkle crossed wrinkle, whereby her face resembled a crumpled-up net. The black pupil seemed to fill the whole eye. She laughed, and looked at the same time both seriously and fixedly at me, as if she were a mummy which some one had set up under the trees.

"Rosemary flowers," she said, at length, "become more beautiful in thy hands ; thou hast a lucky star in thy eyes."

I looked at her with astonishment, and pressed the garland which I was weaving to my lips.

"There is poison in the beautiful laurel-leaves* ; bind thy garland, but do not taste of the leaves."

"Ah, the wise Fulvia of Frascati !" exclaimed Angeline, stepping from among the bushes, "art thou also making garlands for to-morrow's festival ? or," continued she, in a more subdued voice, "art thou binding another kind of nosegay while the sun goes down on the Campagna ? "

"An intelligent eye," continued Fulvia, gazing at me without intermission ; "the sun went through the bull he had nourished, and there hung gold and honour on the bull's horns."

"Yes," said my mother, who had come up with Mariuccia, "when he gets on the black coat and the broad hat we shall then see whether he must swing the censer or go through a thorn-hedge."

That she intended by this to indicate my being of the clerical order, the sibyl seemed to comprehend ; but there was quite another meaning in her reply than we at that time might imagine.

* Prunus laurocerasus, which grows abundantly among these mountains.— *Author's note.*

" The broad hat," said she, " will not shadow his brow when he stands before the people, when his speeches sound like music, sweeter than the song of nuns behind the grating, and more powerful than thunder in the mountains of Albano. The seat of Fortune is higher than Monte Cave, where the clouds repose upon the mountains among the flocks of sheep."

" Oh, God !" sighed my mother, shaking her head somewhat incredulously, although she listened gladly to the brilliant prophecy, " he is a poor child — Madonna only knows what will become of him ! The chariot of Fortune is loftier than the car of a peasant of Albano, and the wheel is always turning; how can a poor child mount it ? "

" Hast thou seen how the two great wheels of the peasant's car turn round ? The lowest spoke becomes the highest, and then goes down again ; when it is down, the peasant sets his foot upon it, and the wheel which goes round lifts him up : but sometimes there lies a stone in the path, and then it will go like a dance in the market-place." *

" And may not I, too, mount with him into the chariot of Fortune ? " asked my mother, half in jest, but uttered at the same moment a loud cry, for a large eagle flew so near us down into the lake that the water at the same moment splashed into our faces from the force with which he struck it with his great wings. High up in the air his keen glance had discovered a large fish, which lay immovable as a reed upon the surface of the lake ; with the swiftness of an arrow he seized upon his prey, stuck his sharp talons into the back of it, and was about to raise himself again, when the fish, which, by the agitation of the waters, we could see was of great size, and almost of equal power to his enemy, sought on the contrary, to drag him below with him. The talons of the bird were so firmly fixed into the back of the fish, that he could not release himself from his prey, and there now, therefore, began between the two such a contest that the quiet lake

---

* The peasants mount into their tall cars by standing upon the spoke of the ascending wheel.— *Author's note.*

trembled in wide circles. Now appeared the glittering back of the fish, now the bird struck the water with his broad wings, and seemed to yield. The combat lasted for some minutes. The two wings lay for a moment still, outspread upon the water, as if they rested themselves; then they were rapidly struck together, a crack was heard, the one wing sank down, whilst the other lashed the water to foam, and then vanished. The fish sunk beneath the waves with his enemy, where a moment afterwards they must both die.

We had all gazed on this scene in silence; when my mother turned herself round to the others, the sibyl had vanished. This, in connexion with the little occurrence, which, as will be seen, many years afterwards had an influence on my fate, and which was deeply stamped upon my memory, made us all somewhat silently hasten home. Darkness seemed to come forth from the thickset leaves of the trees, the fire-red evening clouds reflected themselves in the mirror of the lake, the mill-wheel rushed round with a monotonous sound; all seemed to have in it some-thing demoniacal. As we went along, Angeline related to us in a whisper strange things which had been told to her of the old woman, who understood how to mix poisons and love-potions; and then she told us about poor Therese of Olevano — how she wasted away day by day from anxiety and longing after the slender Guiseppe, who had gone away beyond the mountains to the north — how the old woman had boiled herbs in a copper vessel, and let them simmer over the hot coals for several days, until Guiseppe also was seized upon by a longing, and was obliged to speed back again, day and night, without rest or stay, to where the vessel was boiling holy herbs and a lock of his and Therese's hair. I said an Ave Maria softly, and did not feel easy until I was again in the house with Angeline.

The four wicks in the brass lamp were lighted, one of our garlands hung around it, and a supper of *mongana al pomidoro** was set out for us, together with a bottle full

---

* Veal and tomatoes.

of wine. The peasants in the room below us drank and improvised ; it was a sort of duet between two of them, and the whole company joined in the chorus, but when I went with the other children to sing before the image of the Virgin, which hung beside the great chimney where the fire burned, they all listened and praised my beautiful voice, which made me forget the dark wood and the old Fulvia who had told my fortune. I would gladly now have begun to improvise in emulation of the peasant's, but my mother damped my vanity and my wish by the inquiry whether I thought it becoming for me, who swung the censer in the church, and, perhaps, some day should have to explain the word of God to the people, to set myself up there like a fool ; that it was not now carnival time, and that she would not allow it. But when in the evening we were in our sleeping-room, and I had climbed up into the broad bed, she pressed me tenderly to her heart, called me her comfort and her joy, and let me lay my head upon her arm, where I dreamed till the sun shone in at my window, and awoke me to the beautiful feast of flowers.

How shall I describe the first glance into the street — that bright picture as I then saw it ? The entire, long, gently ascending street was covered over with flowers ; the ground colour was blue : it looked as if they had robbed all the gardens, all the fields, to collect flowers enough of the same colour to cover the street ; over these lay in long stripes, green, composed of leaves, alternately with rose-colour ; at some distance from this was a similar stripe, and between this a layer of dark red flowers, so as to form, as it were, a broad border to the whole carpet. The middle of this represented stars and suns, which were formed by a close mass of yellow, round, and star-like flowers ; more labour still had been spent upon the formation of names — here flower was laid upon flower, leaf upon leaf. The whole was a living flower-carpet, a mosaic floor, richer in pomp of colouring than any thing which Pompeii can show. Not a breath of air stirred — the flowers lay immovable, as if they were heavy, firmly set precious stones. From all windows were hung upon the walls large carpets, worked in leaves and flowers, representing holy pictures. Here Joseph led the ass on which sat the Madonna and the child; roses formed the faces, the feet, and the arms; gilly-flowers and anemones their fluttering garments; and crowns were made of white water-lilies, brought from Lake Nemi. Saint Michael fought with the dragon; the holy Rosalia showered down roses upon the dark blue globe; wherever my eye fell flowers related to me biblical legends, and the people all round about were as joyful as myself. Rich foreigners, from beyond the mountains, clad in festal garments, stood in the balconies, and by the side of the houses moved along a vast crowd of people, all in full holyday costume, each according to the fashion of his country. Beside the stone basin which surrounds the great fountain, where the street spreads itself out, my mother had taken her place, and I stood just before the satyr's head which looks out from the water.

The sun burnt hotly, all the bells rung, and the procession moved along the beautiful flower-carpet; the most charming music and singing announced its approach. Choristers swung the censer before the host, the most beautiful girls of the country followed, with garlands of flowers in their hands, and poor children, with wings to their naked shoulders, sang hymns, as of angels, whilst awaiting the arrival of the procession at the high altar. Young fellows wore fluttering ribands around their pointed hats, upon which a picture of the Madonna was fastened; silver and gold rings hung to a chain around their necks, and handsome, bright-coloured scarfs looked splendidly upon their black velvet jackets. The girls of Albano and Frascati came, with their thin veils elegantly thrown over their black, plaited hair, in which was stuck the silver arrow; those from Villetri, on the contrary, wore garlands around their hair, and the smart neckerchief, fastened so low down in the dress as to leave visible the beautiful shoulder and the round bosom. From Abruzzi, from the Marshes, from every other neighbouring district, came all in their peculiar national costume, and produced altogether the most brilliant effect. Cardinals, in their mantles woven with silver, advanced under canopies adorned with flowers, monks of various orders followed, all bearing burning tapers. When the procession came out of the church an immense crowd followed. We were carried along with it, — my mother held me firmly by the shoulder, that I might not be separated from her. Thus I went on, shut in by the crowd; I could see nothing but the blue sky above my head. All at once there was sent forth a piercing cry — it rang forth on all sides; a pair of unmanageable horses rushed through — more I did not perceive: I was thrown to the earth, it was all black before my eyes, and it seemed to me as if a waterfall dashed over me.

Oh! Mother of God, what a grief! a thrill of horror passes through me whenever I think of it. When I again returned to consciousness, I lay with my head in Mariuccia's lap, she sobbed and cried: beside us lay my mother stretched out, and there stood around a little circle of strange people. The wild horses had gone over us, the wheel had gone over my mother's breast, blood gushed out of her mouth — she was dead.

I looked at the heavy, closed eyes, and folded the lifeless hands which lately had so lovingly protected me. The monks carried her into the convent, and as I was altogether without injury, excepting that one hand was a little scratched, Mariuccia took me back again to the hostel where I had been yesterday so joyful, had bound garlands, and slept in my mother's arms. I was most deeply distressed, although I did not apprehend how entirely forlorn I was. They gave me playthings, fruit, and cakes, and promised me that on the morrow I should see my mother again, who, they said, was to-day with the Madonna, with whom there was a perpetual flower-feast and rejoicing. But other things which Mariuccia said also did not escape my attention. I heard her whisper about the hateful eagle yesterday, about Fulvia, and about a dream which my mother had had; now she was dead every one had foreseen misfortune.

The runaway horses had, in the mean time, gone right through the city, and, striking against a tree, had been stopped, and a gentleman of condition, upwards of forty years of age, half dead with terror, had then been helped from the carriage. He was, it was said, of the Borghesa family, and owned a villa between Albano and Frascati, and was known for his singular passion for collecting all kinds of plants and flowers; nay, in the dark sciences it was believed that he was as knowing as even the wise Fulvia. A servant in rich livery brought a purse containing twenty scudi from him for the motherless child.

The next evening, before the ringing of the Ave Maria, I was conducted into the convent, to see my mother for the last time; she lay in the narrow wooden coffin, in her holyday apparel, as yesterday at the flower-feast. I kissed her folded hands, and the women wept with me.

There stood already at the door the corpse-bearers and the attendants, wrapped in their white cloaks, with the hoods drawn over their faces. They lifted the bier on their shoulders, the Capuchins lighted their tapers, and began the song for the dead. Mariuccia went with me close behind the corpse, the red evening heaven shone upon my mother's face; she looked as if she lived. The other children of the city ran gaily around me, and collected in little paper bags the drops of wax which fell from the monks' tapers.

We went through the streets where yesterday had passed the festival-procession — it lay scattered over with leaves and flowers; but the pictures, the beautiful figures, were all vanished like the happiness of my childhood, the bliss of my past days. I saw when we reached the church-yard how the great stone was lifted aside which covered the vault into which the corpses were lowered. I saw the coffin descend, and heard the dull sound as it was set down upon the others. Then all withdrew except Mariuccia, who let me kneel upon the grave-stone, and repeat an " Ora pro nobis !"

In the moonlight night we journeyed back from Genzano; Federigo and two strangers were with us. Black clouds hung upon the mountains of Albano. I saw the light mists which flew in the moonlight across the Campagna. The others spoke but very little, and I soon slept, and dreamed of the Madonna, of the flowers, and my mother, who lived, smiled, and talked to me.

CHAPTER IV.

UNCLE PEPPO. — THE NIGHT IN THE COLOSSEUM. — THE DISMISSAL.

WHAT should really now be done with me? that was the question which was asked when we came back to Rome, and into my mother's house. Fra Martino advised that I should go to the Campagna to Mariuccia's parents, who kept flocks, and were honest people, to whom the twenty scudi would be wealth, and who would not hesitate to take me home to them, and to treat me as their own child; but, then, I was in part a member of the church, and, if I went out to the Campagna, I should no longer swing the censer in the church of the Capuchins. Federigo also thought it better that I should remain in Rome with some decent people; he should not like, he said, that I should be only a rough, simple peasant.

Whilst Fra Martino counselled with himself in the convent, my uncle Peppo came stumping upon his wooden clogs. He had heard of my mother's death, and that twenty scudi had fallen to me, and for this reason he also now came to give his opinion. He declared, that as he was the only relative I had in the world, he should take me to himself; that I was to follow him, and that every thing which the house contained was his, as well as the twenty scudi. Mariuccia maintained with great zeal that she and Fra Martino had already arranged every thing for the best, and gave him to understand that he, a cripple and a beggar, had enough to do with himself, and could not have any voice in the matter.

Federigo left the room, and the two who remained reproached each other mutually with the selfish ground of their regard for me. Uncle Peppo spit forth all his venom, and Mariuccia stood like a Fury before him. She would, she said, have nothing to do with him, nor with the boy; she would have nothing to do with any thing. She said he might take me and get me a pair of wooden crutches made, and so like a cripple I could help to fill his bag!

He might take me with him, but the money she would keep till Fra Martino came back ; not a single stiver of it should his false eyes behold ! Peppo threatened to knock a hole in her head, as big as the Piazzo del Popolo, with his wooden hand-clogs. I stood weeping near to them. Mariuccia pushed me from her, and Peppo drew me to him. I must follow him, he said, must attach myself to him ; but if he bore the burden he also would have the reward. The Roman senate knew well enough how to do right to an honest man : and then he drew me against my will out of the house door, where a ragged lad held his ass : for on great occasions, and when haste was required, he cast aside his board, and held himself fast on the ass with his withered legs ; he and it were, so to say, one body. Me he set before him upon the beast ; the lad gave it a blow, and so we trotted off, whilst he caressed me in his own way.

"Dost thou see, my child?" he said, "is it not an excellent ass? and fly can he, fly like a racer through the Corso ! Thou wilt be well off with me, like an angel of heaven, my fine fellow !" And then followed a thousand curses and maledictions against Mariuccia.

"Where hast thou stolen that pretty child?" inquired his acquaintance as we rode onward, and so my history was told and told again almost at every corner. The woman who sold citron-peel water reached to us a whole glass for our long story, and gave me a pine-apple to take with me, the inside of which was all gone. Before we got under his roof the sun had gone down. I said not one word, but pressed my hands before my face, and cried. In the little room which adjoined the larger room, he showed me in a corner a bed of maize-leaves, or rather the dried husks of the maize ; here I was to sleep. Hungry I could not be, he said, nor thirsty either, for we had drunk the excellent glass of citron-water. He patted me on the cheek with that same hateful smile of which I always felt such horror. He then asked me how many silver pieces there were in the purse, whether Mariuccia had paid the vetturino out of it, and what the strange servant had said when he brought the money. I would give him no ex-

planation, and asked with tears whether I was always to
remain here, and whether I could not go home to-morrow.

"Yes, surely! yes, surely!" said he; "sleep now, but
do not forget thy Ave Maria; when people sleep the devil
wakes: make the sign of the cross over thee, it is an iron
wall which a raging lion cannot break through! Pray
piously; and pray that the Madonna will punish with
poison and corruption the false Mariuccia, who would
overreach thy innocence, and cheat thee and me of all thy
property. Now go to sleep, the little hole above can stand
open, the fresh air is half a supper. Don't be afraid of
the bats — they fly past, the poor things! Sleep well, my
Jesus-child!" And with this he bolted the door.

For a long time he busied himself in the other room;
then I heard other voices, and the light of a lamp came in
through a chink in the wall. I raised myself up, but
quite softly, for the dry maize-leaves rustled loudly, and
I was afraid that he would hear them and come in again.
I now saw through the chink that two wicks were lighted
in the lamp, bread and radishes were set on the table, and
a flask of wine went round the company. All were beggars, all cripples; I knew them all well, although there
was quite another expression on their countenances than I
was accustomed to see there. The fever-sick, half-dead
Lorenzo, sat there merry and noisy, and talked without
intermission; and by day I had always seen him lying
stretched out on the grass on Monte Pincio*, where he
supported his bound-up head against a tree-stem, and
moved his lips as if half-dying, whilst his wife pointed out
the fever-sick, suffering man, to the passers-by. Francia,
with his fingerless hands, drummed with the stumps upon
the shoulders of the blind Cathrina, and sang half aloud
"Cavalier Torchino." Two or three others sat near the
door, but so much in the shadow, that I did not know
them. My heart beat violently with fear. I heard that
they talked about me.

"Can the boy do any thing?" asked one. "Has he
any sort of a hurt?"

* This is the public promenade which extends from the Spanish Steps to
the French Academy, and down to Porta del Popolo, looking over the greatest
part of Rome and the sea, with the Villa Borghese. — *Author's note.*

"No, the Madonna has not been so kind to him," said Peppo ; "he is slender and well formed, like a nobleman's child."

"That is a great misfortune," said they all. The blind Cathrina added that I could have some little hurt, which would help me to get my earthly bread until the Madonna gave me the heavenly.

"Ay," said Peppo, "if my niece had been wise the lad might have made his fortune ! He has a voice, oh, like the dear angels of heaven ! he was meant for the Pope's chapel ! he ought to have been a singer !"

They talked of my age, and of what could yet be done, and how my fortune must be made. I did not understand what they would do with me, but thus much, I saw clearly that it was something bad they meant, and I trembled for fear. But how should I get away ? This alone filled my whole soul. Whither should I go ? No, of that I thought not. I crept along the floor to the open hole ; by the help of a block of wood I climbed up to it. I saw not a single person in the street. The doors were all closed. I must take a great leap if I would reach the ground ; I had not courage for the leap until I seemed to hear some one at my door : they were coming in to me. A shudder went through me, I let myself slide from the wall. I fell heavily, but only upon earth and green turf.

I started up and ran, without knowing whither, through the narrow, crooked streets. A man who sang aloud, and struck with his stick upon the stone pavement, was the only person I met. At length I stood in a great square : the moon shone brightly. I knew the place : it was the Forum Romanum, the cow-market as we called it.

The moon illumined the back of the Capitol, which, like a perpendicular wall of rock, seemed to divide the closely-built part of Rome from that which was more open. Upon the high steps of the arch of Septimus Severus lay several beggars asleep, wrapped in their large cloaks. The tall columns which yet remain of the old temple cast long shadows. I had never been there before after sunset : there was something spectral to me in the whole ; and as I went along I stumbled over the marble capitals which lay

in the long grass. I rose up and gazed upon the ruins of
the city of the Cæsars. The thick ivy made the walls
still darker ; the black cypresses raised themselves so
demon-like and huge in the blue air, that I grew more
and more fearful. In the grass, amid the fallen columns
and the marble rubbish, lay some cows, and a mule still
grazed there : it was a sort of consolation to me, that
here were living creatures which would do me no harm.

The clear moonlight made it almost as bright as day;
every object showed itself distinctly. I heard some one
coming — was it some one in search of me ? In my
terror I flew into the gigantic Colosseum, which lay before
me like a vast mass of rock. I stood in the double-vaulted
passage which surrounds one half of the building, and is
large and perfect as if only completed yesterday. Here it
was quite dark, and ice-cold. I advanced a few steps
from between the pillars, but softly, very softly, for the
sound of my own footsteps made me more fearful. I saw
a fire upon the ground, and could distinguish before it the
forms of three human beings : were they peasants who
had here sought out a resting-place for the night, that they
might not ride over the desolate Campagna during the
hours of darkness? or were they, perhaps, soldiers who
kept watch in the Colosseum? or they might be robbers.
I fancied that I heard the rattling of their weapons, and I
therefore withdrew softly back again to where the tall
pillars stand without any other roof than that which is
formed by bushes and climbing plants. Strange shadows
fell in the moonlight upon the lofty wall ; square masses
of stone shot out from their regular places, and, overgrown
with evergreen, looked as if they were about to fall, and
were only sustained by the thick climbers.

Above, in the middle gallery, people were walking, travellers, certainly, who were visiting these remarkable ruins
late in the beautiful moonlight: a lady, dressed in white,
was in the company. Now I saw distinctly this singular
picture, as it came into view, vanished, and again showed
itself between the pillars, lighted by the moonbeams and
the red torch. The air was of an infinitely dark blue, and
tree and bush seemed as if made of the blackest velvet;

every leaf breathed night. My eye followed the strangers. After they were all gone out of sight, I still saw the red glare of the torch ; but this also vanished, and all around me was as still as death.

Behind one of the many wooden altars which stand not far apart within the ruins, and indicate the resting-points of the Saviour's progress to the cross, I seated myself upon a fallen capital, which lay in the grass. The stone was as cold as ice, my head burned, there was fever in my blood ; I could not sleep, and there occurred to my mind all that people had related to me of this old building ; of the captive Jews who had been made to raise these huge blocks of stone for the mighty Roman Cæsar ; of the wild beasts which, within this space, had fought with each other, nay, even with men also, while the people sat upon stone benches, which ascended, step-like, from the ground to the loftiest colonnade. *

There was a rustling in the bushes above me ; I looked up, and fancied that I saw something moving. Ah, yes, my imagination showed to me pale, dark shapes, which hewed and builded around me: I heard distinctly every stroke which fell, saw the meagre, black-bearded Jews tear away grass and shrubs to pile stone upon stone, till the whole monstrous building stood there newly erected ; and now all was one throng of human beings, head above head, and the whole seemed one infinitely vast, living giant-body.

I saw the Vestals in their long white garments ; the magnificent court of the Cæsar ; the naked, bleeding gladiators : then I heard how there was a roaring and a howling round about in the lowest colonnades. From various sides sprung in whole herds of tigers and hyænas ; they sped close past the spot where I lay ; I felt their burning

---

* The Colosseum is of an oval form and is built of Travertine marble. There are four stories, each of which is of a different order, Doric, Ionic, and Corinthian. It was built under Vespasian, about seventy years after Christ. Twelve thousand captive Jews laboured at its erection. There are eighty arches, and its circumference is about 1641 feet. There was room within it for 86,000 persons sitting, and upwards of 20,000 standing. The ruins are now used for Christian worship.

" Whilst stands the Colosseum, Rome shall stand ;
When falls the Colosseum, Rome shall fall ;
And when Rome falls — the world." — BYRON.
Author's Note.

breath; saw their red, fiery glances, and held myself fast upon the stone upon which I was seated, whilst I prayed the Madonna to save me: but wilder still grew the tumult around me; yet I could see in the midst of all the holy cross as it still stands, and which, whenever I had passed it, I had piously kissed. I exerted all my strength, and perceived distinctly that I had thrown my arms around it; but every thing that surrounded me tumbled violently together — walls, men, beasts. Consciousness had left me, I perceived nothing more.

When I again opened my eyes, my fever was over, but I was enfeebled, and as if oppressed with weariness.

I lay actually upon the steps of the great wooden cross. I noticed now all that surrounded me: there was nothing at all terrific in it; a deep solemnity lay upon the whole; a nightingale sang among the bushes on the wall: I thought upon the dear child Jesus, whose mother, now that I had none, was mine also, threw my arms around the cross, rested my head against it, and soon sank into a calm, refreshing sleep.

This must have lasted several hours. I was awoke by the singing of a psalm. The sun shone upon the highest part of the wall: the Capuchins went with burning tapers from altar to altar, and sang their " Kyrie eleison," in the beautiful morning. They stood now around the cross where I lay; — I saw Fra Martino bending over me. My forlorn appearance, my paleness, and my being here at this hour, made him uneasy. Whether I explained all to him I know not; but my terror of Uncle Peppo, and my forlorn condition, was clear enough to him; I held fast by his brown cloak, prayed him not to leave me, and it seemed as if the brethren sympathised in my misfortune. They all, indeed, knew me; I had been in the cells of all of them, and had sung with them before the holy altar.

How glad then was I when Fra Martino led me back with him to the convent, and how entirely I forgot all my need as I sat in his little cell, where the old woodcuts were pasted upon the wall, and the orange-tree stretched its green, fragrant twigs in at the window. Fra Martino also had promised me that I should not again be sent back to Peppo. "A beggar," I heard him say to the others,—— "a begging cripple that lies in the streets craving alms; the boy never shall be given up to!"

At mid-day he brought me radishes, bread, and wine, and said to me, with such solemnity that my heart trembled within me, "Poor lad! if thy mother had lived, then had we not been separated; the church would have possessed thee, and thou wouldst have grown up in its peace and protection. Now must thou go forth upon the restless sea, floating upon an insecure plank; but think upon thy bleeding Saviour, and on the heavenly Virgin! Hold fast by them! Thou hast in the whole wide world only them!"

"Where then shall I go?" I asked. And now he told me that I was to go to the Campagna, to the parents of Mariuccia, and besought me to honour them as father and mother, to be obedient to them in all things, and never to forget my prayers and the learning which he had given me.

In the evening Mariuccia came with her father to the convent-gate to fetch me; Fra Martino led me out to them. With regard to dress, Peppo looked almost more respectable than this herdsman, to whom I was now consigned. The torn leather boots, the naked knees, the pointed hat in which was stuck a sprig of flowering heather, were the things which first caught my eye. He knelt down, kissed Fra Martino's hand, and said of me that I was a pretty lad, and that he and his wife would divide every morsel with me. Mariuccia gave him the purse which contained all my wealth, and afterwards all four went into the church: they prayed silently to themselves. I kneeled too, but I could not pray; my eyes sought out all the well-known pictures: Jesus sailing in the ship, high above the church door; the angels in the great altar-piece, and the holy St. Michael; even to the death's heads, with ivy garlands around them, must I say farewell. Fra Martino laid his hand upon my head, and gave me at parting a little book, in which were woodcuts "*Modo di servire la sancta messa*," and so we parted

As we went across the Piazza Barberini, I could not help looking up to my mother's house; all the windows stood open, the rooms had new inmates.

CHAPTER V.

THE CAMPAGNA.

THE immense desert which lies around old Rome was now my home.   The stranger from beyond the mountains, who, full of love for art and antiquity, approaches the city of the Tiber for the first time, sees a vast page of the world in this parched-up desert; the isolated mounds all here are holy ciphers, entire chapters of the world's history.   Painters sketch the solitary standing arch of a ruined aqueduct, the shepherd who sits under it with his flock figures on the paper ; they give the golden thistle in the foreground, and people say that it is a beautiful picture.   With what an entirely different feeling my conductor and I regarded the immense plain !   The burnt-up grass ; the unhealthy summer air, which always brings to the dwellers of the Campagna fevers and malignant sickness, were doubtless the shadow side of his passing observations.   To me there was a something novel in all ; I rejoiced to see the beautiful mountains, which in every shade of violet-colour inclosed one side of the plain ; the wild buffalo, and the yellow Tiber, on whose shore oxen with their long horns went bending under the yoke, and drawing the boat against the stream.   We proceeded in the same direction.

Around us we saw only short, yellow grass, and tall, half-withered thistles.   We passed a crucifix, which had been raised as a sign that some one had been murdered there, and near to it hung a portion of the murderer's body, an arm and a foot : this was frightful to me, and all the more so as it stood not far from my new home.   This was neither more nor less than one of the old decayed tombs, of which so many remain here from the most ancient times. Most of the shepherds of the Campagna dwell in these, because they find in them all that they require for shelter, nay, even for comfort. They excavate one of the vaults, open a few holes, lay on a roof of reeds, and the dwelling is ready. Ours stood upon a height, and consisted of two stories. Two Corinthian pillars at the narrow door-way bore witness to the antiquity of the building, as well as the three broad buttresses to its after-repairs. Perhaps it had been used in the middle ages as a fort; a hole in the wall above the door served as a window; one half of the roof was composed of a sort of reed and of twigs; the other half consisted of living bushes, from among which the honeysuckle hung down in rich masses over the broken wall.

"See, here we are!" said Benedetto; and it was the first word he had said to me on the whole way.

"Do we live here?" I asked, and looked now at the gloomy dwelling, now back again to the mutilated remains of the robber. Without giving me any reply, he called to an old woman, "Domenica!—Domenica!" and I saw an aged woman, whose sole clothing consisted of a coarse shift, with bare arms and legs, and hair hanging loosely. She heaped upon me kisses and caresses; and, if father Benedetto had been silent, she was only the more talkative; she called me her little Ishmael, who was sent out into the desert, where the wild thistles grow. "But thou shalt not be famished with us!" said she. "Old Domenica will be to thee a good mother in the place of her who now prays for thee in heaven! And I have made thy bed ready for thee, and the beans are boiled, and my old Benedetto and thou shalt sit down to table together! And Mariuccia is not then come with you? And thou hast seen the holy father? Yet hast not forgotten some presciutto, nor the brass-hook, nor the new picture of the Madonna, for us to paste on the door beside the old one, which is black with our kissing. No, thou art a man who canst remember, who canst think, my own Benedetto!"

Thus she proceeded with a torrent of words, and led us into the small room, which was called the chamber, but

which afterwards appeared to me as large as the hall of
the Vatican. I believe, indeed, that this home operated
very much upon my poetical turn of mind. This little
narrow room was, to my imagination, what a weight is to
the young palm-tree — the more it is compressed into
itself, the more it grows. The house was, as has been
said already, in the very ancient times, a family burial-
place, which consisted of a large room, with many small
niches, side by side, in two rows, one above the other, all
covered over with the most artistical mosaic. Now was
each put to very different purposes; the one was a store-
room, another held pots and pans, and a third was the
fireplace, where the beans were cooked.

Domenica prepared the table and Benedetto blessed the
food: when we had had enough, the old mother took me
up a ladder, through the broken vault in the wall, to the
second story, where we all slept in two great niches which
had once been graves. In the farthest was the bed which
was prepared for me; beside it stood two posts supporting a third, from which swung a sort of cradle, made of
sail-cloth, for a little child: I fancy Mariuccia's: it was
quite still. I laid myself down; a stone had fallen out of
the wall, and through the opening I could see the blue air
without, and the dark ivy which, like a bird, moved itself
in the wind. As I laid myself down, there ran a thick,
bright-coloured lizard over the wall, but Domenica consoled me by saying that the poor little creature was more
afraid of me than I of it; it would do me no harm! and,
after repeating over me an Ave Maria, she took the cradle
over into the other niche where she and Benedetto slept.
I made the sign of the holy cross, thought on my mother,
on the Madonna, on my new parents, and on the executed
robber's bloody hand and foot which I had seen near the
house, and these all mingled strangely in my dreams this
first night.

The next day began with rain, which continued for a
whole week, and imprisoned us in the narrow room, in
which was a half twilight, although the door stood open
when the wind blew the rain the other way. I had to rock
the baby which lay in the cradle. Domenica spun with

her spindle; told me tales of the robbers of the Campagna, who, however, did no harm; sang pious songs to me, taught me new prayers, and related to me new legends of saints which I had not heard before. Onions and bread were our customary food, and I thought them good; but I grew weary of myself shut up in that narrow room; and then Domenica just outside the door dug a little canal, a little winding Tiber, where the yellow water flowed slowly away. Little sticks and reeds were my boats, which I made to sail past Rome to Ostia; but, when the rain beat in too violently, the door was obliged to be shut, and we sat almost in the dark. Domenica spun, and I thought about the beautiful pictures in the convent church; seemed to see Jesus tossing past me in the boat; the Madonna on the cloud borne upwards by angels, and the tombstones with the garlanded heads.

When the rainy season was over, the heavens showed for whole months their unchangeable blue. I then obtained leave to go out, but not too far, nor too near to the river, because the soft ground might so easily fall in with me, said Domenica; many buffaloes also grazed there, which were wild and dangerous, but, nevertheless, those had for me a peculiar and strange interest. The something demon-like in the look of the buffalo — the strange, red fire which gleamed in its eyeballs, awoke in me a feeling like that which drives the bird into the fangs of the snake. Their wild running, swifter than the speed of a horse, their mutual combats, where force meets with force, attracted my whole attention. I scrawled figures in the sand to represent what I had seen, and, to make this the more intelligible, I sang it all in its own peculiar words to its own peculiar melody, to the great delight of old Domenica, who said that I was a wise child, and sang as sweetly as the angels in heaven.

The sun burnt hotter day by day: its beams were like a sea of fire which streamed over the Campagna. The stagnant water infected the air. We could only go out in the morning and evening. Such heat as this I had not known in Rome upon the airy Monte Pincio, although I well remembered then the hot time when the beggars had prayed for a small coin, not for bread, but for a glass of iced water. I thought in particular about the delicious, green water-melons which lay one on another, divided in halves, and showed the purple-red flesh with the black seeds : my lips were doubly parched with thinking of these. The sun burned perpendicularly : my shadow seemed as if it would vanish under my feet. The buffaloes lay like dead masses upon the burnt-up grass, or, excited to madness, flew, with the speed of arrows, round in great circles. Thus my soul conceived an idea of the traveller's suffering in the burning deserts of Africa.

During two months we lay there like a wreck in the world's sea. Not a single living creature visited us. All business was done in the night, or else in the early hours of morning. The unhealthy atmosphere and the scorching heat excited fever-fire in my blood : not a single drop of any thing cold could be had for refreshment ; every marsh was dried up ; warm, yellow water, flowed sleepily in the bed of the Tiber ; the juice of the melon was warm ; even wine, although it lay hidden among stones and rubbish, tasted sour and half-boiled, and not a cloud, not a single cloud, was to be seen on the horizon, — day and night always the everlasting, never-changing blue. Every evening and morning we prayed for rain, or else a fresh breeze ; every evening and morning, Domenica looked to the mountains to see if no cloud raised itself, but night alone brought shade — the sultry shade of night ; the sirocco alone blew through the hot atmosphere for two long, long months.

At the sun's rise and setting alone was there a breath of fresh air ; but a dulness, a death-like lethargy produced by the heat, and the frightful weariness which it occasioned, oppressed my whole being. Flies and all kind of tormenting insects, which seemed destroyed by the heat, awoke at the first breath of air to redoubled life. They fell upon us in myriads with their poison-stings : the buffaloes often looked as if they were covered over with this buzzing swarm, which beset them as if they were carrion, until, tormented to madness, they betook themselves to the Tiber, and rolled themselves in the yellow water. The Roman, who in the hot summer days groans in the almost expiring streets, and crawls along by the house-sides, as if he would drink up the shadow which is cast down from the walls, has still no idea of the sufferings in the Campagna, where every breath which he draws is sulphurous, poisonous fire; where insects and crawling things, like demons, torment him who is condemned to live in this sea of flame.

September brought with it milder days; it sent out also Federigo one evening to make sketches of the burned-up landscape. He drew our singular house, the gallows, and the wild buffaloes. He gave me paper and pencils, that I also might draw pictures, and promised that when he came next time he would take me with him for a day to Rome, that I should visit Fra Martino and Mariuccia, and all my friends, who seemed really to have quite forgotten me; — but Federigo forgot me also.

It was now November, and the most beautiful time which I had yet spent here. Cool airs were wafted from the mountains, and every evening I saw in the clouds that rich colouring which is only found in the south, and which the painter cannot and dare not give to his pictures. The singular, olive-green clouds, on a grey ground, were to me floating islands from the garden of paradise; the dark blue, on the contrary, those which hung like crowns of fir-trees in the glowing fire of the evening heaven, seemed to me mountains of felicity, in whose valleys the beautiful angels played and fanned cool breezes with their white wings.

One evening as I sat sunk in my reveries, I found that I could gaze on the sun by looking through a finely-pricked leaf. Domenica said that it would injure my eyes, and, to put an end to the sport, she fastened the door. The time went on wearily: I prayed her to let me go out, and, as she consented, I sprang up gladly, and opened the door; but at the same moment a man darted in so suddenly, that I was thrown to the ground: with equal speed he closed the door again. Scarcely had I perceived his pale, agitated countenance, and heard him, in a tone of distress, utter the name of the Madonna, when a violent blow so shattered the door, that it gave way and fell inward, and the whole opening was filled with the head of a buffalo, which glared upon us with his malicious, fiery eyes.

Domenica gave a scream, seized me by the arm, and sprang up several steps of the ladder which led to the upper room. The stranger, pale as death, cast his eyes timidly around him, and perceiving Benedetto's gun, which, in case of nocturnal inroads, always hung on the wall ready-charged, he seized it in a moment. I heard the report, and saw in the cloud of smoke how he had shot the beast through the forehead. It stood immoveably there, squeezed into the narrow doorway, and could neither come forward nor be moved backward.

"But, all ye saints!" exclaimed Domenica, "what have you done? You have really taken the life of the beast!"

"Blessed be Madonna!" replied the stranger; "she has saved my life, and thou wast my good angel!" said he, lifting me from the ground. "Thou openedst the door of salvation for me!" He was yet quite pale, and the cold sweat-drops stood upon his forehead.

We heard immediately by his speech that he was no foreigner, and saw that he must be a noble from Rome. He related, moreover, that it was his pleasure to collect flowers and plants; that for this purpose he had left his carriage at Ponte Molle*, and was going along the banks of the Tiber. Not far from us he had fallen upon the buffaloes, one of which had immediately followed him, and he alone was saved by the nearness of our house, and by the door suddenly opening, as if by miracle.

"Holy Maria, pray for us!" exclaimed Domenica; "yes, she has saved you, the holy mother of God! and my little Antonio was one of her elect! yes, she loves him! Excellenza does not know what a child that is! read can he every thing, whether it is printed or written! and draw so naturally, that one can see directly whatever it is meant for. The dome of St. Peter's, the buffaloes, ay, even fat Father Ambrosius, has he drawn; and then for his voice! Excellenza should hear him sing; the Pope's singers could not excel him; and besides that, he is a good child, a strange child. I would not praise him when he is present, because children cannot bear praise; but he deserves it!"

* Pons Milvius.

"He is, then, not your own son?" inquired the stranger; "he is too young for that."

"And I am too old," replied she. "No, an old fig-tree has no such little heart-shoots; the poor child has no other father and mother in the world than me and my Benedetto. But we will not part with him, even when we have not a stiver left of the money! But then, Holy Virgin!" said she, interrupting herself, and taking hold of the horns of the buffalo, from the head of which the blood streamed into the room, "we must have this beast away! one can neither come in nor go out. Ah, yes! it is jammed in quite fast. We can't get out before Benedetto comes. If it only do not bring us into trouble that the beast is killed!"

"You may be quite easy, good woman," said the stranger; "I will answer for all. You have heard, perhaps, of the Borghese?"

"O Principe!" exclaimed Domenica, and kissed his clothes; but he pressed her hand, and took mine between his, as he desired her to take me in the morning to Rome, to the Borghese Palace, where he lived, and to which family he belonged. Tears filled the eyes of my old foster-mother on account of his great favour, as she called it. My abominable scratches upon bits of paper, which she had preserved with as much care as if they had been the sketches of a Michael Angelo, must now be brought out. Excellenza must see every thing which had pleased her, and I was proud because he smiled, patted my cheeks, and said that I was a little Salvator Rosa.

"Yes," said Domenica, "is it not extraordinary for a child? and is it not so natural that one can plainly see what all is meant for? The buffaloes, the boats, and our little house. See! and that is meant for me! it is just like me; only it wants colouring, for that he can't do with pencil. Now, sing for Excellenza!" said she to me; "sing as well as thou canst, with thy own words! Yes, he can put together whole histories and sermons as well as any monk! Nay, let us hear! Excellenza is a gracious gentleman, he wishes it, and thou knowest how to keep tune."

The stranger smiled, and amused himself with us both. That Domenica should think my improvisation quite a masterpiece was a thing of course; but what I sang, and how, I remember not, and yet that the Madonna, Excellenza, and the buffalo, were the poetical triad of the whole, I recollect distinctly. Excellenza sat silent, and Domenica read in this silence astonishment at my genius.

" Bring the boy with you," were the first words which he spoke. " I will expect you early to-morrow morning. Yet, no—come in the evening, an hour before the Ave Maria. When you come, my people shall be instructed immediately to admit you. But how am I to get out? Have you any other mode of exit than this where the beast lies? and how shall I, without any danger from the buffaloes, get to my carriage at Ponte Molle?"

" Yes, getting out," said Domenica; " there is no possibility of that for Excellenza. I can, to be sure, and so can the rest of us; but it is no way for such a great gentleman! Above here there is a hole where one can creep out, and then slide down quite well; that even I can do in my old age! but it is, as I said, not quite the thing for strangers and grand gentlefolks!"

Excellenza mounted in the meantime up the narrow steps, stuck his head through the hole in the wall, and declared it was as good a way as the steps of the Capitol. The buffaloes had betaken themselves long ago to the Tiber, and on the road, not far from us, went a crowd of peasants sleepily and slowly along the great highway. These he would join: behind their waggon, laden with reeds, he was safe from the buffaloes, if these ventured on a new attack. Yet once more he impressed it upon old Domenica to come the next day, an hour before the Ave Maria, extended his hand to her to kiss, stroked my cheek, and let himself slide down the thick ivy. We soon saw him overtake the waggon, behind which he vanished.

CHAPTER VI.

THE VISIT IN THE BORGHESE PALACE. — END OF THE HISTORY OF MY CHILDHOOD.

BENEDETTO and a couple of herdsmen afterwards removed the animal from the doorway ; there was a great talking and gossiping ; but that which I distinctly remember was, that next morning, before break of day, I was awake and up, because towards evening I was going to the city with Domenica. My Sunday clothes, which had lain for many months under lock and key, were now brought out, and a lovely rose was fastened into my little hat. My shoes were the worst part of my habiliments, and it would have been a difficult thing to decide whether they were that which they were called, or were not rather a pair of antique Roman sandals.

How long was it across the Campagna now, and how the sun burned ! Never in later times has the wine of Falernia and Cyprus tasted more delicious to me than the water which now poured from the mouth of the stone lion in the Piazzo del Popolo.* I pressed my warm cheek to the jaws of the lion, and let the water spout over my head, to the great horror of Domenica, since by so doing my dress was wet and my hair disorderly. In the meantime we strolled down the Via Ripetta, towards the Borghese Palace. How often before now had I, and Domenica no less, gone past this building without regarding it otherwise than any other indifferent object: but now we stood and contemplated it in regular silence ; all seemed so great to us, so magnificent, so rich, and especially the

---

* In coming to Rome from the north, the way passes through the gate del Popolo, and the traveller then finds himself in the large, beautiful Piazzo del Popolo, which lies between the Tiber and Monte Pincio. On either hand he sees, under the shade of cypresses and acacias, modern statues and fountains ; and in the middle of the square, between the well-known four stone lions, stands an obelisk of the time of Sesostris. Beyond lie the three straight streets, Via Babuino, Il Corso, and Via Ripetta, two uniform churches terminating the principal one, Il Corso. No city can have a more pleasant, more gay cheerful appearance than old Rome from this point.—*Author's note.*

long silken curtains in the windows. We knew Excellenza within there; he was actually at our house yesterday; that gave a peculiar interest to the whole. I shall never forget the strange tremor which the pomp of the building and of the rooms produced in me. I had talked quite familiarly with Excellenza: he was, in reality, a human being like all the rest of us; but all this possession, this magnificence!—yes, now I saw the glory which. shows the difference between saints and men. In the centre of the palace four lofty whitewashed colonnades, filled with statues and busts, inclosed a little garden *; tall aloes and cactuses grew up the pillars; citron-trees stood there with grass-green fruit which was not yet yellowed by the sun. Two dancing Bacchantes held a water-bowl aloft, but so obliquely that the water streamed upon their shoulders; tall water-plants drooped over them their juicy, green leaves. How cool, green, and fragrant, was every thing here in comparison with the sterile, burnt-up, burning Campagna!

We ascended the broad marble steps. Beautiful statues stood in niches, before one of which Domenica knelt, and piously made the sign of the cross. She thought that it was the Madonna; afterwards I learned that it was Vesta, the holy virgin also of a more ancient time. Servants in rich livery received us: they met us so kindly that my fear would somewhat have abated had not the hall been so large and so magnificent! The floor was of marble, as smooth as glass, and on all the walls hung beautiful pictures; and where these were not, the walls were covered with looking-glass, and painted with angels that bore garlands and sprays of flowers, and with beautiful birds that extended their broad wings and pecked at red and golden fruit. Never had I seen any thing so splendid!

We had to wait a few moments, and then Excellenza entered, accompanied by a beautiful lady dressed in white, with large, lively eyes, which she riveted upon us. She looked at me with a singularly penetrating but kind glance, stroked my hair from my forehead, and said to him, "Yes, as I

---

* This little garden has been since then altered into a flagged court.—*Author's note.*

said, an angel has saved you! I'll wager that there are wings under that ugly, narrow jacket."

"No," replied he, "I read in his red cheeks that the Tiber will send many waves to the sea before his wings shoot out; the old mother will rather not that he should fly away. That's true, is it not? You would not like to part with him?"

"No; that would be the same as blocking up the door and window of my little house! then it would be dark and lonesome; no, I can't part with the sweet child!"

"But for this one evening," said the lady, "he can stop some hours with us, and then you can fetch him; you have beautiful moonlight to go back in, and you are not afraid of robbers?"

"Yes, the boy stops here for an hour, and you, in the meantime, can go and buy one thing and another that you have need of at home," said Excellenza, and thrust a little purse into Domenica's hand. I heard no more, for the lady took me with her into the hall, and left him and the old mother together.

The rich splendour, the high-born company, quite dazzled me. Now I looked at the smiling angel-children that peeped forth from among the green vine-leaves on the walls; now on the violet-stockinged senators and the red-legged cardinals, who had always appeared to me as a sort of demi-gods, but in whose circle I seemed now to be received. But, above all, my eye was attracted to the beautiful Cupid which, like a lovely child, rode upon the ugly dolphin, which threw up two great streams of water, that fell back again into the basin in which it swam in the middle of the hall.

The high-bred company, nay, even the cardinals and senators, smiled to me a welcome, and a young, handsome man, dressed as an officer of the papal guard, extended to me his hand, when the young lady introduced me as her uncle's good angel. They asked me a thousand questions, to which I readily replied, and soon resounded laughter and the clapping of hands. Excellenza came up, and said that I must sing them a song, which I did willingly. The young officer gave me a glass of foaming wine, which he

E

invited me to drink, but the young lady shook her head and took the glass from me before I had emptied it. Like fire and flame the wine went through my blood. The officer said that I must sing about the handsome lady who stood smiling beside me, and I joyfully did as he desired. Heaven knows what I mixed up together; but my stream of words passed for eloquence, my boldness for wit; and because I was a poor lad from the Campagna, the whole bore the stamp of genius. All applauded me, and the officer himself took a beautiful wreath of laurel from a bust which stood in a corner, and placed it, half smiling, on my head. The whole was a jest, yet I regarded it as sober earnestness—as a homage which made me happy, and made this the brightest moment of my life. I sang to them the songs which Mariuccia and Domenica had taught me; described to them the wicked eyes of the buffaloes and our room in the ruined tomb. Only too quickly passed the time; I must now go home again with my old foster-mother. Laden with cakes, fruit, and several silver coins, I followed her: she was as happy as I was; had made many purchases — articles of clothing, cooking-vessels, and two great bottles of wine. The evening was infinitely beautiful. The night slumbered upon trees and shrubs, but high above us hung the full moon which, like a lovely golden boat in the far outspread dark blue sea of air, sent down coolness over the burnt-up Campagna.

I thought upon the rich saloon, the kind lady, and the many applauding claps; dreamed, both waking and sleeping, the same delicious dream, which was speedily to be reality—beautiful reality.

More than once was I fetched to Rome. The lovely, friendly lady, amused herself with my peculiar turn of mind; she made me tell her tales, talk to her just as I did to old Domenica; she had great delight in it, and praised me to Excellenza. He, too, was kind to me, doubly kind, inasmuch as he was the innocent cause of my mother's death; for he it was who sat in the carriage when the runaway horses passed over her head. The beautiful lady was called Francesca; she often took me with her into the rich picture-gallery which the Borghese Palace contained;

my *naïve* questions and observations on the glorious pictures made her smile she told them again to others, and all laughed with her. In the mornings the hall was filled with strangers, who came from beyond the mountains. Artists sate and copied various paintings; but in the afternoons the pictures were left to their own solitude; then Francesca and I went in, and she related to me many histories, to which the pictures gave occasion.

"The Seasons," by Francesca Albani, were, beyond all others, my favourite pieces; the beautiful, joyous, angel-children, Loves, as she taught me to call them, were as if creations of my own dreams. How deliciously they were staggering about in the picture of Spring! A crowd of them were sharpening arrows, whilst one of them turned round the great grindstone, and two others, floating above, poured water upon it. In summer they flew among the tree branches which were loaded with fruit, which they plucked. They swam in the fresh water, and played with it. Autumn brought the pleasures of the chase. Cupid sits with a torch in his hand, in his little chariot, which two of his comrades draw; whilst Love beckons to the brisk hunter, and shows him the place where they can rest themselves side by side. Winter has lulled all the little ones to sleep; soundly and fast they lie slumbering around. The Nymphs steal their quivers and arrows, which they throw on the fire, that there may be an end of the dangerous weapons.

Why angels were called Loves? why they went about shooting?—yes, there were many things of which I wanted to have a plainer explanation than Francesca at this moment gave me.

"Thou must read thyself about them," said she; "there is a great deal with which thou must become acquainted, but the beginning is not attractive! The whole day long thou must sit on a bench with thy book, not play with the goats in the Campagna, or go here and there looking after thy little friends! Which now shouldst thou like best, either to ride with a helmet and sword beside the coach of the holy father, and wear a fine suit of armour from head to foot, like that in which thou hast seen Fabiani, or to understand all the beautiful pictures which thou seest here, know the whole world around thee, and a thousand histories far more beautiful than those which I have told thee?"

"But can I then never again come to thee?" asked I; "can I not live with good Domenica?"

"Dost thou still remember thy mother, thy dear home with her? Then thou desiredst ever to remain there; thought not of Domenica, not of me; and now we are both of us so much to thee. In a short time this may be again the case; and so it goes through one's whole life."

"But you two are not dead, like my mother!" I replied, with tears in my eyes.

"Die or part must we all! There will come a time when we shall not be altogether as we are now, and I then would know thee joyful and happy."

A torrent of tears was my answer; I felt very unhappy, without properly knowing how to explain the cause of my being so. Francesca patted me on the cheek, and said that I was quite too sensitive, and that this was not at all good in the world. Now came Excellenza, and the young officer with him, who had placed the garland on my head the first time I had improvised before him. He was called Fabiani, and was also very fond of me.

"There is a marriage, a splendid marriage at the Villa Borghese," was shouted some evenings afterwards, till it reached Domenica's poor house on the Campagna. Francesca was the bride of Fabiani, and must now, in a few days, accompany him to his seat near Florence. The marriage was celebrated at the Villa Borghese, just in the neighbourhood of Rome, in the beautiful thick grove of laurels and evergreen oaks, where the lofty pines, winter and summer, lift up their perpetually bright green crowns into the blue air. Then, as now, was that grove a place of recreation for the Romans, as well as for strangers. Rich equipages rolled along the thick oak-alleys; white swans swam on the still lakes, within which the weeping willow was mirrored, and where artificial cascades fell over blocks of stone. High-breasted Roman women, with flashing eyes, rolled forth to the festival, and looked proudly down upon the life-enjoying peasant-girl, who danced upon the highway to the music of her tambourine. Old Domenica went with me all the long way across the Campagna, that we also might be together at the bridal of our benefactress. Outside the garden, where the tall aloes grew up like espaliers along the white wall, we stood and saw the lights shine in the windows. Francesca and Fabiani were married. From the saloon came forth to us the sound of music; and from the green plain, on which the amphitheatre was erected, rockets mounted, aud beautiful fireworks played in the blue air. The shadows of a lady and gentleman were seen on the curtains of one of the lofty windows. " It is he and she !" said Domenica. The shadows bent towards each other in the half-darkened window as if to unite in a kiss. I saw my old foster-mother fold her hands and pray; I also sank down involuntarily before the black cypresses, and prayed for my excellent signora : Domenica kneeled with me. " May they be happy !" and now rained the fire like a thousand fallen stars, as if in token of assent from heaven. But my good old mother wept, wept for me, who was soon to be separated from her. Excellenza had purchased me a place in the Jesuits' school, where I was to be brought up with other children, and to a more splendid life than old Domenica and the Campagna could afford me.

" It is now for the last time," said the old mother, " that we two, whilst my eyes are yet open, shall go together over the Campagna ! Thy feet will tread on polished floors, and on gay carpets : these old Domenica has not; but thou hast been a good child; thou wilt remain so, and never forget me and poor Benedetto ! Oh, God ! yet can a dish of roasted chesnuts make thee happy ? Thou shalt sit and blow up the reeds, and I will see God's angel in thy eyes, when the reeds burn, and the poor chesnuts roast ; so glad wilt thou never more be with so small a gift ! The thistles of the Campagna bear yet red flowers ; upon the polished floors of the rich there grow no straws, and the ground is smooth, one falls so easily there ! Never forget that thou wast a poor child, my little Antonio. Remember that thou must see and not see, hear and not hear; then thou wilt get through the world. Some day, when our Lord has called away me and Benedetto, when the little child which thou hast rocked goes creeping through life with a poor husband in the Campagna, thou wilt, perhaps, then go past in thy own chariot, or on a fine horse; halt thou before the old tomb-chamber where thou hast slept, played, and lived with us, and thou wilt see strangers living there, who will bow themselves deeply before thee. Haughty thou wilt not be, but think upon old times, think upon old Domenica! Look in at the place where the chesnuts were cooked, and where thou rockedst the little child. Thou wilt think upon thy own poor childhood, thou heart's darling child!" With this she kissed me, and clasped me closely to her breast and wept: it seemed to me as if my heart would break.

Our return home and her words were to me far more distressing than our parting, even somewhat later; then she said nothing, but only wept; and when we were outside the door she ran back, and took down the old, half-blackened picture of the Madonna, which was pasted behind the door, and gave it to me; I had kissed it so often—it was the only thing which she had to give me.

CHAPTER VII.

SCHOOL-LIFE. —— HABBAS DAHDAH. —— DIVINA COMEDIA. —— THE
SENATOR'S NEPHEW.

SIGNORA had journeyed away with her husband; I was become a scholar in the school of the Jesuits; new occupations engrossed me; new acquaintances presented themselves; the dramatical portion of my life began to unfold itself. Here years compress themselves together; every hour is rich in change, a whole cycle of pictures, which, now seen from a distant point of view, melt together into one great painting—my SCHOOL-LIFE. As it is to the stranger who for the first time ascends the mountains, and now looks down from above over a sea of clouds and mist, which, by degrees, raises itself or separates, so that now a mountain-top with a city peeps forth; now the sun-illumined part of a valley reveals itself. Thus comes forward and changes the world of my mind. Lands and cities, about which I had never dreamed, lay hid behind the mountains which bounded the Campagna: history peopled every portion of the earth for me, and sang to me strange legends and adventures: every flower, every plant, contained a meaning; but most beautiful to me appeared my fatherland, the glorious Italia! I was proud of being a Roman; every point in my native city was dear and interesting to me; the broken capitals, which were thrown down as corner-stones in the narrow streets, were to me holy relics—Memnon's pillars, which sang strangely to my heart. The reeds by the Tiber whispered to me of Romulus and Remus; triumphal arches, pillars, and statues, impressed upon me yet more deeply the history of my fatherland. I lived in its classical antiquity, and the present time, that will speak for itself: my teacher of history gave me praise and honour for it.

Every society, the political as well as the spiritual, assemblies in the taverns, and the elegant circles around the card-tables of the rich, all have their harlequin; he bears now a mace, orders, or ornaments: a school has him no less. The young eyes easily discover the butt of their jests. We had ours, as well as any other club, and ours was the most solemn, the most grumbling, growling, preaching of harlequins, and, on that account, the most exquisite. The Abbé Habbas Dahdah, an Arab by descent, but educated from his earliest childhood in the papal jurisdiction, was at this time the guide and director of our taste, the æsthetical head of the Jesuit school, nay, of the Academia Tiberina.

In later years I have often reflected on poetry, that singular, divine inspiration. It appears to me like the rich gold ore in the mountains; refinement and education are the wise workmen who know how to purify it. Sometimes purely unmixed ore-dust is met with, the lyrical improvisation of the poet by nature. One vein yields gold, another silver; but there are also tin, and even more ordinary metals found, which are not to be despised, and which sometimes can, with polishing and adorning, be made to look like gold and silver. According to these various metals I now rank my poets, as golden, silver, copper, and iron men. But after these comes a new class, who only work in simple potter's clay — the poetasters — yet who desire as much to be admitted to the true guild. Habbas Dahdah was one of these, and had just ability sufficient to make a sort of ware, which with a kind of poetical facility he overwhelmed people, with whom, as regarded deep feeling and poetical spirit, he could not measure himself. Easy, flexile verses, and the artistical formation of them, so that they only brought before the eye existences, hearts, and other such things, obtained from him admiration and applause.

It might be, therefore, perhaps only the very peculiar melody of Petrarch's sonnets that attracted him to this poet. Perhaps, also, only fashion, or a fixed idea, a bright gleam in the sickliness of his views, for Petrarch and Habbas Dahdah were extremely different beings. He compelled us to learn by heart almost a fourth part of the long epic poem, " Africa," where salt tears and blows rained down in honour of Scipio.*

The profoundness of Petrarch was daily impressed upon us. " Superficial poets," said he, " those who only paint with water-colours, children of fancy, are the very spawn of corruption ; and among the very greatest of these *that* Dante, who set heaven, earth, and hell, in movement to obtain immortality, which Petrarch has already won by a single little sonnet — is, in my estimation, petty, very petty ! To be sure he could write verse ! It is these billows of sound which carry his Tower of Babel to the latest age. If he had only followed his first plan, and had written in Latin, he would have shown study ; but that was inconvenient to him, and so he wrote in the vulgate, which we now have. ' It is a stream,' says Boccaccio,

---

* In order to immortalise himself and the Scipios, Petrarch wrote an epic poem called " Africa," which is now forgotten in the glory of his melodious sonnets to Laura, which he himself did not set any high value upon.—*Author's note.*

'through which a lion can swim, and a lamb may walk.'
I find not this depth and this simplicity. There is in him
no right foundation, an eternal swaying between the past
and the present ! But Petrarch, that apostle of the truth,
did not exhibit his mettle with the pen by placing a dead
pope or emperor in hell : he stood in his time like the
Chorus in the Greek tragedy, a male Cassandra, warning
and blaming popes and princes. Face to face he dared to
say to Charles the Fourth, ' One can see in thee that virtues
are not heritable !' When Rome and Paris wished to
offer him the garland, he turned to his contemporaries
with a noble self-consciousness, and bade them to declare
aloud whether he were worthy to be crowned as a poet.
For three days he submitted to an examination as if he
were a regular schoolboy like you, before he would ascend
the Capitol, where the King of Naples hung around him
the purple mantle, and the Roman senate gave to him the
laurel crown which Dante never obtained."

Such was every oration which he made, to elevate Petrarch and depreciate Dante, instead of placing the noble
pair side by side, like the fragrant night-violet and the
blooming rose. We had to learn all his sonnets by heart.
Of Dante we read not a word ; and I only learned through
the censure of Habbas Dahdah that he had occupied himself with heaven, purgatory, and hell, — three elements
which attracted me in the highest degree, and inspired me
with the greatest desire to become acquainted with his
works. But this could only be done in secret ; Habbas
Dahdah would never have forgiven me meddling with this
forbidden fruit.

One day as I was walking on the Piazzo Navone, among
the piled-up oranges, and the iron wares which lay on the
ground, among the old clothes, and all that chaos of rags
which this place exhibits, I came upon a table of old books
and prints. There lay caricatures of maccaroni-swallowers,
Madonnas with the sword in the bleeding heart, and suchlike highly dissimilar things. A single volume of Metastasio drew my attention ; I had a paolo in my pocket — a
great sum for me, and the last remains of the scudi which
Excellenza had given me half a year before for pocket-

money.   I was willing to expend a few bajocci* on Metastasio, but I could not separate myself from my whole
paolo.   The bargain was nearly closed, when my eyes
caught a titlepage, " Divina Commedia di Dante "—my forbidden fruit of the tree of the knowledge of good and evil !
I threw down Metastasio, and seized the other ; but the
price of this was too high for me, three paoli I could not
raise.   I turned the money in my hand till it burned like
fire, but it would not double itself, and I could only beat
down the seller to that price.   This was the best book in
Italy — the first poetical work in the world, he said ; and
a stream of eloquence over Dante, the depreciated Dante
of Habbas Dahdah, poured from the lips of the honest
man.

"Every leaf," said he, " is as good as a sermon.   He is
a prophet of God, under whose guidance one passes through
the flames of hell, and through the eternal paradise.   You
do not know him, young gentleman ! or otherwise you
would immediately give the price if I asked a scudi for
him !   For your whole life long you have then the most
beautiful book of the fatherland, and that for two poor
paoli !"

Ah ! I would willingly have given three if I had but
had them, but now it was with me as with the fox and the
sour grapes ; I also would show my wisdom, and retailed
a part of Habbas Dahdah's oration against Dante, whilst
I exalted Petrarch.

"Yes, yes !" said the bookseller, after he had vindicated
his poet with much violence and warmth, " you are too
young, and I am too much of a layman to be able to judge
such people.   They may both be very good in their way !
You have not read him ! you cannot !   A young, warm
fellow cannot cherish bitterness against a world's prophet !"

As I now honestly confessed to him that my opinion was
merely founded upon the judgment of my teacher, out of
inspiration for his poet's works he seized the book and threw
it to me, demanding only, in return for the paolo short,

---

* A scudo contains ten paoli, and a paolo ten bajocci : these last are copper
coins, the other silver.—*Author's note.*

that I would now read it, and not condemn the pride of Italy, his beloved, divine Dante.

O how happy that book made me! It was now my own, my own for ever. I had always cherished a doubt of the bitter judgment of Habbas Dahdah; my curiosity and the warmth of the bookseller excited me in the highest degree, so that I could hardly wait for the moment when, unseen by others, I could begin the book.

A new life was now opened to me; my imagination found in Dante an undiscovered America, where nature operated on a larger and more luxuriant scale than I had before seen, where were more majestic mountains, a richer pomp of colour. I took in the great whole, and suffered and enjoyed with the immortal singer. The inscription over the entrance to hell rung within me, during my wandering with him below, like the tolling for the last judgment. —

> " Through me ye enter the abode of woe ;
> Through me to endless sorrow are ye brought ;
> Through me amid the souls accurst ye go.
> Justice did first my lofty Maker move ;
> By power Almighty was my fabric wrought,
> By highest wisdom, and by primal love." *

I saw in that air, ever black, like the sand of the desert which is whirled by the tempest, the race of Adam falling like leaves in autumn, whilst lamenting spirits howled in the torrent of air. Tears filled my eyes at the sight of noble, lofty beings who, unparticipants of Christianity, had here their abode. Homer, Socrates, Brutus, Virgil, and many others, the noblest and best of antiquity, were here, for ever remote from Paradise. It was not enough for me that Dante had made every thing as comfortable and well as it could be in hell. Existence there was yet a grief without suffering, a hopeless longing; they belonged still to the realm of the damned, were inclosed by the deep marshes of hell, from which the sighs of the damned rose up bubble on bubble of poisonous and pestilent vapour. Wherefore had not Christ, when he was down in hell, and again ascended to the right hand of the

* Wright's Dante.

Father, taken all with him out of the Valley of Longing? Could love make a selection among the equally unfortunate? I forgot entirely that the whole was but a fiction. The deep sigh from the sea of boiling pitch went to my heart; I saw them, saw the herd of Simonists come up, and the demons that pushed them down again with their sharp forks. The living descriptions stamped themselves deeply on my soul, and mingled in my ideas by day and my dreams by night. Often when I slept they heard me exclaim, " Pape Satan, alepp Satan Pape ! " They fancied that I had combats with the Devil, and it was reminiscences of that which I had read that I repeated.

In the hours of instruction my mind wandered — a thousand ideas thronged in upon me. With the utmost willingness to do so, I could not drive them away. " What art thou thinking of, Antonio ? " they exclaimed to me ; and shame and terror overwhelmed me, for I knew very well what I was thinking of, — but to leave Dante, and not to finish wandering, was to me impossible.

The day seemed to me long and oppressive, like the gilded mantle of lead which the hypocrite was compelled to wear in the hell of Dante. With uneasiness of heart I crept to my forbidden fruit, and drew in images of terror, which punished me for my imagined sins. Nay, I felt even the sting of the snakes of the pit, which stung and writhed about in flames, wherefrom they, revivified like the phœnix, ascended again to spit out their poison.

The other scholars who slept in the same room with me were often awoke in the night by my cries, and told of my strange, disconnected talk about hell and the damned. The old custodian had seen one morning, to his terror, that I had raised myself up in bed, with my eyes open, yet fast asleep, called upon Lucifer, and wrestled with him, until quite exhausted I had sunk back on the pillow.

It was now the universally received opinion that I had combats with the Evil One ; my bed was sprinkled with holy water, I was enjoined to repeat a certain number of prayers before I laid myself in bed. Nothing could operate more injuriously on my health than exactly this mode of treatment ; my blood was put only into a greater state of ferment thereby, and I myself into a more anxious condition, for I knew the cause of all this, and saw how I betrayed it. At length I reached the point of transition, and came out of the storm into a sort of calm.

Among all the scholars no one stood higher, either by abilites or birth, than Bernardo, the life-rejoicing, almost dissolute Bernardo. It was his daily jest to ride upon the projecting spout high above the fourth story, and to balance himself upon a board between the two corner windows under the roof. All the uproars in our little school kingdom were attributed to him, and that mostly with justice. It was wished that the stillness and repose of the convent might be diffused over us and the whole building, but Bernardo was the disturbing Kobold, yet he never showed himself to be malicious. It was only with regard to Habbas Dahdah that he played a little with the black colouring, and then these two were always on bad terms. But this did not annoy Bernardo. He was the nephew of a senator of Rome, was possessed of great wealth, and had brilliant prospects in life, " for Fortune," said Habbas Dahdah, " threw her pearls into the hollow trees and passed over the slender pines."

Bernardo had his determined opinion in every thing; and when, among his school companions, he could not make his word effective, his hands came to his service, in order to inoculate his sap-green ideas upon the back of the refractory: he was always, therefore, the dominant spirit. Although we were of natures extremely dissimilar, there still existed between us the best understanding. I was, to be sure, always the one who yielded; but even this gave him occasion to deride me.

"Antonio!" said he, "I would cudgel you if I only knew that, by so doing, I could excite a little gall in you. If you would only for once show some character—strike me in the face with your clenched fist when I laugh at you, then I could be your most faithful friend; but now I must give up every hope of you!"

One morning, when we were alone together in the great hall, he seated himself upon the table before me, looked into my face, laughing, and said,—

" You are, however, a greater villain than I ! You play, indeed, an excellent comedy ! For this, folks have their bed sprinkled, and their persons fumed. If you do not guess why, I do. You read Dante's ' Commedia !' "

I grew crimson, and inquired how he could accuse me of such a thing.

" Have you not to-night described the devil to me in sleep, just out of the ' Divina Commedia ? ' Shall I tell you a story ? You are possessed of much fancy, and can enjoy yourself over such descriptions. In hell, there are not merely fire-seas and infected moors, as you know very well from Dante, but also great pools all frozen over ; ice, and ice, where the souls are eternally frozen fast : when one has passed these, one descends to the very deepest depth, where they are who have betrayed their benefactors ; con- sequently there is Lucifer, the rebel against God, —— our greatest benefactor. He stands sunk up to the breast in ice, with outstretched jaws, in which he holds fast Brutus, Cassius, and Judas Iscariot ; and this last has his head downwards, whilst the grim Lucifer shakes his monstrous bat's wings. See, my son, when one has once seen the fellow, one does not very soon forget him. I made ac- quaintance with him in Dante's hell; and you have described him to a hair this night, in your sleep. There- fore, I say to you, how it is you have been reading Dante ; but then you were honester than now. You bade me be silent, and mentioned by name our amiable Habbas Dahdah. Confess it only, now you are awake ! I will not betray you. That is at last something in you that I can like. Yes, yes, I had always a sort of hope of you. But how have you got hold of the book ? From me you might have had it ; I possessed myself of it immediately, for, when Habbas Dahdah spoke ill of it, I conceived the idea that it was worth the trouble of reading. The thick volume regularly terrified me ; but, that I might laugh at him, I took it in hand, and now I am reading it for the third time. Is not hell brilliant ? Where do you think that Habbas Dahdah will go ? He may do with either hot or cold ! "

My secret was now betrayed ; but I could depend on

Bernardo's silence. A more confidential connexion was knit between us. Our conversation, when we were alone, turned upon the " Divina Commedia ;" that occupied and inspired me ; and I must converse on that which employed my soul and my thoughts. " Dante, and his immortal work," was, therefore, the first of my poems which I wrote down.

In my edition of the " Divina Commedia," there was a life of the author, a mere sketch, to be sure, but sufficient to enable me to comprehend his peculiar character. I sang of pure, spiritual love in him and Beatrice, described his suffering in the struggle between the black and the white, the weary wanderings of the excommunicated over the mountains, and his death among strangers. I spoke with most animation of the flight of the enfranchised soul, — its glance backwards upon earth, and down to the deep. The whole thing was borrowed, in small features, from his immortal poem. Purgatory, as he himself had sung it, opened itself again ; the miracle-tree shone with glorious fruit upon its bended branches, which were sprinkled by an eternally rushing waterfall. He sat in the boat where the angel spread out his large white wings as sails, whilst the mountains around trembled as the purified soul ascended to paradise, where the sun and all the angels, like mirrors, reflected the beams of the Eternal God ; where all was bliss, and where the lowest as well as the highest, participated equally of happiness, according to the degree in which every heart could comprehend it.

Bernardo heard my poem, and considered it quite a masterpiece. " Antonio," said he, " you must repeat that at the festival. It will vex Habbas Dahdah ! It is splendid ! Yes, yes, this, and none other shall you repeat !"

I made a movement of dissent.

" How ? " exclaimed he, " you will not ? Then I will ! I will torment him with the immortal Dante. Glorious Antonio, give me your poem. I will repeat it. But then it must really be given to me ! Will you not be unwilling to give up your beautiful plumage to deck out the jackdaw ? You are really an incomparably good-natured fellow ; and this will be a beautiful act in you ! You will consent?"

How willingly would I oblige him ; how willingly even would I see the fun ! There did not need much persuasion.

It was at this time the custom in the Jesuit school, as now in the Propaganda in the Spanish square, that on the 13th of January, *" in onore dei santi re magi,"* the greater part of the scholars made speeches in public ; either a poem in one of the various languages which was taught here, or in that of his home or native country. We ourselves could make choice of the subject, which was only submitted to the censorship of our teacher, after which we were permitted to work it out.

" And you, Bernardo," asked Habbas Dahdah, on the day on which we announced our themes—" you, Bernardo, have not chosen any thing ? You do not belong to the race of singing-birds—we may certainly pass by you !"

" Oh, no," was the reply, " I shall venture this time. I have thought of singing of a poet—certainly not one of the greatest—I have not courage for that ; but I have thought on one of the least—on Dante !"

" Ay, ay," returned Habbas Dahdah ; " he will come out,—and come out with Dante ! that will be a masterpiece !—that will I gladly hear. But as all the cardinals will come, and strangers from all parts of the world, would it not be best to defer this piece of merriment till carnival-time ?" And with these words he went on : but Bernardo was not to be put off in this way, and obtained permission from the other teachers.

Every one now had his theme ; mine was the beauty of Italy.

Each scholar was expected wholly to work out his subject himself ; but a sure way of winning over Habbas Dahdah, and diffusing a sort of sunshine over his bad-weather countenance, was to give him a poem to read through, and to ask from him assistance and advice ; in that case, he commonly worked the whole poem over again, botched and mended it, so that it remained as bad as at first, only in a different way ; and, if it so happened that a stranger praised the poem, he would let fall the remark, that there were a few sparkles of his own wit which had polished away the rough, &c. &c.

My poem on Dante, which was now Bernardo's, he never saw.

At length the day came. The carriages rolled up to the gate; the old cardinals, in their red cloaks with long trains, came in, and took their places in the stately arm-chairs. Tickets, on which our names were inscribed, in the languages in which we were to write our poems, were handed about. Habbas Dahdah made the opening oration, and now followed poems in Syriac, Chaldaic, Coptic, nay, even in Sanscrit, English, and other strange tongues,—nay, the more outlandish and odd the languages sounded, the greater were the applause and bravos, and clapping of hands, mingled with the heartiest laughter.

With a beating heart I came forward, and spoke a few strophes of my "Italy." Repeated acclamations saluted me; the old cardinals clapped their hands in token of applause, and Habbas Dahdah smiled as kindly as it was possible for him to do, and moved prophetically the garland between his hands; for, in Italian, Bernardo only followed me, and it was not to be imagined that the English poem which succeeded him would win any laurels.

Now stepped Bernardo before the chair. My eye and ear followed him with uneasiness. Boldly and proudly he recited my poem on Dante; a deep silence reigned in the hall. The wonderful force which he gave it seemed to seize upon every one. I knew every word of it; but it sounded to me like the song of the poet when it is raised on the wings of music,—the most unanimous applause was awarded to him. The cardinals arose—all was at an end; the garland was given to Bernardo, for although, for order's sake, the succeeding poem was listened to, and received also its applause, people immediately afterwards turned again to the beauty and the spirit of the poem on Dante.

My cheeks burned like fire, my breast heaved, I felt an infinite. unspeakable happiness, my whole soul drank in the incense which was offered to Bernardo. I looked at him, he was become quite other than I had ever seen him before. Pale as death, with his eyes riveted to the ground, he stood there like a criminal—he, who otherwise had looked so unabashedly into every one's face. Habbas Dahdah seemed

F

just like a companion piece to him, and appeared ready to pluck the garland to pieces in his abstraction, when one of the cardinals took it from him and placed it on the head of Bernardo, who bent his knee, and bowed his face into both his hands.

After the festival I sought out Bernardo. " To-morrow ! " he exclaimed, and tore himself loose from me.

On the following day, I observed that he shunned me ; and it grieved me, for my heart was infinitely attached to him, — it needed one trusty soul in this world, and it had selected him.

Two evenings passed, he then threw himself on my neck, pressed my hand, and said, " Antonio, I must speak with you ; I cannot bear it any longer, and will not, either. When they pressed the garland on my head, it was as if they had pressed in a thousand thorns. The acclamations sounded like jeering ! It was to you that the honour belonged ! I saw the joy in your eye, and, do you know, I hated you ! you were to me no longer that which you had been. That is a wicked feeling, I pray you for forgiveness ; but we must now part, I am no longer at home here. I will hence, and not for the next year be the jest of the others when they find that I have not the stolen plumes. My uncle shall and must provide for me. I have told him so — I have besought it from him — I have done that which is repugnant to my nature ; and it seems to me as if you were the cause of it all ! I feel a bitterness towards you, which wounds me to the soul ! We can only be friends under entirely new circumstances !—and we will be so, promise me, Antonio ? "

" You are unjust to me," said I, " unjust to yourself ! Do not let us think any more about that miserable poem, or any thing connected with it. Give me your hand, Bernardo, and do not distress me with such strange talk."

" We will always be friends," said he, and left me. It was late in the evening before he came to his chamber ; and the next morning it was announced that he had left the school to follow another profession.

" He is gone like a falling star," observed Habbas Dahdah, ironically ; " he vanished as soon as one noticed the brightness! The whole was a crack——and so was the poem, too. I shall manage, indeed, that this treasure is preserved! Thou, Holy Virgin! when one looks closely at it, what is it? Is it poetry,——that which runs in and out, without shape or consistency? At first, I thought it was a vase, then a French wine-glass, or a Median sabre; but, when I turned it and drew it, there came out the self-same unmeaning, cut-and-dried shape. In three places there is a foot too many; there are horrible hiatuses; and five-and-twenty times has he used the word 'divina,' as if a poem became divine by the repetition of this word. Feeling, and feeling! that is not all which makes the poet! What a combating with fancies,—— now one is here! now one is there! Neither is it thought, no, discretion, golden discretion! The poet must not let himself be run away with by his subject. He must be cold——ice-cold, must rend to pieces the child of his heart, that he may understand every single portion of it: it is only thus that a work of art can be put together. Not with all this driving and chasing, and all this wild inspiration! And then they set a garland on such a lad! Flogged he should have been for his historical errors, his hiatuses, his miserable work! I have vexed myself, and that does not suit my constitution! The abominable Bernardo!"

Such, probably, was Habbas Dahdah's speech of praise.

CHAPTER VIII.

A WELCOME AND AN UNWELCOME MEETING. —— THE LITTLE
ABBESS. —— THE OLD JEW.

WE all missed the wild, wilful Bernardo, and none missed him more than I did. It seemed to me as if all was empty and deserted around me: I could not enjoy my books; there were dissonances in my soul which I could not even silence; music alone brought a momentary harmony. In the tones of the world, my life and my whole endeavours first received clearness. Here I found more than any poet, than even Dante had expressed; not merely the feelings comprehended from the soul-breathing picture, but the sensitive part, the ear, drank in from living existence. Every evening, before the image of the Madonna on the wall childrens' voices sang to me remembrances from my own childhood, which sounded like a cradle-song from the melancholy bagpipe of the Pifferari. I heard, indeed, in them the monotonous song of the muffled corpse-bearers who carried the coffin of my mother. I began to think about the past and of that which was to come. My heart seemed so strangely to want room; I felt as if I must sing; old melodies intoned within me, and the words came aloud from my lips; yes, too much aloud, for they disturbed Habbas Dadhah, at several rooms distance, who sent to inform me that this was neither an opera-house nor a sing-ing-school, and that there could be no quavering in the school of the Jesuits, excepting such as was in honour of the Virgin. Silently I laid my head against the window-frame and looked into the street, but with my thoughts introverted.

" Felicissima notte, Antonio ! "* reached my ear. A handsome, proud horse was prancing under the window, and then sprang forward with its proud rider. It was a papal officer; with youthful rapidity he bowed himself to his horse, waved his hand again and again till he was out of sight ! but I had recognised him—it was Bernardo, the fortunate Bernardo ! How different had his life been to mine ! No ! I could not think of it ! I drew my hat deeply over my brows, and, as if pursued by an evil spirit, hastened out, and forth wherever the wind would carry me. I thought not then how it was a regulation that no scholar in the Jesuits' school, Propaganda, or any establishment of learning in the Papal States, should go out of the building without being accompanied by a fellow-student of equal or superior age, and might never show themselves alone without an especial permission. Such a universally known

* The inhabitants of the north wish each other " good night, sleep well !" The Italians wish " the happiest night !" The nights of the south have more than dreams. — *Author's Note.*

law as this was never inculcated upon us. I forgot that my freedom in this way was circumscribed, and from this cause went out quite calmly. The old custodian thought perhaps that I had obtained permission.

The Corso was crowded with equipages. A succession of carriages, filled with the natives of Rome and strangers, followed each other: they were taking their evening drive. People stood in throngs around the print-sellers' windows looking at the engravings, and beggars came up to them craving for a bajocco. It was difficult to make one's way through, unless one would venture among the carriages. I had just slipped through in this manner, when a hand took fast hold of my dress, and I heard a well-known horrible voice whisper, " Bon giorno, Antonio ! " I looked down : there sat my uncle, the horrible Peppo, with the two withered legs fastened up to his sides, and with the wooden frame on which he shoved himself onwards. We had never been 'for many years so near to each other. I had always made great circuits to escape him — had avoided the Spanish Steps, where he sat; and when I had been obliged to pass by him in a procession, or with the other scholars, I had always used my utmost endeavours to conceal my face.

" Antonio, my own blood ! " said he, holding fast by my coat, " dost thou not know thy own mother's brother, Peppo ? Think upon St. Joseph *, and then thou hast my name ! Oh, how manly and tall thou hast grown ! "

" Release me ! " exclaimed I, for the people around us looked on.

" Antonio ! " said he, " hast thou forgotten how we two rode together upon the little ass ? Thou sweet child ! Yes, now thou sittest upon a loftier horse, thou wilt not know thy poor uncle — wilt not come to me upon the steps. Yet thou hast kissed my hand, slept upon my poor straw. Don't be ungrateful, Antonio ! "

" Then let me go ! " I cried, and tore the coat out of his hands, and, slipping between the intersecting carriages, came into a side street. My heart trembled for horror of

---

* Peppo is the Italian abbreviation of the name Giuseppe — Joseph. — *Author's Note.*

—yes, what shall I call it?—wounded pride. I fancied
myself to be scorned by every body who had seen us; but
this feeling prevailed only for a moment, and then gave
place to another and a much more bitter one. Every word
which he had said was indeed the truth: I was really the
only child of his sister. I felt that my behaviour had
been cruel, was ashamed before God and myself: it burned
liked fire in my heart. Had I now been alone with Peppo,
I would have kissed his ugly hands, and prayed him for
forgiveness. I was shaken to my inmost soul.

At that moment, the bells of the church of St. Agostino
rang for the Ave Maria. My sin lay heavy upon my soul,
and I went in, that I might pray to the Mother of God.
All was empty and dark in the lofty building; the lights
upon the various altars burned feebly and dreamily without rays, like tinder in the night when the damp sirocco
blows. My soul drank in consolation and pardon.

" Signore Antonio," said a voice close to me, " Excellenza is come and the handsome signora. They are here
from Firenza, and have brought with them their little
angel. Will not you come directly and pay your visit,
and give your welcome? "

It was old Fenella, the wife of the porter at the Palazzo
Borghese. My benefactress was here with her husband
and child. I had not seen her for some years. My soul
was full of joy; I hastened there, and soon the old friendly
faces greeted me again.

Fabiani was gentle and gracious, Francesca glad as a
mother to see me again. She brought to me her little
daughter, Flaminia, a kind-hearted child with wonderfully
bright eyes. She put forth her mouth immediately for
me to kiss, came willingly to me, and we were, in two
minutes, old acquaintances and friends. She sat upon my
arm, and laughed aloud for joy when I danced round the
hall with her, and sang her one of my merry old songs.

" Make not my little abbess * a child of the world,"

---

* It is the custom in most of the Italian families, that when one of the
daughters is destined to the convent from childhood, she bears one or other
name of honour, indicative of her destination, as " Jesus' Bride," " the Nun,"
" the Abbess," &c. — *Author's Note.*

said Fabiani, smiling ; "dost thou not see that she bears already the token of her honour ? " He then showed to me a little silver crucifix, which hung by a cord upon the child's breast. " The holy father gave her this : she bears already her soul-bridegroom upon her heart."

In the plenitude of their love, the young couple had vowed to the church their first female child, and the Pope had bestowed upon the little one in the cradle this holy sign. As a relation of the rich Borghese family, the highest place in the female convents of Rome was open to her ; and, therefore, with them and with all her connexions she bore the honourable name of the Little Abbess. Every story, therefore, that was told her, and every sport, was calculated to fix her ideas on the world to which she peculiarly belonged, on the happiness which awaited her.

She showed me her Jesus-child, her little white-garmented nuns, which went every day to mass, set them up in two rows at the table, as the nurse had taught her, and told me how beautifully they sang and prayed to the Jesus-child. I drew for her merry peasants, who, in their long woollen cloaks, danced around the stone Tritons, and pulchinellos that sat upon one another's shoulders ; and the new pictures unspeakably amused the little one. She kissed them many times, then tore them in her wantonness, and I must draw new ones, till the time came when we must part, by the nurse coming to take her to bed, for her bed-time was long past.

Fabiani and Francesca asked me about the Jesuit school, about my health, and whether I were contented, and promised to be always kind to me, and wished me the best fortune.

" We must see you every day," said they ; "come very often whilst we are here."

They inquired also about old Domenica on the Campagna, and I told how happy she was when I went in spring and autumn to see her ; how she roasted chesnuts for me, and seemed to become young again in talking of the days which we had spent together ; and how I must every time see the little nook where I had slept, and the pictures which I had drawn, and which she preserved with her rosary and her old prayer-book.

"How queerly he bows!" said Francesca to Fabiani, as, in the evening, I bowed in taking leave. "It is very excellent to cultivate the mind, but neither must the body be neglected: that is of much consequence in the world! But that will come, will it not, Antonio?" said she, smiling, and extended her hand for me to kiss.

It was yet early in the evening when I again found myself in the street on my homeward way, but still it was pitch-dark. There were at that time no lamps in Rome; they belong, as is well known, to the last few years. The lamps before the images of the Virgin were the only lights in the narrow ill-paved streets. I was obliged to feel my way before me, that I might not stumble against any thing; and thus I went on slowly, occupied with the thoughts of the adventures of this afternoon.

In going forward, I struck my hand against some object.

"The devil!" resounded from a well-known voice; "don't knock out my eyes, for then I should see still less!"

"Bernardo!" I joyfully exclaimed; "have we met once more?"

"Antonio! my dear Antonio!" cried he, and caught me by the arm; "this is indeed a merry meeting. Where do you come from? From some little adventure? That I did not expect from you; but you are caught in the path of darkness. But where is the slave corporal, the cicisbeo, or whatever you call your faithful companion?"

"I am quite alone," said I.

"Alone?" repeated he; "you are at bottom a fine fellow; you should be in the papal guard: then, perhaps, we should make something out of you."

I related to him in a few words the arrival of Excellenza and Signora, and expressed my delight at this our meeting. His pleasure was not less than mine. We thought not of the darkness around us, and talked as we went along, without thinking where or in what direction we went.

"Do you see, Antonio," said he, "I have only just now learned what life is : you know nothing about it. It is too gay a thing to sit there on the hard school-bench and listen to Habbas Dahdah's mouldy harangues. I know how to manage my horse — you saw me, perhaps, to-day ; and the handsome signoras cast glances at me — oh, such burning ones ! I am, to be sure, a very good-looking fellow, whom the uniform becomes ; in this cursed darkness here, you cannot see me ! My new comrades have led me out into the world ; they are not such recluses as you. We empty our glasses to the well-being of the state, and have also little adventures of which his holiness would not endure to hear. What a foolish fellow you are, Antonio ! I have had ten years' experience in these few months. Now I feel my youth, it boils in my blood, it wells forth in my heart, and I enjoy it — enjoy it in copious draughts, whilst my lips burn, and this exciting thirst is unallayed."

"Your companions are not good, Bernardo," said I.

"Not good!" interrupted he ; "don't preach me any sermon! What can you say about my goings on? My companions are of the purest patrician blood that Rome possesses ; we are the holy father's guard of honour ; his blessing absolves our little sins. After I had left school, I too had some of these conventual notions about me, but I was wise enough not to let my new companions observe it ; I did as they did ; my flesh and blood, my whole proper I, thrilled with joy and life, and I followed this impulse because it was the strongest ; but I perceived, at the same time, a hateful, bad voice within me — it was the Propagandist convent breeding, and the last remains of good-childism, which said, ' Thou art no longer innocent as a child!' Since then I laugh at it, I understand it better. I am a man! the child is shook off : it was that which cried when it could not have its way. But here we are really at the Chiavica, the best inn where artists assemble. Come in ; we must empty a bottle of wine together, for our happy meeting's sake — come in ; it is merry within!"

"What are you thinking of?" replied I. "If they should know at the Jesuit school that I have been here with an officer of the papal guard ! "

"Yes, that would be a great misfortune! To drink a glass of wine, and to hear the foreign artists sing their songs in their native speech, German, French, English, and the Lord knows what tongues! It's a merry thing, you may think!"

"What may be suitable for you is forbidden to me; do not talk to me about it, and ——" I interrupted myself, because I heard laughter and shouting from a little side-street, and was desirous of turning the conversation to other subjects: "there is such a crowd of people together —what can it be? I think the sport goes on under the image of the Madonna;" and, so saying, I drew him towards it.

Rude men and boys of the lowest class had closed up the street; they made a large circle around an old Jew, whom, as we found, they would compel to jump over a stick, which one of the fellows held, because he wished to go out of the street.

It is well known that in Rome, the first city of Christendom, the Jews are only permitted to live in their allotted quarter, the narrow and dirty Ghetto, the gate of which is closed every evening, and soldiers keep watch that none may come in or go out. Once a-year, the oldest amongst them are obliged to go to the Capitol, and, kneeling, pray for permission to live yet one year longer in Rome; which they obtain by binding themselves to bear the expenses of the carnival, and promising that all of them, once in the year, on an appointed day, shall go to a Catholic church and hear a sermon for their conversion.

The old man whom we here saw had come alone on this dark evening through the street, where the boys were pursuing their sport, and the men were playing at mora.

"Do you see the Jew?" one of them had said, and began to scoff at and ridicule the old man; and then, as he pursued his way in silence, they closed up the street. One of the fellows, a thick, broad-shouldered man, held a long stick stretched out, and cried, "Nay, Jew, take thy legs with thee, however; they will shut Ghetto, thou wilt not get in to-night. Let us see how nimble thou art in the legs!"

"Leap, Jew!" cried all the boys; "Abraham's God will help thee!"

"What harm have I done you?" said he. "Let me, an old man, go on my own way, and make not a jest of my grey hair before her to whom you yourselves pray for pardon:" and he pointed to the image of the Madonna just by.

"Dost thou think," said the fellow, "that Madonna troubles herself about a Jew? Wilt thou jump, thou old hound?" and he now clenched his fist in his face, and the boys pressed in a closer circle around him.

With this Bernardo sprang forth, pushed the nearest aside, snatched in an instant the stick out of the fellow's hand, swung round his sword above him, held the stick which he had taken from him before him, and cried in a strong, manly voice, "Jump thou, or I will cleave thy head!—delay not!—by all the saints, I'll split thy skull if thou do not jump over it!"

The fellow stood as if all heaven had fallen amid the astonished crowd. The thundering words, the drawn sabre, the papal officer uniform, all electrified him, and, without replying one word, he gave a great spring over the stick, which he had just held before the poor Jew. The whole assembly appeared equally surprised; no one ventured to say a word, but looked astonished by that which had happened.

Scarcely had the fellow leapt over, than Bernardo seized him by the shoulder, and, striking him lightly on the cheek with the flat of his sabre, said, —

"Bravo, my hound! well done! Yet once more this trick, and then, I think, thou wilt have had enough of this dog's play!"

The fellow was obliged to leap, and the people, who went over to the merry side of the thing, cried "Bravo!" and clapped their hands.

"Where art thou, Jew?" asked Bernardo. "Come, I will lead thee!" But nobody replied; the Jew was gone.

"Come," said I, when we were out of the crowd, — "come, let them say what they may, I will drink a bottle of wine with you. I will drink your health. May we always be friends in whatever circumstances we may be!"

"You are a fool, Antonio!" replied he, "and I also at bottom, to have vexed myself about the rude fellow. I think that he will not speedily be making any body jump again."

We went into the hostel; none of the lively guests observed us. There stood in a corner a little table, and here we bade them bring us a bottle of wine, and drank to our happy meeting and to the endurance of our friendship; then we parted.

I returned to the Jesuit school, where the old custodian, my particular friend, let me in unobserved of any one, and I was quickly asleep and dreaming of this evening's many adventures.

CHAPTER IX.

THE JEW MAIDEN.

THAT I had been out for an evening without permission, nay, drunk wine also in an inn with Bernardo, troubled me afterwards; but Fortune favoured me — nobody missed me, or, if they did, they supposed, like the old custodian, that I had received permission, for I was indeed considered to be the quietest and the most conscientious of the scholars. The days glided on smoothly for weeks; I studied industriously, and visited in the mean time my noble benefactress: these visits were my highest recreation. The little abbess became dearer to me every day; I took to her the pictures which I myself when a child had drawn; but when she had played some minutes with them they flew in many pieces about the floor: these I collected, and joined again for her.

At that time I was reading Virgil. The sixth book, where the Cumæan sibyl conducts Æneas down to the lower regions, interested me greatly, for it bore a relationship to that of Dante. With this I thought of my poem, and that brought Bernardo vividly to my mind, whom I had not seen for so long a time. I longed for him. This was precisely on one of those days in the week on which the gallery of the Vatican stood open to the public. I obtained leave of absence to go and see the glorious marble gods and the beautiful pictures; but that which I particularly wished for was to meet with my dear Bernardo.

I was already in the great open colonnade where the most beautiful bust of Raphael stands, and where the whole ceiling is covered with exquisite pictures from the Bible, drawn by this great master and finished by his scholars. The strange arabesques on the walls, the legions of angels, which are either kneeling in every arch, or spreading forth their great wings towards the Infinite, were not new to me; yet I lingered here a long time as if contemplating them, but waiting in reality for any lucky chance which might bring Bernardo there. I leaned over the balustrade of masonry, and contemplated the magnificent range of mountains, the proud line of the waves beyond the Campagna, but my eye at the same time looked down into the court of the Vatican to see if it were not Bernardo whenever I heard a sword ring up the broad flag-stones: but he came not.

In vain I wandered through the arcades, visited the Nile-group and the Laocoon,—all my looking was only folly, and I grew out of humour. Bernardo was not to be discovered, and, therefore, my homeward way seemed to me about as interesting as the Torso and the splendid Antinous.

Now skipped a light figure in helmet and with ringing spurs along the passage, and I after it: it was Bernardo. His joy was not less than mine; he drew me hastily along with him, for he had, he said, a thousand things to tell me.

" You do not know what I have suffered and still suffer ! You shall be my doctor — you alone can help me to the magical plants."

With these words he led me through the great hall, where the papal Swiss kept guard, into a large room fitted up for the accommodation of the officer on duty.

"But you are not ill?" I inquired,—"you cannot be so!—your eyes and your cheeks burn with the glow of life."

"Oh, yes, they burn," said he,—"I burn from head to foot; but it is all right! You are my star of luck—you bring with you charming adventures and good ideas. You must help!—sit down. You do not know how much I have lived through since that evening which we two spent together. But I will confide all to you—you are an honest friend, and must have a share in the adventure."

He would not allow me to speak—I must hear that which excited him so much.

"Do you remember the Jew—the old Jew whom the fellow would force to leap over the stick, and who hurried away without thanking me for my knightly help? I soon had forgotten him and the whole history. A few days afterwards chance led me past the entrance into the Ghetto; I did not observe it until the soldier who had his post at the gate presented arms, because I now belong to the people of rank. I returned his greeting, and saw with that a handsome crowd of black-eyed girls of the Hebrew race just within the gate, and so, as you may imagine, I was possessed with the desire to go down through the narrow, dirty street. It was a whole synagogue within; houses jostling one against another high into the air— from every window was heard "Bereschit Bara Elohim!" head to head, just as if they were going to pass over the Red Sea. Round about hung old clothes, umbrellas, and such like Rag-Fair goods. I skipped among iron-wares, pictures, and dirt, of course, and heard what a buzzing and screaming there was whether I would not trade, sell, or buy; they would hardly let me have time to notice a pair of black-eyed, beautiful children, which laughed at me from the door. It was such a wandering, you may trust me, as Dante might have described. All at once an old Jew fell upon me, bowed himself down before me as if I had been the holy father.

"'Excellenza,' said he,—'my noble deliverer—the saviour of my life, blessed be the hour in which I saw you! Think not that old Hanoch is ungrateful!' and much more which I did not understand and cannot now remember. I now recognised him; it was the old Hebrew who should have taken the leap.

"'Here is my poor house,' continued he, 'but the threshold is too humble for me to pray you to cross it;' and with this he kissed my hands and my dress. I wished to get away, for the whole neighbourhood was gazing upon us; but just then I cast my eyes upwards to the house, and I saw the most beautiful head that I ever had seen, — a marble Venus with warm blood in her cheeks, and eyes like a daughter of Arabia. Thus you can very well conceive that I followed the old Jew in — he had, indeed, invited me. The passage was truly as narrow and dark as if it had led into the grave of the Scipios, and the stone steps and the handsome wooden gallery — yes, they were, in particular, formed to teach people stability in walking, and circumspection to the extremest finger-point. In the room itself it did not seem so much amiss, only the girl was not there; and what did I want to see besides? I had now to sit and listen to a long speech of gratitude, in which the multitude of Eastern figures of speech would certainly have charmed your poetical turn of mind. I let it go on, thinking to myself 'she will come at last!' but she came not. In the meantime the Jew started an idea which, under other circumstances, would have been very good. He imagined that I, as a young man who was living in the world, should want money, but yet, at the same time, have no superabundance of it — that I had need occasionally to fly to compassionate souls, who, at from twenty to thirty per cent., showed their Christian love, but that he (and it is a miracle in the Jewish kingdom) would lend to me without any percentage at all. Do you hear? — with no percentage! — I was a noble young man — he would trust himself to my honesty! I had protected a twig of the stem of Israel, and not a splinter of this should rend my clothing!

"As I was not in need of any money, I did not take any; so he then besought me to condescend to taste his wine — the only bottle which he possessed. I know not what reply I made, but this I know, that the loveliest girl

of Oriental descent entered.   There were form and colour
— hair shining and jet-black as ebony.   She presented to
me excellent wine of Cyprus, and that kingly blood of the
line of Solomon crimsoned her cheeks as I emptied a glass
to her happiness.   You should have heard her speak —
heard her thank me for her father, which, indeed, it was
not worth the trouble.   It sounded like music in my ears
— it was no earthly being !   She then vanished again, and
only the old man remained."

"The whole is just like a poem !" I exclaimed, —
"it could be beautifully put into verse."

"You do not know," continued he, "how I have since
tormented myself — how I have formed schemes in my
head, and then pulled them down again, for meeting again
with my daughter of Zion.   Only think, I went down
there to borrow money which I did not want ; I borrowed
twenty silver scudi for eight days, but I did not get to see
her.   I took them unchanged back again to him on the
third day, and the old man smiled and rubbed his hands,
for he had not actually so entirely relied upon my boasted
honesty.   I praised his wine of Cyprus, but *she* brought
me none ; he himself presented it with his thin, trembling
hands.   My eyes *peered* into every corner — she was
nowhere.   I saw her not, only as I went down the steps
it seemed to me that a curtain in an open window moved ;
it might be she.

"'Adieu, signora,' I exclaimed, but all was still as a
wall — nothing showed itself.   I have advanced no further
in my adventure — give me counsel.   To give her up I
cannot and will not !   What shall I do ?   Strike out a
brilliant idea, my heart's youth !   Be to me a Juno and
Venus, which led Æneas and Libya's daughter together
into the lonely grotto."

"What will you have me to do ?   I do not comprehend
how I can do any thing here."

"You can do every thing, whatever you will.   The
Hebrew is really a beautiful language, a poetical picture-world ; you shall study it, and take a Jew for your
teacher : I will pay for the lessons.   Do you have the old
Hanoch, for I have discovered that he belongs to the

learned portion in Ghetto. When your true-hearted manner has won him, then you can make the acquaintance of his daughter, and then you must bring me in also, but at full gallop — at full, flying gallop. I have burning poison in my blood — the burning poison of love. You must go to-day to the Jew."

" That I cannot," I replied ; " you do not take into consideration my circumstances — what a part I should have to play; and how can you, dear Bernardo, demean yourself so as to have a love-affair with a Jew girl ? "

" Oh, that you do not understand !" interrupted he ; " Jew-girl or not has nothing to do with it, if she is only good for any thing ! Now, thou beloved youth, my own excellent Antonio, set about studying Hebrew — we will both of us study it, only in different ways. Be reasonable, and think how very much you hereby promote my happiness."

" You know," I said, " how sincerely with my whole soul I am attached to you, — you know how your preponderating force seizes upon my thoughts and my whole will. If you were angry, you could destroy me ! — I should be forced into your magic circle. I judge not your views in life by my own ; every one must follow his own nature. Neither do I consider the mode by which you would seize on pleasure to be sinful, for that is according to your cast of mind. I am quite different ; do not over-persuade me into an undertaking which, even if it turned out favourably, could not tend to your happiness."

" Good — good !" said he, interrupting me ; and I saw the distant, proud glance with which he so often had regarded Habbas Dahdah, when he, from his position, was the deciding party ; " good, Antonio, it is nothing but a jest, the whole of it. You shall not have to do penance on my account. But where would have been the harm of your learning a little Hebrew, and that from my Jew, I cannot comprehend. But not a word about it ! — thanks for your visit ! Will you eat ? — will you drink ? Here they are at your service."

I was cast down ; the tone in which he spoke, his whole manner, showed that he was offended. Icy coldness and formal politeness met the warm pressure of my hand. Troubled and out of spirits, I hastened home.

I felt that he was unjust — that I had acted as was my duty to do ; and yet there were moments in which it seemed as if I had acted unkindly to him. In one of these combats with myself I went through the Jews' quarter, hoping that my fortunate star would conduct me to some adventure which should turn out to the benefit of my dear Bernardo. But I did not once see the old Jew; unknown faces looked out from doors and windows, dirty children lay upon the steps among all sorts of old trash of iron and clothes, and the eternal shouting of whether I would not buy or sell almost deafened me. Some young girls were playing at shuttlecock, from window to window across the street. One of these was very handsome ; could it be Bernardo's beloved ? I involuntarily took off my hat, but the next moment, ashamed of doing so, I stroked my head with my hand, as if it had been on account of the warmth, and not of the girls, that I uncovered my head.

CHAPTER X.

A YEAR LATER. — THE ROMAN CARNIVAL. — THE SINGER.

IF I must uninterruptedly follow the thread which connects together Bernardo's love and my ramble through Ghetto, I must pass over one whole year of my life ; but this year had in its daily progress onward much more for me than the making me twelve months older. It was a sort of interlude in the drama of my life.

I seldom saw Bernardo, and when we did meet he was just the same merry-hearted, bold, young acquaintance as ever ; but confidential as before he never seemed to be, the cold, well-bred air betrayed itself from under the mask of friendship ; it troubled and depressed me, and I had not the courage to ask how it had gone with his love-affair.

I very often went to the Borghese Palace, and found with Excellenza, Fabiani, and Francesca, a true home, yet often, also, found occasion for deep pain. My soul was filled with gratitude to every one of them for all which I had received from them, and, therefore, any grave look from them cast a shade upon my life's happiness. Francesca commended my good qualities, but wished now to perfect me. My carriage, my mode of expressing myself, she criticised, and that with severity — certainly with great severity — so much so as to bring tears to my eyes, although I was a tall youth of sixteen. The old Excellenza, who had taken me from Domenica's hut to his magnificent home, was also just as cordially kind to me as at the first time when we met; but he, too, pursued the signora's mode of education with me. I did not take the same interest as himself in plants and strange flowers, and this he considered as a want of taste for that which was solid : he thought that I was too much occupied by my own peculiar individuality — I did not come sufficiently out of myself — did not let the radius of the mind intersect the great circle of the world.

"Reflect, my son," said he, "that the leaf which is rolled up in itself withers."

But after every warm conversation that he had with me he patted me again upon the cheek, and consoled me by ironically saying that we lived in a bad world, and we must every one of us be pressed like dried flowers, if the Madonna were to have handsome specimens of us. Fabiani looked at every thing on the cheerful side, laughed at both of their well-meant lectures, whilst he assured them that I never should become learned like Excellenza, nor piquant like Francesca, but that I should be of a third character, which also belonged to life, and which was not to be despised either. And then he called for his little abbess, and with her I soon forgot all my small troubles.

The family intended to pass the following year in the north of Italy; the warm summer months they would spend at Genoa, and the winter in Milan. By me, also, at the same time, a great step was to be taken ; I was to enter by a sort of examination into the rank of abbé, and thus gain a higher position in life than I had hitherto possessed.

Before the departure of the family a great ball was given in the Borghese Palace, to which I also was invited. Pitch garlands burned before the house, and all the torches which were borne before the carriages of the guests were stuck into iron arms upon the wall, so that this seemed like a complete cascade of fire. Papal soldiers were stationed at the gates. The little garden was decorated with bright-coloured paper-lamps; the marble steps were magnificently lighted, and upon every step, beside the wall, stood vases filled with flowers or small orange-trees, which diffused their fragrance around. Soldiers leaned their shoulders against the doors. There was a throng of richly dressed servants.

Francesca was splendidly beautiful; the costly bird-of-paradise head-dress which she wore, and her white satin dress with its rich lace, became her most exquisitely, but that she extended to me her hand — yes, *that* I thought the most beautiful of all! In two halls, in each of which was a full orchestra, floated the dancers.

Among these was Bernardo, and he was handsome; the scarlet, gold-embroidered uniform, the narrow, white breeches, all fitted as if but a part of the noble figure; he danced with the most lovely women, and they smiled confidingly and tenderly upon him. That which vexed me was that I could not dance; neither did any body take any notice of me. In my own home it seemed to me that I was the greatest stranger among strangers. But Bernardo offered me his hand, and all my ill-humour was again gone.

Behind the long red curtains, by the open window, we drank together the foaming champagne; he clinked his glass familiarly against mine. Beautiful melodies streamed through the ear into our hearts, and every thought of a friendship less warm than in former days was extinguished. I ventured to mention even the handsome Jewish maiden; he laughed, and seemed quite cured of his deep wound.

" I have found another little golden bird," said he, " which is tamer, and has sung away my whim. We will therefore let the other fly; and it is gone indeed, has escaped away out of the Jews' quarter — nay, even out of Rome, if I am to believe my people!"

Once more we joined glasses; the champagne and the enlivening music infused twofold life to our blood. Bernardo again was in the midst of the dance; I stood alone there, but that great sea of happiness was in my soul, which makes one right glad to embrace the whole world. Down in the street below shouted the poor lads, as they saw the sparks fly from the pitch garlands; I thought upon my own poor childhood, when I also had played like them, and now stood, as if at home, in the splendid ball-room, among the first families of Rome. Thanks and love to the Mother of God, who had led me so tenderly forwards in the world, filled my whole soul; I bent my knees in adoration, and the long thick curtains hid me from the eyes of all. I was infinitely happy!

The night was over; yet two days more, and the whole family left Rome. Habbas Dahdah impressed upon me every hour what this year was to bring me — the name and the dignity of an abbé. I studied industriously, scarcely ever saw Bernardo, or any other acquaintance. Weeks extended themselves into months, and these brought on the day in which, after close examination, I was to assume the black dress and the short silk cloak.

All within me sung *victoria*. The lofty pines, and newly sprung-up anemones, the crier in the streets, and the light cloud which floated through the blue air!

With the short silk cloak of the abbé, I had become a new and happier person. Francesca had sent me a bill of a hundred scudi, for my necessities and my pleasure. In my delight I hastened up the Spanish Steps, threw a silver scudo to uncle Peppo, and hastened away without hearing more from him than his "Excellenza, Excellenza Antonio!"

It was in the first days of February, the almond-tree blossomed, the orange-trees became more and more yellow, the merry carnival was at hand, as if it were a festival to celebrate my adoption into the rank of abbé; heralds on horseback, with trumpets and splendid velvet banners, had already announced its approach. Never before had I yet wholly enjoyed its delights, never rightly understood what is meant in this country by "letting folly loose!"

When I was a little child, my mother feared that I should get hurt in the crowd, and I obtained only momentary glimpses of the whole merriment, as she stood with me in some safe corner of the street. As a scholar in the Jesuits school, I had seen it in the same manner, when permission was given to me, with some of the other scholars, to stand upon the flat roof of the side-buildings of the Doria Palace; but now to be able by myself to wander about from one end of the street to the other, to mount the Capitol, to go to Trastevere, — in short, to go and to be just wherever I myself wished, was a thing hardly to have been thought of. How natural was it then that I should throw myself into the wild stream, and delight myself with every thing just like a child! Least of all did I think that the most serious adventure of my life was now to begin; that an occurrence, which had once occupied me so vividly and so entirely, the lost seedcorn, forgotten and out of sight, should now show itself again like a green, fragrant plant, which had wound itself firmly around my own life's tree.

The carnival was all my thought. I went early in the morning to the Piazza del Popolo that I might see the preparations for the races, walked in the evening up and down the Corso, to notice the gay carnival-dresses which were hung out, figures with masks and in full costume. I hired the dress of an advocate, as being one of the merriest characters, and scarcely slept through the whole night that I might think over and regularly study my part.

The next day seemed to me like a holy festival; I was as happy as a child! All round about in the side-streets the comfit-sellers set up their booths and tables, and displayed their gay wares.* The Corso was swept, and gay carpets were hung out from all the windows. About three o'clock, according to the French mode of reckoning time,

---

* These comfits are small red and white plaster of Paris balls, as large as peas; sometimes also they are grains of corn rolled in a paste of plaster of Paris. During the carnival people throw them at each other.—*Author's note.*

I went to the Capitol, to enjoy for the first time the be_ginning of the festival. The balconies were filled with foreigners of rank ; the senator sat in purple upon a throne of velvet ; pretty, little pages, with feathers in their velvet caps, stood on the left, before the papal Swiss guard. Then came in a crowd of the most aged Jews, who kneeled down, bare-headed, before the senator. I knew one of them, it was Hanoch, the old Jew, whose daughter had so greatly interested Bernardo.

The old man was the speaker, made a sort of oration, in which he prayed, according to old usage, for permission for himself and his people to live yet a year longer in Rome, in the quarter which was appointed to them ; promised to go once during that time into the Catholic church, and prayed furthermore that, according to old custom, they might themselves run through the Corso before the people of Rome, might pay all the expense of the horse-racing, together with the offered prize-money, and might provide the gay velvet banners. The senator gave a gracious nod (the old custom of setting the foot upon the shoulder of the supplicant was done away with), rose up amid a flourish of music in procession, and, descending the steps, entered his magnificent carriage, in which the pages also had a place ; and thus was the carnival opened. The great bell of the Capitol rang for gladness, and I sped home quickly that I might instantly assume my advocate's dress. In this it seemed to me that I was quite another person.

With a kind of self-satisfaction I hastened down into the street, where a throng of masks already saluted mě. They were poor working people, who on these days acted like the richest nobility ; their whole finery was the most original, and at the same time the cheapest in the world. They wore over their ordinary dress a coarse shirt stuck all over with lemon-peel, which was to represent great buttons ; a bunch of green salad on their shoulders and shoes ; a wig of fennel ; and great spectacles cut out of orange-peel.

I threatened them all with actions at law, showed them in my book of laws the regulations which forbade such luxuriousness in dress as theirs, and then, applauded by them all, hastened away to the long Corso, which was changed from a street into a masquerade-hall. From all the windows, and round all the balconies and boxes erected for the occasion, were hung bright-coloured carpets. All the way along, by the house-sides, stood an infinite number of chairs, "excellent places to see from," as those declared who had them to let. Carriages followed carriages, for the greatest part filled with masks, in two long rows—the one up, the other down. Some of these had even their wheels covered with laurel-twigs, the whole seeming like a moving pleasure house; and amid these thronged the merry human crowd. All windows were filled with spectators. Handsome Roman women, in the dress of officers, with the moustachio over the delicate mouth, threw comfits down to their acquaintance. I made a speech to them, summoning them before the tribunal, because they threw, not only comfits into the faces, but fire-glances also into the heart; they cast down flowers upon me, as a reward for my speech.

I met with a decked out little old woman, attended by her cicisbeo; the way was blocked up to us for a few moments by a contest among a crowd of Punchinellos, and the good lady was obliged to listen to my eloquence.

"Signora," said I, "do you call that keeping your vow? Is this maintaining the Roman Catholic customs as you ought to do? Ah, where now is Lucretia, the wife of Tarquinius Collatinus? For this do you and many other women of Rome send out their respectable husbands in the carnival time, and let them go *in exercitia* with the monks of Trastevere. You promise to lead a quiet, God-fearing life in your house, and your husbands mortify their flesh in the time of merriment, and pray and labour night and day within the walls of the convent. Thus you get free play, and flirt about with your gallants on the Corso and about Festino! Ay, signora, I summon you before the tribunal, according to the sixteenth clause of the twenty-seventh law."

An emphatic blow with her fan on my face was my answer, the real cause of which was, we may suppose, that I had, quite innocently, hit upon the truth.

" Are you mad, Antonio ? " whispered her conductor to me, and both made their escape among sbirri, Greeks, and shepherdesses. By those few words I had recognised him : it was Bernardo. But who could the lady be ?

" *Luogi, Luogi ! Patroni !* " cried those who had chairs to let. I was bewildered in my thoughts ; but yet who will think on a carnival's day ? A crowd of harlequins, with little bells on their shoulders and shoes, danced around me, and a new advocate upon stilts, the height of a man, strode in above us. As if he recognised a collegian in me, he joked about the humble position in which I stood, and assured them that it was only he alone who could win any cause, for upon the earth, to which I was stuck fast, there was no justice — it was to be found only above ; and then he pointed into the higher, pure air in which he stood, and stalked on further.

On the Piazza Colonna was a band of music. The merry doctors and shepherdesses danced joyously around, even in the midst of the single troop of soldiers, which, to preserve order, mechanically walked up and down the street among the carriages and the throng of human beings. Here I again began a profound speech, but there came up a writer, and then it was all over with me, for his attendant, who ran before him with a great bell, jingled it so before my ears that I could not even hear my own words ; at that moment also was heard the cannon-shot, which was the signal that all carriages must leave the streets, and that the carnival was at an end for this day.

I obtained a stand upon a wooden scaffolding. Below me moved the crowd, without allowing itself to be disturbed by the soldiers, who warned them to make way for the horses, that would soon pass at a wild speed through the street, where no causeway made a determined path.

At the end of the street, by the Piazza del Popolo, the horses were led up to the barrier. They all seemed half wild. Burning sponges were fastened to their backs, little rockets behind their ears, and iron points hanging loose, which in the race spurred them till the blood came, were secured to their sides. The grooms could scarcely hold them. The cannon was fired. The rope before the barrier fell, and now they flew like a storm-wind past me up the Corso. The tinsel glittered; their manes and the gaudy ribands floated in the air; sparks of fire flew from their hoofs. The whole mass of people cried after them, and, at the same moment in which they had passed, streamed out again into the open mid-path, like the waves, which close again after the ship's keel.

The festival was at an end for the day. I hastened home to take off my dress, and found in my room Bernardo, who was waiting for me.

"You here!" I exclaimed; "and your donna, where, in all the world, have you left her?"

"Hush!" said he, and threatened me jestingly with his finger; "do not let that come to an affair of honour between us! Yet how could you get the whimsical idea of just saying what you did say?—but we will give absolution and show mercy. You must go with me this evening to the Theatre Alibert; the opera of 'Dido' is given there to-night. There will be divine music; many beauties of the first rank will be there; and, besides, there is a foreign singer, who takes the principal character, and who has set the whole of Naples in fire and flame. She has a voice, an expression, a carriage, such as we have no idea of; and then she is beautiful, very beautiful, they say. You must take a pencil with you, for, if she answer only half the description I have heard of her, she will inspire you to write her the most beautiful sonnet! I have kept the last bouquet of violets from the carnival to offer her, in case she should enchant me!"

I was willing to accompany him — I wished to drink up every drop of the merry carnival. It was an important evening for us both. In my *Diario Romano*, also, this 3d of February stands doubly underlined. Bernardo had reasons that it should be so in his.

It was in the Theatre Alibert, the first opera-house in Rome, that we were to see the new singer as Dido. The magnificent ceiling, with the hovering Muses; the curtain, on which is portrayed the whole of Olympus, and the golden arabesques in the boxes, were then all new. The entire house, from the floor to the fifth row, was filled ; in every box burned lights in the lamps, the whole blazed like a sea of light. Bernardo directed my eyes to every new beauty who entered her box, and said a thousand wicked things about the plain ones.

The overture began. It was the exposition-scene of the piece in music. The wild tempest raged on the sea and drove Æneas on the coast of Lybia. The horror of the storm died away in pious hymns, which ascended in triumph, and in the soft tones of the flute a dream-like feeling stole over me of Dido's awakening love — a feeling which I myself had not known till then. The hunting-horns sounded, the storm arose again, and I entered with the lovers into the secret grotto, where all intoned of love, the strong tumultuous passion, which burst into a deep dissonance ; and with this the curtain rose.

Æneas is about to go, to conquer the Hesperian kingdom for Ascanius, to leave Dido, who received him the stranger, who sacrificed for him her honour and her happiness. But as yet she knows it not, " but quickly will the dream vanish," said he, " soon, when the hosts of Teucer, like the black swarms of ants laden with booty, advance to the shore."

Now came forth Dido. As soon as she showed herself upon the boards, a deep silence spread itself over the house ; her whole appearance — her queenly and yet easy, charming carriage seized upon all — me also ; and yet she was not such an one as I had imagined Dido to be. She stood there, a delicate, graceful creature, infinitely beautiful and intellectual, as only Raphael can represent woman. Black as ebony lay her hair upon the exquisite, arched forehead ; the dark eye was full of expression. A loud outbreak of applause was heard ; it was to Beauty, and Beauty alone, that the homage was given, for as yet she had sung not a note. I saw plainly a crimson pass over her brow ; she bowed to the admiring crowd, who now followed with deep silence her beautiful accentuation of the recitative.

" Antonio," said Bernardo half aloud to me, and seized my arm, " it is she! I must have lost my senses, or it is she — my flown bird! Yes, yes, I cannot be wrong; the voice also is hers; I remember it only too well!"

" Who do you mean?" I inquired.

" The Jewish maiden from Ghetto" replied he; " and yet it seems impossible, purely impossible, she cannot really be the same!"

He was silent, and lost himself in the contemplation of the wonderfully lovely, sylph-like being. She sang the happiness of her love; it was a heart which breathed forth, in melody, the deep, pure emotion which, upon the wings of melodious sounds, escapes from the human breast. A strange sadness seized upon my soul; it was as if those tones would call up in me the deepest earthly re-membrances; I also was about to exclaim, with Bernardo, " It is she! — yes, she whom I for these many years had not thought or dreamed of stood now with wonderful vi-vidness before me — she, with whom I, as a child, had preached at Christmas, in the church *ara cœli:* that sin-gularly delicate little girl, with the remarkably sweet voice, who had won the prize from me. I thought of her, and the more I saw and heard this evening, the more firmly was it impressed on my mind, " it is she — she, and no other!"

When, afterwards, Æneas announces to her that he will go — that they are not married — that he knows not of their nuptial torch, how astoundingly did she express all that which passed in her soul — astonishment, pain, rage; and, when she sang her great aria, it was as if the waves of the deep had struck against the clouds. How, indeed, shall I describe the world of melody which she revealed? My thoughts sought for an outward image for these tones, which seemed not to ascend from a human breast, and I saw a swan breathing out its life in song, whilst it now cut, with outspread pinions, the wide ethereal space, now descended into the deep sea, and clave the billows only again to ascend. A universal burst of acclamation re-sounded through the house, " Annunciata! Annunciata!" cried they; and she was obliged again, and yet again, to present herself to the enraptured crowd.

And yet this aria was not at all equal to the duet in the second act, in which she prays Æneas not immediately to go, not thus to forsake her — her who for his sake had disgraced the race of Lybia, the princes of Africa, her virginity and duty. " I sent no ships against Troy ; I disturbed not the manes of Anchises and his ashes !" There was a truth, a pain in the whole of her expression, which filled my eyes with tears ; and the deep silence which reigned around showed that every heart felt the same.

Æneas left her, and now she stood for a moment cold and pale as marble, like a Niobe. But quickly boiled the blood in her veins : it was no longer Dido — the warm, the loving Dido — the forsaken wife : it was a Fury. The beautiful features breathed forth poison and death. Annunciata knew so completely how to change her whole expression, to call up the icy shudder of horror, that one was compelled to breathe and to suffer with her.

Leonardo da Vinci has painted a Medusa's head, which is in the gallery at Florence. Every one who sees it is strangely captivated by it, and cannot tear themselves away. It is as if the deep, out of froth and poison, had formed the most beautiful shape — as if the foam of the abyss had fashioned a Medicean Venus. The look, the expression of the mouth even, breathe forth death. Thus stood Dido now before us.

We saw the funereal pile which her sister Anna had erected ; the court was hung with black garlands and night-shade ; in the far distance sped the bark of Æneas over the agitated sea. Dido stood with the weapons which he had forgotten ; her song sounded deep and heavy, and then again ascended into power and strength, like the lamentation of the fallen angels. The funereal pile was lighted : her heart broke in melody.

Like a tempest burst forth the applause : the curtain fell. We were all out of ourselves with admiration of the glorious actress, her beauty, and her indescribably exquisite voice.

" Annunciata ! Annunciata !" rang from the pit and all the boxes ; the curtain moved, and she stood there, bashful and charming, with eyes full of love and gentleness. Flowers rained down around her; ladies waved their white pocket-handkerchiefs, and the gentlemen, enraptured, repeated her name. The curtain fell, but the acclamation seemed only the more to increase; she again made her appearance, and with her the singer who had performed the part of Æneas; but again and again they shouted, " Annunciata ! " She appeared with the whole corps who had contributed to her triumph; but yet once more they stormed forth her name: and for the fourth time she now came forth, quite alone, and thanked them, in a few cordial words, for the rich encouragement which they had given to her efforts. I had written a few lines in my excitement on a piece of paper, and these, amid flowers and garlands, flew to her feet.

The curtain did not rise again; but still again and again resounded her name; people could not weary of seeing her, could not weary of paying her homage. Yet once more was she obliged to come forth from the side of the curtain ; pass along before the lamps, and send kisses and thanks to the exultant crowd. Delight beamed from her eyes; there was an indescribable joy in her whole look: it was certainly the happiest moment of her life. And was it not also the happiest of mine? I shared in her delight as well as in the acclamation of the others; my eye, my whole soul imbibed her sweet image; I saw only, thought only, Annunciata.

The crowd left the theatre; I was carried away with the stream which bore onward to the corner where the carriage of the singer stood; I was pushed to the wall, for all wished yet once more to see her. All took off their hats and shouted her name. I spoke her name also, but my heart swelled strangely the while. Bernardo had pressed forward to the carriage, and opened the door for her. I saw that in a moment the horses would be taken out, and that the enthusiastic young men would themselves draw her home. She spoke, and besought of them, with a trembling voice, not to do so; but only her name in the most exultant shout sounded through the street. Bernardo mounted on the step, as the carriage was set in motion, in order to compose her, and I seized hold of the pole, and felt myself as happy as the rest. The whole thing was too soon over, like a beautiful dream.

It was a happiness to me now to stand beside Bernardo; he had actually talked with her — had been quite close to her!

" Now what do you say, Antonio?" cried he; " is not your heart in a commotion? If you do not glow through marrow and bone, you are not worthy to be called a man! Don't you now see how you stood in your own light when I wanted to take you to her; and would it not have been worth while to have learned Hebrew, to have sat on the same bench with such a creature? Yes, Antonio, however incomprehensible it may seem, I have not any doubt but that she is my Jewish maiden! She it was whom, a year ago, I saw with old Hanoch; she it was who presented to me Cyprus wine, and then vanished. I have her again; she is here, and like a glorious phœnix ascended from her nest, that hateful Ghetto!"

" It is impossible, Bernardo," I replied; " she has also awoke remembrances in me, which make it impossible that she can be a Jewess; most assuredly is she one of the only blessed church. Had you observed her as closely as I have done, you would have seen that hers is not a Jewish form; that those features bear not the Cain's mark of that unhappy, despised nation. Her speech itself, her accent, come not from Jewish lips. O Bernardo, I feel so happy, so inspired by the world of melody which she has infused into my soul! But what did she say? You have actually talked with her, stood close by her carriage; was she right happy, as happy as she has made us all?"

" You are regularly inspired, Antonio!" interrupted he; " now melts the ice of the Jesuit school! What did she talk about? Yes, she was frighted, and yet she was proud that you wild cubs drew her through the streets. She held her veil tight over her face, and pressed herself into the corner of the carriage; I composed her, and said every thing that my heart could have said to the Queen of Beauty and Innocence; but she would not even take my hand when I would have helped her out!"

" But how could you be so bold ! she did not know you.
I should never have ventured on such audacity."

" Yes, you know nothing of the world — nothing of
women. She has observed me, and that always is something."

I now read him my impromptu to her ; he thought it
was divine, and declared that it must be printed in the
Diario di Roma. We drank together her health. Every
one in the coffee-house talked of her ; every one, like us,
was inexhaustible in her praise. It was late when I parted
from Bernardo ; I hastened home, but sleep was not
to be thought of. It was to me a delight to go over the
whole opera in my own mind ; Annunciata's first appearance ; the aria, the duet, the closing scene, which seized so
strangely on the souls of all. In my rapture I spoke forth
my applause aloud, and called her name. Then in thought
I went through my little poem, wrote it down, and thought
it pretty ; read it a few times to myself ; and, if I must be
candid, my love to her was almost increased by the poem.
Now, many years afterwards, I see it with very different
eyes. I then thought it a little masterpiece. She certainly
took it up, I thought, and now she sits half undressed upon
the soft silken sofa, supports her cheek upon her beautiful
arm, and reads that which I breathed upon paper : —

> My soul went with thee, trembling and unshriven,
>   On that proud track where only Dante stays ;
> In music, through the depths and up to heaven,
>   Thy song has led me and thy seraph-gaze !
> What Dante's power from stony words hath wrung,
> Deep in my soul hast thou in music sung !

I knew no spiritual world more rich and beautiful than
that in Dante's poem, but this now, it seemed to me, revealed itself in a higher vitality, and with much greater
clearness than before. Her melting song, her look, the
pain and the despair which she had represented, had most
completely been given in the spirit of Dante. She must
think my poem beautiful ! I imagined her thoughts, her
desire to know the author, and I almost fancy that, before
I went to sleep, I was, with all my imaginings about her,
still most occupied with myself and my own little insig-
nificant poem.

CHAPTER XI.

BERNARDO AS DEUS EX MACHINA. — LA PRUOVA D'UN OPERA
SERIA. — MY FIRST IMPROVISATION. THE LAST DAY OF THE
CARNIVAL.

THE next forenoon I saw nothing of Bernardo ; in vain I
sought for him. Many were the times that I went across
the Piazza Colonna, not to contemplate the pillar of Anto-
ninus, but to see, if it were only the sleeve of Annunciata,
for she lived there. There were visitors with her, the
lucky people ! I heard a piano ; I listened, but no Annunciata sung : a deep bass voice gave forth some tones ;
certainly it was the master of the musical chapel, or one of
the singers in her company — what an enviable lot ! Were
one only in the place of him who acted Æneas with her !
thus to look into her eyes, drink in her looks of love, travel
with her from city to city, gaining admiration and renown !
I was quite lost in the thought. Harlequins with shells,
Punchinellos, and magicians, danced around. I had quite
forgotten that it was carnival time, and that it even now
was the hour when the sports began for to-day.

The whole gaudy crowd, the noise and the screams, made
an unpleasant impression upon me. Carriages drove past ;
almost all the drivers were dressed as ladies, but it looked
to me horrible ; those black whiskers under womens' caps ;
the vigorous movements, all were painted to me in frightful
colours, nay, were detestable, as it seemed to me. I did
not feel myself, like as yesterday, given up to mirth. I
was about to depart, and now, for the last time, cast a
glance at the house in which Annunciata lived, when Bernardo rushed from the door towards me, and, laughing,
exclaimed, —

" Come along, then, and don't stand staring there ! I
will introduce you to Annunciata ; she expects you already. Look you, is not this a piece of friendship in me ? "

" She ! " I stammered, the blood seeming to boil in my
ears, " she ! don't make any sport of me ! Where will
you take me ? "

H

"To her, of whom you have sung," he replied — "to her, about whom you and I and every body are raving — to the divine Annunciata!"

And, so saying, he drew me into the door with him.

"But explain to me how you got here yourself — how you can introduce me here."

"Presently, presently, you shall know all that," replied he; "now call up a cheerful face."

"But my dress," I stammered, and tried hastily to arrange it..

"Oh, you are handsome, my friend! perfectly charming! See now, then, we are at the door."

It opened, and I stood before Annunciata. She wore a black silk dress of the richest material, which fell in ample folds around her, whilst its simple, unadorned style showed the exquisite bust and the sweep of the delicate shoulders to the greatest advantage; the black hair was put back from the noble, lofty forehead, upon which was placed a black ornament, which seemed to me to be an antique stone. At some distance from her, and towards the window, sat an old woman in a dark brown, somewhat worn dress, whose eyes, and the whole form of whose countenance, said, at the first glance, that she was a Jewess. I thought upon Bernardo's assertion, that Annunciata and the beauty of Ghetto were the same person; but this was impossible, said I again in my heart, when I looked at Annunciata. A gentleman also whom I did not know was in the room; he rose, and she rose also, and came towards me, half smiling, as Bernardo led me in, and said, jestingly, —

"My gracious signora, I have here the honour to present the poet, my friend, the excellent Abbé Antonio, a favourite of the Borghese family."

"Signora will forgive," said she; "but it is in truth no fault of mine that my acquaintance is thrust upon you, however desirable yours may be to me! You have honoured me with a poem," she continued, and crimsoned; "your friend mentioned you as the author, begged to introduce you to me, when suddenly he saw you in the street, and said, 'Now you shall see him instantly,' and was gone before I could reply or prevent—that is his way; but you know your friend better than I do."

Bernardo knew how to make a joke of it, and I stammered out a few words about my good fortune, my joy at being introduced to her.

My cheeks glowed; she extended her hands to me, and in my rapture I pressed them to my lips. She introduced the stranger gentleman to me; it was the chapel-master, or company's leader of the band. The old lady, whom she called her foster-mother, looked gravely, almost sternly, at Bernardo and me; but I soon forgot that in Annunciata's friendship and gay humour.

The chapel-master expressed himself as obliged by my poem, and, offering me his hand, invited me to write opera text for him, and to begin at once.

" Do not listen to him," interrupted Annunciata; " you do not know into what misery he will plunge you. Composers think nothing of their victims, and the public still less. You will this evening, in *La Pruova d' un Opera Seria*, see a good picture of a poor author; and yet this is not painted sufficiently strongly."

The composer wished to make some exception; Annunciata smiled, and turned herself to me.

" You write a piece," she said; " infuse your whole soul into its exquisite verse. Unities, characters, all have been well considered: but now comes the composer; he has an idea that must be brought in; yours must be put aside: here he will have fifes and drums, and you must dance after them. The prima donna says that she will not sing unless you bring in an aria for a brilliant exit. She understands the *furiose maestoso*, and whether it succeed or not the author must answer for. The prima tenor makes the same demands. You must fly from the prima to the tertia donna, to the bass and tenor, must bow, flatter, endure all that our humours can inflict; and that is not a little."

The chapel-master wished to interrupt her; but Annunciata noticed it not, and continued : —

" Then comes the director, weighing, measuring, throwing away; and you must be his most humble servant, even

in folly and stupidity. The mechanist assures you that
the strength of the theatre will not bear this arrangement,
this decoration; that they cannot have it new painted:
thus you must alter this and that in the piece, which is
called, in theatrical language, 'to mend.' The theatrical
painter does not permit that this sea-piece should be brought
out in his new decoration: this, like the rest, must also
be mended. Then the signora cannot make a *roulade* on
the syllable with which one of the verses ends: she will
have one that ends with an a, let it come from where it
may. You must mend yourself, and mend your text;
and if so be that the whole, like a new creation, comes on
the stage, you may have the pleasure of having it hissed,
and the composer exclaim, " Ah, it is that miserable text
which has ruined the whole! The pinions of my melody
could not sustain the colossus: it must fall!"

Merrily came up the sound of music to us from below.
The carnival maskers came buzzing over the square, and
through the streets. A loud acclamation mingled itself
with the clapping of hands, and called us all to the open
window. To be now so near to Annunciata, to see my
heart's first wish so suddenly fulfilled, made me unspeakably happy; and the carnival seemed to me as merry as it
did yesterday, when I played my part in it.

About fifty punchinellos had assembled under the window, and had chosen their king, who mounted a little car,
hung over with gaudy flags and garlands of laurels and
orange-peel, which waved about as if they had been ribands
and lace. The king ascended into the car. They set upon
his head a crown made of gilded and brightly painted eggs,
and gave to him, as a sceptre, a gigantic child's rattle,
covered with macaroons. All danced around him, and he
nodded graciously on all sides; then they harnessed themselves to his carriage, to drag him through the streets. At
that moment his eye fell on Annunciata; he recognised her,
nodded familiarly to her, and said, as he was drawn along,
" Yesterday, thee; to-day, me! Pure Roman blood before
the chariot!"

I saw Annunciata become crimson and step back; but in
a moment, recovering herself, she bent forward over the

balcony, and said to him aloud, " Enjoy thy good fortune !
Thou art unworthy of it, like me !"

They had seen her, heard her words, and her reply. A
" vivat !" resounded through the air, and bouquets of
flowers flew up around her. One of them struck her
shoulder, and flew into my bosom. I pressed it close : it
was to me a treasure which I would not have lost.

Bernardo was indignant at what he called the punchinellos' audacity, and wished to go down immediately and
chastise the fellows ; but the chapel-master, as well as the
rest, prevented him, and treated the whole as a jest.

The servant announced the first tenor singer : he brought
with him an abbé and a foreign artist, who desired to be
introduced to Annunciata. The next moment came fresh
visitors, foreign artists, who introduced themselves, and
brought her their homage. We were altogether a large
party. They spoke of the merry Festino the last evening,
at the Theatre Argentina ; of the various artist masks that
represented the celebrated statues Apollo Musagetes, the
Gladiators, and the Discus-throwers. The only one who
took no part in the conversation was the old lady whom I
took for a Jewess : she sat silent, busied over her stocking,
and nodded very slightly when Annunciata several times
during the conversation turned to her.

. Yet how different was Annunciata from the being which
my soul had imagined her, as I saw and heard her the
evening before. In her person she seemed to be a life-
enjoying, almost wilful being : and yet this suited her indescribably well, and attracted me wonderfully. She knew
how to fascinate me and every one with her easy, sportive
remarks, and the sensible, witty manner in which she expressed herself.

Suddenly she looked at her watch, sprang up hastily, and
excused herself, saying that her toilet awaited her ; that
she was that evening to appear in *La Pruova d' un Opera
Seria.* With a friendly nod of the head she vanished into
a side room.

" How happy you have made me, Bernardo !" I exclaimed aloud to him, when we were scarcely out of the
house-door. " How lovely she is, lovely as in song and

acting! But how, in all the world, did you get admitted
to her?—how so suddenly make her acquaintance? I
cannot understand it: it all seems to me a dream, even
that I myself have been near to her!"

"How did I get admitted?" replied he; "Oh, quite
simply! I considered it my duty as one of the young nobility of Rome, and as one of his Holiness's guard of
honour, and as an admirer of all beauty, to go and pay my
respects. Love did not require one-half of these reasons.
It was thus that I introduced myself; and that I could introduce myself equally well as those whom you yourself
saw arrive without announcer or keeper needs no doubt
whatever. When I am in love, I am always interesting;
and thus you can very well see that I should be very
amusing. We all had become, after the first half-hour, so
well acquainted with each other, that I could very well
bring you in, as soon as I saw you."

"You love her?" I inquired, "love her, right honestly?"

"Yes, more than ever!" exclaimed he; "and what I
told you, of her being the girl who gave me wine at the
old Jew's, I have now no doubt about. She recognised
me, when I stepped before her,—I saw that plainly; even
the old Jew mother, who did not say a word, but only sat
and beat time with her head, and lost her knitting-needle,
is to me a Solomon's seal to the truth of my conjecture.
Yet Annunciata is not a Jewess. It was her dark hair—
her dark eyes—the circumstances and the place where I
saw her first, which misled me. Your own picture is
more correct: she is of our faith, and shall enter into our
Paradise."

In the evening, we were to meet at the theatre. The
crowd was great. In vain I looked for Bernardo; he was
not to be seen. I found one place: all around me was
thronged; the heat was heavy and oppressive. My blood
was already beforehand in a strange, feverish agitation; I
seemed half to have dreamed the last two days' adventures.
No piece could be less calculated to give an equilibrium to
my agitated mind than that which had now begun.

The farce *La Pruova d' un Opera Seria* is, as is well

known, the fruit of the most wanton, fantastical humour, scarcely any connecting thread goes through the whole. Poet and composer have had no other intention than to excite laughter, and to give the singers opportunity of shining. There is here a passionate, whimsical prima donna, and a composer who plays in the same spirit together with caprice on caprice of the other theatrical people, that strange race, which must be managed in their own way, probably as poison, which can both kill and cure. The poor poet skips about among them, like a lightly esteemed victim.

Shouts and garlands of flowers greeted Annunciata. The humour, the liveliness which she showed, was called the highest art. I called it nature. It was exactly thus that she had been at home ; and now, when she sung, it was as if a thousand silver bells were ringing the changes of a delicious harmony, which infused that gladness into every heart which beamed from her eyes.

The duet between her and *il compositore della musica,* in which they change parts, she singing that of the man, and he that of the lady, was a triumph to them both as performers; but in particular was every one captivated by her transitions from the deepest counter-tenor to the highest soprana. In her light, graceful dancing she resembled Terpsichore upon the Etruscan vase ; every motion might have been a study for a painter or a sculptor. The whole graceful animation seemed to me a development of her own individuality, with which I had to-day become acquainted. The personation of Dido was to me artistic study : her " prima donna " this evening was a realisation of the most complete actuality.

Without having particular relation to the piece, there are great bravura-arias introduced into it from other operas. By the archness with which she sang these, all was evidently natural : it was wilfulness and love of fun that excited her to these magnificent representations.

At the close of the piece the composer declares that every thing was excellent, and that now the overture may begin ; he therefore distributes the music to the actual orchestra. The prima donna assists him ; the sign is

given, and both of them join in with the most horrible
ear and heart-rending dissonances, clapping their hands,
and shouting, " Bravo ! bravo ! " in which the public join
them.   Laughter almost overpowers the music ; but I was
captivated to my very soul, and felt myself half faint with
exultation.

Annunciata was a wild, wilful child, but most loveable
in her wilfulness.   Her song burst forth like the wild
dithyrambics of the bacchantes ; even in gaiety I could
not follow her : her wilfulness was spiritual, beautiful, and
great, and, as I looked at her, I could not but think on
Guido Reni's glorious ceiling-painting of Aurora, where
the Hours dance before the chariot of the Sun.   One of
these has a wonderful resemblance to the portrait of Beatrice
Cinci, but, as one must see, in the gayest time of her life.
This expression I found again in Annunciata.   Had I
been a sculptor, I should have designed her in marble, and
the world would have called the statue Innocent Joy.

Higher and yet higher, in wild dissonances, stormed the
orchestra ; the composer and prima donna accompanied
them.   " Glorious ! " they now exclaimed, " the overture
is at an end ; let the curtain rise ! "   And so it falls, and
the farce was ended ; but, as on the preceding night,
Annunciata must again come forth, and garlands, and
flowers, and poems, with fluttering ribands, flew towards
her.

Several young men of my age, some of whom I knew,
had arranged that night to give her a serenade : I was to
be one of them.   It was an age since I had sung.

An hour after the play, when she had arrived at home,
our little band advanced to the Piazza Colonna.   The
musicians were stationed under the balcony, where we still
saw light behind the long curtains.   My whole soul was in
agitation.   I thought only on her.   My song mingled
itself fearlessly with the others ; I sang also a solo-aria.   I
felt all that which I breathed forth.   Every thing in the
world passed away from me.   My voice had a power, a
softness which I had never imagined before.   My companions could not restrain a faint bravo, but yet sufficient
to make me attentive to my own song.   A wondrous joy

stole into my soul; I felt the god which moved within me, and, when Annunciata showed herself upon the balcony, bowed deeply, and thanked us, it seemed to me that it was alone with reference to me. I heard my voice distinctly above that of the others, and it seemed like the soul of the great harmony. I returned home in a whirl of enthusiasm; my vain mind dreamed only of Annunciata's delight in my singing. I had, indeed, astonished myself.

The next day I paid her a visit, and found Bernardo and several acquaintances with her. She was in raptures with the delicious tenor voice which she had heard in the serenade. I crimsoned deeply. One of the persons present suggested that I might be the singer; on which she drew me to the piano, and desired that I would sing a duet with her. I stood there like one about to be condemned, and assured them that it was impossible to me. They besought me, and Bernardo scolded because I thus deprived them of the pleasure of hearing the signora. She took me by the hand, and I was a captive bird: it mattered but little that I fluttered my wings, I must sing. The duet was one with which I was acquainted. Annunciata struck up and raised her voice. With a tremulous tone I began my adagio. Her eye rested upon me as if she would say, " Courage! courage! follow me into my world of melody!" and I thought and dreamed only on this and Annunciata. My fear vanished, and I boldly ended the song. A storm of applause saluted us both, and even the old silent woman nodded to me kindly.

" My good fellow," whispered Bernardo to me, "you have amazed me!" and then he told them all that I possessed yet another gift equally glorious— I was an Improvisatore also, and that I must delight them by giving them a proof of it. My whole soul was in excitement. Flattered on account of my singing, and tolerably secure of my own power, there needed only that Annunciata should express the wish for me, for the first time, as a youth, to have boldness enough to improvise.

I seized her guitar; she gave me the word " Immortality." I rapidly thought over the rich subject, struck a few chords, and then began my poem as it was born in my soul. My genius led me over the sulphur-blue Mediterranean to the wildly fertile valleys of Greece. Athens lay in ruins ; the wild fig-tree grew above the broken capitals, and the spirit heaved a sigh ; then onwards to the days of Pericles, when a rejoicing crowd was in motion under the proud arches. It was the festival of beauty ; women, enchanting as Lais, danced with garlands through the streets, and poets sang aloud that beauty and joy should never pass away. But now every noble daughter of beauty is dust, mingled with dust, the forms forgotten which had enchanted a happy generation : and, whilst my genius wept over the ruins of Athens, there arose before me from the earth glorious images, created by the hand of the sculptor, mighty goddesses slumbering in marble raiment ; and my genius recognised the daughters of Athens, beautifully exalted to divinity, which the white marble preserves for future generations. " Immortality," sang my genius, " is beauty, but not earthly power and strength," and wafting itself across the sea to Italy, to the city of the world, it gazed silently from the remains of the Capitol over ancient Rome. The Tiber whirled along its yellow waters, and, where Horatius Cocles once combated, boats now pass along, laden with wood and oil, for Ostia. Where Curtius sprang from the forum into the flaming gulph, the cattle now lie down in the tall grass. Augustus and Titus ! proud names, which now the ruined temple and arch alone commemorate ! Rome's eagle, the mighty bird of Jupiter, is dead in its nest. Rome, where is thy immortality ? There flashed the eye of the eagle. Excommunication goes forth over ascending Europe. The overturned throne of Rome was the chair of St. Peter ; and kings came as barefoot pilgrims to the holy city — Rome, mistress of the world ! But in the flight of centuries was heard the toll of death — death to all that the hand can seize upon, that the human eye can discern ! But can the sword of St. Peter really rust ? The eagle flies forth from the east to the west. Can the power of the Church decline ? Can the impossible happen ? Rome still stands proudly in her ruins with the gods of antiquity and her holy pictures which rule the world by eternal art. To thy mount, O Rome! will the sons of Europe come as pilgrims for ever; from the east and from the west, from the cold north will they come hither, and in their hearts acknowledge—"Rome, thy power is immortal!"

The most vehement applause saluted me as I concluded this stanza. Annunciata alone moved not a hand, but, silent and beautiful as an image of Venus, she looked into my eyes with a confiding glance, the silent language of a full heart, and again words flowed from my lips in easy verses, the offspring of the moment's inspiration.

From the great theatre of the world, I went to a more confined scene, and described the fair *artiste,* who, with her acting and her singing, attracted to her all hearts. Annunciata cast down her eyes—for it was she of whom I thought—she, who could not but be recognised in· the description which I gave. "And," continued I, "when the last tone has died away, the curtain fallen, and even the roar of applause is over, then also her beautiful labour is dead, and, as a beautiful corpse, lies in the bosom of the spectators. But a poet's heart is like the grave of the Madonna; all becomes flowers and odour; the dead ascend from it more beautiful, and his mighty song intones for her—'Immortality!'"

My eye rested on Annunciata; my thoughts had found words; I bowed low, and all surrounded me with thanks and flattering words.

"You have given me the sincerest pleasure," said Annunciata, and looked confidingly into my eyes. I ventured to kiss her hand.

My poetic power had excited in her a higher interest for me. She discovered already that which I myself perceived only afterwards, that my love for her had misled me in placing her art, and she who exercised it, within the range of immortality, which it could never reach. Dramatic art is like a rainbow, a heavenly splendour, a bridge between heaven and earth; it is admired, and then vanishes with all its colours.

I visited her daily. The few carnival-days were over, flown like a dream; but I enjoyed them thoroughly, for with Annunciata I drank in large draughts of life-enjoyment, such as I never had known before.

"You are really beginning to be a man!" said Bernardo, "a man like the rest of us, and yet you have only sipped of the cup. I dare swear now that you never gave a girl a kiss — never rested your head on her shoulder! Suppose now that Annunciata loved you?"

"What are you thinking of?" I replied, half angry; and the blood burned in my cheeks, — "Annunciata, that glorious woman that stands so high above me!"

"Yes, my friend, high or low, she is a woman, and you are a poet, of whose mutual relationship no one can form a judgment. If the poet have the first place in a heart, he is possessed also of the key which can lock the beloved in."

"It is admiration for her which fills my soul; I worship her loveliness, her understanding, and the art of which she is a votary. Love her? the thought has never entered my mind."

"How grave and solemn!" interrupted Bernardo, laughing. "You are not in love! no, that is true indeed. You are one of those intellectual amphibious creatures that one cannot tell whether they rightly belong to the living or the dream-world — you are not in love, not at least in the same way as I am, not in the same way as every body else — you say so yourself, and I will credit you; but still you may be so in your own particular way. You should not let your blood mount to your cheeks when she speaks to you, should not cast those significant fiery glances at her. I counsel you thus for her sake. What do you think others must think of it? But, in the meantime, she goes away the day after to-morrow, and who knows whether she may come back again after Easter, as she has promised."

For five long weeks Annunciata was about to leave us. She was engaged for the theatre at Florence, and the journey was fixed for the first day in Lent.

"Then she will have a new troop of adorers!" said Bernardo. "The old ones will be soon forgotten; yes, even your beautiful improvisation, for the sake of which she casts such loving looks at you, that one is regularly shocked. But he is a fool who thinks only of one woman!

They are all ours!—the field is full of flowers; one can gather every where."

In the evening we were together at the theatre: it was the last time of Annunciata's appearance before her journey. We saw her again as Dido, and in acting and singing she stood as high as at the first time: higher she could not be, it was the perfection of art. She was again to me the pure ideal which I had that evening conceived. The gay humour, the playful petulance, which she had shown in the farcical opera, and even in life, seemed to me a gaudy world-dress which she put on. It became her very well: but in Dido she exhibited her whole soul, her peculiar and spiritual identity. Rapture and applause saluted her; greater it could hardly have been when the enthusiastic Roman people greeted Cæsar and Titus.

With the honest thanks of an agitated heart she spoke her farewell to us all, and promised soon to return. "Bravo!" resounded from the overflowing house. Again and again they demanded to see her; and, in triumph, as at the first time, they drew her carriage through the streets; I was among the first of them! Bernardo shouted as enthusiastically as I, as we took hold on the carriage, in which Annunciata smiled, happy as a noble heart could be.

The next day was the last of the carnival, and the last which Annunciata had now to spend in Rome. I went to pay my farewell visit. She was very much affected at the homage which had been paid to her talent, and delighted herself in the thought of returning here after Easter, although Florence, with its beautiful country, and its glorious picture-gallery, was to her a beloved place of abode. In a few words she gave me so vivid a picture of the city and its neighbourhood, that I distinctly saw the whole — the wooded Apennines scattered over with villas; the Piazza del gran Duca, and all the old magnificent palaces.

" I shall see again the glorious gallery," said she, " where my love for sculpture was first excited, and where I perceived first the greatness of the human soul, which was able, like a Prometheus, to breathe life into the dead! Would that I at this moment could lead you into one of the rooms, the least of them all, but to me the dearest, the very remembrance of which makes me happy. In that little octagon room hang only select master-pieces; but all fade before one living marble figure, the Medicean Venus! Never did I see such a living expression in stone. The marble eye, otherwise without the power of sight, lives here! The artist has so formed it, " that by the help of light it seems to see, to look into our very souls : it is the goddess herself, born of the ocean-foam, that stands before us. Upon the wall behind the statue hang two magnificent pictures of Venus, by Titian : they are, in life and colouring, the goddess of beauty, but only earthly beauty — rich, luxurious beauty; the marble goddess is heavenly! — Raphael's Fornarina, and the superhuman Madonnas, excite my mind and my heart; but I always turn back again to the Venus : it stands before me, not like an image, but full of light and life, looking into my soul with her marble eyes! I know no statue, no group, which speaks to me thus ; no, not even the Laocoon, although the marble seems to sigh with pain. The Apollo of the Vatican, which you certainly know, alone seems to me a worthy companion-piece. The power and intellectual greatness which the sculptor has given to the poet-god is exhibited with more feminine nobility in the goddess of beauty."

"I know the glorious statue in plaster of Paris," replied I; "I have seen good copies in paste."

" But nothing can be more imperfect," she said ; " the dead plaster gives a dead expression. The marble gives life and soul ; in it the stone becomes flesh ; it is as if the blood flowed beneath the fine skin. I would that you were going with me to Florence, that you might admire and worship. I would be your guide there as you shall be mine in Rome, if I come back again."

I bowed low, and felt happy and flattered by her wish.

" We shall see you next after Easter?"

" Yes, at the illumination of St. Peter's and the giron-dola," replied she. " In the meantime think kindly on me, as I, in the gallery at Florence, will often remember you, and wish that you were there; and looking at that treasure!— That is always the way with me whenever I see any thing beautiful — I long for my friends, and wish that they were with me to participate in my pleasure. That is my kind of home-sickness."

She extended to me her hand, which I kissed, and ventured to say, half in jest, " Will you convey my kiss to the Medicean Venus?"

" Then it does not belong to me?" said Annunciata. " Well, I will honestly take care of it;" and with this she nodded to me most kindly, and thanked me for the happy hours which I had caused her with my singing and my improvisation.

" We shall see one another again," said she; and, like a dreamer, I left the room.

Outside the door I met the old lady, who saluted me more kindly than common; and in my excited state of mind I kissed her hand. She slapped me gently on the shoulder, and I heard her say, " He is a good creature!" I was now in the street, happy in the friendship of Annunciata, and enraptured with her mind and her beauty.

I felt myself in the right humour to enjoy this last day of the carnival. I could not imagine to myself that Annunciata was about to leave Rome, our leave-taking had seemed so easy; I could not but think that our meeting again must be on the morrow. All unmasked as I was, I took the liveliest part in the combat of comfits. Every chair through the whole length of the streets was occupied; every balcony and window was full of people; carriages drove up and down, and the gay throng of human beings, like a billowy stream, moved among them. In order to breathe a little more freely, I was obliged to spring boldly before one of the carriages, the little room between them being the only space in which one could in any measure freely move oneself. Music sounded, merry masks were singing, and behind one of the carriages Il Capitano was trumpeting forth his proud deeds on land and water. Wanton boys, on wooden horses, whose hands and hind-parts were only properly visible, whilst the rest

was covered with a bright carpet, which concealed the two
legs of the rider, which personated the four legs of the
horse, thrust themselves into the narrow space between
the carriages, and thus increased the confusion.   I could
neither get forward nor backward from the spot: the foam
of the horses behind me flew about my ears.   In this
press I sprang up behind one of the carriages, in which
sat two masks, who were, as it seemed, a fat old gentleman
in dressing-gown and night-cap, and a pretty flower-girl.
She had instantly seen that it was not out of lawlessness,
but rather from fear, and therefore she patted me with
her hand, and offered me two comfits for refreshment.
The old gentleman, on the contrary, threw a whole basket-
ful into my face, and, as the space behind me was now
somewhat more free, the flower-girl did the same ; so that
I, not having any weapons of the same kind, quite pow-
dered over from top to toe, was compelled to make a hasty
retreat.   Two harlequins brushed me merrily with their
maces ; but when the carriage again, in its turn, passed
me, the same tempest began anew.   I therefore determined
to defend myself, in return, with comfits ; but the cannon
was fired, the carriages were forced into the narrow side-
streets, to give place to the horse-racing, and my two
masks disappeared from my sight.

They seemed to know me.   Who could they be ?   I
had not seen Bernardo in the Corso through the whole day.
A thought occurred to me that the old gentleman in the
dressing-gown and night-cap might be he, and the pretty
shepherdess his so-called " tame bird." Very gladly would
I have seen her face.   I had taken my place on a chair
close to the corner ; the cannon-shot was soon heard, and
the horses rushed through the Corso up towards the Venetian Square.   The human mass immediately filled the
street again behind them, and I was just about to dismount,
when a fearful cry resounded " Cavallo ! "

One of the horses, the first which reached the goal, had
not been secured, and had now, in a moment, turned itself
about, and was pursuing its way back.   When one thinks
upon the thick crowd, and the security with which every
one went forward after the race was at an end, one may

easily imagine the misfortune that was likely to occur. The remembrance of my mother's death passed through me like a flash of lightning : it was as if I felt the frightful moment in which the wild horses went over us. My eyes stared immoveably forward. The crowd fled to the sides as if by a magical stroke — it seemed as if they had shrunk into themselves. I saw the horse snorting, and with bleeding sides and wildly flying mane, pass by ; I saw the sparks which flew from his hoofs, and at once, as if struck with a shot, drop dead to the earth. Anxiously inquired every one from his neighbour whether some misfortune had not happened. But the Madonna had held a protecting hand over her people ; nobody was hurt, and the danger so happily past made the public mind still gayer, and much wilder than ever.

A sign was made, which announced that all order in driving was now at an end, and the glorious *moccolo*, the splendid finale of the carnival, had begun. The carriages now drove one amongst another ; the confusion and the tumult became still greater ; the darkness increased every minute, and every one lighted his little candle, some whole bundles of them. In every window lights were placed ; houses and carriages, in the quiet, glorious evening, looked as if scattered over with these glimmering stars. Paper-lanterns, and pyramids of light, swung upon tall poles across the street. Every one was endeavouring to protect his own light, and to extinguish his neighbour's ; whilst the cry, " *Sia ammazato chi non porta moccolo !* " sounded forth with increasing wildness.

In vain I tried to defend mine : it was blown out every moment. I threw it away, and compelled every body to do the same. The ladies by the sides of the houses stuck their light behind them through the cellar windows, and cried out to me, laughing, " *Senza moccolo.*" They fancied their own lights safe, but the children from within climbed up to the windows, and blew them out. Little paper balloons and lighted lamps came waving down from the upper windows, where people sat with hundreds of little burning lights, which they held on long canes over the street, crying all the time, " Let every one perish who does not carry a taper !" whilst fresh figures, in the meantime, clambered up the spouts with their pocket-handkerchiefs fastened on long sticks, with which to put out every light, holding up theirs aloft the while, and exclaiming, " *Senza moccolo !*" A stranger who has never seen it can form no idea of the deafening noise, the tumult and the throng. The air is thick and warm with the mass of human beings and the burning lights.

Suddenly, when some of the carriages had drawn off into one of the dark cross streets, I saw close before me my two masks. The lights of the cavalier in the dressing-gown were extinguished, but the young flower-girl held a bouquet of burning tapers aloft on a cane four or five ells long. She laughed aloud for joy that nobody could reach it with their handkerchiefs, and the man in the dressing-gown overwhelmed every body with comfits who ventured to approach them. I would not allow myself to be terri-fied ; in a moment I had mounted on the back of the carriage, and seized hold of the cane, although I heard a beseeching " No," and her companion assailed me with gypsum bullets, and that not sparingly. I seized fast hold of the cane, in order to extinguish the lights ; the cane broke in my hand, and the brilliant bouquet fell to the earth amid the shouting of the people.

" Fie, Antonio !" cried the flower-girl. It pierced me through bone and marrow ; for it was Annunciata's voice. She threw all her comfits at my face, and the basket into the bargain. In my astonishment I leaped down, and the carriage rolled on. I saw, however, a nosegay of flowers thrown to me as a token of reconciliation. I caught at it in the air, and would have followed them, but it was im-possible to slip out ; for the carriages were all entangled, and there was the utmost confusion, although some turned to one side and some to the other. At length I escaped into a side-street ; but when I was able to breathe more freely I perceived a heavy weight at my heart. " With whom was Annunciata driving ?"

That she wished to enjoy this, the last day of the car-nival, seemed to me very natural ; but the gentleman in the dressing-gown ? Ah, yes, my first conjecture was certainly correct: it must be Bernardo! I determined to convince myself of it. I ran in haste through the cross-streets, and came to the Piazza Colonna, where Annunciata lived, and posted myself by the door to await her arrival. Before long the carriage drove up, and, as if I had been the servant of the house, I sprang towards it. Annunciata skipped out without seeming to notice me. Now came the gentleman in the dressing-gown: he descended too slowly to be Bernardo. "Thanks, my friend!" said he; and I heard that it was the old lady-friend, and saw, by her feet and her brown gown, which hung below the dressing-gown, as she stepped out, how much I had erred in my conjecture.

"*Felicissima notte, Signora!*" cried I aloud in my joy.

Annunciata laughed, and said jestingly that I was a bad man, and that she therefore would set off to Florence; but her hand pressed mine.

Happy, and with a light heart, I left her, and shouted aloud the wild cry, "Perish every one who carries not a taper!" and all the while had not one myself. I thought in the meantime only on her and the good old woman, who had donned the dressing-gown and night-cap in order to enjoy the carnival fun, for which she did not seem created. And how beautiful and natural it was of Annunciata, that she had not gone driving about with strangers, and had not given a seat in her carriage to Bernardo, nor even to the chapel-master! That I, the moment I recognised her, had become jealous of the night-cap, was a something which I would not acknowledge. Happy and merry as I was, I resolved to spend in pleasure the few hours which yet remained before the carnival had passed like a dream.

I went into the Festino. The whole theatre was decorated with garlands of lamps and lights — all the boxes were filled with masks, and strangers without masks. From the pit a high broad step led to the stage, covering in the narrow orchestra, and was decorated with drapery and garlands for a ball-room. Two orchestras played alternately. A crowd of *quaqueri* and *vetturini* masks danced a merry ring-dance around the Bacchus and Ariadne. They drew me into their circle; and, in the gladness of my heart, I made my first dancing-essay, and found it so delightful that it did not remain the last.   No! for as, somewhat late at night, I hastened home, I danced about yet once more with the merry masks, and cried with them, " The happiest night after the most beautiful carnival!"

My sleep was only short.   I thought in the lovely morning-hour on Annunciata, who now, perhaps, at this moment left Rome — thought upon the merry carnival-days, which seemed to have created a new life for me, and which now, with all their exultation and tumult, were vanished for ever.   I had no rest — I must out into the free air.   Every thing was all at once changed — all doors and shops were closed — but few people were in the streets — and in the Corso, where yesterday one could hardly move for the joyous throng, there were now to be seen only a few slaves in their white dresses with the broad blue stripes, who swept away the comfits, which lay upon the streets like hail, while a miserable horse with its hay-bundle, from which it kept eating, hanging by its side, drew along the little car into which the litter of the street was thrown.   A vetturino drew up at a house, then fastened at the top of his coach trunks and bandboxes, drew a great mat over the whole, and then hooked the iron chain fast around the many boxes that were put behind. From one of the side-streets came another similarly laden coach.   All went hence.   They went to Naples or Florence. Rome would be as if dead for five long weeks, from Ash-Wednesday till Easter.

CHAPTER XII.

LENT. — ALLEGRI'S MISERERE IN THE SIXTINE CHAPEL. — VISIT TO
BERNARDO. — ANNUNCIATA.

STILL and deathlike slid on the weary day.   In thought I recalled and revived the spectacle of the carnival, and the great adventure of my own life, in which Annunciata played the chief part. And day as it succeeded to day brought with it again this uniformity and this gravelike stillness. I was conscious of an emptiness which my books could not fill. Bernardo had formerly been every thing to me ; now it was as if there lay a gulf between us. I felt myself constrained in his presence, and it became more and more clear to me that Annunciata alone occupied me.

For some moments I was happy in this consciousness ; but there came also days and nights in which I thought on Bernardo, who had loved her before I had done so. He, indeed, it was also who had introduced me to her. I had assured him that it was admiration, and nothing more, which I felt for her — him, my only friend — him, whom I had so often assured of my heart's fidelity towards him. I was false and unjust. There burned in my heart the fire of remorse, but still my thoughts could not tear themselves from Annunciata. Every recollection of her, of my most happy hours spent with her, sunk me into the deepest melancholy. Thus contemplate we the smiling image, beautiful as life, of the beloved dead ; and the more lifelike, the more kindly it smiles, the stronger is the melancholy which seizes us. The great struggle of life, of which I had so often been told at school, and which I had fancied was nothing more than the difficulties of a task, or the ill-humour or unreasonableness of a teacher, I now, for the first time, began to feel. If I were to overcome this passion which had awoke within me, would not my former peace certainly return ? To what, also, could this love tend ? Annunciata stood high in her art ; yet the world would condemn me if I forsook my calling to follow her. The Madonna, too, would be angry ; for I had been born and brought up as her servant. Bernardo would never forgive me ; and I did not know, either, whether Annunciata loved me. That was at the bottom the bitterest thought to me. In vain I cast myself, in the church, before the image of the Madonna ; in vain I besought her to strengthen my soul in my great struggle, for even here my sin was increased — the Madonna was to me like Annunciata. It seemed to me that the countenance of every beautiful woman wore that intellectual expression which existed in that of Annunciata. No; I will rend these feelings out of my soul! I will never again see her!

I now fully comprehended what I never could understand before — why people felt impelled to torture the body, that by the pain of the flesh they might conquer in the spiritual combat. My burning lips kissed the cold marble feet of the Madonna, and for the moment peace returned to my soul. I thought upon my childhood, when my dear mother yet lived; how happy I had then been, and what a many delights even this dead time before Easter had brought me.

And all, indeed, was just the same as then. In the corners and the squares stood, as then, the little green huts of leaves, ornamented with gold and silver stars; and all round still hung the beautiful shields like signs, with their verses, which told that delicious dishes for Lent were here to be obtained. Every evening they lighted the gay-coloured paper lamps under the green boughs. How had I, as a child, delighted myself with these things! how happy had I been in the splendid booth of the bacon dealer, which in Lent glittered like a world of fancy! The pretty angels of butter danced in a temple, of which sausages, wreathed with silver, formed the pillars, and a Parmesan cheese the cupola! My first poem, to be sure, had been about all this magnificence; and the bacon dealer's lady had called it a *Divina Commedia di Dante!* Then I had heard not Annunciata, but neither did I know any singer. Would that I could forget Annunciata!

I went with the procession to the seven holy churches of Rome, mingled my song with those of the pilgrims, and my emotions were deep and sincere. But one day Bernardo whispered into my ear, with demon-like mirth, "The merry lawyer on the Corso — the bold improvisatore, with penitence in his eyes, and ashes on his cheeks! Ay, how well you can do it all! how you understand every part! I cannot imitate you here, Antonio!" There was a jeer, and yet, at the same time, an apparent truth in his words, which wounded me deeply.

The last week of Lent was come, and strangers streamed

back towards Rome. Carriage after carriage rolled in through the Porta del Popolo and the Porta del Giovanni. On Wednesday afternoon began the Miserere in the Sixtine chapel. My soul longed for music; in the world of melody I could find sympathy and consolation. The throng was great, even within the chapel — the foremost division was already filled with ladies. Magnificent boxes, hung with velvet and golden draperies, for royal personages and foreigners from various courts, were here erected so high, that they looked out beyond the richly carved railing which separated the ladies from the interior of the chapel. The papal Swiss guards stood in their bright festal array. The officers wore light armour, and in their helmets a waving plume : this was particularly becoming to Bernardo, who was greeted by the handsome young ladies with whom he was acquainted.

I obtained a seat immediately within the barrier, not far from the place where the papal singers were stationed. Several English people sat behind me. I had seen them during the carnival, in their gaudy masquerade dresses : here they wore the same. They wished to pass themselves off for officers, even boys of ten years old. They all wore the most expensive uniforms, of the most showy and ill-matched colours. As, for example, one wore a light blue coat, embroidered with silver, gold upon the slippers, and a sort of turban with feathers and pearls. But this was not any thing new at the festivals in Rome, where a uniform obtained for its wearer a better seat. The people who were near smiled at it, but it did not occupy me long.

The old cardinals entered in their magnificent violet-coloured velvet cloaks, with their white ermine capes ; and seated themselves side by side, in a great half-circle, within the barrier, whilst the priests who had carried their trains seated themselves at their feet. By the little side-door of the altar the holy father now entered in his purple mantle and silver tiara. He ascended his throne. Bishops swung the vessels of incense around him, whilst young priests, in scarlet vestments, knelt, with lighted torches in their hands, before him and the high altar.

The reading of the lessons began.* But it was impossible to keep the eyes fixed on the lifeless letters of the Missal — they raised themselves, with the thoughts, to the vast universe which Michael Angelo has breathed forth in colours upon the ceiling and the walls. I contemplated his mighty sybils and wondrously glorious prophets, every one of them a subject for a painting. My eyes drank in the magnificent processions, the beautiful groups of angels; they were not to me painted pictures, all stood living before me. The rich tree of knowledge, from which Eve gave the fruit to Adam; the Almighty God, who floated over the waters, not borne up by angels, as the older masters had represented him — no, the company of angels rested upon him and his fluttering garments. It is true I had seen these pictures before, but never as now had they seized upon me. My excited state of mind, the crowd of people, perhaps even the lyric of my thoughts, made me wonderfully alive to poetical impressions; and many a poet's heart has felt as mine did!

The bold foreshortenings, the determinate force with which every figure steps forward, is amazing, and carries one quite away! It is a spiritual Sermon on the Mount, in colour and form. Like Raphael, we stand in astonishment before the power of Michael Angelo. Every prophet is a Moses like that which he formed in marble. What giant forms are those which seize upon our eye and our thoughts as we enter! But, when intoxicated with this view, let us turn our eyes to the back-ground of the chapel, whose whole wall is a high altar of art and thought. The great chaotic picture, from the floor to the roof, shows itself there like a jewel, of which all the rest is only the setting. We see there the LAST JUDGMENT.

Christ stands in judgment upon the clouds, and the apostles and his mother stretch forth their hands beseechingly for the poor human race. The dead raise the grave-stones under which they have lain; blessed spirits float upwards, adoring to God, whilst the abyss seizes its victims.

* Before the commencement of the Miserere, fifteen long lessons are read; and, at the close of each one. a light in the grand candelabra is extinguished, there being a light for every lesson. — *Author's note.*

Here one of the ascending spirits seeks to save his condemned brother, whom the abyss already embraces in its
snaky folds. The children of despair strike their clenched
fists upon their brows, and sink into the depths! In bold
foreshortening, float and tumble whole legions between
heaven and earth. The sympathy of the angels; the expression of lovers who meet; the child that, at the sound
of the trumpet, clings to the mother's breast, is so natural
and beautiful, that one believes oneself to be one among
those who are waiting for judgment. Michael Angelo has
expressed in colours what Dante saw and has sung to the
generations of the earth.

The descending sun, at that moment, threw his last
beams in through the uppermost window. Christ, and
the blessed around him, were strongly lighted up; whilst
the lower part, where the dead arose, and the demons thrust
their boat, laden with damned from shore, were almost in
darkness.

Just as the sun went down the last lesson was ended,
and the last light which now remained was extinguished,
and the whole picture-world vanished in the gloom from
before me; but, in that same moment, burst forth music
and singing. That which colour had bodily revealed arose
now in sound: the day of judgment, with its despair and
its exultation, resounded above us.

The father of the church, stripped of his papal pomp,
stood before the altar and prayed to the holy cross; and
upon the wings of the trumpet resounded the trembling
quire, " *Populus meus, quid feci tibi?* " Soft angel tones
rose above the deep song, tones which ascended not from a
human breast: it was not a man's nor a woman's: it belonged to the world of spirits: it was like the weeping of
angels dissolved in melody.

It this world of harmony my soul imbibed strength and
the fulness of life. I felt myself joyful and strong, as I
had not been for a long time. Annunciata, Bernardo, all
my love, passed before my thought. I loved, in this moment, as blessed spirits may love. The peace which I had
sought in prayer, but had not found, flowed now, with
these tones, into my heart.

When the Miserere was ended, and the people all had gone away, I was sitting with Bernardo in his room. I offered him my hand in sincerity, spoke all that my excited soul dictated. My lips became eloquent. Allegri's Miserere, our friendship, all the adventures of my singular life, furnished material. I told him how morally strong the music had made me, how heavy my heart had been previously — my sufferings, anxiety, and melancholy, during the whole of Lent; yet, without confessing how great a share he and Annunciata had had in the whole: this was the only little fold of my heart which I did not unveil to him. He laughed at me, and said, that I was a poor sort of a man; that the shepherd-life, with Domenica and the Signora, all that woman's education, and, last of all, the Jesuit school, had quite been the ruin of me; that my hot Italian blood had been thinned with goat's milk; that my Trappist-hermit life had made me sick; that it was necessary for me to have a little tame bird, which would sing me out of my dream-world; that I ought to be a man, like other folks, and then I should find myself sound both body and soul.

"We are very different, Bernardo," said I; "and yet my heart is wonderfully attached to you; at times I wish that we could be always together."

"Then it would not go well with our friendship," replied he; "no, then it would be all over with it before we were aware. Friendship is like love, all the stronger for separation. I think sometimes how wearisome it must be in reality to be married. For ever and for ever to see one another, and that in the smallest things. Most married folks are disgusting to one another; it is a sort of propriety, a species of good nature, which holds them together in the long-run. I feel very well, in myself, that if my heart glows ever so fiercely, and hers whom I love burns the same, yet would these flames, if they met, be extinguished. Love is desire, and desire dies when gratified."

"But if, now, your wife were beautiful and discreet as ———"

"As Annunciata," said he, seeing that I hesitated for the name which I wanted. "Yes, Antonio, I would look at the beautiful rose as long as it were fresh; and when the leaves withered, and the fragrance was lost, God knows what I then should have a fancy for. At this moment, however, I have a very curious one, and I have felt something like it before. I have a wish to see how red your blood is, Antonio! But I am a reasonable man—you are my friend, my honest friend; we will not fight, even if we cross each other in the same love adventure." And with this he laughed loud, pressed me violently to his breast, and said, half-jestingly, " I will make over to you my tame bird; it begins to be sensitive, and will certainly please you. Go with me this evening; confidential friends need not hide any thing from one another; we will have a merry evening. On Sunday the holy father will give us all his blessing."

" I shall not go with you," I replied.

" You are a coward, Antonio," said he; " do not let the goat's milk entirely subject your blood. Your eye can burn like mine; it can truly burn; I have seen it. Your sufferings, your anxiety, your penitence in Lent — yes, shall I openly tell you the reason of them? I know it very well, Antonio; you cannot hide it from me. Now, then, clasp Beauty to your heart — only you have not the courage — you are a coward, or ——"

" Your conversation, Bernardo," replied I, " offends me."

" But you must endure it, though," he answered. At these words the blood mounted into my cheeks, whilst my eyes filled with tears.

" Can you thus sport with my devotion for you? " I cried. " Do you fancy that I have come between you and Annunciata? — fancy that she has regarded me with more kindness than yourself? "

" Oh, no! " interrupted he; " you know very well that I have not such a vivid fancy. But do not let her come into our conversation. And with regard to your devotion to me, of which you are always talking, I do not understand it. We give one another the hand; we are friends, reasonable friends; but your notions are over-strained — me you must take as I am."

This probably was the sting in our conversation — the part which went to my heart, and, so to say, went into the blood; I felt myself wounded, and yet in his hand-pressure, at parting, there was a something cordial.

The next day, which was Green-Thursday, called me to the church of St. Peter's, into whose magnificent vestibule the greatness of which has indeed led some strangers to imagine that it was the whole church, as great a throng was found as was seen in the streets and across the bridge of St. Angelo. It was as if the whole of Rome flocked here to wonder even as much as strangers did at the greatness of the church, which seemed more and more to extend itself to the throng.

Singing resounded above us; two great choirs, in different parts of the nave of the church, replied to each other. The throng crowded to witness the feet-washing, which had just begun.* From the barrier behind which the stranger ladies were seated, one of them nodded kindly to me. It was Annunciata. She was come — was here in the church; my heart beat violently. I stood so near to her that I could bid her welcome.

She had arrived the day before, but still too late to hear Allegri's Miserere; yet she had been present at the Ave Maria in the church of St. Peter's.

"The extraordinary gloom," said she, "made all more imposing than now by daylight. Not a light burned, excepting the lamps at St. Peter's tomb; these formed a wreath of light, and yet not strong enough to illumine the nearest pillar. All marched around in silence; I, too, sank down, feeling right vividly how very much can be comprised in nothing; what force there lies in a religious silence."

Her old friend, whom I now first discovered, and who wore a long veil, nodded kindly. The solemn ceremony was in the meantime concluded, and they looked in vain for their servant, who should have attended them to their carriage. A crowd of young men had become aware of

---

* On Green-Thursday the pope washes the feet of thirteen priests, old and young; they kiss his hand, and he gives to them a bouquet of blue stocks. — *Author's note.*

Annunciata's presence; she seemed uneasy, and wished to go. I ventured to entreat that I might conduct them out of the church to their carriage. The old lady immediately took my arm; but Annunciata walked beside of us. I had not courage to offer her my arm; but when we neared the door, and were carried along with the crowd, I felt her arm within mine: it went like fire through my blood.

I found the carriage. When they were seated, Annunciata asked me to dine with them that day. "Only to eat a meagre dinner," said she, "such as we may enjoy in Lent."

I was happy! The old lady, who did not hear well, understood, however, by the expression of Annunciata's face, that it was an invitation, but imagined that it was to take a seat with them in the carriage. She, therefore, in a moment put aside all the shawls and cloaks which lay on the seat opposite, and extended to me her hand, saying, " Yes, be so good, Mr. Abbé! there is room enough ! "

That was not Annunciata's meaning: I saw a slight crimson pass over her cheek; but I sat directly opposite to her, and the carriage rolled away.

A delicious little dinner awaited us. Annunciata spoke of her residence in Florence, and of the festival of to-day; inquired from me about Lent in Rome, and how I had passed the time; a question which I could not answer quite candidly.

" You will certainly see the christening of the Jews on Easter Day ? " asked I, casting, at the same time, a glance at the old woman, whom I had quite forgotten.

" She did not hear it ! " replied Annunciata, " and, if she had you need not have minded. I only go to such places as she can accompany me to, and for her it would not be becoming to be present at the festival in the baptismal chapel of Constantine.* Neither is it very interesting to me ; for it so rarely happens that it is from conviction that either Jews or Turks receive baptism. I remember, in my childhood, what an unpleasant impression

* Annually, on Easter day, some Jews or Turks are baptized. In the *Diario Romano* this day is thus marked ; *si fà il battesimo degl' Ebrei e Turchi.* — *Author's note.*

this whole scene made upon me. I saw a little Jew-boy, who seemed to be seven years old ; he came forth with the dirtiest shoes and stockings, with thin, uncombed hair ; and, in the most painful contrast with this, in a magnificent white silk dress, which the church had given him. The parents, filthy as the boy, followed him ; they had sold his soul for a happiness which they did not know themselves ! "

" You saw that as a child here in Rome ? " asked I.

" Yes ! " returned she, crimsoning, " but yet, for all that I am not a Roman."

" The first time I saw you, and heard you sing," said I, " it seemed to me that I had known you before. I do not even know, but I fancy so still ! If we believed in the transmigration of souls, I could fancy that we both had been birds, had hopped upon the same twigs, and had known one another for a very long time. Is there any kind of recollection in your soul? nothing which says to you that we have seen each other before ? "

" Nothing at all ! " replied Annunciata, and looked me steadfastly in the face.

" As you have just told me that you were a child in Rome, and consequently not, as I thought, had passed all your young years in Spain, a remembrance awoke in my soul, the same which I felt the first time that you stood before me as Dido. Have you never, as a child, at Christmas, made a speech before the little Jesus, in the church Ara Cœli, like other children ? "

" That I have ! " exclaimed she, " and you, Antonio, were the little boy who drew all attention ? "

" But was supplanted by you ! " returned I.

" It was you, Antonio ! " exclaimed she aloud, seizing both my hands, and looking into my face with an indescribably gentle expression. The old lady drew her chair nearer to us, and looked gravely at us. Annunciata then related the whole to her, and she smiled at our recognition-scene.

" How my mother and every body talked about you," said I ; " of your delicate, almost spirit-like form, and your sweet voice ! yes, I was jealous of you, my vanity could not endure to be cast so wholly in the shade by any one. How strangely paths in life cross one another!"

" I remember you very well!" said she; " you had on a little short jacket, with many white buttons, and these at that time excited most my interest for you!"

" You," replied I, " had a beautiful red scarf upon your breast; but yet it was not that, but your eyes, your jet-black hair, which most of all captivated me! Yes, I could not but recognise you, you are the same as then, only the features more developed; I should have known them, even under a greater change. I said so immediately to Bernardo, but he gainsaid me, and thought it must be quite another ——"

" Bernardo!" she exclaimed; and it seemed to me that her voice trembled.

" Yes!" I replied, somewhat confused, " he fancied also that he knew you, that he had seen you, I should say; seen you, and connected in such a way, as did not agree with my conjecture. Your dark hair, your glance, — yes, you will not be angry with me, he immediately changed his opinion; he fancied at the first moment that you were —" I hesitated, — " that you were not of the Catholic church, and thus that I could not have heard you preach in Ara Cœli."

" That I was, perhaps, of the same faith as my friend here?" said Annunciata, indicating the old lady. I nodded involuntarily, but seized her hand at the same time, and asked, " Are you angry with me?"

" Because your friend took me for a Jewish maiden?" asked she, smiling; " you are a strange creature!"

I felt that our connexion in childhood had made us more familiar; every care was forgotten by me, and also every resolution never to see, never to love her. My soul burned only for her.

The galleries were closed these two days before Easter; Annunciata said how charming it must be, if, at this time, and quite at one's ease, one could wander through them; but that was hardly possible. The wish from her lips was a command; I knew the custodian and the porter, all the dependants who now were returned to the Palazzo Borghese, where was one of the most interesting collections in Rome, through which I, as a child, had gone with Francesca, and made acquaintance with every little Love in Francesco Albani's Four Seasons.

I entreated that I might take her and the old lady there the following day ; she consented, and I was infinitely happy.

In my solitude at home I again thought on Bernardo ! no, he loved her not, I consoled myself with thinking ; " his love is only sensual, not pure and great, like mine !" Our last conversation seemed to me still more bitter than it had done before ; I saw only his pride, felt myself very much offended, and worked myself up into a greater passion than I had ever done before. His pride had been wounded by Annunciata's apparently greater kindness towards me than him. To be sure it was he who introduced me to her, but perhaps his intention only was to make fun of me, and therefore he had expressed astonishment at my singing, and at my improvisation — he had never dreamed that I could outshine his handsome person, his free and bold manner. Now, it had been his intention to deter me from again visiting her. But a good angel had willed it otherwise ! her gentleness, her eyes, all had told me that she loved me, that she had a kindness for me, nay more than a kindness, for she must have felt that I loved her !

In my joy I pressed hot kisses upon my pillow, but with this feeling of the happiness of love a bitterness arose in my heart towards Bernardo. I grew angry with myself for not having had more character, more warmth, more gall ; now a hundred excellent answers occurred to me, which I might have given him when he treated me the last time like a boy ; every little affront which he had given now stood livingly before me. For the first time I felt the blood regularly boil in my veins ; hot anger and the purest and best emotions, mingled with a hateful bitterness, deprived me of sleep. It was not until towards morning that I slumbered a little, and then awoke stronger and lighter of heart.

I announced to the custodian that I was about to bring a foreign lady to see the gallery, and then went to Annunciata. We drove all three to the Palazzo Borghese.

CHAPTER XIII.

THE PICTURE GALLERY. — A MORE PRECISE EXPLANATION. — EASTER.
— THE TURNING POINT OF MY HISTORY.

I⊤ was to me quite a peculiar feeling to conduct Annunciata to where I had played as a boy — where the signora had shown to me the pictures, and had amused herself with my *naïve* inquiries and remarks. I knew every piece, but Annunciata knew them better than I did ; her observations were most apposite ; with an accustomed eye, and natural taste, she detected every beauty. We stood before that celebrated piece of Gerardo del Notti, Lot and his Daughters. I praised it for its great effect — Lot's strong countenance, and the life-enjoying daughter who offered him wine, and the red evening heaven which shone through the dark trees.

"It is painted with soul and flame!" exclaimed she. "I admire the pencil of this artist, as regards colouring and expression ; but the subjects which he has chosen do not please me. I require, even in pictures, a kind of fitness, a noble purity in the selection of the subject ; therefore Correggio's Danaë pleases me less than it might do ; beautiful is she, divine is the little angel with the bright wings, which sits upon the couch, and helps her to collect together the gold, but the subject is to me ignoble, it wounds, so to say, my heart's feeling of beauty. For this reason is Raphael so great in my judgment ; in every thing that I have seen of his, he is the apostle of innocence, and he, therefore, alone has been able to give us the Madonna!"

"But beauty, as a work of art," interrupted I, "can, however, make us overlook the want of nobility in a subject."

"Never!" replied Annunciata ; "art in every one of its branches is high and holy ; and purity in spirit is more attractive than purity of form ; and therefore the *naïve* representations of the Madonna, by the olden masters, excite

K

us so deeply, although, with their rough forms, they often seem more like Chinese pictures, where all is so stiff and hard. The spirit must be pure in the pictures of the painter, as well as in the song of the poet; some extravagances I can forgive, call them something startling, and lament that the painter has fallen into such, but I can nevertheless please myself with the whole."

"But," I exclaimed, "variety in subject is interesting; to see always ———"

"You mistake me!" she returned. "I do not desire that people should always paint Madonnas! no; I am delighted with a glorious landscape, a living scene out of the life of the people, a ship in a storm, and the robber-scenes of Salvator Rosa! But I will not have any thing revolting in the region of art, and so I call even Scidoni's well-painted sketch in the Sciara Palazzo. You have not forgotten it? Two peasants upon asses ride past a stone wall, upon which lies a death's head, within which sit a mouse, a gadfly and a worm, and on the wall these words are to be read, ' Et ego in Arcadia! '"

"I know it," replied I; "it hangs by the side of Raphael's charming Violin Player."

"Yes," returned Annunciata; "would that the inscription was placed under this, and not upon the other hateful picture!"

We now stood before Francesco Albani's Four Seasons. I told her what an impression the little Loves had made upon me as a child, when I lived and played about in this gallery.

"You enjoyed happy life-points in your childhood!" said she, repressing a sigh, which perhaps had reference to her own.

"You, doubtless, no less so," replied I; "you stood, the first time I saw you, like a happy, admired child, and, when we met the second time, you captivated the whole of Rome, and — seemed happy. Were you so really at heart?"'

I had bowed myself half down to her. She looked directly into my face with an expression of singular melancholy, and said, "The admired, happy child was fatherless and motherless——a homeless bird upon the leafless twig; it might have perished of hunger, but the despised Jew gave it shelter and food till it could flutter forth over the wild, restless sea?"

She ceased, and then, shaking her head, added, "But these are not adventures which could interest a stranger; and I cannot tell how I have been induced to gossip about it."

She would have moved on, but I seized her hand, whilst I inquired, "Am I, then, such a stranger to you?"

She gazed for a moment before her in silence, and said, with a pensive smile, "Yes, I, too, have also had beautiful moments in life. And," added she, with her accustomed gaiety, "I will only think on these! Our meeting as children——your strange dreaming about that which is past, infected me also, and made the heart turn to its own pictures, instead of the works of art which surround us here!"

When we left the gallery and had returned to her hotel, we found that Bernardo had been there to pay his respects to her. They told him that she and the old lady had driven out, and that I had accompanied them. His displeasure at the knowledge of this I had foreseen already; but, instead of grieving over this, as I should have done formerly, my love for Annunciata had awoke defiance and bitterness towards him. He had so often wished that I was possessed of character and determination, even if it made me unjust to him; now he would see that I had both.

For ever rung in my ear Annunciata's words about the despised Jew who took the homeless bird under his wings; she must then be the same whom Bernardo had seen at the old Hanoch's. This interested me infinitely; but I could not again induce her to renew the subject.

When I made my appearance the next day, I found her in her chamber, studying a new piece. I entertained myself for a long time with the old lady, who was more deaf than I had imagined, and who seemed right thankful that I would talk with her. It had occurred to me that she had seemed kindly disposed to me since my first improvisation; and from that I had imagined that she had heard it.

"And so I have done," she assured me; "from the expression of your countenance, and from some few words which reached me, I understood the whole. And it was beautiful! It is in this way that I understand all Annunciata's recitative, and that alone by the expression : my eye has become acuter as my ear has become duller."

She questioned me about Bernardo, who had called yesterday when we were out, and lamented that he was not with us. She expressed an extraordinary good-will towards him, and great interest. "Yes," said she, as I assented to it, "he has a noble character! I know one trait of him. May the God of the Jew and the Christian defend him for it!"

By degrees she became more eloquent. Her affection for Annunciata was touching and strong. Thus much became clear to me out of the many broken and half-darkly expressed communications which she made. Annunciata was born in Spain, of Spanish parents. In her early childhood she came to Rome ; and when she became there suddenly fatherless and motherless, the old Hanoch, who, in his youth , had been in her native land, and had known her parents, was the only one who befriended her. Afterwards, whilst yet a child, she was sent back to her native country, to a lady who cultivated her voice and her dramatic talent. A man of great influence had fallen in love with the beautiful girl ; but her coldness towards him had awoke in him bitterness, and a desire to obtain her by craft. The old woman seemed unwilling to lift the mysterious veil which covered this terrible time. Annunciata's life was in danger ; she secretly fled to Italy, where it would be difficult to discover her, with her old foster-father, in the Jews' quarter in Rome. It was only a year and a half since this happened ; and during this time it was that Bernardo had seen her, and when she had presented him with the wine of which he had spoken so much. How indiscreet it seemed to me to show herself thus to a stranger, when she might have expected an assassin in every one of them. Yes, she knew indeed that Bernardo was not such a one ; she had heard nothing, indeed, but the praises of his boldness and of his noble conduct.

Shortly after this they heard that her persecutor was dead. She flew forth, therefore, inspired by her sacred art, and enraptured the people by it and her beauty. The old lady accompanied her to Naples, saw her gather her first laurels, and had not yet left her.

" Yes," continued the eloquent old lady, " she is also an angel of God! Pious is she in her faith, as a woman ought to be ; and understanding has she as much as one could wish for the best heart."

I left the house just as the joy-firing commenced. In all the streets, in the squares, from balconies and windows, people stood with small cannons and pistols, which was a sign that Lent was now at an end. The dark curtains with which, for five long weeks, the pictures in churches and chapels had been covered, fell off at the same moment. All was Easter gladness. The time of sorrow was over ; to-morrow was Easter, the day of joy, and of two-fold joy for me ; for I was invited to accompany Annunciata to the church festival, and the illumination of the dome.

The bells of Easter rang — the cardinals rolled abroad in their gay carriages, loaded with servants behind — the equipages of rich foreigners — the crowd of foot-passengers, filled the whole narrow streets. From the Castle of St. Angelo waved the great flag on which were the papal arms and the Madonna's holy image. In the square of St. Peter's there was music, and round about garlands of roses, and woodcuts, representing the Pope distributing his blessing, were to be purchased. The fountains threw up their gigantic columns of water, and all around by the colonnades were *loges* and benches, which already, like the square itself, were almost filled.

Anon, and almost as great a throng proceeded from the church, where processions and singing, exhibitions of holy relics, fragments of food, nails, &c., had refreshed many a pious mind. The immense square seemed a sea of human beings ; head moved itself to head ; the line of carriages drew itself closer together ; peasants and boys climbed up the pedestals of the saints. It seemed as if all Rome at this moment lived and breathed only here.

The Pope was borne in procession out of church. He

K 3

sat aloft on the shoulders of six priests apparelled in lilac-coloured robes, upon a magnificent throne-chair; two younger priests waved before him colossal peacocks' tails on long staves; priests preceded him swinging the vessels of incense, and cardinals followed after, singing hymns.

As soon as the procession had issued from the portal, all the choirs of music received him with triumph. They bore him up the lofty steps to the gallery, upon whose balcony he soon showed himself, surrounded by cardinals. Every one dropped on their knees — long lines of soldiers — the aged person like the child — the Protestant stranger alone stood erect, and would not bow himself for the blessing of an old man. Annunciata half kneeled in the carriage, and looked up to the holy father with soul-full eyes. A deep silence reigned around, and the blessing, like invisible tongues of fire, was wafted over the heads of us all.

Next fluttered down from the Papal balcony two different papers; the one containing a forgiveness of all sins, the other a curse against all the enemies of the church. And the people struck about them to obtain even the smallest scrap of them.

Again rang the bells of all the churches; music mingled itself in the jubilant sound. I was as happy as Annunciata. At the moment when our carriage was set in motion, Bernardo rode close up to us. He saluted both the ladies, but appeared not to see me.

" How pale he was!" said Annunciata, " is he ill ? "

" I fancy not," I replied ; but I knew very well what had chased the blood from his cheeks.

This matured my determination. I felt how deeply I loved Annunciata; that I could give up every thing for her if she yielded me her love. I resolved to follow her. I doubted not of my dramatic talent; and my singing — I knew the effect which my singing had produced. I should certainly make my *début* with honour when I had once ventured on this step. If she loved me, what pretension had Bernardo? He might woo her if his love were as strong as mine ; and, if she loved him, — yes, then I would instantly withdraw my claim.

I wrote all this to him in a letter that same day, and I

will venture to believe that there breathed in it a warm and true heart, for many tears fell upon the paper as I spoke of our early acquaintance, and how wonderfully my heart had always clung to him. The letter was despatched, and I felt myself calmer, although the thought of losing Annunciata, like the vulture of Prometheus, rent my heart with its sharp beak ; yet, nevertheless, I dreamed of accompanying her for ever, and of winning at her side honour and joy. As singer, as improvisatore, I should now begin the drama of my life.

After the Ave Maria I went with Annunciata and the old lady in their carriage to see the illumination of the Dome. The whole of the church of St. Peter's, with its lofty cupola, the two lesser ones by its side, and the whole façade, were adorned with transparencies and paper lanterns ; these were so placed in the architecture that the whole immense building stood with a fiery outline amid the blue air. The throng in the neighbourhood of the church seemed greater than in the forenoon ; we could scarcely move at a foot's pace. We first saw from the bridge of St. Angelo the whole illuminated giant structure, which was reflected in the yellow Tiber, where boat-loads of rejoicing people were charmed with the whole picture.

When we reached the square of St. Peter's, where all was music, the ringing of bells and rejoicing, the signal was just given for the changing of the illumination. Many hundreds of men were dispersed over the roof and dome of the church where, at one and the same moment, they shoved forwards great iron pans with burning pitch-garlands ; it was as if every lantern burst forth into flame ; the whole structure became a blazing temple of God, which shone over Rome, like the star over the cradle in Bethlehem.* The triumph of the people increased every moment, and Annunciata was overcome by the view of the whole.

" Yet it is horrible ! " she exclaimed. " Only think of the unhappy man who must fasten on and kindle the top-

* The church is entirely built of stone : so are the surrounding edifices ; thus there is no danger from leaving the pitch-garlands and iron-pans to burn out of themselves. All is, therefore, in flame through the whole night.— *Author's note.*

most light on the cross upon the great cupola.   The very
thought makes me dizzy."

" It is as lofty as the pyramids of Egypt," said I ; " it
requires boldness in the man to swing himself up there,
and to fasten the string.   The holy father gives him the
sacrament, therefore, before he ascends."

" Thus must the life of a human being be risked,"
sighed she ; " and that merely for the pomp and gladness
of a moment."

" But it is done for the glorifying of God," I replied ;
" and how often do we not risk it for much less ? "

The carriages rushed past us ; most of them drove to
Monte Pincio, in order to see from that distance the illuminated church, and the whole city which swam in its
glory.

" Yet it is," said I, " a beautiful idea, that all the
light over the city beams from the church.   Perhaps
Correggio drew from this the idea for his immortal night."

" Pardon me," she said ; " do you not remember that
the picture was completed before the church ?   Certainly
he derived the idea from his own heart ; and it seems to
me also far more beautiful.   But we must see the whole
show from a more distant point.   Shall we drive up to
Monte Maria, where the throng is not so great, or to
Monte Pincio !   We are close by the gate."

We rolled along behind the colonnade, and were soon in
the open country.   The carriage drew up at the little inn
on the hill.   The cupola looked glorious from this point ;
it seemed as if built of burning suns.   The façade, it is
true, was not to be seen, but this only added to the effect ;
the splendour which diffused itself through the illumined
air caused it to appear as if the cupola, burning with stars,
swam in a sea of light.   The music and the ringing of
bells reached us, but all around us reigned a twofold night,
and the stars stood only like white points high in the blue
air, as if they had dimmed their shine above the splendid
Easter fire of Rome.

I dismounted from the carriage, and went into the little
inn to fetch them some refreshment.   As I was returning
through the narrow passage where the lamp burned before

the image of the Virgin, Bernardo stood before me, pale as when, in the Jesuit school, he received the garland. His eyes glowed as if with the delírium of fever, and he seized my hand with the force and wildness of a madman.

"I am not an assassin, Antonio," said he, with a strangely suppressed voice, "or I would drive my sabre into your false heart; but fight with me you shall, whether your cowardice will or will not. Come, come with me!"

"Bernardo, are you mad?" inquired I, and wildly tore myself from him.

"Only cry aloud," returned he, with the same suppresseᴊ voice, "so that the crowd may come and help you, for you dare not stand single-handed against me. Before they bind my hands you will be a dead man!"

He offered me a pistol. "Come, fight with me, or I shall become your murderer!" and, so saying, he drew me forth with him. I took the pistol which he had offered to defend myself from him.

"She loves you," whispered he; "and, in your vanity, you will parade it before all the Roman people, before me, whom you have deceived with false, hypocritical speeches, although I never gave you cause to do so."

"You are ill, Bernardo," I exclaimed; "you are mad; do not come too near me."

He threw himself upon me. I thrust him back. At that moment I heard a report; my hand trembled; all was in smoke around me, but a strangely deep sigh, a shriek it could not be called, reached my ear, my heart! My pistol had gone off; Bernardo lay before me in his blood.

I stood there like a sleep-walker, and held the pistol grasped in my hand. It was not till I perceived the voices of the people of the house around me, and heard Annunciata exclaim, "Jesus Maria!" and saw her and the old lady before me, that I was conscious of the whole misfortune.

"Bernardo!" I cried in despair, and would have flung myself on his body; but Annunciata lay on her knees beside him, endeavouring to stanch the blood.

I can see even now her pale countenance and the stead-
fast look which she riveted upon me.   I was as if rooted
to the spot where I stood.

"Save yourself! save yourself!" cried the old lady,
taking hold of me by the arm.

"I am innocent!" I exclaimed, overcome by anguish;
"Jesus Maria! I am innocent! He would have killed me;
he gave me the pistol, which went off by accident!" and
that which I perhaps otherwise should not have dared to
say aloud, I revealed in my despair: "Yes, Annunciata, we
loved thee.   For thy sake would I die, like him! Which
of us two was the dearer to thee?   Tell me, in my despair,
whether thou lovest me, and then will I escape."

"Away!" stammered she, making a sign with her hand,
whilst she was busied about the dead.

"Fly!" cried the old lady.

"Annunciata," besought I, overcome with misery,
"which of us two was the dearer to thee?"

She bowed her head down to the dead; I heard her
weeping, and saw her press her lips to Bernardo's brow.

"The *gens d'armes!*" cried some one just by me.
"Fly, fly!" and, as if by invisible hands, I was torn out
of the house.

CHAPTER XIV.

THE PEASANTS OF ROCCA DEL PAPA. — THE ROBBER'S CAVE. —
THE PARCÆ OF MY LIFE.

"SHE loves Bernardo!" rung in my heart: it was the
arrow of death which poisoned my whole blood, which
drove me onward, and silenced even the voice which cried
within me, "Thou hast murdered thy friend and brother!"

I instinctively rushed through bushes and underwood,
climbing over the stone walls which fenced in the vineyards
on the hill-side.   The cupola of St. Peter's lit up the

atmosphere to a great distance: thus shone forth the altar of Cain and Abel, when the murderer fled.

For many hours I wandered uninterruptedly forwards; nor did I pausè until I reached the yellow Tiber, which cut off my farther progress. From Rome onwards, down to the Mediterranean, no bridge was to be met with, nor even a boat, which could have conveyed me over. This unexpected impediment was as the stab of a knife, which, for a moment, cut in sunder the worm that gnawed at my heart; but it speedily grew together again, and I felt that my whole misfortune was twofold.

Not many paces from me I perceived the ruins of a tomb, larger in circumference, but more desolate, than that in which I had lived as a child with the old Domenica. Three horses were tied to one of the overturned blocks of stone, and were feeding from the bundles of hay which were fastened to their necks.

A wide opening led, by a few deep steps, into the vault of the tomb, within which a fire was burning. Two strong-built peasants, wrapped in their sheep-skin cloaks, with the wool outwards, and in large boots and pointed hats, in which was fastened a picture of the Virgin, stretched themselves before the fire, and smoked with their short pipes. A shorter figure, wrapped in a large grey cloak, and with a broad slouching hat, leaned against the wall, while he drank from a flask of wine to a farewell and a happy meeting. Scarcely had I contemplated the whole group, before I was myself discovered. They snatched up their weapons which lay beside them, as if they apprehended a surprise, and stepped hastily towards me.

" What do you seek for here?" they asked.

" A boat to take me across the Tiber," I replied.

" You may look for that a long time," they returned. " Here is neither bridge nor boat, unless folks bring them with them."

" But," began one of them, while he surveyed me from top to toe, " you are come a long way out of the high-road, signore, and it is not safe out o' nights. Cæsar's band may still have long roots, although the holy father has been using the spade, till he has perhaps worked his own hand off."

"You should, at least," remarked another, "have taken some arms with you. See what we have done—a threefold charge in the gun, and a pistol in the belt, lest the piece should miss fire."

"Yes, and I have also taken a good little caseknife with me," said the first speaker, and drew out of his belt a sharp and bright knife, with which he played in his hand.

"Stick it again in its sheath, Emidio," said the second; "the strange gentleman gets quite pale: he is a young man who cannot bear such sharp weapons. The first best villain will get from him his few scudi—us he would not so easily manage. Do you see?" said the fellow to me; "give us your money to keep, and so it will be quite safe."

"All that I have you can take," replied I, weary of life, and obtuse from suffering; "but no great sum will you get."

It was evident to me in what company I now found myself. I quickly felt in my pocket, in which I knew there to be two scudi; but, to my astonishment, found there a purse. I drew it forth: it was of woman's work; I had seen it before, in the hands of the old lady at Annunciata's: she must have thrust it into my pocket, at the last moment, that I might have spare money for my unhappy flight. They snatched all three at the full purse; and I shook out its contents upon the flat stone before the fire.

"Gold and silver!" cried they, as they saw the white louis-d'or shining among the piastres. "It would have been a sin if the beautiful soûls had fallen into robbers' hands."

"Kill me now," said I, "if such be your intention; so there may be an end of my sufferings."

"Madonna mia!" exclaimed the first, "what do you take us for? We are honest peasants from Rocca del Papa. We kill no Christian brother. Drink a glass of wine with us, and tell us what compels you to this journey."

That remains my secret," said I, and eagerly took the

wine which they offered to me; for my lips burned for a refreshing draught.

They whispered to each other; and then the man in the broad hat rose up, nodded familiarly to the others, looked jestingly into my face, and said, "You'll pass a cold night after the warm merry evening!" He went out, and we soon heard him galloping.

"You wish to go over the Tiber?" said one: "if you will not go with us, you will have to wait a long time. Seat yourself behind me on my horse, for to swim after its tail would not be much to your liking."

Secure I was not in this place: I felt my home was with the outlawed. The fellow assisted me upon a strong fiery horse, and then placed himself before me.

"Let me fasten this cord around you," said the fellow, or else you may slip off, and not find the ground." He then threw a cord fast round my back and arms, flinging it round himself at the same time, so that we sat back to back: it was not possible for me to move my hands. The horse advanced slowly into the water, trying every step before he took it. Presently the water reached the saddle-bow; but, labouring powerfully, he gained at length the opposite shore. As soon as we had reached this, the fellow loosened the cord which bound me to him, yet only to secure my hands still more firmly to the girths.

"You might fall off and break your neck," said he. "Hold only fast, for now we cut across the Campagna."

He struck his heels into the sides of the horse; the other did the same; and away they sped, like well-accustomed horsemen, over the great desolate plain. I held myself fast, both with hands and feet. The wind caught up the fellow's long, black hair, which flapped upon my cheeks. We sped on past the fallen gravestones: I saw the ruined aqueduct, and the moon which, red as blood, rose upon the horizon, whilst light, white mists flew past us.

That I had killed Bernardo — was separated from Annunciata and my home, and now, in wild flight, bound upon the horse of a robber, was speeding across the Campagna — seemed all to me a dream, a horrible dream!

Would that I might speedily awake, and see these images of terror dissipate themselves! I closed my eyes firmly, and felt only the cold wind from the mountains blowing upon my cheek.

" Now we shall be soon under grandmother's petticoat," said the rider when we approached the mountains. " Is it not a good horse which we have? Then it has also had this year St. Antonio's blessing: my fellow decked him out with bunches of silken ribands, opened the Bible before him, and sprinkled him with holy water; and no devil, or evil eye, can have any influence on him this year."

Daylight began to dawn on the horizon when we reached the mountains.

" It begins to get light," said the other rider, " and the signore's eyes may suffer: I will give him a parasol;" and with that he threw a cloth over my head, which he bound so fast, that I had not the slightest glimmering of sight. My hands were bound: I was thus entirely their captive, and, in my distress of mind, submitted to every thing.

I observed that we were ascending for some time: then we rapidly descended again; twigs and bushes struck me in the face; we were upon an altogether unused path. At length I was made to dismount: they conducted me forwards, but not a word was said: at length we descended one step through a narrow opening. My soul had been too much occupied with itself for me to remark in what direction we had entered the mountains; yet we could not have gone very deep into them. It was not till many years afterwards that the place became known to me: many strangers have visited it, and many a painter has represented on canvass its character and colouring. We were at the old Tusculum. Behind Frascati, where the sides of the hills are covered with chesnut woods and lofty laurel hedges, lie these ruins of antiquity. Tall white thorns and wild roses shoot up from the steps of the amphitheatre. In many places of the mountains are deep caves, brick-work vaults, almost concealed by a luxuriant growth of grass and underwood. Across the valley may be seen the lofty hills of Abruzzi, which bound the Marshes, and which give to the whole landscape a character of great wildness, that here, amid the ruins of a city of antiquity, is doubly impressive. They conducted me through one of these openings in the mountain, half concealed with depending evergreen and twining plants. At length we came to a stand. I heard a low whistle; and, immediately afterwards, the sound of a trap-door, or door which opened. We again descended some steps deeper, and I now heard several voices. The cloth was removed from my eyes, and I found myself in a spacious vault. Large-limbed men, in sheep-skin cloaks, like my conductors, sat and played at cards around a long table, upon which burned two brass lamps, with many wicks, which strongly lighted up their dark expressive countenances. Before them stood wine in great bottles. My arrival excited no astonishment: they made room for me at the table, gave me a cup of wine, and a piece of their sausage, keeping up a conversation, in the meantime, in a dialect which I did not understand; which seemed, however, to have no reference to me.

I felt no hunger, but only a burning thirst, and drank the wine. I cast my eyes around me, and saw that the walls were covered with arms and articles of clothing. In one corner of the vault was a still deeper apartment. From its roof depended two hares, which were partly skinned, and beneath these I perceived yet another being. A meagre old woman, with a singular, almost youthful bearing, sat there immovably, and spun flax upon a hand-spindle. Her silver-white hair had loosened itself from the knot into which it had been fastened, and hung down over one cheek, and round her yellow-brown neck, and her dark eye was steadfastly fixed upon the spindle. She was the living image of one of the Parcæ. Before her feet lay a quantity of burning wood-ashes, as if they were a magical circle which separated her from this world.

I did not long remain left to myself. They commenced a sort of examination of me, of my condition in life, and of every thing connected with my circumstances and family. I declared to them that they had already had all that I possessed, and that nobody in Rome, if they demanded a ransom for me, would give as much as a scudo, and that I was a poor bird, which, for a long time, had the intention of going to Naples, to try my talents as an improvisatore. I concealed not from them the peculiar ground of my flight, the unfortunately accidental going off of the piece, yet without explaining the immediate circumstances of it.

"The only ransom which you are likely to obtain for me," added I, "is the sum which the law will give you for delivering me up. Do it; for I myself, at this moment, have no higher wish!"

"That's a merry wish!" said one of the men. "You have perhaps, however, in Rome, a little girl who would give her gold earrings for your liberty. You can, however, improvise at Naples; we are the men to get you over the barriers. Or the ransom shall be the earnest-money of our brotherhood; so here is my hand! You are among honourable fellows, you shall see! But sleep now, and think of it afterwards. Here is a bed, and you shall have a coverlet which has proved the winter's blast and the sirocco rain —— my brown cloak there on the hook."

He threw it to me, pointed to the straw mat at the end of the table, and left me, singing as he went the Albanian folks' song, "*Discendi, o mia bettina!*"

I threw myself down on the couch, without a thought of repose. All the late occurrences passed before my mind as a horrible picture; nevertheless my eyes closed; my bodily strength was exhausted; I slept deeply through the whole day.

When I again awoke I felt myself wonderfully invigorated. All that had so agitated my soul seemed to me like a dream; but the place in which I was, and the dark countenances around me, told me immediately that my recollections were reality.

A stranger, with pistols in his girdle, and a long grey cloak thrown loosely over his shoulder, sat astride on the bench, and was in deep conversation with the other robbers. In the corner of the vault sat yet the old Mulatto-coloured woman, and twirled her spindle immovably as ever, a picture painted on a dark background. Fresh-burning wood was laid on the floor before her, and gave out warmth.

" The ball went through his side," I heard the stranger say; " he lost some blood, but, in a month, all will be over."

" Ei, Signore," cried my horseman, as he again saw me awake; " a twelve-hours' sleep is a good pillow? Nay, Gregorio brings news from Rome which will certainly please you! You have trodden heavily on the train of the Senate! Yes; it is actually you! All circumstances agree together. You have actually shot the nephew of the senator! That was a bold shot!"

" Is he dead?" were the only words I could stammer forth.

" No, not entirely!" replied the stranger, " and will not die this time. At least the doctors say so. The foreign handsome signora, who sings like a nightingale, watched through the whole night by his bed, till the doctors assured her that she might be easy, for that there was no danger."

" You missed your mark," exclaimed the other, " both in regard to his heart and hers! Let the bird fly, they'll make a pair, and you stop with us. Our life is merry and free. You may become a little prince; and the danger of it is no greater than hangs over every crown. Wine you shall have, and adventures and handsome girls for the one which has jilted you. Better is it to drink of life in copious draughts than to sip it up by drops."

" Bernardo lives! I am not his murderer!" This thought gave new life to my soul; but my distress on account of Annunciata could not be alleviated. Calmly and resolutely I replied to the man, that they could deal with me as they liked, but that my nature, my whole education, my intentions in life, forbade me to form any such connection with him as he proposed.

" Six hundred scudi is the lowest sum for which we will liberate you!" said the man, with a gloomy earnestness. " If these are not forthcoming in six days, then you are ours, either dead or alive! Your handsome face, my kindness towards you, will avail nothing! Without the six hundred scudi you will only have your choice between brotherhood with us, or brotherhood with the many who lie arm in arm, embracing in the well below. Write to your friend, or to the handsome singer ; they must both of them be grateful to you at bottom, for you have brought about an explanation between them. They will certainly pay this miserable sum for you. We have never let any body go so cheaply out of our inn before. Only think," added he, laughing, "your coming here cost you nothing ; and now, board and lodging for a whole six days, nobody can say that it is unreasonable."

My answer remained the same.

"Perverse fellow !" said he. "Yet I like it in thee ; that I will say, even if I have to put a bullet through thy heart. Our jolly life must, however, captivate a young spirit ; and thou, a poet, an improvisatore, and not charmed with a bold flight ! Now, if I had desired thee to sing 'The Proud Strength among the Rocks,' must not thou have praised and cried up this life, which thou seemest to despise ? Drink of the cup, and let us hear your art. You shall describe to us that which I have just said — the proud struggle which the mountains see ; and, if you do it like a a master, why, then, I'll extend your time yet one day longer."

He reached to me a guitar from the wall ; the robbers gathered around me, demanding that I should sing.

I bethought myself for some moments. I was to sing of the woods, of the rocks — I who, in reality, had never been amid them. My journey the night before had been made with bandaged eyes, and during my abode in Rome, I had visited only the pine-woods of the Villa Borghese and the Villa Pamfili. Mountains had, indeed, occupied me as a child, but only as seen from the hut of Domenica. The only time in which I had been amongst them was on that unfortunate going to the flower-feast at Gensano. The darkness and stillness of the woods lay in the picture which my memory retained of our ramble under the lofty plantains by Lake Nemi, where we bound garlands that evening. I again saw all this, and ideas awoke in my soul. All these images passed before me in one half of the time which it requires me to speak of them.

I struck a few accords, and the thoughts became words, and the words billowy verse. I described the deep calm, shut in among woods, and the cliffs which reared themselves high amid the clouds. In the nest of the eagle sat the mother-bird, and taught her young ones the strength of their pinions and the practice of their keen gaze, by bidding them look at the sun. " You are the king of birds," said she ; " sharp is your eye, strong are your talons. Fly forth from your mother ; my glance will follow you, and my heart will sing like the voice of the swan when death embraces her. Sing will I of ' proud strength !' And the young ones flew from the nest. The one flew only to the next peak of the cliff and sat still, with his eye directed to the beams of the sun, as if he would drink in its flames ; but the other swung itself boldly in great circles, high above the cliff and the deep-lying lake. The surface of the water mirrored the woody margin and the blue heaven. A huge fish lay still, as if he had been a reed which floated on its surface. Like a lightning flash darted the eagle down upon its prey, struck its sharp talons in its back, and the heart of the mother trembled for joy. But the fish and the bird were of equal strength. The sharp talon was too firmly fixed to be again withdrawn, and a contest began, which agitated the quiet lake in great circles. For a moment, and it was again calm ; the huge wings lay outspread upon the waters like the leaves of the lotus-flower ; again they fluttered aloft ; a sudden crack was heard— one wing sunk down, whilst the other lashed the lake into foam, and then vanished. The fish and the bird sank into the deep water. Then was sent forth the lamenting cry of the mother, and she turned again her eye upon the second son, which had rested above upon the cliff, and he was not there ; but far away, in the direction of the sun, she saw a dark speck ascending and vanishing in his beams. Her heart was agitated with joy, and she sang of the proud strength which only became great by the lofty object for which it strove ! "

My song was at an end ; a loud burst of applause saluted

me, but my eye was arrested by the old woman. In the midst of my song I had indeed observed that she let the hand-spindle drop, riveted upon me a keen, dark glance, which made it exactly seem to me as if the scene of my childhood, which I had described in my song, again was renewed. She now raised herself up, and, advancing to me with quickening steps, exclaimed, —

"Thou hast sung thy ransom ! the sound of music is stronger than that of gold ! I saw the lucky star in thy eye when the fish and the bird went down into the deep abyss to die ! Fly boldly towards the sun, my bold eagle ! the old one sits in her nest and rejoices in thy flight. No one shall bind thy wings !"

"Wise Fulvia !" said the robber who had required me to sing, and who now bowed with an extraordinary gravity to the old woman, "dost thou know the signore ? Hast thou heard him improvise before now ?"

"I have seen the star in his eye — seen the invisible glory which beamed around the child of fortune ! He wove his garland ; he shall weave one still more beautiful, but with unbound hands. Dost thou think of shooting down my young eagle in six days, because he will not fix his claws into the back of the fish ? Six days he shall remain here in the nest, and then he shall fly towards the sun !"

She now opened a little cupboard in the wall, and took out paper, upon which she was about to write.

"The ink is hard," said she," like the dry rock ; but thou hast enough of the black moisture ; scratch thy hand, Cosmo, the old Fulvia thinks also on thy happiness !"

"Without saying a word, the robber took his knife, and, putting aside the skin, wetted the pen with the blood. The old woman gave it to me to write the words, "I travel to Naples !"

"Thy name under it !" said she, "that is a papal seal !"

"What is the meaning of this ?" I heard one of the younger men say, as he cast an angry glance at the old woman.

"Does the worm talk?" said she; "defend thyself from the broad foot that crushes thee!"

"We confide in thy prudence, wise mother," rejoined one of the elder ones; "thy will is the tabernacle of blessing and good luck!"

No more was said.

The former lively state of feeling returned; the wine-flask circulated. They slapped me familiarly on the shoulder; gave me the best pieces of the venison which was served up; but the old woman sat as before immovably at work with her hand-spindle, whilst one of the younger men laid fresh ashes at her feet, saying, "Thou art cold, old mother!"

From their conversation, and from the name by which they had addressed her, I now discovered that she it was who had told my fortune, as a child, when I, with my mother and Mariuccia, wove garlands by Lake Nemi. I felt that my fate lay in her hand; she had made me write, "I travel to Naples!" That was my own desire, but how was I to get across the barrier without a passport? how was I to maintain myself in this foreign city, where I knew no one? To make my *début* as an improvisatore, whilst I was a fugitive from a neighbouring city, was a thing I dared not to do. My power of language, however, and a singular childish reliance on the Madonna, strengthened my soul; even the thought of Annunciata, which dissolved into a strange melancholy, brought peace to my soul — a peace like that which descends upon the seaman, when, after his ship is gone down, he alone is driven in a little boat towards an unknown shore.

One day after another glided on; the men came and went, and even Fulvia was absent for one whole day, and I was alone in the cave with one of the robbers.

This was a young man of about one-and-twenty, of ordinary features, but with a remarkably melancholy expression, which almost bordered on insanity; this, and his beautiful long hair which fell upon his shoulders, characterised his exterior. He sat silent for a long time, with his head sunk upon his arm. At length he turned himself to me and said, "Thou canst read: read me a prayer out of this book!" and with that he gave me a little prayer-book. I read, and the most heartfelt devotion beamed in his large, dark eyes.

"Why wilt thou leave us?" asked he, offering me his hand good-naturedly; "perjury and falsehood dwell in the city as in the wood; only in the wood one has fresh air and fewer people."

A sort of confidential feeling arose between us; and whilst I shuddered at his wild manner I was touched by his unhappiness.

"Thou knowest, perhaps," said he, "the legend of the Prince of Savelli? of the gay wedding at Ariccia? It was, to be sure, only a poor peasant and a simple country-girl, but she was handsome, and it was her wedding. The rich lord of Savelli gave a dance in honour of the bride, and sent her an invitation to his garden; but she revealed it to her bridegroom, who dressed himself in her clothes, and put on her bridal veil, and went instead of her, and then, when the count would have pressed her to his breast, a dagger was driven into his noble heart. I knew a count and a bridegroom like these, only the bride was not so open-hearted: the rich count celebrated the bridal night, and the bridegroom the feast of death with her. Her bosom shone like snow when the pale knife found its way to her heart!"

, I looked silently into his face, and had not a word wherewith to express my sympathy.

"Thou thinkest that I never knew love — never, like the bee, drank from the fragrant cup!" exclaimed he. "There travelled a high-born English lady to Naples; she had a handsome serving-maid with her — health on her cheeks and fire in her eyes! My comrades compelled them all to dismount from the carriage, and to sit in silence on the ground whilst they plundered it. The two women, and a young man, the lover of one I fancy he was, we took up among the hills. By the time that the ransom came for all three the girl's red cheeks were gone, and her eyes burned less brightly: that came from so much wood among the hills!"

I turned myself from him, and, as if half to excuse

himself, he added, " The girl was a Protestant, a daughter of Satan ! "

In the evening Fulvia returned, and gave me a letter which she commanded me not to read.

" The mountains have their foggy mantles around them ; it is time to fly away. Eat and drink, we have a long journey before us, and there grow no cakes upon the naked rocky path."

The young robber placed food on the table in haste, of which I partook, and then Fulvia threw a cloak over her shoulders, and hurried me along through dark, excavated passages.

" In the letter lie thy wings," said she, "not a soldier on the barrier shall ruffle a feather of thine, my young eagle ! The wishing rod also lies beside it, which will afford thee gold and silver till thou hast fetched up thy own treasures."

She now divided, with her naked, thin arm, the thick ivy, which hung like a curtain before the entrance to the cavern : it was dark night without, and a thick mist enwrapt the mountains. I held fast by her dress, and scarcely could keep up with her quick steps along the untrodden path in the dark : like a spirit she went forward ; bushes and hedges were left behind us on either hand.

Our march had continued for some time, and we were now in a narrow valley between the mountains. Not far from us stood a straw hut, one of those which is met with in the Marshes, without walls, and with its roof of reeds down to the ground. Light shone from a chink in its low door. We entered, and found ourselves as if in a great beehive, but all around was quite black from the smoke, which had no other exit than through the low door. Pillars and beams, nay, even the reeds themselves, were shining with the soot. In the middle of the floor was an elevation of brickwork, a few ells long, and probably half as broad ; on this lay a fire of wood ; here the food was cooked, and by this means, also, the hut was warmed. Further back was an opening in the wall, which led to a smaller hut, which was attached to the greater, just as one sees a small onion

grow to the mother bulb; within this lay a woman sleeping, with several children. An ass poked forth his head
from above them, and looked on us. An old man,
almost naked, with a ragged pair of drawers on made of
goat-skin, came towards us; he kissed Fulvia's hands, and,
without a word being exchanged, he threw his woollen skin
over his naked shoulders, drew forth the ass, and made a
sign for me to mount.

"The horse of fortune will gallop better than the ass of
the Campagna," said Fulvia.

The peasant led the ass and me out of the hut. My
heart was deeply moved with gratitude to the singular old
woman, and I bent down to kiss her hand; but she shook
her head, and then, stroking the hair back from my forehead, I felt her cold kiss, saw her once more motioning
with her hand, and the twigs and hedges hid us from each
other. The peasant struck the ass, and then ran on beside
him up the path: I spoke to him; he uttered a low sound,
and gave me, by a sign, to understand that he was dumb.
My curiosity to read the letter which Fulvia had given
me let me have no rest; I therefore drew it out and
opened it. It consisted of various papers, but the darkness
forbade me to read a single word, however much I strained
my eyes.

When the day dawned, we were upon the ridges of the
mountains, where alone was to be seen naked granite, with
a few creeping plants, and the grey-green strong-scented
wormwood. The heavens were quite clear, scattered over
with shining stars; a sea-like cloud world lay below us, it
was the Marshes which stretched themselves out from the
mountains of Albano, between Veletri and Terracina,
bounded by Abruzzi and the Mediterranean Sea. The
low, wavy clouds of mist shone below us, and I quickly
saw how the infinitely blue heaven changed to lilac, and
then into rose colour, and the mountains even became like
bright blue velvet. I was dazzled with the pomp of
colouring; a fire burned upon the side of the mountain,
which shone like a star upon the light ground. I folded
my hands in prayer; my head bowed itself before God in

the great church of nature, and silently besought, " Let Thy will be done !"

The daylight was now sufficiently clear for me to see what my letter contained ; it was a passport in my own name, prepared by the Roman police, and signed by the Neapolitan ambassador—an order on the house of Falconet, in Naples, for five hundred scudi, and a small note containing the words, " Bernardo's life is out of danger ; but do not return to Rome for some months."

Fulvia said justly that here were my wings and wishing-rod. I was free, a sigh of gratitude arose from my heart.

We soon reached a more trodden path, where some shepherds were sitting at their breakfasts. My guide stopped here ; they seemed to know him, and he made them understand, by signs with his fingers, that they should invite us to partake of their meal, which consisted of bread and buffalo-cheese, to which they drank asses' milk. I enjoyed some mouthfuls, and felt myself strengthened thereby.

My guide now showed me a path, and the others explained to me that it led down the mountains along the Marshes to Terracina, which I could reach before evening. I must continually keep this path to the left of the mountains, which would, in a few hours, bring me to a canal, which went from the mountains to the great highroad, the boundary trees of which I should see as soon as the mist cleared away. By following the canal, I should come out upon the highroad, just beside a ruined convent, where now stood an inn, called *torre di tre ponti.*

Gladly would I have bestowed upon my guide a little gift ; but I had nothing. It then occurred to me that I still had, however, the two scudi, which were in my pocket when I left Rome ; I had only given up the purse with the money which I had received as needful in my flight. Two scudi were thus, for the moment, all my ready money ; the one I would give to my guide, the other I must keep for my own wants till I reached Naples, where I could only avail myself of my bill. I felt in my pocket, but vain was all my search ; they had long ago taken from me all my little property.   I had nothing at all : I therefore took off the silk-handkerchief which I had round my neck, and gave it to the man, offered my hand to the others, and struck alone into the path which led down to the Marshes.

END OF THE FIRST VOLUME.

VOLUME THE SECOND.

CHAPTER I.

THE PONTINE MARSHES. —— TERRACINA.—— AN OLD ACQUAINTANCE. ——
FRA DIAVOLO'S NATIVE CITY. —— THE ORANGE GARDEN AT MOLO
DI GAETA. —— THE NEAPOLITAN SIGNORA. —— NAPLES.

MANY people imagine that the Pontine Marshes are only marshy ground, a dreary extent of stagnant, slimy water, a melancholy road to travel over: on the contrary, the marshes have more resemblance to the rich plains of Lombardy ; yes, they are like them, rich to abundance ; grass and herbage grow here with a succulence and a luxuriance which the north of Italy cannot exhibit.

Neither can any road be more excellent than that which leads through the marshes, upon which, as on a bowling-green, the carriages roll along between unending alleys of lime trees, whose thick branches afford a shade from the scorching beams of the sun. On each side the immense plain stretches itself out with its tall grass, and its fresh, green marsh-plants. Canals cross one another, and drain off the water which stands in ponds and lakes covered with reeds and broad-leaved water-lilies.

On the left hand, in coming from Rome, the lofty hills of Abruzzi extend themselves, with here and there small towns, which, like mountain castles, shine with their white walls from the grey rocks. On the right the green plain stretches down to the sea where Cape Cicello lifts itself, now a promontory, but formerly Circe's Island, where tradition lands Ulysses.

As I went along, the mists, which began to dissipate, floated over the green extent where the canals shone like linen on a bleaching-ground. The sun glowed with the warmth of summer, although it was but the middle of

March.   Herds of buffaloes went through the tall grass.
A troop of horses galloped wildly about, and struck out
with their hind feet, so that the water was dashed around
to a great height; their bold attitudes, their unconstrained
leaping and gambolling, might have been a study for an
animal painter.   To the left I saw a dark monstrous
column of smoke, which ascended from the great fire which
the shepherds had kindled to purify the air around their
huts.   I met a peasant, whose pale, yellow, sickly exterior
contradicted the vigorous fertility which the marshes presented.   Like a dead man arisen from the grave, he rode
upon his black horse, and held a sort of lance in his hand
with which he drove together the buffaloes which went
into the swampy mire, where some of them lay themselves
down, and stretched forth only their dark ugly heads with
their malicious eyes.

The solitary post-houses, of three or four stories high,
which were erected close by the road-side, showed also, at
the first glance, the poisonous effluvia which steamed up
from the marshes.   The lime-washed walls were entirely
covered with an unctuous, grey-green mould.   Buildings,
like human beings, bore here the stamp of corruption,
which showed itself in strange contrast with the rich
luxuriance around, with the fresh verdure, and the warm
sunshine.

My sickly soul presented to me here in nature an image
of the false happiness of life ; thus people almost always
see the world through the spectacles of feeling, and it appears
dark or rose-coloured according to the hue of the glass
through which they look.

About an hour before the Ave Maria I left the marshes
behind me ; the mountains, with their yellow masses of
rock, approached nearer and nearer, and close before me
stood Terracina in the fertile, Hesperian landscape.   Three
lofty palm-trees, with their fruit, grew not far from the
road.   The vast orchards, which stretched up the moun-
tain-sides, seemed like a great green carpet with millions of
golden points.   Lemons and oranges bowed the branches
down to the ground.   Before a peasant's hut lay a quantity of lemons, piled together into a heap, as if they had

been chesnuts which had been shaken down. Rosemary and wild dark-red gillyflowers grew abundantly in the crevices of the rock, high up among the peaks of the cliffs where stood the magnificent remains of the castle of the Ostrogothic king Theodoric*, and which overlook the city and the whole surrounding country.

My eyes were dazzled with the beautiful picture, and, quietly dreaming, I entered Terracina. Before me lay the sea, which I now beheld for the first time—the wonderfully beautiful Mediterranean. It was heaven itself in the purest ultra-marine, which, like an immense plain, was spread out before me. Far out at sea I saw islands, like floating clouds of the most beautiful lilac colour, and perceived Vesuvius where the dark column of smoke became blue in the far horizon. The surface of the sea seemed perfectly still, yet the lofty billows, as blue and clear as the ether itself, broke against the shore on which I stood, and sounded like thunder among the mountains.

My eye was riveted like my foot : my whole soul breathed rapture. It seemed as if that which was physical within me, heart and blood, became spirit, and infused itself into it that it might float forth between these two, the infinite sea and the heaven above it. Tears streamed down my cheeks, and I was compelled to weep like a child.

Not far from the place where I stood was a large white building, against the foundations of which the waves broke. Its lowest story, which lay to the street, consisted of an open colonnade, within which stood the carriages of travellers. It was the hotel of Terracina, the largest and the handsomest upon the whole way between Rome and Naples.

The cracking of whips re-echoed from the wall of rocks; a carriage with four horses rolled up to the hotel. Armed servants sat on the seat at the back of the carriage ; a pale, thin gentleman, wrapped in a large bright-coloured dressing-gown, stretched himself within it. The postilion dismounted and cracked his long whip several times, whilst fresh horses were put to. The stranger wished to proceed, but as he desired to have an escort over the mountains

---

* Diderik of Born. — *Author's note.*

where Fra Diavolo and Cesari had bold descendants, he was obliged to wait a quarter of an hour, and now scolded, half in English and half in Italian, at the people's laziness, and at the torments and sufferings which travellers had to endure, and at length knotted up his pocket-handkerchief into a night-cap, which he drew on his head, and then throwing himself into a corner of the carriage, closed his eyes, and seemed to resign himself to his fate.

I perceived that it was an Englishman, who already, in ten days, had travelled through the north and the middle of Italy, and in that time had made himself acquainted with this country; had seen Rome in one day, and was now going to Naples to ascend Vesuvius, and then by the steam-vessel to Marseilles, to gain a knowledge also of the south of France, which he hoped to do in a still shorter time. At length eight well-armed horsemen arrived, the postilion cracked his whip, and the carriage and the out-riders vanished through the gate between the tall yellow rocks.

" With all his escort and all his weapons, he is, how-ever, not so safe as my strangers," said a little, square-built fellow, who played with his whip. " The English must be very fond of travelling; they always go at a gallop; they are queer birds— *Santa Philomena di Napoli!*"

" Have you many travellers in your carriage?" inquired I.

" A heart in every corner," replied he; " you see, that makes a good four: but in the cabriolet there is only one. If the Signore wishes to see Naples, that he can the day after to-morrow, while the sun still shines on Sant Elmo."

We soon agreed, and I was thus relieved from the embarrassment in which my entire want of money had placed me.*

" You will, perhaps, wish to have earnest-money, signore?" asked the *vetturino*, and held out a five-paolo piece between his fingers.

---

* When people travel with *vetturini*, they pay nothing beforehand; but, on the contrary, receive money from them as an earnest that their honesty is to be relied upon. The *vetturini* also provide board and lodging for the whole journey. All these expenses are included in the agreement which is then made. — *Author's note.*

" Reserve the place for me, with board and a good bed,"
replied I. " Do we set off in the morning ? "

" Yes, if it please Saint Antonio and my horses," said
he, " we shall set off at three o'clock. We shall have
twice to go to the Pass-Bureau, and three times to be written in the papers : to-morrow is our hardest day." With
these words he lifted his cap, and, nodding, left me.

They showed me to a chamber which looked out to the
sea, where the fresh wind blew, and the billows heaved
themselves, presenting a picture very dissimilar to the
Campagna, and yet its vast extent led my thoughts to my
home there, and the old Domenica. It troubled me now
that I had not visited her more industriously ; she loved
me with her entire heart, and was certainly the only one
who did so. Excellenza, Francesca, yes, they also had
some affection for me, but it was of a peculiar kind.
Benefits bound us together, and where these could not be
mutual, there must always remain, between giver and re-
ceiver, a gulf, which years and days indeed might cover
with the climbing-plants of devotion, but never could fill
up. I thought upon Bernardo and Annunciata ; my lips
tasted salt drops which came from my eyes ; or, perhaps,
from the sea below me, for the billows actually dashed high
upon the walls.

Next morning, before day, I rolled with the *vetturino*
and his strangers away from Terracina. We drew up at
the frontiers just at dawn. All dismounted from the carriage while our passports were inspected. I now for the
first time saw my companions properly. Among these was
a man of about thirty, rather bland, and with blue eyes,
who excited my attention : I must have seen him before,
but where I could not remember : the few words which I
heard him speak betrayed him to be a foreigner.

We were detained a very long time by the passports,
because most of them were in foreign languages, which
the soldiers did not understand. In the meantime the
stranger, of whom I have spoken, took out a book of blank
paper, and sketched the place where we stood — the two
high towers by the gate through which the road passed,

the picturesque caves just by, and, in the background, the little town upon the mountain.

I stepped nearer to him, and he turned my attention to the beautiful grouping of the goats which stood in the largest cave. At the same moment they sprang out; a great bundle of faggots, which had lain in one of the lesser openings of the cave, and which served as door to the descent, was withdrawn, and the goats skipped out two and two, like the animals which went out of Noah's ark. A very little peasant lad brought up the rear; his little pointed hat, round which a piece of twine was tied, the torn stockings, and sandals, with the short brown cloak, which he had thrown around him, gave him a picturesque appearance. The goats tripped up above the cave among the low bushes, whilst the boy, seating himself upon a piece of rock which projected above the cave, looked at us and the painter, who drew him and the whole scene.

"*Maledetto!*" we heard the *vetturino* exclaim, and saw him running towards us at full speed: there was something amiss about the passports. "It was certainly with mine," thought I, anxiously, and the blood mounted to my cheeks. The stranger scolded because of the ignorance of the soldiers who could not read, and we followed the *vetturino* up into one of the towers, where we found five or six men half-stretched over the table, on which our passports lay spread out.

"Who is called Frederick?" inquired one of the most important-looking of the men at the table.

"That is I," replied the stranger, "my name is Frederick, in Italian Federigo."

"Thus, then, Federigo the Sixth."

"Oh, no! that is my king's name which stands at the top of my passport."

"Indeed!" said the man, and slowly read aloud, "'Frédéric Six, par la grace de Dieu Roi de Danemarc, des Vandales, des Gothes, &c.'—But what is that?" exclaimed the man; "are you a Vandal? they are actually a barbarous people?"

"Yes," replied the stranger, laughing; "I am a barbarian who am come to Italy to be civilised. My name stands below, it is Frederick like my king's, Frederick, or Federigo."

" Is he an Englishman ? " asked one of the writers.

" Oh, no ! " replied another, " thou confoundest all nations together ; thou canst surely read that he is out of the north ; he is a Russian."

Federigo — Denmark — the name struck my soul like a flash of lightning. It was, indeed, the friend of my childhood, my mother's lodger ; him with whom I had been into the catacombs, who had given me his beautiful silver watch, and drawn lovely pictures for me.

The passport was correct, and the barrier soldier found it doubly so, when a paolo was put into his hand that he might not any longer detain us.

As soon as we were out again I made myself known to him ; it was actually he whom I supposed our Danish Federigo, who had lived with my mother. He expressed the most lively joy at again meeting with me, called me still 'his little Antonio. There were a thousand things to be inquired after, and mutually communicated. He induced my former neighbour in the cabriolet to exchange places with him, and we now sat together ; yet once more he pressed my hand, laughed and joked.

I related to him in a few words the occurrences of my life, from the day when I went to Domenica's hut, till the time when I became abbé, and then, making a great leap forwards, without touching upon my late adventures, ended by shortly saying, " I now go to Naples."

He remembered very well the promise which he had made, the last time we saw each other in the Campagna, to take me with him for one day to Rome ; but shortly after that he received a letter from his native country, which obliged him to take the long journey home, so that he could not see me again. His love for Italy, however, in his native land, became only stronger every year, and at length drove him there again.

" And now, for the first time, I enjoy every thing properly," said he ; " drink in great draughts of the pure air, and visit again every spot where I was before. Here my heart's fatherland beckons me ; here is colouring ; here is form.   Italy is a cornucopia of blessing !"

Time and the way flew on so rapidly in Federigo's society, that I marked not our long detention in the Pass-Bureau at Fondi.   He knew perfectly how to seize upon the poetically beautiful in every thing ; he became doubly dear and interesting to me, and was the best angel of consolation for my afflicted heart.

" There lies my dirty Itri !" exclaimed he, and pointed to the city before us.   " You would hardly credit it, Antonio, but in the north, where all the streets are so clean, and so regular, and so precise, I have longed for a dirty Italian town, where there is something characteristic, something just for a painter.   These narrow, dirty streets, these grey, grimy stone balconies, full of stockings and shirts ; windows without regularity, one up, one down, some great, some small ; here steps four or five ells wide leading up to a door, where the mother sits with her hand spindle ; and there a lemon-tree, with great yellow fruit, hanging over the wall.

" Yes, that does make a picture !   But those cultivated streets, where the houses stand like soldiers, where steps and balconies are shorn away, one can make nothing at all of !"

" Here is the native city of Fra Diavolo !" exclaimed those inside the carriage, as we rolled into the narrow, dirty Itri, which Federigo found so picturesquely beautiful. The city lay high upon a rock beside a deep precipice. The principal street was in many places only wide enough for one carriage.

The greater part of the first stories of the houses were without windows, and instead of these, a great broad doorway, through which one looked down as if into a dark cellar.   Every where was there a swarm of dirty children and women, and all reached out their hands to beg : the women laughed, and the children screamed and made faces at us.   One did not dare to put one's head out of the carriage, lest it should get smashed between it and the projecting houses, from which the stone balconies in some places hung out so far above us that it seemed as if we drove through an archway. I saw black walls on either hand, for the smoke found its way through the open doors up the sooty walls.

" It is a glorious city !" said Federigo, and clapped his hands.

" A robber city it is," said the *vetturino*, when we had passed through it ; the police compelled one half of the people to flit to quite another city behind the mountains, and brought in other inhabitants, but that helped nothing. All runs to weed that is planted here. But then poor folks must live."

The whole neighbourhood here, upon the great high road between Rome and Naples, invites to robbery. There are places of deep concealment on every hand, in the thick olive-woods, in the mountain-caves, in the walls of the Cyclops, and many other ruins.

Federigo directed my attention to an isolated colossal wall overgrown with honeysuckle and climbing plants. It was Cicero's grave ! it was here that the dagger of the assassin struck the fugitive, here the lips of eloquence became dust.

" The *vetturino* will drive us to Cicero's villa in Mola di Gaeta," said Federigo ; " it is the best hotel, and has a prospect which rivals that of Naples."

The form of the hills was most beautiful, the vegetation most luxuriant ; presently we rolled along an alley of tall laurels, and saw before us the hotel which Federigo had mentioned. The head-waiter stood ready with his napkin, and waited for us on the broad steps which were ornamented with busts and flowers.

" Excellenza, is it you ?" exclaimed he, as he assisted a somewhat portly lady out of the carriage.

I noticed her ; her countenance was pretty, very pretty, and the jet-black eyes told me immediately that she was a Neapolitan.

" Ah, yes, it is I," replied she ; " here am I come with my waiting-woman as *cicisbeo ;* that is my whole train— I have not a single man-servant with me. What do you think of my courage in travelling thus from Rome to Naples ?"

She threw herself like an invalid on the sofa, supported her pretty cheek upon her round little hand, and began to study the list of eatables. "*Brodettò, cipollette, facioli.* You know that I cannot bear soup, else I should have a figure like Castello dell' Ovo. A little *animelle dorate,* and some fennel, is enough for me; we must really dine again in Santa Agatha. Ah, now I breathe more freely," continued she, untying the strings of her cloak, "Now I feel my Neapolitan air blowing—*bella Napoli!*" exclaimed she, hastily opening the door of the balcony, which looked on the sea, and spreading out her arms, she drank in great draughts of the fresh air.

"Can we already see Naples?" inquired I.

"Not yet," replied Federigo; "but Hesperia, Armida's enchanted garden."

We went out into the balcony, which was built of stone, and looked out over the garden. What magnificence!—richer than fancy can create to itself! Below us was a wood of lemon and orange-trees which were overladen with fruit; the branches bent themselves down to the ground with their golden load; cypresses gigantically tall as the poplars of the North of Italy, formed the boundary of the garden; they seemed doubly dark against the clear, heaven-blue sea which stretched itself behind them, and dashed its waves above the remains of the baths and temples of antiquity, outside the low wall of the garden. Ships and boats, with great white sails, floated into the peaceful harbour, around which Gaeta*, with its lofty buildings, stretches itself. A little mountain elevates itself above the city, and this is crowned with a ruin.

My eye was dazzled with the great beauty of the scene.

"Do you see Vesuvius?—How it smokes!" said Federigo, and pointed to the left, where the rocky coast elevated itself, like light clouds, which reposed upon the indescribably beautiful sea.

With the soul of a child I gave myself up to the rich magnificence around me, and Federigo was as happy as myself. We could not resist going below under the tall

---

* There Æneas buried his nurse, Cajeta, after whom this city is called.— *Author's note.*

orange-trees, and I kissed the golden fruit which hung upon the branches ; took from the many which lay on the ground, and threw them like golden balls up in the air, and over the sulphur-blue lake.

" Beautiful Italy !" shouted Federigo, triumphantly. " Yes, thus stood thy image before me in the distant North. In my remembrance blew this air which I now inspire with every breath I draw. I thought of thy olive-groves when I saw our willows ; I dreamed of the abundance of the oranges when I saw the golden apples in the peasants' gardens beside the fragrant clover-field ; but the green waters of the Baltic never become blue like the beautiful Mediterranean ; the heavens of the North never become so high, so rich in colour, as the warm, glorious south. Its gladness was inspiration : its speech became poetry.

" What longings I had in my home ? " said he ; " they are happier who have never seen Paradise, than they who, having seen it, are driven forth, never to return. My home is beautiful ; Denmark is a flowery garden, which can measure itself with any thing on the other side the Alps ; it has beech-woods and the sea. But what is earthly beauty compared with heavenly ? Italy is the land of imagination and beauty ; doubly happy are they who salute it for the second time ! "

And he kissed, as I had done, the golden oranges ; tears ran down his cheeks, and throwing himself on my neck, his lips burned on my forehead. With this my heart opened itself to him entirely ; he was not indeed a stranger to me, he was the friend of my childhood. I related to him my life's last great adventure, and felt my heart lighter by the communication, by speaking Annunciata's name aloud ; by telling of my suffering and my misfortune ; and Federigo listened to me with the sympathy of an honest friend. I told him of my flight, of my adventure in the robber's cave ; of Fulvia, and what I knew of Bernardo's recovery. He offered me his hand with the truest friendliness, and looked, with his light blue eyes, sympathisingly into my soul.

A suppressed sigh was heard close to us behind the hedge ; but the tall laurels, and the orange-branches, bowed

down with their fruit, concealed all; any one might very
well have stood there and heard every word I said; of that
I had not thought.   We turned the branches aside, and
close beside us, before the entrance to the ruins of Cicero's
bath, sat the Neapolitan Signora, bathed in tears.

"Ah, young gentleman," exclaimed she, "I am entirely
guiltless of this.   I was sitting here already when you
came with your friend, it is so charming here and so cool!
You talked so loud, and I was in the middle of your history before I remarked that it was quite a private affair.
You have affected me deeply.   You shall have no cause to
repent that I have become privy to it; my tongue is as
dumb as the dead."

Somewhat embarrassed, I bowed before the strange Signora, who had thus become acquainted with my heart's
history.   At length Federigo sought to console me by saying that nobody knew to what it might lead.

"I am," said he, "a real Turk in my reliance on fate;
besides, after all, there are no state secrets in the whole of
it; every heart has, in its archives, such painful memoirs.
Perhaps it was her own youth's history which she heard
in yours; I can believe it, for people have seldom tears
for others' troubles, except when they resemble their own.
We are all egotists, even in our greatest sufferings and
anxieties."

We were soon again in the carriage, rolling on our way.
The whole country round us was of a luxuriant character;
the broad-leaved aloe grew close by the road to the height
of a man, and was used as a fence.   The large weeping-
willow seemed to kiss, with its depending, ever-moving
branches, its own shadow upon the ground.

Towards sunset we crossed the river Garigliano, where
formerly stood the old Minturnæ; it was the yellow Liris,
which I saw overgrown with reeds, as when Marius concealed himself here from the cruel Sylla.   But we were yet
a long way from Santa Agatha.

The darkness descended, and the Signora became extremely uneasy on account of robbers, and looked out continually to see that nobody cut away the luggage from behind
the carriage.   In vain the *vetturino* cracked his whip, and
repeated his *maledetto,* for the dark night advanced faster

than he did. At length we saw lights before us. We were at Santa Agatha.

The Signora was wonderfully silent at supper; but it did not escape me how much her eye rested upon me. And the next morning, before our journey, when I went to drink my glass of coffee*, she came up to me with great amiability. We were quite alone: she offered me her hand, and said, good-humouredly and familiarly—

" You do not bear any ill-will towards me ? I am perfectly ashamed before you ; and yet I am quite guiltless of the whole thing."

I prayed her to make herself easy, and assured her that I had the greatest confidence in her womanly spirit.

" Yet you know nothing of me," said she ; " but you may do ; probably my husband can be useful to you in the great foreign city. You can visit me and him. You, perhaps, have no acquaintance ; and a young man can so easily make an error in his choice."

I thanked her heartily for her sympathy. It affected me. One, however, meets with good people every where.

" Naples is a dangerous city !" said she ; but Federigo entered, and interrupted us.

We were soon again seated in the carriage. The glass-windows were put down ; we became all better acquainted as we approached our common goal — Naples. Federigo was enraptured with the picturesque groups which we met. Women, with red cloaks turned over their heads, rode past on asses, a young child at the breast, or sleeping with an elder one in the basket at their feet. A whole family rode upon one horse ; the wife behind the husband, and rested her arm or her head against his shoulder, and seemed to sleep ; the man had before him his little boy, who sat and played with the whip. It was such a group as Pignelli has given in his beautiful scenes out of the life of the people.

The air was grey, it rained a little ; we could neither see Vesuvius nor Capri. The corn stood juicy and green

* In Italy people do not drink their coffee in cups, but in wine-glasses.— *Author's note.*

in the field under the tall fruit-trees and poplars, round which the vines enwreathed themselves.

" Do you see," said the Signora, " our Campagna is a table well spread with bread, fruit, and wine ; and you will soon see our gay city and our swelling sea !"

Towards evening we approached it. The splendid Toledo Street lay before us ; it was really a corso. On every hand were illumined shops ; tables which stood in the street, laden with oranges and figs, were lit up by lamps and gaily-coloured lanterns. The whole street, with its innumerable lights in the open air, looked like a stream sprinkled over with stars. On each side stood lofty houses, with balconies before every window, nay, often quite round the corner, and within these stood ladies and gentlemen, as if it were still a merry carnival. One carriage passed another, and the horses slipped on the smooth slabs of lava with which the street was paved. Now a little cabriolet on two wheels came by ; from five to six people sat in the little carriage, ragged lads stood behind it, and beneath, in the shaking net, lay quite snugly, a half-naked lazzarone. One single horse drew the whole crowd, and yet it went at a gallop. There was a fire kindled before a corner-house, before which lay two half-naked fellows, clad only in drawers, and with the vest fastened with one single button, who played at cards. Hand-organs and hurdygurdies were playing, to which women were singing ; all were screaming, all running one among another — soldiers, Greeks, Turks, English. I felt myself transported into quite another world ; a more southern life than that which I had known breathed around me. The Signora clapped her hands at the sight of her merry Naples. " Rome," she said, " was a grave beside her laughing city."

We turned into the Largo del Castello, one of the largest squares in Naples, which leads down to the sea, and the same noise and the same crowd met us here. Around us we saw illuminated theatres, on the outside of which were bright pictures, which represented the principal scenes of the pieces which were being performed within. Aloft, on a scaffold, stormed a Bajazzo family.

The wife cried out to the spectators; the husband blew the trumpet, and the youngest son beat them both with a great riding-whip, whilst a little horse stood upon its hind-legs in the back-scene, and read out of an open book. A man stood, and fought and sang in the midst of a crowd of sailors, who sat in a corner; he was an improvisatore. An old fellow read aloud, out of a book, Orlando Furioso, as I was told: his audience were applauding him just as we passed by.

"Monte Vesuvio!" cried the Signora; and I now saw, at the end of the street where the light-house stood, Vesuvius, lifting itself high in the air, and the fire-red lava, like a stream of blood, rolling down from its side. Above the crater hung a cloud, shining red from the reflected glow of the lava; but I could only see the whole for a moment. The carriage rolled away with us across the square to the Hotel Casa Tedesca. Close beside this stood a little puppet theatre, and a still smaller ·one was erected before it, where Punchinello made his merry leaps, peeped, twirled himself about, and made his funny speeches. All around was laughter. Only very few paid attention to the monk who stood at the opposite corner, and preached from one of the projecting stone steps. An old broad-shouldered fellow, who looked like a sailor, held the cross, on which was the picture of the Redeemer. The monk cast flaming glances at the wooden theatre of the puppets, which drew the attention of the people away from his speech.

"Is this Lent?" I heard him say. "Is this the time consecrated to Heaven? the time in which we should, humbled in the flesh, wander in sackcloth and in ashes? Carnival-time is it? Carnival always, night and day, year out and year in, till you post down into the depths of hell! There you can twirl, there you can grin, can dance, and keep festino in the eternal pool and torment of hell!"

His voice raised itself more and more; the soft Neapolitan dialect rung in my ear like swaying verse, and the words melted melodiously one into another. But all the more his voice ascended, ascended also that of Punchinello, and he leaped all the more comically, and was all the more applauded by the people; then the monk, in a holy rage, snatched the cross from the hand of the man who bore it, rushed forward with it, and exhibiting the crucified, exclaimed, " See, here is the true Punchinello! Him shall you see, him shall you hear! For that you shall have eyes and ears! Kyrie, eleison!" and, impressed by the holy sign, the whole crowd dropped upon their knees, and exclaimed with one voice, " Kyrie, eleison!" Even the puppet-player let fall his Punchinello. I stood beside our carriage, wonderfully struck by the whole scene.

Federigo hastened to obtain a carriage to take the Signora to her home. She extended her hand to him, with her thanks; then, throwing her arm around my neck, I felt a warm kiss upon my lips, and heard her say, " Welcome to Naples!" And, from the carriage which conveyed her away, she waved kisses with her hand, and we ascended to the chamber in the hotel which the waiter assigned to us.

CHAPTER II.

PAIN AND CONSOLATION. —— NEARER ACQUAINTANCE WITH THE SIGNORA. —— THE LETTER. —— HAVE I MISUNDERSTOOD HER.

AFTER Federigo was in bed, I continued sitting in the open balcony, which looked into the street, with Vesuvius before me. The extraordinary world, in which I seemed to be as in a dream, forbade me to sleep. By degrees it became more and more quiet in the street below me: the lights were extinguished: it was already past midnight. My eye rested upon the mountain, where the pillar of fire raised itself up from the crater, towards the blood-red broad mass of cloud, which, united to this, seemed like a mighty pine-tree of fire and flame: the lava streams were the roots with which it embraced the mountain.

My soul was deeply impressed by this great spectacle—
the voice of God, which spoke from the volcano, as from
the still silent night-heaven. It was one of those moments
which occurs now and then, when, so to say, the soul
stands face to face with its God. I comprehended something of His omnipotence, wisdom, and goodness—comprehended something of Him, whose servants are the lightning and the whirlwind; yet, without whose permission,
not even a sparrow falls to the earth. My own life stood
clearly before me: I saw in the whole a wonderful guiding
and directing; every misfortune even, and every sorrow,
had brought about a change for the better. The unhappy
death of my mother by the runaway horses, whilst I stood
a poor helpless child, seemed to shape out for me a better
future; for was not, perhaps, the peculiar and nobler reason which afterwards induced Excellenza to take charge of
my bringing up the circumstance of his having been the
innocent cause of my misfortune? The strife between
Mariuccia and Peppo, the fearful moments which I passed
in his house, drove me out upon the stream of the world;
for unless I had dwelt with old Domenica, on the dreary
Campagna, the attention of Excellenza had perhaps never
been directed to me.

Thus I reviewed in thought scene after scene of my
life, and found the highest wisdom and goodness in the
chain of events; nor was it until I came to that last link
that all seemed to fall asunder. My acquaintance with
Annunciata was like a spring day, which in a moment had
expanded every flower-bud in my soul. With her I could
have become every thing: her love would have perfected
the happiness of my life. Bernardo's sentiment towards
her was not pure like mine: even had he suffered for a
moment by losing her, his pain would have been short:
he would soon have learned to console himself; but that Annunciata loved him annihilated all my life's happiness. Here
I comprehended not the wisdom of the Almighty, and felt
nothing but pain, because of all my vanished dreams. At
that moment a cithern sounded under the balcony; and I
saw a man, with a cloak thrown over his shoulders, who
touched the strings from which trembled notes of love.

Shortly afterwards, the door of the opposite house opened quite softly, and the man vanished behind it — a happy lover, who went to kisses and embraces.

I looked up to the star-bright air — to the brilliant dark blue sea which gleamed redly with the reflected light of the lava and the eruption.

" Glorious nature ! " burst forth from my heart. " Thou art my mistress ! Thou claspest me to thy heart — openest to me thy heaven, and thy breath kisses me on my lips and brow ! Thee will I sing, thy beauty, thy holy greatness ! I will repeat before the' people the deep melodies which thou singest in my soul ! Let my heart bleed ; the butterfly which struggles upon the needle becomes most beautiful : the stream which, hurled as a waterfall from the rock, scatters itself in foam, is more glorious ! — that is the poet's lot. Life is, indeed, only a short dream. When in that other world I again meet Annunciata, she will also love me. All pure souls love one another : arm in arm the blessed spirits advance towards God ! "

Thus dreamed my thoughts ; and courage and power to come forth as an improvisatore, as well as a strong delight in so doing, filled my soul. One thing alone lay heavily on my heart — what would Francesca and Excellenza say to my flight from home, and my *début* as improvisatore ? They believed me industriously and quietly occupied with my books in Rome. This consciousness allowed me to have no rest: I determined, therefore, that same night to write to them.

With filial confidence I related to them every thing which had occurred, every single circumstance — my love for Annunciata, and the consolation which alone I found in nature and in art ; and concluded with an urgent prayer for an answer, as favourable as their hearts could give me; nor before I obtained this would I take one step, or come forward in public. Longer than a month they must not let me languish.

My tears fell upon the letter as I wrote it ; but I felt relieved by it ; and when I had ended it, I quickly slept more soundly and calmly than I had done for a long time.

The following day, Federigo and I arranged our affairs.

He removed into a new lodging, in one of the side streets. I remained at the Casa Tedesca, where I could see Vesuvius and the sea, two world's wonders which were new to me. I industriously visited the *Museo Bourbonico*, the theatres, and the promenades; and during three days' residence in the foreign city had made myself very well acquainted with it.

An invitation for Federigo and me came from Professor Maretti and his wife Santa. At the first moment I believed this to be a mistake, as I knew neither the one nor the other, and yet the invitation seemed to have particular reference to me: I was to bring Federigo with me. On inquiry, I found that Maretti was a very learned man, an antiquarian; and that Signora Santa had lately returned home from a visit in Rome. I and Federigo had made her acquaintance on the journey. Thus then she was the Neapolitan Signora.

In the course of the evening Federigo and I went. We found a numerous company in a well-lighted saloon, the polished marble floor of which reflected the lights; whilst a large scaldino, with a loose iron grating, diffused a mild warmth.

Signora or, as we now indeed know her name, Santa, met us with open arms. Her light blue silk dress was very becoming to her: had she not been so stout, she would have been very lovely. She introduced us to her company, and prayed us to make ourselves quite at home.

" Into my house," said she, " enter none but friends: you will soon become acquainted with them all. With this she mentioned several names, pointing to different persons.

" We talk, we dance, we have a little singing," said she, " and so the time flies on."

She pointed out seats to us. A young lady was seated at the piano, and sang: it was precisely the very same aria which Annunciata had sung in Dido; but it sounded with quite another expression, and seized upon the soul with a much less powerful effect. Yet I was compelled, with the rest, to applaud the singer: and now she struck a few accords, and played a lively dance: two or three gentlemen took their ladies, and floated over the polished smooth floor. I withdrew myself into a window; a little half-famished-looking man, with ever-moving glassy eyes, bowed himself deeply before me. I had remarked him, like a little kobold, incessantly popping in and out of the door. In order to get up a conversation, I began to speak of the eruption of Vesuvius, and how beautiful the lava-stream was.

"That is nothing, my friend," replied he, "nothing to the great revolution of 96, which Pliny describes: then the ashes flew as far as Constantinople. We have also, in my time, gone with umbrellas in Naples, because of the ashes; but between Naples and Constantinople there is a difference. The classical time excelled us in every thing — a time in which we should have prayed, "*Serus in cœlum redeas !*"

I spoke of the theatre of San Carlo; and the man went back to the car of Thespis, and gave me a treatise on the tragic and comic Muses. I dropped a word about the mustering of the royal troops; and he immediately went into the ancient mode of warfare, and commanding of the whole phalanx. The only question which he himself asked me was, whether I studied the history of art, and gave myself up to antiquities. I said that the whole world's life, every thing lay near to my heart; that I felt called upon to be a poet; and the man then clapped his hands, and began to declaim about my lyre —

> " O decus Phœbi, et dapibus supremi
> Grata testudo Jovis !"

"Has he now got hold of you?" said Santa, laughing, and coming up to us; "then are you already deep in Sesostris' age. But your own times have demands upon you: there sit ladies on the opposite side with whom you must dance."

"But I do not dance; never did dance," replied I.

"But if I," said she, "the lady of the house, were to ask you to dance with me, you would not refuse."

"Yes, indeed; for I should dance so badly that we should both of us fall on the smooth floor."

"A beautiful idea!" exclaimed she, and skipped across

to Federigo, and soon were they two floating through the room.

" A lively woman !" said the husband, and added, " and handsome, very handsome, Signor Abbé."

" Very handsome," replied I politely, and then we were, heaven knows how, deep in the Etruscan Vases. He offered himself as my guide in the Museo Bourbonico, and explained to me what great masters they had been who had painted these brittle treasures, in which every line contributed to the beauty of the figures in expression of attitude, and who were obliged to paint them whilst the clay was warm, it not being possible to rub any thing out, whilst, on the contrary, every line which had once been made must remain there."

" Are you yet deep in history ? " inquired Santa, who again came up to us ; " the consequence then follows !" exclaimed she, laughing, and drew me away from the pedant, whilst she whispered, half aloud, " Do not let my husband annoy you ! You must be gay, must take part in the gaiety ! I will seat you here ; you shall relate to me what you have seen, heard, and enjoyed."

I then told her how much Naples pleased me ; told her of that which had given me most delight ; of a little trip I had this afternoon made through the grotto of Posilippo, besides which I had discovered, in a thick vine-grove, the ruins of a little church, which had been converted into a family dwelling, whilst the friendly children, and the handsome woman who had served me with wine, had greatly contributed to make it all only the more romantic.

" Then you have been making acquaintances ? " said she, laughing, and lifting her forefinger ; " nay, there is no need for you to be confused about it : at your age the heart does not amuse itself with a Lent sermon."

This was about all that I learned this evening of Signora Santa and her husband. There was a something in her manner that expressed itself in an ease, a *naïveté* peculiar to the Neapolitans, a cordiality which wonderfully attracted me to her. Her husband was erudite, and that was no fault ; he would be the best guide for me in the Museum. And so he was ; and Santa, whom I often visited, became to me more and more attractive. The attentions which she showed to me flattered me, and her sympathy opened my heart and my lips. I knew but very little of the world, was in many things a complete child, and grasped, therefore, the first hand which extended itself kindly towards me, and, in return for a hand-pressure, gave my whole confidence.

One day, Signora Santa touched upon the most important moment of my life, my separation from Annunciata, and I found consolation and relief in speaking freely of it to the sympathising lady. That she could see many faults in Bernardo, after I had given a description of him, was a sort of consolation to me; but that she could also find failings in Annunciata I could not pardon.

"She is too small for the stage," said she, "altogether too slenderly made; that certainly you will concede to me? Some substance there must be as long as we belong to this world. I know, to be sure, right well, that here, in Naples, all the young men were captivated by her beauty. It was the voice, the incomparably fine voice, which transported them into the spirit-world, where her fine form had its abode. If I were a man, I should never fall in love with such a being: I should actually fear her falling to pieces at my first embrace."

She made me smile, and that, perhaps, thought I, was her intention. To Annunciata's talent, mind, and pure heart, she did the fullest justice.

During the last evening, inspired by the beauty of the surrounding country and my own excited state of feeling, I had written some short poems: "Tasso in Captivity," "The Begging Monk," and some other little lyrical pieces, which perfectly expressed my unhappy love, and the shattered picture-world which floated in my soul. I began to read them to Santa, but in the middle of the first my feelings, which I had there described, so entirely overpowered me, that I burst into tears; with that, she pressed my hand and wept with me.

With these tears she bound me for ever!

Her house became to me a home. I regularly longed for the hour when I should again converse with her. Her humour, the comical ideas which she often started, made me frequently laugh, although I was compelled to feel how very different was Annunciata's wit and merriment — how much nobler and purer ; but then, as no Annunciata lived for me, I was grateful and devoted to Santa.

" Have you lately," she asked me one day, " seen the handsome woman, near Posilippo, and the romantic house which is half a church ? "

" Only once since," I replied.

" She was very friendly ? " inquired Santa, " the children were gone out as guides, and the husband was on the lake ?   Take care of yourself, Signore: on that side of Naples lies the under-world ! "

I honestly assured her that nothing but the romantic scenery drew me towards the grotto of Posilippo.

" Dear friend," said she, confidentially, " I know the thing better !   Your heart was full of love, of the first strong love to her, whom I will not call unworthy, but who, however, did not act openly towards you !   Do not say one word to me against this : she occupied your soul, and you have torn yourself from this image — have given her up, as you yourself have assured me, and therefore there is a vacancy in your soul which craves to be filled. Formerly you lived alone in your books and your dreams ; the singer has drawn you down into the world of human life ; you are become flesh and blood, like the rest of us, and these assert their right.   And why should they not ? I never judge a young man with severity ; and, besides this, they can act as they will ! "

I objected to this last assertion ; but as to the desolation which remained in my soul after the loss of Annunciata, she was right in that ; but what could supply the place of that lost image ?

" You are not like other people ! " continued she ; " you are a poetical being ; and do you see, even the ideal Annunciata required something more of a realist ; for that reason she preferred Bernardo, who was so much inferior to you in soul.   But," added she, " you beguile me to talk to you as it is hardly becoming for me, as a lady, to do ; your wonderful simplicity and your little knowledge of the world make one become as *naïve* in speech as you are in thoughts ;" and with this she laughed aloud, and patted me on the cheek.

In the evening, when I sat alone with Federigo, and he became merry and confidential, he told me of the happy days which he had spent in Rome, in which his heart also had beaten strongly ; Mariuccia had played her part in these adventures.

Many young men came to the house of the Professor Maretti ; they danced well, talked excellently in company, received glances of favour from the ladies, and were esteemed by the men.   I had known them but for a short time, and yet they confided to me already their hearts' affairs, which I shrunk from doing, even with Bernardo, and which only my ingrained affection for him made me tolerate in him ! Yes, they were all different from me.   Was Santa actually right ? should I be only a poetical being in this world ? That Annunciata really loved Bernardo was a sufficient proof thereof ; my spiritual *I* was perhaps dear to her, but I myself could not win her.

I had now been a month in Naples, and yet had heard nothing either of her or of Bernardo.   At that time the post brought me a letter ; I seized it with a throbbing heart, looked at the seal and the direction to divine of its contents.   I recognised the Borghese arms and the old Excellenza's hand-writing.   I hardly dared to open it.

" Eternal mother of God !" I prayed, " be gracious to me !   Thy will directs all things for the best !"

I opened the letter and read : —

" Signore, — Whilst I believed that you were availing yourself of the opportunity which I afforded you, of learning something, and of becoming a useful member of society, all is going on quite otherwise ; quite differently to my intentions regarding you.   As the innocent occasion of your mother's death, have I done this for you.   We are quits.

" Make your *début* as improvisatore, as poet, when and how you will, but give me this one proof of your so-much-talked-of gratitude, never to connect my name, my solicitude for you, with your public life.   The *very great* service which you might have rendered me by learning something, you would not render; the *very small* one of calling me benefactor is so repugnant to me, that you cannot do any thing more offensive to me than to do that!"

The blood stagnated at my heart; my hands dropped powerless on my knees; but I could not weep; that would have relieved my soul.

"Jesus Maria!" stammered I; my head sank down on the table. Deaf, without thought, without pain even, I lay immovably in this position. I had not a word with which to pray to God and the saints; they also, like the world, seemed to have forsaken me.

At that moment Federigo entered.

"Art thou ill, Antonio?" asked he, pressing my hand; "one must not thus wall oneself in so with one's grief. Who knows whether thou wouldst have been happy with Annunciata? That which is best for us always happens; that I have found more than once, although not in the most agreeable way."

Without a word I handed to him the letter, which he read; in the meantime my tears found a free course, but I was ashamed to let him see me weeping, and turned away from him, but he pressed me in his arms and said, "Weep freely; weep all thy grief out, and then thou wilt be better."

When I was somewhat calmer, he inquired from me whether I had taken any resolve. A thought then passed through my soul; I would reconcile the Madonna to me, to whose service I was dedicated as a child; in her had I found a protector, and my future belonged to her.

"It is best," said I, "that I become a monk; for that my fate has prepared me; there is nothing more for me in this world. I am besides that only a poetical being, not a man, like the rest of you! Yes, in the bosom of the church is a home and peace for me!"

"Be reasonable, however, Antonio!" said Federigo to me. "Let Excellenza, let the world see that there is power in thee, let the adverse circumstances of life elevate and not depress thee. I think and hope, however, that

N 2

thou wilt only be a monk for this evening; to-morrow, when the sun shines warmly into thy heart, thou wilt not be one. Thou art really an improvisatore, a poet, and hast soul and knowledge. Every thing will be glorious, excellent. To-morrow we will take a cabriolet, and drive to Herculaneum and Pompeii, and will ascend Vesuvius. We have not been there; thou must be amused and brought again into humour, and when all the dark fumes are dissipated then we will talk about the future quite rationally. Now thou goest with me to the Toledo; we will amuse ourselves. Life speeds on at a gallop, and all of us have, like the snail, our burden upon our backs, it matters not whether of lead or mere playthings, if they are alike oppressive."

His solicitude for me affected me; I was still supported by a friend. Without a word I took my hat and followed him.

Music was merrily sounding in the square from one of the little wooden theatres; we remained standing before it among a great crowd of people. The whole artistic family stood as usual upon the stage; the man and woman, in gay clothes, hoarse with shouting; a pale little boy, with a care-depressed countenance, and in a white dress, stood and played upon the violin, whilst two little sisters twirled about in a lively dance. The whole thing appeared to me very tragical.

"The unhappy beings!" thought I, "uncertain as theirs, lies also my fate." I linked my arm closely in Federigo's, and could not repress the sigh which ascended from my breast.

"Now be calm and rational," whispered Federigo. "First of all, we will take a little walk to let the wind blow on thy red eyes, and then we will visit Signora Maretti; she will either laugh thee quite gay again, or else weep with thee, till thou art tired; she can do that better than I can."

Thus for some time we wandered up and down the great street, and then went to the house of Maretti.

"At length you are come one evening out of the common course," exclaimed Santa kindly as we entered.

" Signore Antonio is in his elegiac mood ; it must be removed by mirth, and to whom could I bring him better than to you ?   To-morrow we drive to Herculaneum and Pompeii, ascend Vesuvius ; if we could only be blessed with an eruption."

" *Carpe diem*," broke forth from Maretti.   " I should delight to make the journey with you ; but not to ascend Vesuvius, only to see how it goes with the excavations in Pompeii.   I have just received from there some little glass ornaments of various colours ;   these I have arranged according to their shades, and have within an opusculum on them.   You must see these treasures," said he, turning to Federigo, " and give me a hint with regard to colour. And you," continued he, clapping me on the shoulder, " you shall begin to be merry, and then afterwards we will empty a glass of Falernian, and sing with Horace, —

> " ' Ornatus viridi tempora pampino,
> Liber vota bonos ducit ad exitus.' "

I remained alone with Santa.

" Have you written any thing lately ? " inquired she. " You look as if you had been composing one of those beautiful pieces which so wonderfully speak to the heart. I have thought many times on you and your Tasso, and have felt myself quite pensive, although you very well know that I do not belong to the weeping sisterhood.   Be now in a good humour.   Look at me ; you say nothing complimentary ; you see nothing, say nothing about my new dress.   See how becoming it is ; a poet must have an eye for every thing.   I am slender as a pine ; regularly thin ?   Is it not so ? "

" That one sees immediately," was my reply.

" Flatterer ! " interrupted she, " am I not as usual ? My dress hangs quite loosely upon me !   Now what is there to blush about ?   You are, however, a man !   We must have you more in women's society, and thus educate you a little ; that we can do excellently.   Now sit down, my husband and Federigo are up to the ears in their blessed antiquity ; let us live for the present ; one has much more enjoyment in that !   You shall taste our excellent Falernian wine, and that directly; you can drink of it again with the other two."

I refused, and attempted to begin an ordinary conversation on the events of the day; but I found, only too plainly, how abstracted I was.

"I am only a burden to you," said I, rising, and about to take my hat. "Pardon me, Signora; I am not well, and that it is which makes me unsociable."

"You will not leave me?" said she, drawing me back to my chair, and looking sympathisingly and anxiously into my face. "What has happened? Have confidence in me. I mean it so honestly and kindly towards you! Do not let my petulance wound you. It is only my nature. Tell me what has happened; have you had letters? Is Bernardo dead?"

. "No, God be praised," returned I; "it is another thing, quite another."

I wished not to have spoken of Excellenza's letter; yet, in my distress, I disclosed every thing to her quite openheartedly, and with tears in her eyes she besought me not to be troubled.

"I am thrust out of the world;" said I, "forsaken by every one; nobody — nobody at all loves me."

"Yes, Antonio," exclaimed she, "you are loved. You are handsome; you are good; my husband loves you, and I love you;" and with these words I felt a burning kiss upon my brow, her arm clasped my neck, and her cheek touched mine.

My blood became like flame, a trembling went through my limbs; it was as if my breath stood still; never had I felt so before; the door opened, and Federigo and Maretti entered.

"Your friend is ill," said she, in her usual tone; "he has almost terrified me. Pale and red in one moment; I thought he would have fainted in my arms, but now he is better; is it not so, Antonio?"

And then, as if nothing had happened, as if nothing had been said, she jested about me. I felt my own heart beat, and a feeling of shame and indignation arose in my soul; I turned from her, the beautiful daughter of sin.

"*Quæ sit hiems Veliæ, quod cœlum, Vala Salerni!*"
said Maretti. "How is it with heart and head, Signor?
What has he now done, the *ferus Cupido*, who always
sharpens the bloody arrow on the glowing whetstone?"

The Falernian wine sparkled in the glass. Santa
clinked her glass against mine, and said, with an extraordinary expression, "To better times!"

"To better times!" repeated Federigo; "one must
never despair."

Maretti touched his glass to mine also, and nodded,
"To better times!"

Santa laughed aloud, and stroked my cheek.

CHAPTER III.

RAMBLE THROUGH HERCULANEUM AND POMPEII. — THE EVENING ON VESUVIUS.

THE next morning Federigo fetched me. Maretti joined
us. Fresh morning breezes blew from the sea, and our
carriage rolled round the bay from Naples to Herculaneum.

"How the smoke whirls from Vesuvius!" said Federigo, and pointed to the mountain. "We shall have a
glorious evening."

"The smoke whirled in another manner," said Maretti;
"it went like the shadow of a cloud over the whole
country, *anno* 79 *post Christum*. At that time the cities
which we now go to visit were buried under lava and
ashes!"

Exactly where the suburbs of Naples end, begin the
cities Sant Giovanni, Portici, and Recina, which lie so
close that they may be regarded as one city. We had
reached the goal before I was aware of it, and drew up
before a house in Recina. Under the street here, under
the whole city, lies Herculaneum buried. Lava and ashes

covered the whole city in a few hours; people forgot its existence, and the city of Recina rose above it.

We entered the nearest house, in the garden of which was a large open well, through which a spiral staircase descended.

"See you, gentlemen," said Maretti; "it was *post Christum* 1720 that the Prince of Elbœuf had this well dug. As soon as they had descended a few feet, they found statues; and so the excavation was forbidden (*mirabile dictu!*) ♦For thirty years not a hand moved itself before Charles of Spain came here, ordered the well to be dug deeper, and they stood upon a great stone staircase, such as we now see here!"

The daylight descended here but to a short distance; and these were the seats of the great theatre of Herculaneum. Our guides kindled a light for each of us to carry, and we descended to the depth of the well, and now stood upon the seats on which the spectators, seventeen hundred years before, had sat; like a giant body, had laughed, been affected by, and had applauded, the scenes of life which had been represented!

A little low door, close by, led us into a large, spacious passage. We descended to the orchestra; saw there the different apartments for the different musicians, the dressing-room, and the scenes themselves. The greatness of the whole deeply impressed me. It could be lighted for us only piecemeal, yet it seemed to me much larger than the theatre of San Carlo. Silent, dark, and desolate, lay all around us, and a world rioted above us. As we imagine that a vanished race may, as spirits, enter into our scene of life and action, seemed I now to have stepped out of our age, and to be wandering, like a ghost, in the far-off antiquity. I literally longed for daylight, and we soon breathed again the warm air.

We walked straight forward along the street of Recina, and an excavation lay before us, but much less than the former. This was all the remains of Herculaneum on which the sun shone. We saw one single street, houses with small, narrow windows, red and blue painted walls; very little in comparison with that which awaited us in Pompeii.

Recina lay behind us, and now we saw around us a plain, which seemed like a pitch-black, foaming sea, which had run into iron-dross. Yet here buildings had raised themselves; little vine-gardens grew verdantly, and the church was half buried in this land of death.

"I myself saw this destruction!" said Maretti. "I was a child, in the age between *lactens* and *puer*, as one may say. Never shall I forget that day! The black dross over which we are now rolling was a glowing river of fire; I saw how it rolled down from the mountain towards Torre del Greco. My father (*beati sunt mortui*) has even plucked ripe grapes for me where now lies the black, stone-hardened rind. The lights burned blue within the church, and the outer walls were red from the strong glow of fire. The vineyards were buried, but the church stood like a floating ark upon this glowing sea of fire!"

Like vine-branches laden with heavy bunches swung from tree to tree, and looking like one single garland, thus united themselves city to city around the bay of Naples.* The whole way, with the exception of the already-mentioned desolate extent, appears a Toledo street. The light cabriolets full of people, riders on horseback and on asses, passed one another; whole caravans of travellers, ladies and gentlemen, contribute to the life of the picture.

I had always imagined Pompeii, like Herculaneum, below the earth, but it is not so. It looks down from the mountain over the vineyards to the blue Mediterranean. We ascended at every step, and stood now before an opening made in a wall of dark-grey ashes, to which grim hedges and cotton-plants attempted to give a friendly appearance. Soldiers on guard presented themselves, and we entered the suburb of Pompeii.

"You have read the letters of Tacitus?" said Maretti. "You have read those of the younger Pliny; now you shall have such commentaries on his work as no other author has."

The long street in which we stood is called the Tomb

---

* Where Torre del Greco ends begins immediately Torre del Annunciata. —*Author's note.*

Street. Here are monuments on monuments. Before two of these one finds round, handsome seats, with beautiful ornaments. Here, in those former times, the sons and daughters of Pompeii rested themselves, on their rambles out of the city. From the tombs they looked out over the blooming landscape, the lively bend of the road, and the bay. Next we saw a row of houses on each side, all shops; like so many skeletons with hollow eye-sockets they seemed to stare upon us. On every hand were traces of the earthquake which, earlier than the great destruction, had shaken the city. Many houses plainly showed that they were in the progress of building exactly when the fire and ashes buried them for centuries; unfinished marble cornices lay on the ground, and near to them the models, in terra cotta, from which they were being worked.

We had now reached the walls of the city; up these, flights of broad steps led us to an amphitheatre. Before us stretched out a long, narrow street, paved, as in Naples, with lava-flags, the remains of a much earlier eruption than that which, seventeen hundred years before, had devastated Herculaneum and Pompeii. Deep tracks of wheels are visible in the stone; and upon the houses one still reads the names of the inhabitants, hewn in whilst they yet lived there. Before a few of the houses there yet hung out signs, one of which announced that here, in this house, mosaic-work was done.

All the apartments were small; the light was admitted through the roof, or by an opening above the door, a square portico inclosed the court, which was usually only large enough for a single little flower-bed or basin, in which the fountains played; for the rest, the courts and floors were ornamented with beautiful mosaics, in which artistical forms, circles, and quadrants, cut through each other. The walls were brightly painted with deep red, blue, and white colours, with female dancers, genii, and light floating figures around upon a glowing ground. All was indescribably graceful in colouring and drawing, and as fresh as if they had been painted only yesterday. Federigo and Maretti were in deep conversation on the wonderful composition of colours which resist time so uncommonly well, — yes, before I was aware of it, were deep in the middle of Bayardi's ten folio volumes on the "Antique Monuments of Herculaneum." They, like a thousand others, forgot the poetical reality which lay before them, and busied themselves with criticism, and treatises thereon. Pompeii itself was forgotten amid their learned researches. I had not been thus consecrated to these outwardly learned mysteries; the reality around me was a poetical world, in which my soul felt itself at home. Centuries melted together into years, revealed themselves in moments in which every care slumbered, and my thoughts won anew repose and inspiration.

We stood before the house of Sallust.

"Sallust!" shouted Maretti, and lifted his hat, "*corpus sine animo!* The soul is hence, but we salute reverentially the inanimate body."

A large picture of Diana and Actæon occupied the opposite wall. The workmen exclaimed aloud and joyfully, and brought forth to the light a magnificent marble table, white as the stone of Carrara, supported by two glorious sphinxes; but that which deeply affected me, was the yellow bones which I saw, and, in the ashes, the impression of a female breast of infinite beauty.

We went across the forum to the temple of Jupiter. The sun shone upon the white marble pillars; beyond lay the smoking Vesuvius; pitch-black clouds whirled out from the crater, and white as snow hung the thick steam over the stream of lava, which had formed to itself a path down the side of the mountain.

We saw the theatre, and seated ourselves upon the step-formed benches. The stage, with its pillars, its walled background, with doors for exit, all stood as if people had played there yesterday; but no tone more will sound from the orchestra, no Roscius speak to the exulting crowd. All was dead around us; the great stage of Nature alone breathed of life. The succulent green vineyards, the populous road which led down to Salerno, and in the background the dark blue mountain, with its sharp outline in the warm ethereal colouring was a great theatre, upon

which Pompeii itself stood like a tragic chorus, which sang
of the power of the angel of death. I saw him, even himself, whose wings are coal-black ashes, and overflowing
lava which he spreads over cities and villages.

We were not to ascend Vesuvius till evening, when the
glowing lava and moonlight would have great effect. We
took asses from Recina, and rode up the mountain; the
road lay through vineyards and lonesome farms; very soon,
however, the vegetation diminished into small, woeful-
looking hedges, and dry, reed-like, blades of grass. The
wind blew colder and stronger, otherwise the evening was
infinitely beautiful. The sun seemed, as it sank, like a
burning fire; the heavens beamed like gold, the sea was
indigo, and the islands pale blue clouds. It was a fairy
world in which I stood. On the edge of the bay Naples
grew more and more indistinct; in the far distance lay the
mountains covered with snow, which shone gloriously like
the glaciers of the Alps, whilst aloft, quite close to us,
glowed the red lava of Vesuvius.

At length we came to a plain, covered with the iron
black lava, where was neither road nor track. Our asses
carefully assayed their footing before they advanced a step,
and thus we only very slowly ascended the higher part of
the mountain, which, like a promontory, raised itself out
of this dead, petrified sea. We approached the dwelling
of the hermit through a narrow excavated road, where
only reed-like vegetation was found. A troop of soldiers
sat here around a blazing fire, and drank from their bottles
lacrymæ Christi. They serve as an escort for strangers
against the robbers of the mountains. Here the torches
were lighted, and the winds seized upon their flames as if
they would extinguish them, and rend away every spark.
By this wavering, unsteady light, we rode onward in the
dark evening along the narrow, rocky path, over loose
pieces of lava, and close beside the deep abyss. At length,
like a mountain, reared itself before us the coal-black peak
of ashes : this we had to ascend ; our asses could no longer
be serviceable to us; we left them, therefore, behind us
with the lads who had driven them.

The guide went first with the torches, we others followed after, but in a zig-zag direction, because we went through the ashes, in which we sank at every step up to the knee; nor could we keep a regular line behind one another, because there lay great loose stones and blocks of lava in the ashes, which rolled down when we trod upon them; at every other step we slid one backwards, every moment we fell into the black ashes; it was as if we had leaden weights fastened to our feet.

"Courage!" cried the guide before us, "we shall quickly be at the summit!" But the point of the mountain seemed for ever to be at the same height above us. Expectation and desire gave wings to my feet; an hour elapsed before we reached the top—I was the first who did so.

A vast platform, scattered over with immense pieces of lava thrown one upon another, spread itself here before our eyes, in the midst of which stood a mount of ashes. It was the cone of the deep crater. Like a ball of fire hung the moon above it; thus high had it ascended; and now, for the first time, the mountain permitted us to see it, but only for a moment; in the next, with the rapidity of thought, a coal-black cloud whirled out of the crater, and it became dark night around us; deep thunder rolled within the mountain; the ground trembled under our feet, and we were compelled to hold firmly one by another that we might not fall. The same moment resounded an explosion which a hundred cannon could only faintly imitate. The smoke divided itself, and a column of fire, certainly a mile high, darted into the blue air; glowing stones, like blood-rubies, were cast upwards in the white fire. I saw them like rockets falling above us, but they fell in a right line into the crater, or else rolled down the mound of ashes.

"Eternal God!" stammered my heart, and I hardly ventured to breathe.

"Vesuvius is in a Sunday humour!" said the guide, and beckoned us onwards. I had imagined that our journey was at an end, but the guide pointed forward over the plain, where the whole horizon was a brilliant fire, and where gigantic figures moved themselves like black shades upon the strong fire-ground. These were travellers who stood between us and the down-streaming lava. We had gone round the. mountain in order to avoid this, and had ascended it from the opposite, the eastern side. In its present restless state we could not approach the crater itself, but could only stand where the lava-streams, like fountains of water, poured out of the sides of the mountain. We therefore left the crater on our left, advanced across the mountain plain, and climbed over the great blocks of lava, for here was neither road nor path. The pale moonlight, and the red glare of the torches upon this uneven ground, caused every shadow, and every cleft, to seem like a gulf, whilst we could see only the deep darkness.

Again the loud thunder resounded below us, all became night, and a new eruption glared before us.

Only slowly, and feeling before us with our hands at every step, crept we onwards towards our goal, and quickly we perceived that every thing which we touched was warm. Between the blocks of lava it steamed forth hot as from an oven.

A smooth plain now lay before us ; a lava-stream which was only about two days old ; the upper rind of which was already black and hard from the operation of the air, although scarcely half an ell thick, under which lay, fathoms deep, the glowing lava. Firm as the ice-rind on an inland lake, lay here the hardened crust above this sea of fire. Over this we had to pass, and, on the other side, lay again the uneven blocks, upon which the strangers stood, and looked down upon the new torrent of lava, which they could see only from this point.

We advanced singly, with the guides at our head, upon the crust of lava ; it glowed through the soles of our shoes ; and around us, in many places, where the heat had caused great chinks, we could see the red fire below us ; if the rind had broken, we should have been plunged into the sea of fire ! We assayed every footstep before we took it, and yet went on hastily in order to pass this space, for it burned our feet, and produced the same effect as iron when it begins to cool and become black, which, when put in motion, instantly emits again fiery sparks ; on the snow, the footprints were black, here red. Neither of us spoke a word ; we had not imagined this journey to have been so fearful.

An Englishman turned back to us with his guide; he came up to me upon the very crust of the lava where we were surrounded by the fiery red rents.

" Are there any English among you ? " he inquired.

" Italian only, and a Dane," I replied.

" The devil ! " That was all that was said.

We had now arrived at the great blocks on which many strangers were standing. I also mounted one, and before me, down the mountain-side, glided slowly the fresh torrent of lava ; it was like a redly glowing fiery slime, as of melted metal streaming from a furnace, and which spread it out below us far and wide, to a vast extent. No language, no picture, can represent this in its greatness and its fearful effect. The very air appeared like fire and brimstone ; a thick steam floated upwards over the lava stream, red with the strongly reflected light; but all around was night. It thundered below in the mountain, and above us ascended the pillar of fire, with its glowing stones. Never before had I felt myself so near to God. His omnipotence and greatness filled my soul. It was as if the fire around me burned out every weakness within me ; I felt strength and courage ; my immortal soul lifted its wings.

" Almighty God ! " breathed forth my spirit, " I will be Thy apostle. Amid the storms of the world I will sing Thy name, Thy might, and majesty ! Higher shall my song resound than that of the monk in his lonely cell. A poet I am ! Give me strength ; preserve my soul pure, as the soul of Thy priest and of Nature's ought to be ! " I folded my hands in prayer, and, kneeling amid fire and cloud, poured out my thanks to Him whose wonders and whose greatness spoke to my soul.

We descended from the block of lava on which we stood, and were scarcely more than a few paces from the place when, with a loud noise, it sank down through the broken crust, and a cloud of sparks whirled aloft in the air ; but I did not tremble ; I felt that my God was near to me : it was one of those moments in life in which the soul is conscious of the bliss of its immortality, in which there is neither fear nor pain, for it knows itself and its God.

All around us sparks were cast upwards from small

craters, and new eruptions followed every minute from the large one ; they rushed into the air like a flock of birds which flew all at once out of a wood. Federigo was as much transported as I was, and our descent from the mountain in the loose ashes corresponded with our excited state of mind ; we flew ; it was a falling through the air : we slid, ran, sank. The ashes lay as soft as new-fallen snow upon the mountains. We needed only ten minutes for our descent, whereas we had required an hour in ascending. The wind had abated ; our asses were waiting for us below, and in the hut of the hermit sat our learned man, who had declined making the wearisome ascent with us.

I felt myself animated anew. I turned my glance continually backwards ; the lava lay in the distance like colossal, falling stars ; the moon shone like day. We travelled along the edge of the beautiful bay, and saw the reflection of the moon and the lava in two long stretches of light, the one red, the other blue, trembling on the mirror of the waters. I felt a strength in my soul, a clearness in my comprehension ; yes, if I may compare the small with the great, I was so far related to Boccacio, that the impression of a place, and its momentary inspiration, determined the whole operation of the spirit. Virgil's grave saw his tears, the world his worth as a poet ; the greatness and terror of the volcano had chased away depression and doubt ; therefore, that which I saw this day and this evening is so vividly impressed upon my soul, therefore have I lingered over this description, and have given that which then stamped itself upon my breast, and which I otherwise must have spoken of at a later period.

Our learned man invited us to accompany him home. At the first moment I felt some embarrassment, a strange reluctance, after the last scene between me and Santa, to see her again ; but the greater and more important decision in my soul soon annihilated this lesser one.

She took me kindly by the hand, poured us out wine, was natural and lively, so that at last I upbraided myself for my severe judgment upon her ; I felt that the impure thought existed in myself; her compassion and sympathy, which she had evidently expressed so strongly, I had mistaken for unworthy passion. I sought now, therefore, by friendliness and jest, which was quite accordant with my present state of mind, to make up for my strange behaviour the day before. She seemed to understand me, and I read in her glance a sister's heartfelt sympathy and love.

Signora Santa and her husband had never yet heard me improvise; they urged me to do so. I sang of our ascent to Vesuvius, and applause and admiration saluted me. That which Annunciata's silent glance had spoken was poured in eloquent language from Santa's lips, and they became doubly beautiful from these words: the eye burned with looks of gratitude into my very soul.

CHAPTER IV.

AN UNEXPECTED MEETING. — MY *DÉBUT* IN SAN CARLO.

IT was decided that I should make my *début* as Improvisatore. Day by day I felt my courage to do so increase. In Maretti's house, and in the few families whose acquaintance I had made there, I contributed, by my talent, to the entertainment of the company, and received the warmest praise and encouragement. It was a refreshment for my sick soul; I experienced a joy therefrom, and a gratitude towards Providence, and nobody who could have read my thoughts would have called the fire which burned in my eyes vanity; it was pure joy! I had really a sort of anxiety about the praise which they bestowed upon me; I feared that I was unworthy of it, or that I should not always be able to preserve it. I felt it deeply, and ventured to express it, although it concerned me so much. Praise and encouragement are the best school for a noble soul; where, on the contrary, severity and unjust blame either render it timid, or else awaken defiance and scorn. I had learned this by my own experience.

o

Maretti showed me much attention, and went out of his way to serve me, and introduced me to persons who could be useful to me in the path which I had chosen for myself. Santa was infinitely mild and affectionate towards me ; and yet it seemed to me that a something within me ever repelled me from her. I always went with Federigo, or when I knew that they had company with them ; I feared lest the late scene should be renewed. Yet my eye dwelt upon her when she was not aware of it ; and I could not help thinking her beautiful. It happened with me, as it so often happens in the world, people are jested with ; they are told that they love somebody that they have never thought about, nor have paid much attention to. But then comes the desire to see what there may be in this person, and why they should be fixed upon for our choice. One begins with curiosity, which becomes interest ; and one has had examples of interest in a person becoming love. With me, however, it only went no farther than to attention — a sort of outward regard which I had never known before, but just sufficient to excite a beating of the heart — an anxiety which made me bashful, and kept me at a distance from her.

I had now been two months in Naples ; on the next Sunday I was to make my *début* in the great theatre of San Carlo. The opera of the Barber of Seville was given that night ; and, after this, I was to improvise on given subjects. I called myself Cenci ; I had not the boldness to have my family name placed on the bill.

An extraordinary longing for the decisive day which was to establish my fame filled my soul ; but with it there often went also an anxiety, a feverish terror, through my blood. Federigo comforted me : said that that came from the air — he, and almost everybody else, felt the same ; it proceeded from Vesuvius, whose eruptions increased so greatly. The lava-stream was already come below the mountain, and had taken the direction towards Torre del Annunciata. We could hear, in an evening, the thundering reports in the mountain ; the air was filled with ashes, which lay thickly upon the trees and flowers. The top of the mountain stood enveloped in dark tempest-brooding clouds, from which, with every eruption, darted forth the zig-zag pale-blue lightning. Santa was unwell, like the rest. "It is fever," she said, and her eye burned. She looked pale, and expressed herself very much troubled about it; because she must, and would, be in San Carlo on the evening of my *début.*

"Yes," said she, "that I shall, even though I have a fever three times as severe the day after. I shall not remain away. One must venture one's life for one's friends, even if they know nothing about it!"

I passed my time now on the promenades, in the coffee-houses, and the various theatres. Again, my excited state of mind drove me to the churches, to the foot of the Madonna; there I confessed every sinful thought, and prayed for courage, and for strength to follow the powerful impulses of my soul. "Bella ragazza!" whispered the tempter in my ear, and my cheeks burned as I tore myself away. My spirit and my blood strove for the mastery; I felt, as it were, a period of transition in my individual I. The next Sunday evening I regarded as the culmination-point.

"We must just for once go to the great gambling-house," Federigo had said many a time. "A poet must know every thing!"

We had not been there; and I felt a kind of bashfulness in going. Bernardo had not said of me, without some degree of justice, that my bringing up with the good Domenica, and in the Jesuits' school, had infused a little goat's milk in my blood — cowardice, as he had also offensively called it.

I needed more decision; I must live more in the world if I meant to describe it! These thoughts passed impressively through my mind, as somewhat late in the evening, I went to the most celebrated gaming-house in Naples.

"I will go up there, just because I feel the want of courage to do so!" said I within myself. "I need not play; Federigo and my other friends will say that I have done very rationally."

Yet how weak one can be! My heart beat all the time as if I were about to commit a sin, whilst my reason whis-

pered to me that there really was no harm in it all. Swiss
guards stood at the doors; the staircase was magnificently
lighted. In the lobby stood a crowd of servants, who
took from me my hat and stick, and opened the door for
me, which revealed to me a suite of well-lighted rooms.
There was a large assembly of people, gentlemen and
ladies. Endeavouring not to appear embarrassed, I went
quickly forward into the first saloon, and no one took the
least notice of me. The company sat around the great
gaming-table, with piles of colonati and louis-d'or lying
before them.

A lady advanced in years, who certainly had once been
handsome, sat with painted cheeks, and richly apparelled,
grasping the cards in her hands, whilst she fixed a falcon
glance upon the piles of gold. Several young and very
lovely girls stood in very confidential conversation with some
gentlemen — all of them the beautiful daughters of sin.
Even the old lady with the falcon eye had once won hearts,
as she could now win with their colour.

In one of the smallest of the chambers, there stood a
red and green diced table. I saw that they set one or
more colonati upon one of these colours; the balls were
rolled, and, if they lay upon the selected colour, the stake
was won double. It went on like the beating of my pulse;
gold and silver played over the board. I also took out my
purse, threw a colonati upon the table, which fell on the
red colour. The man who stood before it looked at me
with an inquiring glance, as to whether it should remain
lying there. I nodded involuntarily; the ball rolled, and
my money was doubled. I became quite embarrassed
thereby; it remained lying there, and the ball rolled again
and again. Fortune favoured my play; my blood was put
into motion. It was only my lucky piece which I ventured; presently there lay a heap of silver before me, and
the louis-d'or shone beside it as a balance. I swallowed a
glass of wine, for my mouth was parched. The great
heap of silver increased more and more, for I took none of
it away. The ball rolled again, and, with the most
cold-blooded mien, the banker swept the whole glittering
heap to himself. My beautiful golden dream was at an

end ; but it also awoke me. I played no more ; I had only lost the colonati which I had risked at first. This consoled me, and I went into the next saloon.

Among the young ladies there was one who attracted my attention, by a wonderful likeness to Annunciata, only she was taller and stouter. My eye rested continually upon her. She observed it, stepped up to me, and, pointing to a little table, asked whether we should make up a party. I excused myself, and returned to the room from which I was just come ; she followed me with her eye. In the innermost room a number of young men were playing at billiards ; they were playing without their coats, although ladies were in their company. I did not remember what freedom was permitted in this company. Before the door, but with his back towards me, stood a young man of fine figure ; he steadied the queue on the ball, and made a masterly stroke, for which he was applauded. The lady even, who had attracted my attention, nodded kindly, and seemed to say something amusing. He turned himself round, and wafted her a kiss with his hand, whilst she jestingly struck him on the shoulder. My heart beat ; it was actually Bernardo !

I had not courage to advance nearer, yet I desired to have perfect knowledge. I stole along the wall towards the open door of a large, half-lighted saloon, where, unseen myself, I could more narrowly observe him. A twilight pervaded this apartment ; red and white glass lamps cast a faint light ; an artificial garden adjoined it, adorned with bowers, which, however, were only formed with painted, leaden foliage, surrounded by beautiful orange-trees ; stuffed parrots, with brilliant plumage, swung among the branches, whilst a hand-organ played, in low tones, soft, graceful melodies, that went to the heart. A mild coolness was wafted through the open door from the arcade. Scarcely had I cast a hasty glance over the whole, when Bernardo approached with light footsteps : I drew myself mechanically into an arbour ; he saw me standing there, smiled and nodded to me, and, hastening into the next arbour, threw himself upon a seat, and hummed an air half aloud. A thousand emotions agitated my breast : —

he here ?   I so near him ?   I felt a trembling in all my
limbs, and was obliged to seat myself.   The fragrant
flowers, the half-suppressed music, the twilight, even the
soft, elastic sofa, all carried me into a sort of dream-world,
and only in such a one could I expect to meet with Bernardo.   Whilst I thus sat, the young lady whom I have
already mentioned entered the room and approached the
arbour where I was ; seeing this, Bernardo hummed
aloud, and she, recognising his voice, turned towards him.
I heard a kiss ; it burned into my soul.

Him — the faithless, fickle Bernardo, had Annunciata
preferred to me !   Already, so shortly after the happiness
of his love, he could forget her, could consecrate his lips
to an image of beauty formed of clay !   I darted out of
the room, out of the house ; my heart trembled with indignation and pain.   I got no rest till morning.

The day was now come on the evening of which I was
to make my *début* in the theatre of San Carlo.   The
thoughts of this and the adventures of yesterday had set
my whole soul in motion.   Never had my heart prayed
more inwardly to the Madonna and the saints.   I went to
church, received the sacrament from the priest ; prayed
that it might strengthen and purify me, and felt its wonderful power !   One thought only seized disturbingly
upon the rest which was so necessary for me, and this
was, whether Annunciata were here — whether Bernardo
had followed her.   Federigo brought me the certain intelligence that she was not here ; he, on the contrary, as the
list of arrivals showed, had been here four days.   Santa, I
knew, was ill of fever ; but, notwithstanding, she insisted
on going to the theatre.   The playbills were pasted up ;
Federigo told histories, and Vesuvius threw up fire and
ashes more violently than usual ; all was in activity.

The opera had begun when the carriage conveyed me to
the theatre.   Had the Fates sat at my side, and my life's
thread been between the shears, I believe I should have
exclaimed, " Cut away ! "   My prayer and my thought
were, " God lets all things be for the best."

In the green-room I found a crowd of artists of the
stage, and some fine spirits, and even an improvisatore,

and a professor of the French language, Santini, · with whom Maretti had made me acquainted. The conversation was easy ; they jested and laughed ; the singers in " The Barber" came and went as if it were from a party ; the stage was their accustomed home.

" We shall give you a theme," said Santini ; " oh, a hard nut to crack ; but it will succeed. I remember how I trembled the first time that I made my appearance ; but it succeeded! I had my tricks — little innocent artifices which reason permits ; certain little stanzas about love and antiquity, the beauty of Italy, poetry and art, which one knows how to bring in, to say nothing of a few standing poems ; that is a matter of course ! "

I assured him that I had never thought of preparing myself in this way.

" Yes, that one says ? " said he, laughing, " but good ! good ! You are a rational young man, it will succeed gloriously with you ! "

The piece came to an end, and I stood alone upon the empty stage.

" The scaffold is ready !" said the manager, laughing, and gave the sign to the mechanist. The curtain drew up.

I saw only a black abyss, could only distinguish the first heads in the orchestra and the first boxes of the five heights in that lofty building ; a thick, warm air wafted towards me. I felt a strong resolution within me which was amazing to myself ; to be sure, my soul was in a state of excitement, but it was, as it ought to be, flexible and susceptible of every thought. As the air is the clearest when in winter severe cold penetrates it, thus felt I an elasticity and clearness all at once. All my spiritual abilities were awake, as in this case they must and should be.

Any one could give me a subject on a slip of paper, upon which I was to improvise, a secretary of the police having in the first place examined that nothing contrary to the law was suggested. From these subjects I could make my selection. In the first I read " il cavalier servente ; " but I had never rightly thought over this kind of business. I knew, certainly, that the *cicisbeo*, as they are also called, was the knight of the present time, who, now that he can no longer enter the lists for his lady, is her faithful attendant, who stands in the place of her husband. I recollected the well-known sonnet, " *Femina di costume, di maniere*,"* but at the moment not a thought would arise in my mind to embellish this subject. I opened with impatience the second paper; in it was written " Capri ; " this, also, was embarrassing to me ; I had never been upon the island, had only seen its beautiful mountain outline from Naples. What I did not know I could not sing ; I preferred rather " Il cavalier servente."

I opened the third paper, and here I read, " The Cata_ combs of Naples ; " neither had I been here ; but with the word catacombs a life's moment stood before me ; the ramble in my childhood with Federigo, and our adventure, arose livingly before my soul. I struck a few notes ; the verses came of themselves ; I related what I had felt and gone through, only that it was in the catacombs of Naples instead of Rome. I seized for a second time the thread of happiness, and repeated, stormy plaudits saluted me ; they streamed like champagne through my blood.

They gave me now as a subject, " Fata Morgana ; " I had not seen this beautiful ethereal appearance, peculiar to Sicily and Naples ; but I knew very well the beauty fairy Phantasy, which dwelt in those splendid castles ; I could describe my own dream-world, in which floated, also, her gardens and castles. In my heart, indeed, abode life's most beautiful " Fata Morgana."

I rapidly thought over my subject; a little story fashioned itself therewith, and new ideas presented themselves in my song. I began with a little description of the ruined church at Posilippo, without precisely mentioning

---

* This sonnet is in W. Müller's Rom, Römer, und Römerin. The *cicisbeo* was established in Genoa, among the merchants. Business took these men much from home, and, in order not to confine their wives to the house, they were placed under the care of a friend, to become their attendant ; commonly this friend was a priest. Afterwards it became the fashion : nobody could do without a *cicisbeo*. The connexion was noble and pure, and there are instances in which the dead have been praised on their monuments for the exact and faithful fulfilment of their duty as *cicisbeos*. From morning till night must the *cicisbeo* attend his lady, must show her the greatest attention, and, on the contrary, be indifferent to others : this is his duty. — *Author's Note.*

its name. This romantic house had captivated me, and I gave a picture of the church, which now had become the home of the fisherman ; a little child lay asleep on his bed below the window on which the picture of Saint George was painted on the glass. In the still moonlight night a beautiful little girl came to him, she was as lovely and as light as air, and had beautiful, bright-coloured wings upon her shoulders. They played together, and she led him out into the green vine-grove, showed him a thousand glorious things which he had never seen before; they went out into the mountains, which opened themselves into large, splendid churches, full of pictures and altars ; they sailed upon the beautiful blue sea over against the smoking Vesuvius, and the mountain appeared as if of glass ; they saw how the fires burned and raged within it ; they went below the earth and visited the old cities, of which he had heard tell, and all the people were living; he saw their wealth and pomp, greater even than we have any conception of from their ruins. She loosened her wings, bound them upon his shoulders, for she, without these, was light as air, and needed them not. Thus flew they over the orange-woods, over the mountains, the luxuriant green Marshes to ancient Rome, amid the dead Campagna; flew over the beautiful blue sea, far past Capri, rested upon the crimson, shining clouds, and the little girl kissed him, called herself Fancy, and showed him her mother's beautiful castle, built of air and sunbeams, and there they played so happily and so joyously ! But, as the boy grew up, the little girl came to him less frequently, peeped only at him in the moonlight between the green vine-leaves, and the oranges nodded to him, and he became troubled and full of longing. But he must now help his father on the sea, learn to work the oars, to pull the ropes, and steer the boat in the storm ; but all the more he grew, all the more turned his thoughts towards his beloved play-fellow, who never more visited him. Late in the moon-light nights, when he lay upon the quiet sea, he let the oars rest, and down in the deep, clear water, he saw the sandy, seaweed-strewn bottom of the ocean. Fancy then looked upwards at him, with her dark, beautiful eyes, and seemed to beckon and call him downward to her.

One morning many fishermen stood together on the shore. Floating in the ascending beams of the sun, not far from Capri, lay a new, wondrously beautiful island formed of rainbow colours, with glittering towers, stars, and clear, purple-tinted clouds. *"Fata Morgana!"* exclaimed they all, and triumphed joyfully in the charming apparition; but the young fisher knew it well: there had he played; there had he abode with his beautiful Fancy: a strange melancholy and yearning seized upon his soul; but, amid his tears, grew dim, and vanished the whole well-known image.

In the clear moonlight evening again ascended, from the promontory on which the fisherman stood, castles and islands fashioned of brightness and of air; they saw a boat with the speed of an arrow dart towards the strangely floating land and vanish; and suddenly was extinguished the whole creation of light, and, instead, a cold-black cloud spread itself over the sea, a water-spout advanced along the peaceful surface, which now began to heave its dark green billows. When this had vanished, the ocean was again calm; the moon shone upon the azure waters, but they saw no boat; the young fisher had vanished — vanished with the beautiful *Fata Morgana!*

The same applause as before greeted me again; my courage and my inspiration increased. The next subject which was given furnished recollections out of my own life, which it was only needful for me to relate. I was to improvise of Tasso. He was myself; Leonora was Annunciata; we saw each other at the court of Ferrara. I suffered with him in captivity; breathed again freedom with death in my heart, as I looked from Sorrento over the billowy sea towards Naples; sat with him under the oak at the Convent of St. Onophrius; the bell of the Capitol sounded for his coronation-feast, but the angel of death came and first placed upon his head the crown of immortality.

My heart beat violently; I was engrossed, was carried away by the flight of my thoughts. Yet was one more poem given to me, it was " The Death of Sappho." The pangs of jealousy I had felt as I remembered Bernardo;

Annunciata's kiss upon his brow burned into my soul. Sappho's beauty was that of Annunciata; but the sufferings of her love were my own. The ocean waters closed over Sappho!

My poem had called forth tears; the most extraordinary applause resounded from all sides, and after the curtain had fallen, I was twice called for. A happiness, a nameless joy, filled my soul, and yet seemed so to oppress my heart till it was ready to break; and when I had left the stage, amid the embraces and congratulations of my friends and acquaintance, I burst into tears, into violent, convulsive sobs.

With Santini, Federigo, and some of the singers, a very lively evening was spent; they drank to my well-being, and I was happy, but my lips were sealed!

"He is a pearl!" exclaimed Federigo in his gay delight, speaking of me; "his only fault is, that he is a Joseph the second, whom we Danes, for the sake of clearness, should call Joseph the son of Jacob! Enjoy life, Antonio; pluck the rose before it be withered!"

It was late when I reached home; and with prayers and thanks to the Madonna, and Jesus Christ, who had not forsaken me, I was soon deeply and soundly asleep.

CHAPTER V.

SANTA. — THE ERUPTION. — OLD CONNEXIONS.

THE next morning I stood before Federigo a new-born man; I was able to express my delight; I could not do it the evening before. Life around me interested me more; I felt myself, as it were, ennobled; I seemed to have become more mature through the dew of encouragement which had fallen upon my life's tree.

It was necessary, also, that I should pay a visit to Santa; she had probably heard me the evening before; I longed also to hear her praise, of which I was sure.

Maretti received me with rapture, but Santa, I was told, had through the whole night, after she returned from the theatre, suffered severely from fever; at this moment she was asleep, and sleep would be beneficial to her. I was made to promise that I would call again in the evening. I dined with Federigo and my new friends; health after health was drunk: the white *lacrymæ Christi* alternated with the wine of Calabria. I would not drink any more: my blood was in flame, champagne must cool it.

We separated gaily, and full of delight. When we came out into the street, we found the atmosphere lighted up by Vesuvius, and the mighty streams of lava. Several of the party drove out to see the fearful, but glorious spectacle. I went to Santa, for it was a little past the Ave Maria. I found that she was quite alone, much better: the servant said the sleep had strengthened her: I was permitted to see her, but nobody else.

I was introduced into a beautiful, snug little room, the long thick window-curtains of which were drawn; a lovely marble statue of Cupid whetting his arrow, and an argand lamp, whose light gave a magical colouring to the whole, were the first things which I saw. Santa lay, in a light wrapping-dress, on a soft silken sofa: she half rose as I entered, held with one hand a large shawl around her, and extended the other to me.

"Antonio!" said she, "it has succeeded gloriously! Fortunate man! you have captivated every one! Oh, you know not what anxiety I had about you: how my heart beat; and with what delight I again breathed when you so far exceeded my greatest expectation!"

I bowed, and inquired after her health. She gave me her hand, and assured me that she was better, "Yes, much better," said she; and added, "you look like some one newly created! You looked handsome, very handsome! When you were carried away by your inspiration, you looked quite ideal. It was you yourself that I saw in every poem, in the little boy with the painter, in the catacombs, methought — you and Federigo!"

"It was so," said I, interrupting her; "I have passed through all that I have sung."

" Yes," replied she, " you yourself have passed through all — the bliss of love, the pain of ' love — may you be happy as you deserve ! "

I told her what a change there seemed to be in my whole being — how entirely differently life seemed now to present itself to me ; and she grasped my hand, and looked as if into my soul, with her dark, expressive eyes. She was lovely, more lovely than common : a fine crimson glowed upon her cheeks : the dark, glossy hair was put smoothly back from the beautifully formed brow. The luxuriant figure resembled an image of Juno, beautiful as a Phidias could form it.

" Yes," said she, " you shall live for the world : you are its property : you will rejoice and captivate millions : let not, therefore, the thought of one single one seize distinctively on your happiness. You are worthy of love : you captivate with your spirit, and with your talent, with ——" She panted ; and then, drawing me towards her, continued, " We must talk seriously : we have, indeed, not been able rightly to talk together since that evening, when sorrow lay so heavily upon your soul ! You seemed then — yes, what shall I call it ? — to have misunderstood me —— "

My heart had done so ; and very often had I reproached myself for it. " I am not deserving of your goodness," said I, impressing a kiss upon her hand, and looked into her dark eyes with a purity of soul and thought. Her glance still burned and rested, seriously, almost penetratingly, upon me. Had a stranger seen us, he would have discovered shadow where there was only purity and light. It was, my heart could assert it aloud, as if here met a brother and sister, eye and thought.

She was greatly excited. I saw her bosom heave violently : she loosened a scarf to breathe more freely. " You are deserving of love ! " said she. " Soul and beauty are deserving of any woman's love ! "

She laid her arm on my shoulder, and looked again into my face ; and then continued, with an indescribably eloquent smile, " And I can believe that you only dream in an ideal world ! You are possessed of delicacy and good sense ; and these always gain the victory. Therefore,

Antonio, are you dear to me; therefore is your love my
dream, my thought!" She drew me towards her: her
lips were like fire, that flowed into my very soul!

Eternal Mother of God! Thy holy image, at that moment, fell down from the wall where it stood above my
head. It was not a mere accident! No! thou touchedst
my brow: thou didst seize me, as I was about to sink in
the whirlpool of passion!

"No! no!" exclaimed I, starting up: my blood was
like seething lava.

"Antonio!" cried she, "kill me! kill me! but do not
leave me." Her cheeks, her eyes, her glance, and expression, was passion; and yet she was beautiful — an image
of beauty, painted in flame. I felt a tremour in all my
nerves; and, without replying, I left the apartment; and
rushed down the steps, as if a dark spirit had pursued me.

When I reached the street, all seemed in flame, like my
blood. The current of the air wafted forward heat. Vesuvius stood in glowing fire — eruptions in rapid succession
lit up every thing around. Air! air! demanded my heart.
I hastened to the Molo, in the open bay, and seated myself
exactly where the waves broke on the shore. The blood
seemed to force itself to my eyes: I cooled my brow with
the salt water; tore open my coat, that every breath of air
might cool me; but all was flame — the sea even shone
like the fire of the red lava, which rolled down the mountain. Which ever way I looked, I saw her standing, as if
painted in flame; and looking into my soul with those beseeching, burning gleams of fire. "Kill me! but leave me
not!" resounded in my ears. I closed my eyes, turned my
thoughts towards God; but they relapsed again: it was
as if the flames of sin had scorched the wings of my soul.
An evil conscience must indeed crush the spirit, when
thoughts of sin can thus enfeeble both mind and body.

"Will Excellenza have a boat to Torre del Annunciata?"
said a voice close beside me; and the name of Annunciata
recalled consciousness to my soul.

"The lava-stream runs three ells in a minute," said the
fellow, who with his oar held the boat firm to the land:
"in half an hour we can be there."

" The sea will cool me," thought I, and sprang into the boat. The fellow stood from land ; spread out his sail ; and now we flew, as if borne onward by the wind, across the blood-red, glowing water. A cool wind blew on my cheek, I breathed more freely, and felt myself calmer and better, as we approached land on the opposite side of the bay.

" Never again will I see Santa," I firmly determined in my heart. " I will fly the serpent of beauty, which shows to me the fruit of knowledge. Thousands would ridicule me for doing so ; but rather their laughter than the lamenting cry of my own heart. Madonna, thou didst permit thy holy image to fall from the wall, that thereby I might be preserved from falling ! " Deeply did I feel her protecting grace.

A wonderful joy now penetrated me : all that was noble and good sang hymns of victory in my heart : I was again the child of soul and thought. " Father, direct Thou every thing as is best for me ! " I ejaculated in prayer ; and, full of the enjoyment of life, as if my happiness was established for ever, I rambled through the streets of the little town to the high road.

Every thing was in motion ; carriages and cabriolets laden with people drove past me ; they shouted, huzzaed, and sang, and every thing around was lit up by the flame. The torrent of lava had approached a small city which lay upon the side of the mountain ; families fled therefrom. I saw women with little children at the breast, and with small bundles under their arms, heard their lamentations, and could not help dividing the small sum I had with me with the first that I met. I followed the crowd up among the vineyards, which were inclosed with white walls, and towards the direction which the lava took. A large vine-field lay between us and it, and the torrent, like red-hot, fiery slime many fathoms deep, came moving itself onward, and overwhelming buildings and walls in its course ; the cries of the fugitives, the exultation of the strangers at this imposing scene, the shouting of coachmen, and the vendors of various wares, mingled strangely together, whilst groups of drunken peasants, who stood in crowds around the brandy-sellers, people in carriages, and people on horseback, all lighted up with the red fire-lights, formed a picture of which, in its completeness, no description can be given. One might advance quite close to the lava, which had its determined course; many people stuck in their sticks, or else pieces of money, which they took out again, attached to a piece of lava.

Fearfully beautiful was it when a part of the fiery mass, from its size, tore itself loose; it was like the breakers of the sea: the descending piece lay like a beaming star outside the stream. The air first of all cooled the projecting corners; they became black, and the whole piece appeared like dazzling gold, inclosed in a coal-black net. There had been hung on one of the vines an image of the Virgin, in the hope that the fire would become suspended before the holy form; but it advanced onward in the same uniform course. The heat singed the leaves on the tall trees, which bowed down their crown-like heads to the fiery mass as if they would beseech for mercy. Full of expectation, many a glance rested on the image of the Virgin, but the tree bowed itself deeply with her before the red fire-stream; it was only distant a few ells. At that moment I saw a Capuchin monk close beside me throw his arms aloft and exclaim that the image of the Madonna caught fire. "Save her!" cried he, "so will she save you from the flames of the fire!"

All trembled and drew back, when, at that moment, a woman started forward, cried aloud the name of the Madonna, and hastened towards the glowing death. Whilst this was doing, I saw a young officer on horseback with his drawn sword drive her back, although the fire stood like a wall of rock by his side.

"Mad woman!" exclaimed he, "Madonna needs not thy help. She wills that her badly-painted picture, consecrated by the hand of a sinner, shall be burned in the fire."

It was Bernardo; I knew his voice; his quick decision had saved the life of a fellow-creature, and his speech prevented all offence. I could not but esteem him, and wished in my heart that we had never been separated. But my heart beat more quickly, and I had neither courage nor desire to see him face to face.

The fire-stream swallowed up the trees and the Madonna image ; I withdrew to some distance, and leaned involuntarily against a wall, where several strangers sat around a table.

"Antonio! is it actually thou?" I heard a voice exclaim ; I fancied that it was Bernardo ; a hand pressed mine ; it was Fabiani, the son-in-law of Excellenza, the husband of Francesca, who had known me as a child, and who now, as I must imagine from the letter which I had received, was angry with me like the others, and, like them, had cast me off.

"Nay, that we should meet here !" said he. " It will delight Francesca to see you ! But it is not handsome of you that you have not been to visit us. We have actually been eight days at Castelamare ! "

" I knew nothing of that," replied I, " besides ———"

" Yes, all at once you are become quite another person ; have been in love, and," added he, more gravely, " have also fought a duel, on which account you have regularly eloped, which I cannot at all commend. Excellenza has just now announced it to us, and we were astonished at it. He has, however, written to you, has he not, and that truly not in the mildest manner ? "

My heart beat violently ; I felt myself thrown back into the fetters which benefits had riveted upon me, and expressed the distress which I had experienced in being cast off by them all.

" Nay, nay, Antonio !" said Fabiani, " it is not so bad as that. Come with me to my carriage ! Francesca will be astonished to see you this evening ; we shall soon be at Castelamare, and we will find a place in the hotel for you. You shall tell me what you have seen. It is a sin to despair. Excellenza is violent ; you know him ; but all will be right again."

" No, that it cannot be," replied I, half aloud, falling back again into my former suffering.

" It shall and will !" said Fabiani, with determination, and led me towards his carriage.

He required me to tell him every thing.

" But you are not going to turn improvisatore ?" asked

he, with a smile, when I told him of my flight and of
Fulvia in the robber's cave.

"It sounds so poetic," said he, "as if it were your
fancy, and not your memory, that played the principal
part."

I showed him Excellenza's letter. "Severe, too severe!"
said he, when he had read it; "but cannot you, however,
see by it how much he thinks of you, and therefore it was
so serious? But you really have not made your appearance in the theatre?"

"Yesterday evening," replied I.

"That was too daring," interrupted he; "and how did
it go off?"

"Gloriously! most fortunately!" returned I, joyfully.
"I received the greatest applause — was twice called
for."

"Is it possible?—You have succeeded?"

There was a doubt, a surprise in these words which
wounded me deeply, but the obligations of gratitude bound
my lips, as well as my thoughts.

I felt a sort of embarrassment in presenting myself to
Francesca; I knew, indeed, how grave and severe she could
be. Fabiani consoled me, half jestingly, by saying that
there should be neither confession nor castigatory sermon,
although I had actually so well deserved it.

We reached the hotel.

"Ah, Fabiani!" exclaimed a young, handsomely dressed
and curled gentleman, who sprang forward to meet us. "It
is well you are come, your Signora is quite impatient.
Ah!" said he, breaking off the moment he saw me, "you
are bringing the young improvisatore with you! Cenci,
is it not?"

"Cenci?" repeated Fabiani, and looked at me in
amazement.

"The name under which I appeared in public," I replied.

"Indeed!" said he; "well, that was very rational."

"He can sing about love," said the stranger; "you
should have heard him in San Carlo last evening. That is
a talent!"

He offered me his hand obligingly, and showed his delight in making my agreeable acquaintance.

" I shall sup with you this evening," said he to Fabiani, " and invite myself on account of your excellent singer, and you and your wife will not refuse me."

" You are always welcome, as you know very well," returned Fabiani.

" But you must, however, introduce me to the stranger gentleman," said he.

" There is no need of ceremony here," said Fabiani, " we, he, and I, are sufficiently acquainted; my friends need not be introduced to him. It will be a great honour to him to make your acquaintance."

I bowed, but I was not at all satisfied with the mode in which Fabiani had expressed himself.

" Well, then, I must introduce myself!" said the stranger; " you, I have already had the honour of knowing; my name is Gennaro, officer in King Ferdinand's Guard;" and, added he, laughing, " of a good Neapolitan family! Many people give it even number ONE. It may be that this is right; at least my aunts make very much of that! Inexpressibly delightful is it to me to make the acquaintance of a young man of your talent, your——"

" Be quiet!" interrupted Fabiani, " he is not accustomed to such speeches; now you know one another. Francesca waits for us; there will now be a reconciliation-scene between her and your improvisatore: perhaps you will here find occasion to make use of your eloquence."

I wished that Fabiani had not spoken in this way; but they two were friends, and how could Fabiani place himself in my painful position? He led us in to Francesca; I involuntarily held back a few steps.

" At length, my excellent Fabiani!" she exclaimed.

" At length," repeated he, " and I bring two guests with me."

" Antonio!" exclaimed she, and then again her voice sank; " Signore Antonio!"

She fixed a severe, grave glance upon me and Fabiani; I bowed, wished to kiss her hand, but she seemed not to observe it—offered it to Gennaro, and expressed the great pleasure she had in seeing him to supper.

" Tell me about the eruption," said she to her husband; " has the lava-stream changed its direction ? "

Fabiani told her about it, and ended by saying that there he had met with me; that I was his guest, and that now mercy must be shown before judgment.

" Yes," exclaimed Gennaro, " I cannot at all imagine how he can have sinned; but every thing must be forgiven to genius."

" You are in your very best humour," said she, and nodded very graciously to me, whilst she assured Gennaro that she had really nothing to forgive me. " What do you bring us for news ? " inquired she from him. " What do the French papers say ? and where did you spend last evening ? "

The first question he quickly dismissed; the second he discussed with great interest.

" I was in the theatre," said he, " heard the last act of the ' Barber ! ' Josephine sang like an angel, but when one has once heard Annunciata, nothing can satisfy one. I went there principally to hear the improvisatore ! "

" Did he satisfy you ? " inquired Francesca.

" He surpassed my — nay, every body's highest expect-ations," replied he. " It is not said to flatter him; and of what consequence, indeed, would my poor criticism be to him ? but that *was* indeed improvisation ! He was tho-roughly master of his art, and carried us all along with him. There was feeling, — there was fancy. He sang about Tasso, about Sappho, about the Catacombs; they were poems which were worthy of being preserved ! "

" A beautiful talent ! " said Francesca; " one cannot sufficiently admire it. I wish I had been there."

" But we have the man with us," said Gennaro, and pointed to me.

" Antonio ! " exclaimed she, inquiringly; " has *he* im-provised ? "

" Yes, like a master," replied Gennaro; " but you know him already, and must therefore have heard him."

" Yes, very often," returned she, smiling; " we ad-mired him always as a little boy."

" I myself put the wreath on his head the first time that I heard him," said Fabiani, likewise in jest. " He sang about my lady-love before we were married ; and, as a lover, I thus worshipped her in his song. But now to supper ! Gennaro, you will conduct my Francesca ; and, as we have no more ladies, I will take the improvisatore. Signore Antonio, I request your hand."

He then conducted me after the others into the supper-room.

" But you have never told me about Cenci, or whatever you call the young gentleman," said Gennaro.

" We call him Antonio," replied Fabiani ; " we did not really at all know that it was he who was to make his *début* as improvisatore. You see this is exactly the recon-ciliation-scene of which I spoke. You must know that he is, in a manner, a son of the house. Is it not so, An-tonio ? "

I bowed, with a grateful look, and Fabiani continued, " He is an excellent person ; there is not a stain upon his character ; but he will not learn any thing."

" But if he can now read every thing much better out of the great book of Nature, why should he not do so ? "

" You must not spoil him with your praise," said the Signora, jestingly ; " we believed that he was sitting deep in his classics, and physics, and mathematics, and instead of that he was over head and ears in love with a young singer from Naples."

" That shows that he has feeling," said Gennaro. " And was she handsome ? What was her name ? "

" Annunciata," said Fabiani ; " of extraordinary talent, and a very distinguished woman."

" I myself have been in love with her," said Gennaro. " He has good taste. Here is to Annunciata's health, Sir Improvisatore ! "

He touched his glass against mine ; I could not say a word : it tortured me that Fabiani so lightly could lay bare my wound before a stranger ; but he indeed saw the whole thing from quite a different side to what I did.

" Yes," continued Fabiani, " and he has also fought a duel for her sake, wounded the nephew of the senator in the side, who was his rival, and so he has been obliged to fly. Heaven knows how he has conveyed himself across the frontiers; and, thereupon, he makes his appearance in San Carlo. It is, in fact, an act of temerity which I had not expected from him."

"The senator's nephew!" repeated Gennaro, "now that interests me. He is within these few days come here, has entered into the royal service. I have been with him this very afternoon — a handsome, interesting man. Ah, now I comprehend it all! Annunciata will soon be here; the lover has flown hither before her, settles himself down, and very soon we shall read in the play-bills that the singer makes her appearance for the last — positively for the last time."

"Do you fancy, then, that he will marry her?" inquired Francesca; "but that would, however, be a scandal in his family."

"One has instances of such things," said I, with a tremulous voice; "an instance of a nobleman, who considered himself ennobled and happy by gaining the hand of a singer."

"Happy, perhaps," interrupted she, "but never ennobled."

"Yes, my gracious signora," interposed Gennaro, "I should consider myself ennobled if she chose me, and so I fancy would many others."

They talked a deal — a great deal of her and Bernardo; they forgot how heavily every word must fall upon my heart.

"But," said Gennaro, turning to me, "you must delight us with an improvisation. Signora will give you a subject."

"Yes," said Francesca, smiling, "sing us Love; that is a subject which interests Gennaro, as you indeed know."

"Yes, Love and Annunciata!" exclaimed Gennaro.

"Another time I will do every thing which you can desire from me," said I, "but this evening it is impossible to me. I am not quite well. I sailed across the bay without my cloak, it was so warm by the lava stream; and then I drove here in the cool evening."

Gennaro besought me most pressingly to improvise not-withstanding, but I could not in this place, and upon this subject.

"He has already the artist's way with him," said Fabiani; " he must be pressed. Will you, or will you not, go with us to-morrow to Pæstum? there you will find material enough for your poetry. You should make yourself a little scarce. There cannot be much which binds you to Naples."

I bowed and felt myself in a difficulty, whilst I did not see how I could refuse.

" Yes, he goes with us," exclaimed Gennaro; " and when he stands in the great temple, and the spirit comes over him, he will sing like a Pindar!"

" We set off to-morrow morning," continued Fabiani; " the whole tour will occupy four days. On our return we will visit Amalfi and Capri. You must go with us."

A *no* might, perhaps, as the consequence will show, have changed my whole fate. These four days robbed me, dare I say it, of six years of my youth. And man is a free agent! Yes, we can freely seize upon the threads which lie before us, but how they are firmly twisted together we do not see. I gave my thanks, and said *yes;* and seized hold upon the thread which drew the curtain of my future more closely together.

" To-morrow we shall have more talk together," said Francesca, when, after supper, we separated, and she extended to me her hand to kiss.

" This very evening I shall, however, write to Excellenza," said Fabiani; " I will prepare the reconciliation scene."

" And I will dream about Annunciata," exclaimed Gennaro; " for that I shall not be challenged," added he, laughing, as he pressed my hand.

I, too, wrote a few words to Federigo; told him of my meeting with the family of Excellenza, and that I should make a little journey towards the south with them. I ended the letter; a thousand feelings operated in my breast. How much had not this evening brought me! How many events ran athwart each other!

I thought on Santa, on Bernardo, by the burning picture of the Madonna, and then on the last hours spent amid old connexions. Yesterday a whole public, to whom I was a stranger, had received me with acclamation; I was admired and honoured. This very evening, a woman, rich in beauty, had made me conscious of her love for me; and a few hours afterwards I stood among acquaintance, friends, whom I had to thank for every thing; and as nothing before them but the poor child, whose first duty was gratitude.

But Fabiani and Francesca had really met me with affection; they had received me as the prodigal son, had given me a place at their table; invited me to join them in a pleasure tour on the morrow. Benefit was added to benefit: I was dear to them. But the gift which the rich present with a light hand lies heavily upon the heart of the poor!

CHAPTER VI.

JOURNEY TO PÆSTUM. — THE GRECIAN TEMPLE.— THE BLIND GIRL.

THE beauty of Italy is not found in the Campagna, nor yet in Rome. I knew it only from my ramble by Lake Nemi, and from what I had seen in my journey to Naples. Doubly, therefore, must I have felt its rich beauty, almost more even than a foreigner, who could compare its loveliness with that of other countries. Like a fairy world, therefore, which I have seen in dreams, nay, which lived in them, lies this three days' journey before me. But how can I describe the impressions which my soul received, nay, as it were, actually infused into my blood?

The beauties of nature can never be given by description. Words place themselves in array indeed, like loose pieces of mosaic, one after another, but one understands not the whole picture put together piecemeal. Thus it is in nature; of the entire greatness there must be always something wanting. One gives the single pieces, and thus lets the stranger put them together himself; but if hundreds saw the complete picture, each would represent it very differently. It is with nature, as with a beautiful face, no idea can be formed of it by the mere details of it; we must go to a well-known object, and only when we can say, with mathematical precision, that this resembles that, with the exception of this or that particular, can we have, in any degree, a satisfactory idea.

If it were given to me to improvise on the beauty of Hesperia, I would describe with exact truth the real scenes which my eye here beheld; and thou who hast never seen the beauty of South Italy, thy fancy might beautify every natural charm with which thou wast acquainted, and it would not be rich enough. The ideal of nature exceeds that of man.

In the beautiful morning we set off from Castelamare. I see yet the smoking Vesuvius, the lovely rocky valley, with the great vine-woods, where the juicy green branches ran from tree to tree; the white mountain-castles perched on the green cliffs, or half buried in dark olive-woods. I see the old temple of Vesta, with its marble pillars and its cupola, now the church of Santa Maria Maggiore. A piece of the wall was overthrown; skulls and human bones closed the opening, but the green vine-shoots grew wildly over them, and seemed as if, with their fresh leaves, they would conceal the power and terror of death.

I see yet the wild outline of the mountains, the solitary towers, where nets were spread out to catch the flocks of sea-birds. Deep below us lay Salerno, with the dark-blue sea; and here we met a procession that doubly impressed the whole picture upon my mind. Two white oxen, with their horns an ell in span, drew a carriage, upon which four robbers, with their dark countenances and horrible scornful laugh, lay in chains, whilst dark-eyed, finely formed Calabrians, rode beside them with their weapons on their shoulders.

Salerno, the learned city of the middle ages, was the extent of our first day's journey.

" Old folios have mouldered away," exclaimed Gennaro,

" the learned glory of Salerno is grown dim, but the volume
of nature goes into a new edition every year; and our
Antonio thinks, like me, that one can read more in that
than in any learned musty book whatever."

" We may learn out of both," replied I, " wine and
bread must go together."

Francesca discovered that I spoke very rationally.

" In talking there is no coming short in him," said Fabiani, " but in deeds! You will have an opportunity of
showing us that, Antonio, when you come to Rome."

To Rome! I go to Rome? This thought had never
occurred to me. My lips were silent; but my inmost
heart said to me that I could not — would not again see
Rome, again enter into the old connexions.

Fabiani continued to talk, so did the others, and we
arrived at Salerno. Our first visit was to the church.

" Here I can be cicerone," said Gennaro ; " this is the
chapel of Gregory the Seventh, the holy father who died in
Salerno. His marble statue stands before us upon the
altar. There lies Alexander the Great," continued he,
pointing to a huge sarcophagus.

" Alexander the Great?" repeated Fabiani, inquiringly.

" Yes, certainly ; is it not so?" asked he from the
attendant.

" As Excellenza says," replied he.

" That is a mistake," remarked I, observing the monument more nearly. " Alexander really cannot be buried
here, that is against all history. See only, it is the triumphal procession of Alexander, which is represented on
the sarcophagus, and thence is derived the name."

As soon as we had entered into the church, they showed
us a similar sarcophagus, upon which was delineated a
bacchanalian triumph, which had been brought hither
from the temple in Pæstum, and now had been converted
into the burial-place for a Salernian prince, whose modern
marble statue, the size of life, was raised upon it. I re-
verted to this, and gave it as my opinion, that the circumstances of this so-called grave of Alexander must be similar
to it. Quite pleased with my own penetration, I made a
sort of oration on the subject of the graves, to which Gen-

naro coldly replied, "Perhaps;" and Francesca whispered in my ear, that it was unbecoming of me, wishing to appear wiser than he; that I must not do so. Silently and respectfully I drew back.

At Ave Maria I sat alone with Francesca in the balcony of the great hotel. Fabiani and Gennaro were gone out to walk: it was my place to entertain the gracious lady.

"What a beautiful play of colours!" said I, and pointed to the sea, which, white as milk, stretched itself out from the broad lava-paved street to the rosy-hued, brilliant horizon, whilst the rocky coast was of a deep indigo blue; such a pomp of colouring I had never seen in Rome.

"The clouds have already said, ' *Felicissima notte!* '" remarked Francesca, and pointed to the mountain, where a cloud hung high above the villas and the olive-woods, and yet far below the old castle, which, with its two towers, was nearly perched on the top of the mountain.

"There I should like to dwell and live!" exclaimed I, "high above the cloud, and look out over the eternally changing sea."

"There you could improvise!" said she, smiling; "but then nobody would hear you, and that would be a great misfortune, Antonio!"

"Oh, yes!" replied I, likewise jestingly, "if I must be candid, entirely without applause, is like a tree without sunshine! That, of a certainty, gnawed into the flower of Tasso's life, in his captivity, as much as did the unhappiness of his love!"

"Dear friend!" interrupted she, somewhat gravely, "I am now speaking of you, and not of Tasso. What have we to do with him in this question?"

"Only as an example," replied I: "Tasso was a poet, and ———"

"You believe it to be so," interrupted she, hastily; "but, for Heaven's sake, dear Antonio, do not ever mention an immortal name in conjunction with your own! Do not fancy that you are a poet, an improvisatore, because you have an easily excited temperament of mind, and the art of catching up ideas! Thousands can do this as well as you! Do not go and make yourself unfortunate through it."

"But thousands only lately have awarded to me their applause!" replied I, and my cheeks burned; "and it really is quite natural that I should have these thoughts, this conviction: and I am sure that you will rejoice in my success, and in that which conduces to my well-being!"

"None of your friends would do so more than I!" said she; "we all value your excellent heart, your noble character, and for the sake of these I will venture to promise that Excellenza will forgive you! You have glorious abilities, which must be developed, but that they must actually be, Antonio! Nothing comes of itself! People must labour! Your talent is a charming company talent; you may delight many of your friends by it, but it is not great enough for the public."

"But," I ventured to suggest, "Gennaro, who did not know me, was yet enchanted with my first appearance in public."

"Gennaro!" repeated she, "yes, with all my esteem for him, I set no value at all upon his judgment of art! And the great public? Yes, in the capital, artists very soon hear quite a different opinion! It was very well that you were not hissed; that would really have distressed me. Now it will all blow quietly over, and very soon will be entirely forgotten both you and your improvisation! Then you assumed a feigned name also! In about three days we shall be again in Naples, and the day afterwards we return to Rome. Regard it all as a dream, as it really has been, and show us, by industry and stability, that you are awake again. Do not say a word, now — I intend kindly by you; I am the only one who tells you the truth!"

She gave her hand for me to kiss.

The next morning we set off in the early, grey dawn, in order that we might reach Pæstum in time to spend a few hours there, and be back again the same day in Salerno, because visitors cannot pass the night at Pæstum, and the road thither is unsafe. *Gends'armes* on horseback accompanied us as escort.

Orange-gardens, woods I might call them, lay on either hand. We passed over the river Sela, in whose clear water were reflected weeping-willows and laurel hedges. The wild hills inclosed a fertile corn-country. Aloes and cactuses grew wildly by the road-side; every thing was luxuriant and abundant, and now we saw before us the ancient temple, above two thousand years' old, built in the purest, most beautiful style; this, a miserable public-house, three wretched dwellings, and some huts of reeds, were now all that remained of this renowned city. We saw not a single rose-hedge, and the multitude and affluent beauty of the roses had once given its celebrity to Pæstum. At that time a crimson glow lay upon these fields; now they were blue, infinitely blue, like the distant mountains; fragrant violets covered the great plain, springing up amid thistles and thorns. A wilderness of fertility lay all around; aloes, wild figs, and the red *pyretrum indicum*, twined one among another.

Here are found the characteristics of Sicilian landscape; its abundance and luxuriance; its Grecian temples and its poverty. A whole crowd of beggars stood around us, who resembled the natives of the South Sea Islands. Men clad in long sheep-skins, with the wool outside, with naked, dark brown limbs, and the long black hair hanging loosely around the brown yellow countenance; girls of the most beautiful forms, only half clad, with the short skirt hanging in tatters to the knee; a sort of cloak, of ugly brown stuff, thrown loosely around the bare shoulders, and the long black hair bound together in a knot, and with eyes that flashed fire.

One young girl there was, scarcely more than eleven years old, lovely as the Goddess of Beauty, and yet resembling neither Annunciata nor Santa. I could think of nothing else but the Medicean Venus, as Annunciata had described it, as I looked at her. I could not love, but admire, and bow before the form of beauty.

She stood at a little distance from the other beggars; a brown square piece of cloth hung loosely over one shoulder, the other breast and arm were, like her feet, uncovered. That she thought of ornament, and had the taste for it, was proved by the smoothly bound-up hair, in which a bouquet of blue violets was fastened, and which hung in curls upon her beautiful forehead. Modesty, soul, and a singular, deep expression of suffering, were expressed in her countenance. Her eyes were cast down, as if she sought for something upon the ground.

Gennaro perceived her first, and, although she spoke not a word, he offered her a gift, patted her under the chin, and said that she was too handsome for the rest of her company. Fabiani and Francesca were of his opinion. I saw a fine crimson diffuse itself under the clear brown skin, and raising her eyes, I saw that she was blind.

Gladly would I, too, have given her money, but I ventured not to do it. When the others were gone to the little hostel, followed by the whole troop of beggars, I turned myself quickly round, and pressed a scudo into her hand; by the feeling she seemed to know its worth; her cheeks burned, she bent forward, and the fresh lips of health and beauty touched my hand; the touch seemed to go through my blood; I tore myself away, and followed the others.

Fagots and twigs burned in a great flaming pile in the wide chimney, which almost occupied the whole breadth of the chamber. The smoke whirled out under the sooty roof, which compelled us to go outside, and behind the tall, shadowy weeping willow our breakfast was prepared, whilst we went to the temple. We had to pass through a complete wilderness. Fabiani and Gennaro took hold of each other's hands, to make a sort of seat for Francesca, and thus carried her.

" A fearful pleasure-excursion !" cried she, laughing.

" O Excellenza ! " said one of our guides, " it is now magnificent: three years ago there was no getting through here for thorns, and in my childhood sand and earth lay right up to the pillars."

The rest affirmed to the truth of his remark, and we went forward, followed by the whole troop of beggars, who silently observed us ; the moment our eye met that of one of the beggars, he immediately stretched out his hand mechanically to beg, and a *miserabile* resounded from his lips. The beautiful blind girl I could not see ; she now, indeed, sat alone by the way-side. We went over the ruins of a theatre, and a temple of peace.

" A theatre and peace !" exclaimed Gennaro ; " how could these two ever exist so near to each other ? "

The Temple of Neptune lay before us ; this, the so-called Basilica, and the Temple of Ceres, are the glorious, proud remains which, like a Pompeii, stand forth again to our age, out of oblivion and night.

Buried amid rubbish, and entirely overgrown, they lay concealed for centuries, until a foreign painter, who sought for subjects for his pencil, came to this place, and discovered the uppermost of the pillars; their beauty attracted him ; he made a sketch of them ; they became known ; the rubbish and the wild growth of plants were removed, and again stood forth, as if rebuilded, the large, open halls. The columns are of yellow Travertine marble, wild vines grow up around them ; fig-trees shoot up from the floor, and in clefts and crevices spring forth violets and the dark-red gillyflower.

We seated ourselves upon the pedestal of one of the broken columns. Gennaro had driven the beggars away, that we might enjoy in stillness the rich scene around us. The blue mountains, the near sea, the place itself in which we were, seized strongly upon me.

" Improvise now to us ! " Fabiani said ; and Francesca nodded to me the same wish.

I leaned against one of the nearest pillars, and sang, to a melody of my childhood, that which my eye now beheld; the beauty of nature ; the glorious memorial of art ; and I thought on the poor blind maiden, from whom all magnificent objects were concealed. She was doubly poor, doubly forlorn. Tears came to my eyes : Gennaro clapped his hands in applause ; and Fabiani and Francesca said apart to each other, " He has feeling."

They now descended the steps of the temple. I followed them slowly. Behind the pillar against which I had stood sat, or rather lay, a human being, with her head sunk to her knees, and her hands clasped together: it was the blind maiden. She had heard my song — had heard me sing of her painful yearning and of her deprivations: it smote me to the soul. I bent myself over her: she heard the rustling of the leaves, raised her head, and to me it seemed that she looked much paler. I ventured not to move. She listened.

"Angela!" she exclaimed, half aloud.

I know not why, but I held my breath; and she sat for a moment silent. It was the Grecian goddess of beauty which I saw, with eyes without the power of vision, such as Annunciata had described her to me. She sat on the pedestal of the temple, between the wild fig-tree and the fragrant myrtle-fence. She pressed a something to her lips, and smiled: it was the scudo which I had given to her. I grew quite warm at the sight of it, bowed myself involuntarily, and pressed a hot kiss upon her forehead.

She started up with a cry, a thrilling cry, which sent, as it were, a death-pang through my soul. She sprung up like a terrified deer, and was gone. I saw nothing more, every thing was in motion around me, and I, too, made my escape through thorns and bushes.

"Antonio! Antonio!" I heard Fabiani calling to me a long way behind; and again I bethought myself of time and place.

"Have you started a hare?" asked he; "or was it a poetical flight which you were taking?"

"He will show us," said Gennaro, "that he can fly where we can only get along at a foot's pace; yet I would venture to take the same flight with him;" and, so saying, he placed himself at my side, to race with me.

"Do you think that I, with my Signora on my arm, can go step for step with you?" exclaimed Fabiani. Gennaro remained standing.

When we came to the little hostel, my eye in vain sought for the blind girl: her cry continually resounded in my ear: I heard it within my very heart. It was to me as if I had committed a sin. I it was really, who had, although innocently, sung care and sorrow into her heart, by making her deprivations more intelligible to her. I had excited terror and anxiety in her soul, and had impressed a kiss upon her brow, the first which I had ever given to a woman. If she could have seen me, I had not dared to do it : her misfortune — her defencelessness — had given me courage. And I had passed such severe judgment on Bernardo ! — I, who was a child of sin like him, like every one ! I could have kneeled at her feet, and prayed for forgiveness ; but she was nowhere to be seen.

We mounted the carriage to drive back to Salerno ; yet once more I looked out to see if I could discover her ; but I did not venture to inquire where she could be.

At that moment, Gennaro exclaimed, " Where is that blind girl ? "

" Lara ? " said our guide. " She still sits in the Temple of Neptune : she is generally there."

" *Bella Divina !* " cried Gennaro, and wafted a kiss with his hand towards the temple. We rolled away.

She was then called Lara. I sat with my back to the driver, and saw when the columns of the temple became yet more and more distant ; but within my heart intoned the anguish-cry of the girl, my own suffering.

A troop of gipsies had encamped themselves by the road-side, and had made a great fire in the ditch, over which they were boiling and roasting. The old gipsy mother struck upon the tambourine, and wanted to tell us our fortunes, but we drove past. Two black-eyed girls followed us for a considerable time. They were handsome : and Gennaro made himself merry about their easy motions and their flashing eyes ; but beautiful and noble as Lara were they not.

Towards evening we reached Salerno. The next morning we were to go to Amalfi, and thence to Capri.

" We shall remain," said Fabiani, " only one day in Naples, if we return there at all. Towards the end of the week we must be again in Rome. You can very soon get your things in order, Antonio ? "

I could not — I wished not, to return to Rome ; but a bashfulness, a fear, which my poverty and my gratitude had instilled into me through all the years of my life, per-

Q

mitted me to do no more than stammer forth that Excellenza certainly would be angry at my audacity in coming back again.

" We will take care of all that !" exclaimed Fabiani to me.

" Forgive me, but I cannot !" I stammered, and seized Francesca's hand. " I feel deeply that which I owe you."

" Say nothing of that, Antonio," she replied, and laid her hand upon my mouth.

Strangers at that moment were announced, and I withdrew silently into a corner, feeling how weak I was.

Free and independent as a bird had I been only two days before ! and He who permits not a sparrow to fall unheeded to the ground would have cared for me ; and yet I let the first thin thread which twined itself round my feet grow to the strength of a cable.

In Rome, thought I, thou hast true friends, true and honest, if not so courteous as those in Naples. I thought on Santa, whom I never more would see. I thought on Bernardo, whom I actually should meet in Naples every day — on Annunciata, who would come here — on his and her happiness in love. " To Rome ! to Rome ! it is much better there !" said my heart to me, whilst my soul struggled after freedom and independence.

CHAPTER VII.

THE ADVENTURE IN AMALFI. — THE BLUE GROTTO OF CAPRI.

How beautifully Salerno looked out from the sea, as, in the delicious morning hour, we sailed away from it ! Six stout fellows pulled the oars. A little boy, handsome enough to be painted, sat at the helm : he was called Alphonso. The water was green as glass. The whole coast to the right seemed like magnificent hanging gardens, laid out by the bold Semiramis of fancy. The vast open caves lay like colonnades down in the sea, within which played the heavy billows. Upon the projecting point of rock stood a castle, below whose turreted walls floated a small cloud. We saw Minori and Majori ; and, immediately afterwards, Amalfi, the birthplace of Masaniello and Flavio Giojas, the discoverer of the mariner's compass, which looked forth from amidst green vineyards.

This great affluence of beauty overpowered me. Would that all the generations of the earth could see these glorious scenes ! No storm from the north or west brings cold or winter to the blooming garden upon whose terrace Amalfi is placed. The breezes come only here from the east and the south, the warm breezes from the region of oranges and palms, across the beautiful sea.

Along the shore, high up on the side of the mountain, hangs the city, with its white houses with their flat, oriental roofs ; higher still ascend the vineyards. One solitary pine-tree lifts up its green crown into the blue air, where, on the ridge of the mountain, the old castle, with its encircling wall, serves as a couch for the clouds.

The fishermen had to carry us through the surf from the boats to the land. Deep caves in the cliffs extended even under the city ; into some of these the water flowed, others were empty. Boats lay beside them, in which played crowds of merry children, most of them only in a skirt or little jacket, which constituted their whole clothing. Half-naked lazzaroni stretched themselves in the warm sand, their brown cowls pulled up about their ears, this being their most important covering during their noonday's sleep. All the church bells were ringing ; a procession of young priests in violet-coloured dresses went past us, singing psalms. A fresh garland of flowers hung around the picture which was fastened to the cross.

To the left, high above the city, stands a magnificently great convent, just before a deep mountain-cave ; this is the *herberg* for all strangers. Francesca was carried up in a litter ; we others followed after, along the road cut in the rock, with the clear, blue sea lying deeply below us. We had now reached the gate of the convent, exactly opposite to which a deep cave gapes in the rock. Within this there were three crosses, on which were the Redeemer and

the two thieves ; and above them, upon the stone of the
rock, were kneeling angels in bright-coloured garments,
and great white wings. No artistical work this, but all
carved out of wood, and painted ; but, nevertheless, a
pious, trusting heart breathed its own peculiar beauty
over the rudely-formed images.

We ascended directly up through the convent-court to
the rooms which were appropriated to our use. From my
window I saw the eternal sea, stretching away to Sicily,
the ships standing like silver-white points upon the far
horizon.

"Sir Improvisatore," said Gennaro, "shall not we
descend into the lower regions, and see whether the beauty
there is as great as it is here ! The female beauty is so, of
a certainty ! For the English ladies that we have here for
neighbours are cold and pale ! And you have a taste for
the ladies ! I beg your pardon. It is this exactly which
has driven you out into the world, and will give me a charming evening, and an interesting acquaintance !"

We descended the rocky path.

" The blind girl in Pæstum was, however, very handsome !" said Gennaro. " I think that I shall send for
her to Naples when I send for my Calabrian wine ! Both
one and the other would set my heart in a glow !"

We arrived at the city, which lay, if I may so say, singularly piled upon itself. Beside of it, the narrow Ghetto
in Rome would have been a Corso. The streets were
narrow passages between the tall houses, and right through
them. Now one comes through a door into a long landing-
place, with small openings on the sides leading into dark
chambers, then into a narrow lane between brickwork and
walls of rock, steps up and steps down, a half-dark laby-
rinth of dirty passages : I often did not know whether it
was a room or a lane in which we were. In most places
lamps were burning ; and if it had not been so, although
it was mid-day, it would have been dark as night.

At length we breathed more freely. We stood upon a
great brickwork bridge, which connected together two
ridges of rock ; the little square below us was certainly the
largest in the whole city. Two girls were dancing there

the *saltarello,* and a little boy, entirely naked, beautifully formed, and with brown limbs, stood looking on, like a little Cupid. Here, they told me, it never freezes. The severest cold Amalfi has known for many years has been eight degrees above zero.

Close beside the little tower, upon the projecting platform of rock from which is to be seen the lovely bay of Minori and Majori, a little serpentine path winds between aloes and myrtles ; and, following it, we were soon overshadowed by the lofty arch of entwining vines. We felt a burning thirst, and hastened onwards towards a little white dwelling-house, which, at the end of the vineyard, invited us, as it were, so kindly from among the fresh green. The mild, warm air was filled with fragrance, and beautifully bright insects hummed around us.

We stood before the house, which was highly picturesque. There had been built into the wall, by way of ornament, some marble capitals, and a beautifully-chiselled arm and foot, which had been found among the rubbish. Upon the roof even was a charming garden of oranges and luxuriant twining plants, which, like a curtain of green velvet, hung down over the wall ; in the front blossomed a wilderness of monthly roses. Two lovely little girls, of from six to seven years old, played, and wore garlands ; but the most beautiful, however, was a young woman with a white linen cloth on her head, who came to meet us from the door. The intellectual glance, the long, dark eye-lashes, the noble form, yes, she was very beautiful ! We both involuntarily took off our hats.

" This most beautiful maiden, then, is the possessor of this house ? " inquired Gennaro. " Will she then, as mistress of the house, give to two weary travellers a refreshing draught ? "

" The mistress of the house will do that with pleasure ! " said she, smiling, and the snow-white teeth parted the fresh, rosy lips. " I will bring out wine to you here ; but I have only of one kind."

" If you serve it, it will be excellent !" said Gennaro. " I drink it most willingly when a young maiden as handsome as you serves it."

Q 3

"But Excellenza must be so good as to talk to a wife to-day!" said she, sweetly.

"Are you married?" asked Gennaro, smiling, "so young?"

"Oh, I am very old!" said she, and laughed also.

"How old?" inquired I.

She looked archly into my face, and replied, "Eight-and-twenty years old!" She was much nearer fifteen, but most beautifully developed; a Hebe could not have been formed more exquisitely.

"Eight-and-twenty!" said Gennaro. "A beautiful age, which is very becoming to you! Have you been long married?"

"Twenty years!" replied she; "only ask my daughters there." And the little girls whom we had seen playing came towards us.

"Is that your mother?" inquired I, although I very well knew that it was not so. They looked up to her, and laughed, nodded thereto an assent, and clung affectionately to her.

She brought us out wine, excellent wine, and we drank her health.

"This is a poet, an improvisatore," said Gennaro to her, pointing to me; "he has been turning the heads of all the ladies in Naples! But he is a stone, a queer sort of fellow. He hates all women; never gave a woman a kiss in his life!"

"That is impossible!" said she, and laughed.

"I, on the contrary," continued Gennaro, "am of quite a different sort; I kiss all the handsome lips that come near me, am the faithful attendant of woman, and thus reconcile the world and her wherever I go! It is awarded to me also, and I assert it as my right with every handsome woman, and I now, of course, require here my tribute also!" and, so saying, he took her hand.

"I absolve both you and the other gentleman," said she; "neither have I any thing to do with paying tribute. My husband always does that!"

"And where is he?" asked Gennaro.

"Not far off," she replied.

" Such a handsome hand I have never seen in Naples !"
said Gennaro ; "what is the price of a kiss upon it ?"

" A scudo," said she.

" And double that price upon the lips ? " said Gennaro.

" That is not to be had," returned she ; " that is my
husband's property !"

And now she poured us out again the enlivening, strong
wine, joked and laughed with us ; and, amid her joking,
we discovered that she was about fifteen, had been married
the year before to a handsome young man, who, at this
moment, was in Naples, and was not expected to return
before the morrow. The little girls were her sisters, and
on a visit to her till her husband's return. Gennaro
prayed them for a bouquet of roses, which they hastened
to gather, and for which he promised them a carlin.

In vain he prayed her for a kiss ; said a thousand
sweet, flattering things ; threw his arm round her waist ;
she tore herself away, scolding him, but yet always came
back again, because she found it amusing. He took a
louis-d'or between his fingers, and told her what charming
ribands she could buy with it, and how beautifully she
might adorn her dark hair with them ; and all this splendour she might have only by giving him a kiss — one
single kiss.

" The other Excellenza is much better !" said she, and
pointed to me. My blood burned ; I took her hand,
saying that she must not listen to him, that he was a bad
man, must not look at his tempting gold, but must revenge
herself upon him by giving *me* a kiss.

She looked at me.

" He has," continued I, " said only one true word in
all his speeches ; and that is, that I have never kissed the
lips of any woman. I have kept my lips pure until I
found the most beautiful ; and now I hope that you will
reward my virtue !"

" He is actually an accomplished tempter !" said Gennaro. " He excels me by being so accustomed to his
work."

" You are a bad man with your money," said she ;

Q 4

" and for that you shall see that I care neither for it nor for a kiss, and so the poet shall have it!"

With this, she pressed her hands on my cheeks, her lips touched mine, and she vanished behind the house.

When the sun went down, I sat up in my little chamber in the convent, and looked from the window over the sea; it was rosy red, and threw up long billows on the shore. The fishermen pulled up their boats on the sand; and, as the darkness increased, the lights became brighter, the billows were of a sulphur-blue. Over every thing prevailed infinite stillness; in the midst of which I heard a choral song of fishermen on the shore, with women and children. The soprano of the children's voices mingled itself with the deep bass, and a sentiment of melancholy filled my soul. A falling star for a moment played in the heavens, and then shot downward behind the vineyards, where the lively young woman had kissed me in the day-time. I thought of her, how lovely she was, and of the blind girl, the image of beauty, amid the ruins of the temple; but Annunciata stood in the background, intellectually and physically beautiful, and thus doubly beautiful! My spirit expanded itself; my soul burned with love, with longing, with a deep sense of what it had lost. The pure flame which Annunciata had kindled in my heart, the altar-fire of which she was the priestess, she had herself stirred out and left; the fire now burned wildly through the whole building.

" Eternal Mother of God!" prayed I; " my breast is full of love, my heart is ready to burst with longing and regret!" And I seized upon the roses which stood in the glass, pressed the most beautiful of them to my lips, and thought on Annunciata.

I could not bear it any longer, and went down to the sea-side, where the shining billows broke along the shore, where the fishermen sang and the wind blew. I mounted the brickwork bridge, where I had stood during the day. A figure wrapped in a large cloak stole close by me; I saw that it was Gennaro. He went up the serpentine road to the little white house, and I followed him. He now softly passed the window, within which a light was burning. Here I took my station, concealed by the depending vine-leaves, and could see distinctly into the room. There was, exactly on the other side of the house, a similar window, and some high steps led to the side-chamber.

The two little girls, undressed to their night-clothes, were kneeling with their elder sister, the mistress of the house, as she really was, between them, before the table, on which stood the crucifix and the lamp, and were singing their evening devotions. It was the Madonna with two angels, a living altar-piece, as if painted by Raphael, which I saw before me. Her dark eyes were cast upwards; the hair hung in rich folds upon her naked shoulders, and the hands were folded upon the youthfully beautiful bosom.

My pulse beat more quickly; I scarcely ventured to breathe. Now all three arose from their knees; she went with the little girls up the steps into the side-room, closed the door, and then went into the first room, where she busied herself about her small household affairs. I saw her presently take out of a drawer a red pocket-book, turn it about in her hand a many times, and smile; she was just about to open it, but shook her head at that moment, and threw it again into the drawer, as if something had surprised her.

A moment afterwards I heard a low tapping upon the opposite window. Terrified, she looked towards it, and listened. It tapped again, and I heard some one speak, but could not distinguish the words.

" Excellenza !" now exclaimed she aloud; " what do you want? Why do you come here at this hour? For Heaven's sake ! I am angry, very angry."

He again said something.

" Yes, yes, it is true," she said, " you have forgotten your pocket-book; my little sister has been down to the inn to give it to you, but you were up in the convent. To-morrow morning she would have gone there to you. Here it is."

She took it from the drawer. He again said something, to which she shook her head.

"No! no!" said she; "what are you thinking of? I shall not open the door; you shall not come in!"

"So saying, she went to the window, and opened it, to give him the pocket-book. He snatched at her hand, she let the book fall, and it remained lying on the window-sill. Gennaro put his head in; the young wife flew to the window behind which I stood, and I could now hear every word which Gennaro said.

"And you will not allow me to kiss your lovely hand as thanks; not receive the smallest reward; not reach me a single cup of wine? I am parched with thirst. There cannot be any thing wrong in that! Why not permit me to come in?"

"No!" said she; "we have nothing to talk about at this hour. Take that which you have forgotten, and let me close the window."

"I will not go," said Gennaro, "before you give me your hand, before you give me a kiss. You cheated me out of one to-day, and gave it to that stupid youth!"

"No! no!" said she, and yet laughed in the midst of her anger. "You want to obtain by force what I would not give freely," said she; "therefore I shall not — will not do it."

"It is the last time," said Gennaro, in a soft and beseeching tone, "of a certainty the last time; and can you refuse only just giving me your hand? More I do not desire, although my heart has a thousand things to say to you! Madonna wills it really that we human beings love one another like brother and sister! Like a brother I will divide my money with you; you can adorn yourself, and be twice as handsome as you are! All your friends will envy you; nobody will know." And with these words he gave a quick spring, and stood within the room.

She uttered a loud scream, "Jesus Maria!"

I shook the window violently where I stood; the glass jingled, and, as if driven by an invisible power, I flew round to the open window, tearing away a support from one of the vine-trellises, that I might have with me some kind of weapon.

"Is it thou, Nicolo?" cried she loudly.

" It is I ! " replied I, in a deep, resolute voice.

I saw Gennaro again fly out of the window, his cloak streaming in the wind. The lamp was knocked out, and it remained quite dark in the room.

" Nicolo ! " she cried from the window, and her voice trembled. " Thou here again ! Madonna be praised ! "

" Signora ! " stammered I.

" All ye saints ! " I heard her say, and shut too the window with all haste. I stood there as if riveted to the spot. After some moments, I heard her go softly across the floor. The door of the side-chamber was opened and then closed again ; I heard her knocking something, as if she were making bolts secure.

" Now she is safe," thought I, and crept softly away. I felt myself so well, so wonderfully gay at heart. " Now I have paid for the kiss which she gave me to-day," said I to myself; " perhaps she would have given me yet another, had she known what a protecting angel I have been to her ! "

I reached the convent exactly as supper was ready ; no one had missed me. Gennaro, however, did not make his appearance, and Francesca became uneasy. Fabiani sent messenger on messenger. At length he came. He had walked, he said, as far as the mountains, and had lost himself, but had had the luck to meet at length with a peasant, who had put him in the right way.

" Your coat is, also, quite in tatters," said Francesca.

" Yes," said Gennaro, taking up the laps, " the missing piece hangs on a thorn-bush ; I saw it, however ! Heaven knows how I could ever lose my way so ! But it was all the lovely evening, and then the darkness came on so quickly, and I thought of shortening my way, and pre- cisely by that means lost it ! "

We laughed at his adventure ; I knew it better ; we drank to his health ; the wine was excellent ; we became regularly excited. When we at length went to our cham- bers, which were only divided by a door from each other, he came before he undressed into mine, laughed, and, laying his hand upon my shoulder, prayed me not to dream too much about the handsome woman that we had seen to-day.

" But I had the kiss!" said I, jestingly.

" Oh, yes, that you had!" said he, laughing, " and do you think, therefore, that I came off with the step-child's portion ? "

" Yes, so I think !" returned I.

" Step-child, however, I never should remain," said he, in a cold tone, in which was a certain degree of bitterness ; but a faint smile played again around his mouth as he whispered, " if you could keep your counsel, I could tell you something ? "

" Tell me," said I, " nobody shall hear a syllable from me ? " I expected now to hear his lamentations over his unfortunate adventure ; his secret was this : —

" I forgot, to-day, intentionally, my pocket-book, at the handsome woman's house, that I might have an excuse for going there in the evening, for then women are not so strict. There it is : I have been there, and with climbing over the garden-wall and up among the bushes I tore ·my coat."

" And the handsome woman ? " I inquired.

" Was twice as handsome !" said he, nodding significantly, — " twice as handsome, and not a bit stern ; we were quite good friends, that I know. She gave you one kiss — she gave me a thousand, and her heart into the bargain. I shall dream about my good luck all the night. Poor Antonio !"

And, so saying, he kissed his hand to me and went to his own room.

The morning heaven was covered as if with a grey veil, when we left the convent. Our stout rowers waited for us on the shore, and again carried us to our boat. Our voyage was now to Capri. The veil of heaven was rent asunder into light clouds ; the air became twofold high and clear ; not a billow moved ; the soft curling of the sea was like a watered ribbon. The beautiful Amalfi vanished behind the cliffs ; Gennaro threw a kiss towards it whilst he said to me, " There we have plucked roses !"

" You, at all events, got among the thorns !" thought I, and nodded assentingly.

The great, infinite sea, stretching on to Sicily and Africa, spread itself before us. To the left lay the rocky coast of Italy, with its singular caves; before some of these stood little cities, which seemed as if they had stepped out of the caves; in others sat fishermen, and cooked their meals and tarred their boats behind the high surf.

The sea seemed to be a fat, blue oil; we put our hands down into it, and they appeared as blue as it. The shadow which the boat threw upon the water was of the purest dark blue, the shadows of the oars a moving snake of every shade of blue.

"Glorious sea!" exclaimed I, in delight, "nothing in all nature, with the exception of Heaven, is so beautiful as thou!"

I called to mind how often I, as a child, had lain upon my back, and dreamed myself up into the blue infinite air; now my dream seemed to have become a reality.

We passed by three small rocky islands, *Il Galli;* they were immense blocks of stone thrown one upon another; giant-towers raised up out of the deep, with others, again, piled upon them. The blue billows dashed up upon these green masses of stone. In storm it must be a Scylla, with her howling dogs.

The surface of the water slumbered around the naked stony Cape Minerva, where in old times the Syrens had their abode. Before us lay the romantic Capri, where Tiberius had luxuriated in joy, and looked over the bay to the coast of Naples. The sail was spread in our boat; and, borne onward by the wind and the waves, we approached the island. Now, for the first time, we remarked the extraordinary purity and clearness of the water. It was as wonderfully transparent as if it had been air. We glided along, every stone, every reed, for many fathoms below us, being visible. I became dizzy when I looked down from the edge of our little boat into the depth over which we were passing.

The island of Capri is approachable only from one side. Around it ascend steep, perpendicular walls of cliff; towards Naples they stretch out, amphitheatre-like, with vineyards, orange and olive-groves; upon the shore stand several cottages of fishermen and a watchhouse; higher up, amid the green gardens, looks the little city of Anna Capri, into which a very small draw-bridge and gates conduct the stranger. We betook ourselves to the small inn of Pagani, where tall palm-trees stand against the door, to rest ourselves.

After dinner we were to ride up on asses to the ruins of Tiberius's Villa, but now, however, we waited for our breakfast, and between that and the following meal Francesca and Fabiani wished to repose themselves, in order to have strength for the afternoon's walk. Gennaro and I felt no necessity for this. The island did not appear so large to me, but that in a few hours we could row round it, and see the lofty portals of rock which, towards the south, rear themselves isolatedly out of the sea.

We took a boat and two rowers; the wind blew a little, so that for half the distance we could make use of the sail. The sea was broken on the low reef. Fishing-nets lay outspread among them, so that we were obliged to go a considerable distance from them; it was a beautiful, merry sail in that little boat! Before long we saw only the perpendicular cliffs ascending from the sea up towards heaven; in the crevices of which, however, here and there sprang up an aloe, or gillyflower, yet with no footing even for the mountain-goat. Below the surf, which flew up like blue fire, grew upon the rocks the blood-red sea-apple, which, wetted by the waves, seemed to have a doubly bright hue; it was as if the rocks bled at every stroke of the billows.

The open sea now lay to the right of us, to the left of us lay the island; deep caves, whose uppermost openings lay but a little above the water, showed themselves in the cliffs, others were only dimly visible in the surf. Down amid these abode the Syrens; the blooming Capri, upon which we had climbed, being only the roof of their rock-fortress.

"Yes, bad spirits live here," said one of the rowers, an old man with silver-white hair. "It may be beautiful, down there," said he; "but they never let their victims escape, and, if by any chance one does come back, he has no longer any understanding for this world!"

He now showed us at some distance an opening, somewhat larger than the others, but yet not large enough for our boat to enter, without a sail, even if we had lain down in it, either for length or breadth.

"That is the Witches' Cave!"* whispered the younger rower, and pushed out further from the rocks; "within, all is gold and diamonds, but any one who goes in there is burned up in a fiery flame! Santa Lucia, pray for us!"

"I wish I had one of the Syrens here in the boat!" said Gennaro; "but she must be beautiful, then all would be right."

"Your luck with the ladies," said I, laughing, "would avail you, then, here also!"

"Upon the swelling sea is the right place for kissing and embracing; that is what the waves are always at! Ah!" sighed he, "if we had but here the handsome woman from Amalfi! That was a woman! was not she? You sipped of the nectar of her lips! Poor Antonio! You should have seen her last evening! She *was* gracious to me!"

"Nay, nay," said I, half indignant at his unabashed boasting, "it is not so; I know better than that!"

"How am I to understand that?" asked he, and looked with much astonishment into my face.

"I saw it myself," continued I; "chance led me there; I doubt not of your great good fortune in other cases; but this time you only wish to joke with me."

---

* This is the name given by the inhabitants of Capri to the Blue Grotto, which was only properly explored in 1831 by two young Germans, Fries and Kopisch, and since then has become the goal of every traveller who visits South Italy. Kopisch was born in Breslau, and is the author of a beautiful novel called " Die Kahlköpfe auf Capri ; " in 1837 his poems were published. — *Author's Note.*

Ernst Fries was a landscape-painter of extraordinary promise, the son of Mr. Fries, the well-known and hospitable banker of Heidelberg. Ernst Fries spent many years in Italy, and his finest pieces are scenes from that beautiful country. He died suddenly, while yet quite young, at Carlsruhe, and lies buried under a beautiful monument in one of the burial-grounds in Heidelberg. In memory of him, his fellow-townspeople have laid out a fine public walk, leading from the splendid ruins of their celebrated castle round the hill to the very ancient site of the Roman Castle. A graceful and beautiful mark of respect to the memory of one who would so truly have enjoyed the luxury of its exquiiste scenery. The road bears the name of the "Friesen Weg," in honour of him. — *Translator's Note.*

He looked at me in silence.

" ' I will not go,' " said I, laughing, and imitating Gennaro, " ' before you give me the kiss which you cheated me out of, and gave it to that foolish youth ! ' "

" Signore ! you have listened to me ! " said he, gravely, and I saw that his countenance became quite pale : " How dare you affront me ? You shall fight with me, or I despise you ! "

This was an effect which I did not anticipate that my remarks would have produced.

" Gennaro, this is not your serious meaning," exclaimed I, and took his hand ; he drew it back, made me no reply, but desired the sailors to make for the land.

" Yes, we must sail round the island," said the old man, " we can only land where we set out from."

They bent to their oars, and we speedily approached the lofty arch of rock in the blue swelling water ; but anger and vexation agitated my mind ; I looked at Gennaro, who lashed the water with his stick.

" *Una tromba !* " exclaimed the youngest of the seamen ; and across the sea from Cape Minerva came floating a coal-black cloud-pillar in an oblique direction from the sea towards heaven, the water boiling around it ; with all speed they took down the sail.

" Where are you steering to ? " inquired Gennaro.

" Back again, back again," said the younger rower.

" Around the whole island again ? " inquired I.

" Close under land ; close to the rocky wall ; the water-spout takes a direction farther out."

" The surf will draw the boat in among the rocks," said the old man, and hurriedly snatched at the oars.

" Eternal God ! " stammered I, for the black cloud-pillar came with the speed of the wind across the water, as if it would sweep along the rocky wall of Capri, in the neighbourhood of which we were, and, if it came, it would either whirl us up with it, or force us down into the deep close by the perpendicular rocky coast. I seized upon the oar with the old man, and Gennaro assisted the younger ; but we already heard the winds howling, and the waters boiled before the feet of the water-spout, which drove us, as it were, before it.

"Santa Lucia, save us ! " cried both the seamen, flinging down their oars, and falling on their knees.

" Snatch hold on the oar," cried Gennaro to me, but looked towards heaven pale as death.

Then rushed the tempest over our heads ; and to the left, not far from us, went the dark night over the waves, which lifted themselves up in the air, and then struck white with foam upon the boat. The atmosphere pressed heavily upon us, as if it would force the blood out of the eyes ; it became night, the night of death. I was conscious but of one thing, and that was, that the sea lay upon me ; that I, that we all, were the prey of the sea, of death ; and further I was conscious of nothing.

More terrible than the might of the volcano ; overpowering as the separation from Annunciata, stands the sight before me which met my eyes, when they again opened to consciousness. Far below me, above me, and around me, was blue ether. I moved my arm, and, like electric sparks of fire, millions of falling stars glittered around me. I was carried along by the current of air. I was certainly dead, I thought, and now was floated through ethereal space up to the heaven of God ; yet a heavy weight lay on my head, and that was my earthly sin, which bowed me down : the current of air passed over my head, and it was like the cold sea. I mechanically put out my hands to grasp whatever might be near me : I felt a solid substance, and clung firmly to it. A weariness, as of death, went through my whole being ; I felt that I had neither life nor strength within me ; my corpse rested certainly within the depths of the sea, it was my soul which now ascended to its fate.

" Annunciata!" sighed I. My eyes again opened. This swoon must certainly have lasted a long time. I breathed again ; I felt that I was stronger, and that my perception was distinct. I lay upon a cold, hard mass, as if on a point of rock, aloft in the infinitely blue ether, which was lighted up around me. Above me vaulted itself the heavens with singular ball-shaded clouds, blue as itself ; all was at rest, infinitely quiet. I felt, however, an icy coldness through my whole being ; I slowly raised my hand.

My clothing was of blue fire ; my hands shone like silver, and yet I felt that they were my bodily hands. My mind constrained itself to action ; did I belong to death or to life? I extended my hand down into the strangely shining air below me ; it was water into which I thrust it, blue, like burning spirit, but cold as the sea. Close beside me stood a column, unshapely and tall, of a sparkling blue, and like the water-spout upon the sea, only of a smaller size. Was it my terror or my remembrance which presented to me this image? After some moments I ventured to touch it; it was as hard as stone, and as cold as it also ; I stretched out my hands into the half-dark space behind me, and felt only hard, smooth wall, but dark-blue, as the night-heavens.

Where was I? Was that below me, which I had taken for air, a shining sea, which burned of a sulphurous blue, but without heat; was the illumined space around me this, or was it light-diffusing walls of rock, and arches high above me? Was it the abode of death, the cell of the grave for my immortal spirit? An earthly habitation it certainly was not. Every object was illumined in every shade of blue ; I myself was enwrapped in a glory which gave out light.

Close beside me was an immense flight of steps which seemed to be made of vast sapphires, every step being a gigantic block of this sparkling stone ; I ascended these, but a wall of rock forbade all further advance. Perhaps I was unworthy to approach any nearer to heaven. I had left the world, burdened with the wrath of a human being. Where was Gennaro? Where were the two seamen? I was alone, quite alone. I thought of my mother, of Domenica, of Francesca, of every'one ; I felt that my fancy created no deception ; the glory which I beheld was, like myself, either spiritual or physical.

In a crevice of the cliff, I saw an object standing ; I touched it. It was a large and heavy copper cup, which was full of gold and silver coins ; I felt the individual pieces, and my situation appeared to me stranger than before. Close to the surface of the water, and not far from where I stood, I saw a clear blue star, which cast a single, long ray of light, pure as ether, over the mirror of the water, and, while I yet looked at it, I saw it darken itself like the moon; a black object showed itself, and a little boat glided onward over the burning blue water. It was as if it had ascended out of the deep, and then floated upon its surface; an old man slowly rowed it forward, and the water shone red as crimson at every stroke of his oars. In the other part of the boat sat also a human figure, a girl, as I soon could see. Silent, immovable as images of stone, they sat, excepting that the old man worked the oars. A strangely deep sigh reached my ear: it seemed to me that I recognised the sound. They rowed round in a circle, and approached the place where I stood. The old man laid his oars in the boat; the girl raised her hand on high, and exclaimed in a voice of deep suffering, " Mother of God, forsake me not ! Here am I indeed, as thou hast said."

" Lara !" I cried aloud.

It was she; I knew the voice; I recognised the form; it was Lara, the blind girl, from the ruined temple in Pæstum.

" Give me my eyesight ! Let me behold God's beautiful world!" said she.

It was as if the dead had spoken; my very soul trembled. She demanded now from me the beauty of the world, after which I, by my song, had breathed into her soul deep longings.

" Give me——" stammered her lips, and she sank back into the boat, and the water splashed like fire-drops around it.

For a moment the old man bent himself over her, and then came out to where I stood. His glance rested upon me; I saw him make the sign of the cross in the air, take up the heavy copper vessel, which he placed in the boat, and then entered himself. I instinctively followed after him. His singularly dark glance was fixed immovably upon me; he now snatched up the oars, and we floated on towards the shining star. A cold current of air rushed towards us; I bent myself over Lara. A narrow opening of rock now shut us in, but only for a moment, and then the sea, the great sea, in its infinite expanse, lay before us, and behind us reared itself up to heaven the perpendicular cliff. It was a little, dark opening through which we had come; close beside us was a low flat, overgrown with scattered bushes and dark red flowers. The new moon shone wonderfully clearly.

Lara raised herself up. I ventured not to touch her hand; she was a spirit, I believed. The whole were spirits; no dream images of my fancy.

"Give me the herbs!" said she, and stretched out her hand. I felt that I must obey the voice of the spirit. I saw the red flowers growing upon the green bushes on the low flat under the high cliffs. I stepped out of the boat, gathered the flowers, which had a very peculiar smell: I offered them to her. A weariness, as of death, went through my limbs, and I sank down on my knee, but not without perceiving that the old man made the sign of the cross, took from me the flowers, and then lifted Lara into a large boat which lay just by: the lesser one remained fastened to the shore. The sail was spread, and they sailed away over the sea.

I stretched my hands after them, but death lay as heavily on my heart as if it were about to break.

"He lives!" were the first words which I again heard. I opened my eyes, and saw Fabiani and Francesca, who stood with yet a third person, a stranger, beside me; he held my hand, and looked gravely and thoughtfully into my face. I was lying in a large, handsome room: it was day. Where was I? Fever burned in my blood, and only slowly and by degrees I became aware how I had come there, and how I had been saved.

When Gennaro and I did not return, they had become very uneasy about us; neither could any tidings be gained of the men who went with us; and, as a water-spout had been seen to pass southward round the coast, our fate became decided. Two fishing-boats were immediately sent out to make the circuit of the island, so that they might meet each other; but not a trace either of us or our boat could they discover. Francesca had wept; she was very kind to me; she lamented with pain the deaths of Gennaro and the two seamen. Fabiani would not be satisfied without himself going out to search: he resolved to examine every little crevice of the rocks, to see whether some of us might not have saved ourselves by swimming, and might perhaps be even then enduring the most horrible of deaths — that of distress and hunger ; for from not one single place was it possible to climb up to human beings. In the early morning, therefore, he had gone out with four strong rowers, had visited the isolated rocky portals of the sea, and every individual chasm of rock. The rowers were unwilling to approach the terrific Witch's Cave, but Fabiani commanded them to steer there towards the little green flat. As he approached the place, he saw, at no great distance, a human being lying outstretched: it was myself. I lay like a corpse among the green bushes : my dress was half dried by the winds ; they took me into the boat ; he covered me with his cloak, rubbed my hands and my breast; and perceived that I breathed faintly. They made for land, and, under the care of the physician, I was again among the number of the living. Gennaro and the two seamen were nowhere to be found.

They made me tell them all that I could remember; and I told them of the singularly beaming cave in which I had awoke, of the boat with the old fisherman and the blind girl, and they said it was my imagination, a feverish dream in the night air : even I myself felt as if I ought to think so; and yet I could not, it stood all so livingly before my soul.

" Was he then found by the Witch's Cave ?" inquired the physician, and shook his head.

" You do not, then, believe that this place has a more potent influence than any other ?" asked Fabiani.

. " Nature is a chain of riddles," said the physician ; " we have only found out the easiest."

It became day in my soul. The Witch's Cave, that world of which our seamen had spoken, where all was gleaming fire and beams ! Had the sea, then, borne me in there ? I remembered the narrow opening through which I had sailed out of it. Was it reality, or a dream ? Had I looked into a spiritual world ? The mercy of the Madonna had saved and protected me. My thoughts dreamed themselves back again into the beamingly beautiful hall where my protecting angel was called Lara.

In truth, the whole was no dream. I had seen that which not until some years afterwards had been discovered, and now is the most beautiful object in Capri, nay, in Italy, the Grotta Azzurra. The female form was really the blind girl from Pæstum. But how could I believe it?—how imagine it to be so? It was, indeed, very strange. I folded my hands, and thought upon my guardian angel.

CHAPTER VIII.

JOURNEY HOME.

FRANCESCA and Fabiani remained yet two days in Capri, that we might be able to make the journey back to Naples together. If I had formerly been many times wounded by their mode of speaking to me, and their treatment of me, I now received so much affection from them, and they had showed so much solicitude about me, that I clung to them with my whole heart.

"Thou must go with us to Rome," they said; "that is the most rational and the best thing for thee."

My singular deliverance, the wonderful appearance in the cave, operated greatly on my excited state of mind. I felt myself so wholly in the hand of the invisible guide who lovingly directs all for the best, that I now regarded all chances as in the ruling of Providence, and was resigned; and, therefore, when Francesca kindly pressed my hand, and asked me whether I had a desire to live in Naples with Bernardo, I assured her that I must and would go to Rome.

"We should have shed a many tears for thee, Antonio," said Francesca, and pressed my hand; "thou art our good child. Madonna has held her protecting hand over thee."

" Excellenza shall know," said Fabiani, " that the Antonio with whom he was angry is drowned in the Mediterranean, and that we are bringing back home with us the old excellent Antonio ! "

" Poor Gennaro ! " sighed Francesca then ; " he possessed a noble heart, life, and spirit. In every thing he was an example ! "

The physician sat beside me for many hours : he was properly from Naples, and was only on a visit in Capri. On the third day he accompanied us back. He said that I was perfectly well, bodily at least, though not spiritually. I had looked into the kingdom of death — had felt the kiss of the angel of death upon my brow. The mimosa of youth had folded together its leaves.

When we were seated in the boat, with the physician in company, and I saw the clear, transparent water, all the recollections of the past crowded themselves upon my soul, and I thought how near I had been to death, and how wonderfully I had been saved. The sun shone warmly upon the glorious, blue sea. I felt that life was still so beautiful, and tears rushed to my eyes. All my three companions occupied themselves alone with me, nay, Francesca herself talked of my beautiful talent — called me a poet ; and when the physician heard that it was I who had improvised, he told what delight I had given to all his friends, and how transported they had been with me.

The wind was in our favour, and instead of sailing direct to Sorrento, as had at first been determined, and of going from thence over land to Naples, we now sailed directly up to the capital. In my lodging I found three letters, one from Federigo ; he had again set off to Ischia, and would not return for three days ; this distressed me, for thus I should not be able to bid him farewell, because our departure was fixed for the noon of the following day. The second letter, the waiter told me, had been brought the morning after I had set out ; I opened it and read : —

" A faithful heart, which intends honourably and kindly towards you, expects you this evening." Then was given the house and the number, but no name, only the words, " Your old friend."

The third letter was from the same hand, and contained : —

" Come, Antonio !' The terror of the last unfortunate moment of our parting is now well over. Come quickly ! — regard it as a misunderstanding. All may be right ; only delay not a moment in coming ! " — the same signature as before.

That these were from Santa was to me sufficiently evident ; although she had chosen another house than hers for our meeting. I resolved not to see her again ; wrote in haste a few polite words to her husband, that I was leaving Naples, that the hurry in which our arrangements were made forbade me to pay him a farewell visit. I thanked him for his and his Signora's politeness to me, and besought them not to forget me. For Federigo I wrote, also, a little note ; promised him a regularly long letter from Rome, because I was not now in a condition to write.

I went out nowhere, for I wished not to meet Bernardo, and saw none of my new friends. The only person whom I visited was the physician, and I drove to his house with Fabiani. His was a charming and friendly home : his eldest sister, an unmarried lady, kept his house. There was a something so affectionate, something so truthful, about her, that I was immediately taken with her. I could not help thinking of old Domenica, only that she was accomplished, was possessed of talents and higher perfections.

The next morning, the last which I was to spend in Naples, my eye dwelt, with a melancholy sentiment, upon Vesuvius, which I now saw for the last time ; but thick clouds enveloped the top of the mountain, which seemed as if it would not say to me farewell.

The sea was perfectly tranquil. I thought upon my dream-pictures — Lara in the glittering grotto — and soon would all my whole residence here in Naples be like a dream ! I took up the paper *Diario di Napoli*, which the waiter brought in : I saw my own name in it, and a critique on my first appearance. Full of curiosity, I read it : my rich fancy and my beautiful versification were in particular most highly praised. It is said that I seemed to be of the

school of Pangetti, only that I had a little too much followed my master. I knew nothing at all about this Pangetti, that was certain ; and, therefore, could not have
formed myself upon this model. Nature and my own
feelings had alone been my guides. But the greatest
number of critics are so little original themselves, that
they believe, that all whom they pass judgment upon must
have some model to copy. The public had awarded me a
greater applause than this ; although the critic said that in
time I should become a master, and that I was now already
possessed of uncommon talent, rich imagination, feeling,
and inspiration. I folded together the paper, and resolved
to keep it : it would some time be a token to me, that all
this which I had lived through here was not a dream. I
had seen Naples, had moved about in it, had won and had
lost much. Was Fulvia's brilliant prophecy all come to
an end ?

We left Naples ; the lofty vineyards disappeared from
our sight. In four days we made the journey back to
Rome ; the same way which, about two months before,
I had travelled with Federigo and Santa. I saw again
Mola di Gaæta and its gardens of oranges : the trees were
now fragrant with blossoms. I went into the path where
Santa had sat and heard my life's adventure : how many
important circumstances had since that time knit themselves to it ! We drove through the dirty Itri, and I
thought upon Federigo. At the frontiers where our passports were given up for inspection, some goats yet stood
in the cave of the rock as he had painted them ; but the
little boy I saw not. We passed the night at Terracina.

The next morning, the atmosphere was infinitely clear.
I said my farewell to the sea, which had pressed me in its
arms, had lulled me into the most beautiful dream, and
had shown me Lara, my image of beauty. In the far distance I yet perceived, on the clear horizon, Vesuvius, with
its pale blue pillar of smoke : the whole was as if breathed
in air upon the brilliant firmament.

"Farewell! farewell! away to Rome, where stands my
grave !" sighed I ; and the carriage bowled us away, over
the green marshes, to Velletri. I greeted the mountains

where I had gone with Fulvia: I saw again Genzano, drove over the very spot where my mother had been killed; where I, as a child, had lost my all in this world. And here I now came, like an educated gentleman; beggars called me Excellenza, as I looked out into the street. Was I now really happier than I had been at that former time?

We drove through Albano: the Campagna lay before us. We saw the tomb of Ascanius, with its thick ivy, by the wayside; farther on, the monuments, the long aqueduct, and now Rome, with the cupola of St. Peter's.

"A cheerful countenance, Antonio," said Fabiani, as we rolled in at the Porta San Giovanni. The Lateran Church, the tall Obelisk, the Coliseum, and Trajan's Square, all told me that I was at home. Like a dream of the night, and yet like a whole year of my life, floated before me the circumstances of the last few weeks. How dull and dead was every thing here, in comparison with Naples! The long Corso was no Toledo street. I saw again well-known countenances around me. Habbas Dahdah went tripping past, and saluted us, as he recognised the carriage. In the corner of the Via Condotti sat Peppo, with his wooden clogs upon his hands.

"Now we are at home," said Francesca.

"Yes, home!" repeated I; and a thousand emotions agitated my breast. In a few moments, I should stand, like a schoolboy, before Excellenza. I shrunk from the meeting; and yet it seemed to me that the horses did not fly fast enough.

We drew up at the Palazzo Borghese.

Two small rooms, in the highest story, were appropriated to me. But I had not yet seen Excellenza. We were now summoned to table. I bowed deeply before him.

"Antonio can sit between me and Francesca," were the first words which I heard him say.

The conversation was easy and natural. Every moment I expected that a bitter remark would be aimed at me; but not a word, not the least reference, was made to my having been away, or to Excellenza having been displeased with me, as his letter had said.

This gentleness affected me. I doubly prized the affection which met me thus; and yet there were times when my pride felt itself wounded, because — I had met with no reproof.

CHAPTER IX.

THE EDUCATION. — THE YOUNG ABBESS.

THE Palazzo Borghese was now my home. I was treated with much more mildness and kindness. Sometimes, however, the old teaching tone, the wounding, depreciating mode of treating me, returned; but I knew that it was intended for my good.

During the hottest months, they left Rome, and I was alone in the great palace: towards winter they returned, and the old results were again produced. They seemed to forget, in the mean time, that I had become older, that I was no longer a child in the Campagna, who regarded every word which was spoken as an article of faith; or a scholar from the Jesuits' school, who continually and continually must be educated.

Like a mighty sea, where billow is knit to billow, lies an interval of six years before me. I had swum over it: God be praised! Thou who hast followed me through my life's adventures, fly rapidly after me. The impression of the whole I will give thee in a few touches. It was the combat of my spiritual education; the journeyman treated as an apprentice, before he could come forth as a master.

I was considered as an excellent young man of talent, out of whom something might be made; and, therefore, every one took upon himself my education. My dependence permitted it to those with whom I stood connected; my good nature permitted it to all the rest. Livingly and deeply did I feel the bitterness of my position, and yet I endured it. That was an education.

Excellenza lamented over my want of the fundamental principles of knowledge : it mattered not how much soever I might read : it was nothing but the sweet honey, which was to serve for my trade, which I sucked out of books. The friends of the house, as well as of my patrons, kept comparing me with the ideal in their own minds, and thus I could not do other than fall short. The mathematician said that I had too much imagination, and too little reflection : the pedant, that I had not sufficiently occupied myself with the Latin language. The politician always asked me, in the social circle, about the political news, in which I was not at home, and inquired, only to show my want of knowledge. A young nobleman, who only lived for his horse, lamented over my small experience in horseflesh, and united with others in a *Miserere* over me, because I had more interest in myself than in his horse. A noble lady-friend of the house, who, on account of her rank and great self-sufficiency, had gained the reputation of great wisdom and critical acumen, but who had actually very little of the sense she pretended to, requested that she might go through my poems, with reference to their beauty and structure ; but she must have them copied out on loose papers. Habbas Dahdah considered me as a person whose talent had, at one time, promised great things ; but which had now died out. The first dancer in the city despised me, because I could not make a figure in the ball-room ; the grammarian, because I made use of a full stop where he placed a semicolon ; and Francesca said, *that I was quite spoiled, because people made so much of me ;* and for that reason she must be severe, and give me the benefit of her instruction. Every one cast his poison-drop upon my heart : I felt that it must either bleed, or become callous.

The beautiful and the noble in every thing seized upon and attracted me. In tranquil moments I often thought on my educators, and it seemed to me that they existed in the whole of nature, and the life of the world for which my thoughts and my soul only existed as active artisans. The world even seemed to me a beautiful girl, whose form, mind, and dress had attracted my whole attention; but the shoemaker said, " Look only at her shoes; they are quite preferable; they are the principal thing!" The dressmaker exclaimed, "No, the dress; see, what a cut! that, above all, must occupy you; go into the colour, the hems, study the very principles of it!" " No," cries the hair-dresser, " you must analyse this plait; you must devote yourself to it!" " The speech is of much more importance!" exclaims the language-master. " No, the carriage!" says the dancing master. " Ah, good Heavens!" I sigh, " it is the whole together which attracts me. I see only the beautiful in every thing; but I cannot become a dress-maker or a shoemaker just for your pleasure. My business is to exalt the beauty of the whole. Ye good men and women, do not, therefore, be angry and condemn me."

" It is too low for him!" " It is not high enough for his poetical spirit!" said they all, deridingly.

No beast is, however, so cruel as man! Had I been rich and independent, the colours of every thing would soon have changed. Every one of them was more prudent, more deeply grounded, and more rational, than I. I learned to smile obligingly where I could have wept; bowed to those whom I lightly esteemed, and listened attentively to the empty gossip of fools. Dissimulation, bitterness, and *ennui,* were the fruit of the education which circumstances and men afforded me. People pointed always to my faults. Was there then nothing at all intellectual, no good points in me? It was I myself who must seek for these, who must make these availing. People riveted my thoughts upon my own individual self, and then upbraided me for thinking too much of myself.

The politician called me an egotist because I would not occupy myself solely and altogether with his calling. A young *dilletante* in Æsthetics, a relation of the Borghese family, taught me what I ought to think, compose, and judge, and that always in one mode, that every stranger might see that it was the nobleman who taught the shepherd boy, the poor lad, who must be doubly grateful to him in that he condescended to instruct him. He who interested himself for the beautiful horse, and for that and that alone, said that I was the very vainest of men because I had no eye for his steed. But were not they all egotists? Or were they right? Perhaps! I was a poor child for whom they had done a great deal. But, if my name had no nobility attached to it, my soul had, and inexpressibly deeply did it feel every humiliation.

I who, with my whole soul, had clung to mankind, was now changed, like Lot's wife, into a pillar of salt. This gave rise to defiance in my soul. There were moments when my spiritual consciousness raised itself up in its fetters, and became a devil of high-mindedness, which looked down upon the folly of my prudent teachers, and, full of vanity, whispered into my ear, " Thy name will live and be remembered, when all theirs are forgotten, or are only remembered through thee, as being connected with thee, as the refuse and the bitter drops which fell into thy life's cup!"

At such moments I thought on Tasso, on the vain Leonora, the proud court of Ferrara, the nobility of which now is derived from the name of Tasso; whose castle is in ruins, and the poet's prison a place of pilgrimage. I myself felt with what vanity my heart throbbed; but, in the manner in which I was brought up, it must be so, or else it must bleed. Gentleness and encouragement would have preserved my thoughts pure, my soul full of affection; every friendly smile and word was a sunbeam, which melted one of the ice-roots of vanity;—but there fell more poison-drops than sunbeams.

I was no longer so good as I had been formerly, and yet I was called an excellent, a remarkably excellent young man. My soul studied books, nature, the world, and myself; and yet they said, he will not learn any thing.

This education lasted for six years, nay, seven, I might say, but that about the close of the sixth year there occurred a new movement in the waves of my life's sea. In six long years there were certainly many circumstances which might have been communicated, many which were of more marked interest than those of which I have been speaking, but all melted themselves, however, into one single drop of poison, as every man of talent, not possessed of either wealth or rank, knows as well as the pulsations of his own heart.

I was an abbé, had a sort of name in Rome as improvisatore, because I had improvised and read poems aloud in the Academia Tiberina, and had always received the most decided applause; but Francesca was right when she said that they clapped every thing which any body read here. Habbas Dahdah stood as one of the first in the Academy; that is to say, he talked and wrote more than any one else: all his fellow-professors said that he was too one-sided, ill-tempered, and unjust, and yet they endured him among them, and so he wrote and wrote on.

He had gone, he said, through my water-colour pieces, as he called my poems, but he could not now discover one trace of the talent which he had at one time, when in the school I bowed myself before his opinion, found in me; it had been strangled in the birth, he said, and my friends ought to prevent any of my poems, which were only poetical misconceptions, from seeing the light. The misfortune was, he said, that great geniuses had written in their youthful years, and thus it had been with me.

I never heard any thing of Annunciata: she was to me like one dead, who, in the moment of death, had laid her cold hand crushingly upon my heart, and thereby it had become more susceptible of every painful emotion. My residence in Naples, all the recollections of it, were as a beautiful paralysing Medusa's head. When the sirocco blew, I bethought myself of the mild breezes at Pæstum, of Lara, and the brilliant grotto in which I had seen her. When I stood like a school-boy before my male and female educators, came to me recollections of the plaudits in the Robber's Cave, and in the great theatre of San Carlo. When I stood unobserved in a corner, I thought of Santa, who stretched forth her arms after me, and sighed, " Kill me, but leave me not!" They were six long instructive years; I was now six-and-twenty years old.

Flaminia, the young abbess, as they called her, the daughter of Francesca and Fabiani, who already had been consecrated in the cradle by the holy father as the bride of heaven, I had not seen since I had danced her upon my arm, and drawn for her merry pictures. She had been educated in a female convent in the Quattri Fontane, from which she never came. Fabiani had not seen her either for six long years ; Francesca only, as her mother, and as a lady, was permitted to visit her. She was, they said, grown quite a beautiful young woman, and the pious sisters had brought her mind to the same state of perfection. According to old custom, the young abbess was now to return home to her parents for some months, to enjoy all the pleasures of the world, and all its joy, before she said for ever farewell to it. She could even then, it was said, choose between the noisy world and the quiet convent ; but as, from the child's play with the dolls dressed as nuns, so through her whole education in the convent, every thing had been done with the design of riveting her soul and her thoughts to her destined life.

Often when I went through Quattri Fontane, where the convent was situated, I thought of the friendly child which I had danced upon my arm, and how changed she must be, and how quietly she lived behind the narrow wall. Once only had I been to the convent church, and had heard the nuns singing between the grating. Was the little abbess seated among them ? thought I, but ventured not to inquire whether the boarders also took part in the singing, and the church music. There was one voice which sounded so high and melancholy above the others, and which had a great resemblance to Annunciata's : I seemed again to hear her, and all the remembrances from that gone time seemed to awaken again in my soul.

"Next Monday our little abbess comes to us," said Excellenza. I long inexpressibly to see her. She seemed to me, like myself, to be like a captive bird, whom they let out of the cage with a string about its leg, that it might enjoy freedom in God's nature."

I saw her for the first time again at the dinner-table. She was, as they had told me, very much grown, somewhat pale, and, at the first moment, no one would have said that she was handsome ; but there was an expression of heart-felt goodness in her countenance, a wonderful gentleness was diffused over it.

There were at the table only a few of the nearest relations. Nobody told her who I was, and she appeared not to recognise me, but replied, with a kindness to which I was not accustomed, to every single word which I said. I felt that she made no difference between us, and drew me also into the conversation. She does not know me most assuredly, thought I.

All the party was cheerful, told anecdotes and droll passages in every-day life ; and the young abbess laughed. This gave me courage, and I introduced several puns, which, just at that time, had produced great effect in many circles in the city. But no one laughed at them, excepting the young abbess ; the others only faintly smiled, said that it was poor wit, and that it was not worth repeating. I assured them that, in almost every other place in Rome, people found a deal to laugh at in them.

" It is but a mere play upon words," said Francesca. " How can any one find pleasure in such superficial wit ? What mere nothings can occupy a human brain !"

I occupied myself very little, in truth, with such things. But I had wished to contribute my part to the general entertainment, and that which I had related appeared to me very amusing, and exactly calculated for the purpose. I became silent and constrained.

Many strangers were there in the evening, and I kept myself prudently in the back-ground. The great circle had gathered around the excellent Perini. He was of my age, but a nobleman, lively, and, in fact, very entertaining; and was possessed of all possible company talents. People knew that he was amusing and witty, and discovered that every thing which he said was so. I stood somewhat behind him, and heard how they were all laughing, especially Excellenza. I approached nearer. It was precisely that very same play of words, which I to-day had so unfortunately brought forward for the first time, that Perini now related. He neither took from it nor added to it, but gave

s

the very same words with the very same mien that I had done, and they all laughed!

" It is most comic," cried Excellenza, and clapped his hands; " most comic, is it not?" said he to the young abbess, who stood by his side and laughed.

" Yes; so it seemed to me at dinner when Antonio told it to us!" returned she. There was nothing at all bitter in this remark of hers: it was spoken with her customary gentleness. I could have fallen at her feet.

" Oh, it is superb!" said Francesca, to Perini's pun.

My heart beat violently. I withdrew to the window, behind the long curtains, and breathed the fresh air.

I bring forward merely this one little trait. Every day, as it went on, gave rise to similar ones. But the young abbess was an affectionate child, who looked into my face with gentleness and love, as if she would pray for forgiveness for the sins of the others. I was also very weak. I had vanity enough, but no pride. That was occasioned, certainly, by my low birth, by my early bringing up, by my dependence, and the unfortunate relationship of benefits received, in which I was placed to those around me. The thought was for ever recurring to my mind how much I was indebted to my circumstances, and that thought bound my tongue to the resolves of my pride. It was assuredly noble; but, at the same time, it was weakness.

Had I stood in an entirely independent position, things could not have come to the state in which they were. Every one acknowledged my sense of duty and my firm conscientiousness; and yet, they said, a genius is not capable of grave business. Those who were the most polite to me said, that I was possessed of too much spirituality for it. If they meant what they said, how ill they judged of a man of mind! I might have perished of hunger, it was said, had it not been for Excellenza; how much gratitude, therefore, did I not owe him?

About this time I had just finished a great poem — " David" — into which I had breathed my whole soul. Day after day, through the last year, spite of the eternal educating, the recollections of my flight to Naples, my adventures there, and the severing of my first strong love, had given my whole being a more determined poetical bent. There were moments which stood before me as a whole life, a true poem, in which I myself had acted a part. Nothing appeared to me without significance, or of every-day occurrence. My sufferings even, and the injustice which was done to me, was poetry. My heart felt a necessity to pour itself forth, and in " David" I found material which answered to my requiring. I felt livingly the excellence of what I had written, and my soul was gratitude and love; for it is the truth, that I never either sang or composed a strophe which appeared to me good, without turning myself with child-like thanks to the eternal God, from whom I felt that it was a gift, a grace which he had infused into my soul! My poem made me happy; and I heard with a pious mind every thing which seemed to be said unreasonably against me; for I thought, when they hear this, they will feel what an injustice they have done me, their hearts will warm towards me with twofold love!

My poem was completed; no human eye excepting my own had yet seen it. It seemed to stand before me like a Vatican Apollo, an unpolluted image of beauty known only to God himself. I gladdened myself with the thought of the day when I should read it in the Academia Tiberina. I resolved that nobody in the house should in the mean time know of it. One day, however, one of the first after the young abbess was come home, Francesca and Fabiani were so gentle and kind to me, that I felt as if I could have no secrets with them. I told them, therefore, of my poem, and they said, " But we ought first of all to hear it."

I was willing that they should, although not without a kind of throbbing of heart, an extraordinary anxiety. In the evening, just as I was about to read it, who should make his appearance but Habbas Dahdah.

Francesca besought him to remain, and to honour my poem by hearing it read. Nothing could have been more repugnant to me. I knew his bitterness, ill-humour, and bad blood; nor were the others particularly prepossessed in my favour. Nevertheless, the consciousness of the excellence of my work gave me a sort of courage. The young abbess looked happy; she delighted herself with the thoughts of hearing my "David." When I first stepped forward in San Carlo, my heart did not beat more violently than now, as I sat before these people. This poem, I thought, must entirely change their judgment of me — their mode of treating me. It was a sort of spiritual operation by which I desired to influence them, and therefore I trembled.

A natural feeling within me had led me only to describe that which I knew. David's shepherd life, with which my poem opened, was borrowed from my childhood's recollections in the hut of Domenica.

"But that is actually yourself," cried Francesca; "yourself out in the Campagna."

. "Yes; that one can very well see," said Excellenza. "He must bring himself in. That is really a peculiar genius that the man has! In every possible thing he knows how to bring forward himself."

"The versification ought to be a little smoother," said Habbas Dahdah. "I advise the Horatian rule, 'Let it only lie by — lie by till it comes to maturity!'"

It was as if they had all of them broken off an arm from my beautiful statue. I, however, read yet a few more stanzas, but only cold slight observations met my ear. Whenever my heart had expressed naturally its own emotions, they said I had borrowed from another poet. Whenever my soul had been full of warm inspiration, and I had expected attention and rapture, they seemed indifferent, and made only cold and every-day remarks. I broke off at the conclusion of the second canto: it was impossible for me to read any more. My poem, which had seemed to me so beautiful and so spiritual, now lay like a deformed doll, a puppet with glass eyes and twisted features; it was as if they had breathed poison over my image of beauty.

"But David does not kill the Philistines!" said Habbas Dahdah. With this exception, they said that there were some very pretty things in the poem; that what related to childhood and to sentiment I could express very nicely.

I stood silent, and bowed, like a criminal for a gracious sentence.

" The Horatian rule," whispered Habbas Dahdah, pressing my hand very kindly and calling me " poet." Some minutes, however, afterwards, when I had withdrawn, greatly depressed, into a corner, I heard him say to Fabiani that my work was nothing at all but desperate bunglingly put-together stuff !

They had mistaken both it and me, but my soul could not bear it. I went out into the great saloon adjoining, where a fire was burning on the hearth ; I convulsively crumpled together my poem in my hand. All my hopes, all my dreams, were in a moment destroyed. I felt myself so infinitely small ; an unsuccessful impression of him in whose image I was made.

That which I had loved, had pressed to my lips, into which I had breathed my soul, my living thoughts, I cast from me into the fire ; I saw my poem kindle up into red flame.

" Antonio ! " cried the young abbess close behind me, and snatched into the fire after the burning leaves ; her foot slipped in her quick movement, and she fell forward on the fire. It was a fearful sight ; she uttered a shriek, I sprang forward to her and caught her up : the poem was all in a blaze, and the others came rushing into the room.

" Jesus Maria ! " exclaimed Francesca.

The young abbess lay pale as death in my arms : she raised her head, smiled, and said to her mother, —

" My foot slipped ; I have only burned my hand a little ; if it had not been for Antonio, it would have been a great deal worse ! "

I stood like a sinner, and could not say one word. She had severely burnt her left hand, and a great excitement was occasioned by it in the house. They had not noticed that I had thrown my poem into the fire. I expected that they would afterwards inquire about it, but, as I did not speak of this, neither was it spoken of by any one, — by no one at all ? Yes, by one, — by Flaminia, the young abbess !

In her I saw the good angel of the house ; through her

gentleness, her sisterly disposition, after some time, my whole childlike confidence returned; I was as if bound to her.

It was more than fourteen days before her hand was healed. The wound burned, but it burned also in my heart.

" Flaminia, I am guilty of the whole!" said I one day as I sat alone with her; "for my sake you have suffered this pain."

" Antonio," said she, "for Heaven's sake be silent! Let no creature hear a word of this; you do yourself an injustice; my foot slipped, it might have been much more unfortunate had not you been there. I owe thanks to you for it, and that my father and mother feel also; they are much attached to you, Antonio, more so than you think."

" I owe every thing to them," I said; "every day lays me under fresh obligation."

" Do not speak of that," said she, with indescribable sweetness; " they have their own mode of behaving to you, but they only think that it is the best. You do not know how much good my mother has told me about you! We have all of us our faults, Antonio, even you yourself" —— she paused. " Yes," continued she, "how could you be so angry as to burn that beautiful poem?"

" It was not worth any thing better," said I; " I ought long before to have thrown it into the flames."

Flaminia shook her head. " It is a bad, wicked world!" said she; " yes, it was very much better there among the sisters in the quiet, friendly convent."

" Yes," exclaimed I; "innocent and good like you am I not; my heart has in its remembrance rather the bitter drops than the refreshing draughts of benefits which have been extended to me."

" In my beloved convent it was much better than it is here, though you all love me so much," she would often say when we were together alone. My whole soul was attracted towards her; for I felt that she was the good angel of my better feelings and my innocence. I seemed also to perceive in others a greater delicacy towards me, a greater gentleness in word and in looks; and I fancied that this was the effect of Flaminia's influence.

She seemed to have such great pleasure in talking to me about the things which occupied me most, — poetry, the glorious, Godlike poetry. I told her a great deal about the great masters, and often inspiration ascended into my soul, and my lips became eloquent, as she sat there before me with folded hands, and looked into my face like the angel of Innocence.

"And yet, how happy you are, Antonio!" said she, "more happy than thousands! And, nevertheless, it seems to me that it must be an anxious thing to belong to the world in the same degree as you and every poet must! How very much good cannot one word of yours produce, and yet how much evil likewise!"

She expressed her astonishment that poets for ever sung of human struggles and troubles; to her it seemed that the prophet of God, as the poet is, should only sing of the eternal God and of the joy of heaven.

"But the poet sings of God in His creatures!" replied I; "he glorifies Him in that which He has created for His glory."

"I do not understand it," said Flaminia; "I feel clearly, however, that which I mean to say, but I have not the words for it. Of the eternal God, of the divinity in His world and in our own hearts, the poet ought to speak, ought to lead us to his heart, and not into the wild world."

She then inquired from me how it was to be a poet; how one felt when one improvised; and I explained to her this state of spiritual operation as well as I could.

"The thoughts, the ideas," said she; "yes, I understand very well that they are born in the soul, that they come from God; we all know that, but the beautiful metre, the mode in which this consciousness expresses itself, that I understand not."

"Have you not," I inquired, "often in the convent learned one or another beautiful psalm or legend which is made in verse? And then often, when you are least thinking about it, some circumstance or another has called up an idea within your mind, by which the recollection is awoke of this or that, so that you could, then and there, have written them down on paper; verses, rhymes, even have led you to remember the succeeding, whilst the thought, the subject, stood clearly before you? Thus is it with the improvisatore and poet,—with me at least! At times it seems to me these are reminiscences, cradle-songs from another world, which awake in my soul, and which I am compelled to repeat."

"How often have I felt the same kind of thing!" said Flaminia, "but never was able to express it. That strange longing, which often took hold upon me, without my knowing wherefore! To me it seemed, therefore, so often, that I was not at home here in this wild world. The whole seemed to me a great and strange dream; and this was the reason why I longed so again for my convent— for my little cell! I know not how it is, Antonio, but there I used so often to see in my dreams my bridegroom Jesus and the Holy Virgin, now they present themselves more seldom: I dream now so much about worldly pomp and joy, about so much that is wicked. I am certainly no longer so good as I was among the sisters! Why should I have been kept from them so long? Do you know, Antonio; I will confess to you, I am no longer innocent, I would too gladly adorn my person; and it gives me so much pleasure when they say that I am lovely! In the convent they told me that it was only the children of sin who thought in this way."

"Oh that my thoughts were as innocent as yours!" said I, bowing myself before her, and kissing her hand.

She then told me that she remembered how I had danced her on my arm when she was little, and had drawn pictures for her.

"And which you tore in pieces after you had looked at them," said I.

"That was hateful of me!" said she; "but you are not angry with me for it?"

"I have seen my heart's best pictures torn in pieces since then," said I; "and yet I was not angry with those who did it."

She stroked me affectionately on the cheek.

More and more dear did she become to my heart, that,

indeed, had been repulsed by all the world; she alone was affectionate and sympathising.

In the two warmest summer months the family removed to Tivoli; I accompanied them, for which I certainly had to thank Flaminia. The glorious scenery there, the rich olive-groves, and the foaming waterfall, seized upon my soul as the sea had seized upon it, when I had seen it for the first time at Terracina. I felt myself so exhilarated to leave Rome, the yellow Campagna around it, and the oppressive heat. The first breath from the mountains, with their dark olive-groves, brought again life's pictures from Naples back to my soul.

Frequently, and with great delight, Flaminia rode, with her maid, upon asses, through the mountain-valley of Tivoli; and I was permitted to attend them. Flaminia had much taste for the picturesque beauty of nature, and I therefore attempted to make sketches of the rich neighbourhood; the boundless Campagna, when the cupola of St. Peter's raised itself upon the horizon; the fertile sides of the mountains, with their thick olive-groves and vineyards; even Tivoli itself, which lay aloft on the cliffs, below which waterfall upon waterfall fell foaming into the abyss.

"It looks," said Flaminia, "as if the whole city stood upon loose pieces of rock, which the water would soon tear down. Up above those, in the street, one never dreams about it, but goes with a light step above an open grave!"

"So, indeed, do we always!" replied I; it is well and happy for us, that it is concealed from our eyes. The foaming waterfalls, which we see hurled down here, have in them something disturbing, but how much more terrible must it be in Naples, where fire is thrown up like water here!"

I then told her about Vesuvius, of my ascent to it; told her about Herculaneum and Pompeii, and she drank in every word of my lips. When we were at home again, she begged me to tell her more about all the glorious things on the other side of the Marshes.

The sea she could not rightly understand, for she had only seen it from the top of the mountains, like a silver riband on the horizon. I told her that it was, like God's heaven, spread out upon the earth, and she folded her hands, and said, " God has made the world infinitely beautiful ! "

" Therefore man ought not to turn himself away from the glory of His works, and immure himself in a dark convent ! " I would have said, but I dared not.

One day we stood beside the old sibyl's temple, and looked down upon the two great waterfalls, which, like clouds, were hurled into the chasm, whilst a column of spray mounted upwards among the green trees, towards the blue air ; the sunbeams fell upon the column, and caused a rainbow. Within the cavern in the cliff, above the lesser waterfall, a flock of doves had established themselves ; they flew in wide circles below us, and above the great mass of water, which is shivered in its fall.

" How glorious ! " exclaimed Flaminia ; " now improvise for me also, Antonio ! " said she ; " now sing to me a poem about what you see ! "

I thought upon my heart's dream, which had all been shivered like the water-stream here, and I obeyed her, and sang. Sang how life burst forth like the stream, but yet every drop of it did not drink in the sunbeam, it was only over the whole, over a whole human race, that the glory of beauty diffused itself.

" No ! any thing sorrowful I will not hear ! " said Flaminia ; " you shall not sing me any thing if you do not like to do it. I do not know how it is, Antonio, but I do not consider you like the other gentlemen whom I know ! I can say any thing to you ! You seem to me almost like my father and my mother ! "

I possessed also her confidence as she did mine ; there was so much which agitated my soul, that I longed for sympathy. One evening I related to her much of my childhood's life, of my ramble in the Catacombs, of the flower-feast in Genzano, and of my mother's death, when the horses of Excellenza went over us. Of that she had never heard.

" O Madonna ! " said she ; " thus are we guilty of your misfortune ! Poor Antonio ! " she took my hand, and

looked sorrowfully into my face. She was greatly interested in old Domenica; inquired whether I frequently
visited her, and I took shame to myself to confess, that
during the last year I had only been twice out there; although in Rome I had seen her more frequently, and had
always divided my little wealth with her; but that was
indeed nothing to speak of.

She besought of me always to tell her more, and so,
when I had related to her all about my life in childhood, I
told her of Bernardo and Annunciata, and she looked with
an inexpressibly pious expression into my very soul. The
nearness of innocence directed my words. I told her about
Naples, touching lightly, very lightly, upon the shadowy
side, and yet she shuddered at what I told, shuddered before Santa, the servant of beauty in my Paradise.

"No, no!" exclaimed she, "thither will I never go!
No sea, no burning mountain can cleanse away all the sin
and abomination of the great city! You are good and
pious, and therefore did the Madonna protect you!"

I thought of the image of the Mother of God, which
had fallen down from the wall when my lips met Santa's;
but this I could not tell to Flaminia: would she then have
called me good and pious? I was a sinner like the others.
Circumstances, the mercy of the Mother of God, had
watched over me. In the moment of temptation I was
weak as any of those whom I knew.

Lara was inexpressibly dear to her. "Yes," said she,
"when your soul was in God's heaven, could she only
come to you! I can very well fancy her, fancy the blue,
beaming grotto, where you saw her for the last time!"

Annunciata did not rightly please her. "How could
she love the hateful Bernardo? I would rather not that
she had been your wife. A woman who thus can come
forward before a whole public; a woman — yes, I cannot
properly make that intelligible which I mean! I feel,
however, how beautiful she was, how wise, how many
advantages she possessed above other women, but it does
not seem to me that she was worthy of you. Lara was a
better guardian angel for you!"

I must now tell her of my improvisation; and to her it

seemed that it would be much more terrible in the great
theatre, than before the robbers in the mountain cave.
I showed her the *Diario Napoli,* in which was the critique
on my first appearance; how often had I read it since
then!

It amused her to see every thing which that paper from
the foreign city contained.   All at once she looked up and
exclaimed, " But you never told me, however, that
Anunciata was in Naples at the same time you were there.
Here it is stated that she will make her appearance on the
morrow, that is on the day upon which you set out!"

" Annunciata!" stammered I, and stared at the paper,
into which I had so often looked before, and yet, truly
enough, had never read any thing but what had reference
to myself.

" That I never saw!" exclaimed I; and we looked
silently at each other.   " God be praised that I did
not meet her, did not see her — she was indeed not
mine!"

" But if it were to happen now," asked Flaminia;
" would it not please you?"

" It would be painful to me!" exclaimed I, " great
suffering.   The Annunciata who captivated me, who still
exists idolised in my memory, I shall never again find;
she would be to me a new creature, who would painfully
excite a remembrance which I must forget, must regard
as the property of death!   She stands among my
dead!"

On one warm afternoon, I entered the large general
sitting-room, where the thick green twining plants overshadowed the window.   Flaminia sat, supporting her head
upon her hand, in a light slumber: it seemed as if she
were keeping her eyes closed only for sport.   Her breast
heaved, she dreamed.   " Lara!" said she. · In dreams
she certainly floated with my heart's dream-image, in that
splendid world where I last had seen her.   A smile parted
her lips; she opened her eyes.

" Antonio!" said she, " I have been asleep, and have
dreamed.   Do you know of whom?"

"Lara!" said I; for I too could not but think of her when I saw Flaminia with closed eyes.

"I dreamt about her!" said she. "We both of us flew far over the great, beautiful sea, which you have told me about. Amid the water there lay a rock, on which you sat, looking very much dejected, as you often do. She then said that we would fly down to you, and she sank through the air down to you. I too wished to go with her, but the air kept me far aloft, and with every stroke of my wings, which I made to follow her, I seemed to fly farther away. But when I fancied that there lay thousands of miles between us, she was at my side, and you also!"

"Thus will death assemble us!" said I. "Death is rich, he possesses every thing which has been dearest to our hearts!"

I spoke with her about my beloved dead, the dead even of my thoughts, of my affections, and we often turned back to these reminiscences.

She then asked me if I would also think of her when we were separated. Very soon she should be really again in the convent, a nun, the bride of Christ, and we should never see each other more.

Deep suffering penetrated my soul at this thought; I felt right livingly how dear Flaminia had become to me.

One day, when she, and her mother, and I, were walking in the garden of the Villa d'Este, where the tall cypresses grow, we went up the long alley which runs up to the artificial fountain. Here lay a ragged beggar pulling up the grass from the walk, and, as soon as he saw us, he prayed for a bajocco. I gave him a paolo, and Flaminia smiled kindly, and gave him another.

"Madonna reward the young Excellenza and his handsome bride!" cried he after us.

Francesca laughed aloud; it ran like burning fire through my blood; I had not courage to look at Flaminia. In my soul a thought had awoke, which I had never dared to unveil before to myself. Slowly, but firmly, had Flaminia grown into my heart: it must bleed, I felt, when we parted from each other. She was the only one to whom my soul now clung; the only one who affectionately met my thoughts and feelings. Was it love? Did I love her? The feeling which Annunciata had awoke in my soul was very different; even the sight of Lara, the remembrance of her, had something much more allied to this feeling. Intellect and beauty had captivated me in Annunciata; ideal beauty mingled itself with the first view of Lara, which made my heart swell. No, this was not my love for Flaminia. It was not the wild, burning passion; it was friendship; a brother's most living love. I felt the connexion in which I stood to her, with regard to her family and her destination, and was in despair at the thought of separation from her; she was to me my all, — my dearest in this world; but I had no wish to press her to my heart, to breathe a kiss upon her lips, as had been my whole thoughts with regard to Annunciata, and which, as an invisible power, had driven me towards the blind girl; no, this was to me quite foreign.

"The young Excellenza and his handsome bride!" as the beggar had cried, resounded continually in my soul. I sought to read every wish on Flaminia's lips, and hung about her like her shadow. When others were present, I became constrained and dejected. I felt the thousand bonds which pressed heavily upon me; I became silent and absent, for her alone was I eloquent. She was so dear to me, and I must lose her.

"Antonio!" said she, "you are unwell, or something has happened which I may not know? Why not? may I not?"

With her whole soul she depended on me, and I desired to be to her a dear, faithful brother; and yet my conversation perpetually tended to lead her out into the world. I told her how I myself had once wished to be a monk, and how unhappy I should have been if I had become so, because sooner or later the heart asserts its right.

"I," said she, "shall feel myself happy, very happy, to return again to my pious sisters — among them I am only rightly at home. Then I shall very often think upon the time when I was out in the world, shall think of every thing of which you have told me. It will be a beautiful dream, I feel it so already. I shall pray for you, pray that the wicked world may never corrupt you ; that you may become very happy, and that the world may rejoice in your song, and that you may feel how good the dear God is to you and to us altogether."

Tears streamed from my eyes ; I sighed deeply, " We shall then never see each other more ! "

" Yes, with God and the Madonna ! " said she, and smiled piously. " There you shall show me Lara ! there also shall she receive the sight of her eyes. Oh, yes, with the Madonna it is the best ! "

We removed again to Rome. In a few weeks, I heard it said, that Flaminia was to return to the convent, and shortly after that to take the veil. My heart was rent with pain, and yet I was obliged to conceal it. How forlorn and desolate should I not be when she had left us! how like a stranger and alone should I not stand ! what grief of heart I should experience ! I endeavoured to hide it — to be cheerful — to be quite different to what I was.

They spoke of the pomp of her investiture as if it had been a feast of gladness. But could she, however, go away from us ? They had befooled her mind, they had befooled her understanding. Her beautiful long hair was to be cut away from her head, the living was to be clothed in a shroud ; she would hear the funeral bells ring, and only as the dead rise up the bride of heaven. I said this to Flaminia : with an anguish as of death besought of her to think about what she was doing, of thus going down alive to the grave.

" Let nobody hear what you are saying, Antonio ! " said she, with a solemnity which I had never seen in her before. " The world has all too firm a hold upon you : look more to that which is heavenly."

She became crimson, seized my hand, as if she had spoken to me with too much severity, and said, with the most heartfelt gentleness, " You will not distress me, Antonio ? "

I then sank down before her feet, she stood like a saint before me, my whole soul clung to her. How many tears did I shed that night! my strong feeling for her seemed to me a sin, she was really the bride of the church. I daily saw her, daily learned to value her more highly. She talked to me like a sister, looked into my face, offered me her hand, said that her soul was filled with desires for me, and that I was dear to her. I convulsively concealed the night of death which lay in my soul, and it made me happy that it was known to no one. God send death to a heart which suffers as mine suffered!

The moment of separation stood horribly before me, and a wicked spirit whispered into my ear, " Thou lovest her!" and I really did not love her as I had loved Annunciata: my heart trembled not as it had done when my lips touched Lara's forehead. " Say to Flaminia, that thou canst not live without her; she also is attached to thee as a sister to a brother. Say that thou lovest her! Excellenza and the whole family will condemn thee, turn thee out into the world: but then in losing her thou losest every think. The choice is easy!"

How often did this confession arise to my lips, but my heart trembled, and I was silent; it was a fever, a fever of death, which agitated my blood, my thoughts!

All was in a state of preparation within the palace for a splendid ball, a flower-festival for the sacrificial lamb. I saw her in the rich, magnificent dress: she was unspeakably lovely.

" Now be gay like the others!" she whispered to me; " it distresses me to see you so dejected. Often shall I certainly, for your sake, when I am sitting in my convent, send my thoughts back to the world, and that is sin, Antonio. Promise me that you will become more cheerful — promise me that you will forgive my father and mother when they are a little severe towards you. They mean it for your good. Promise me that you will not think so much on the bitterness of the world, and will be always good and pious as you now are; then I may dare still to think of you, still to pray for you, and Madonna is good and merciful."

Her words penetrated my heart. I see her yet as she was that last evening before she left us, — she was so tranquil. She kissed her father and the old Excellenza, and spoke of the separation as if it were only for a few days.

" Now say farewell to Antonio," said Fabiani, who was much affected, while the others appeared not to be so. I hastily hurried up to her, and bowed to kiss her hand. " Antonio," said she ; her voice was so low, tears streamed from my eyes. " Mayst thou be happy !"

I knew not how to tear myself away ; for the last time I looked into her pious, gentle countenance.

" Farewell !" said she, scarcely audibly. She bent towards me, and, impressing a kiss upon my forehead, said, " Thanks for thy affection, my dear brother ! "

More I know not ! I rushed out of the hall and into my own chamber, where I could weep freely ; it was as if the world sank away from under my feet.

And I saw her yet once more ! When the time was accomplished I saw her. The sun shone so warm and cheerfully. I saw Flaminia in all her rich pomp and magnificence, as she was led up to the altar by her father and her mother. I heard plainly the singing, and perceived that many people were kneeling all around, but there stood distinctly before me only the pale, mild countenance — an angel it was — which kneeled with the priests before the high altar.

I saw how they took the costly veil from her head, and the abundant hair fell down upon her shoulders ; I heard the shears divide it — they stripped her of her rich clothing — she stretched herself upon the bier, the pall and the black cloth, upon which are painted death's heads, were thrown over her. The church-bells tolled for the burial procession, and the song for the dead was intoned. Yes, dead was she — buried to this world.

The black grate, before the entrance to the interior to the convent, was raised, the sisters stood in their white linen vestments, and sang the angel's welcome to their new sister. The bishop extended to her his hand, and the dead arose as the bride of heaven arose. Elizabeth she was now called. I saw the last glance which she directed to the assembly ; after this she gave her hand to the nearest sister, and entered into the grave of life.

T

The black grating fell! I still saw the outline of her figure—the last wave of her garment—and she was gone!

CHAPTER X.

OLD DOMENICA. — THE DISCOVERY. — THE EVENING IN NEPI. —
THE BOATMAN'S SONG. — VENICE.

CONGRATULATIONS were now offered in the Borghese Palace. Flaminia-Elizabeth was really the bride of heaven. Francesca's seriousness was not concealed by her artificial smile; the tranquillity which lay on her countenance was banished from her heart.

Fabiani, most deeply affected, said to me, "You have lost your best benefactress! You have reason for being very much depressed! She desired me to give you some scudi," continued he, "for old Domenica; you have certainly spoken to her about your old foster-mother. Take her these, they are Flaminia's gift."

The dead lay like a snake around my heart; my thoughts were life's weariness; I trembled before them; before them self-murder seemed to lose its terrors.

"Out into the free air!" thought I; "to the home of my childhood, where Domenica sang cradle-songs to me; where I played and dreamed."

Yellow and scorched lay the Campagna; not a green blade spoke of the hope of life; the yellow Tiber rolled its waves towards the sea in order to vanish there. I saw again the old burial-place, with the thick ivy over the roof, and depending from the walls; the little world which, as a child, I had called my own. The door stood open; a pleasant melancholy feeling filled my heart; I thought of Domenica's affection and her joy at seeing me. It certainly was a year since I had last been out there, and eight months since I had spoken with her in Rome, and she had prayed me to go very often to see her. I had very often thought about her, had talked of her to Flaminia; but our summer residence in Tivoli and my excited state of mind since our return had prevented my going out to the Campagna.

I heard, in thought, her scream of joy as she saw me, and hastened my steps ; but, when I came pretty near the door, walked very softly to prevent her hearing me. I looked into the room ; in the middle of the room stood a great iron pan over a fire, some reeds were laid upon it, and a young fellow blew them ; he turned his head and saw me ; it was Pietro, the little child, which I had nursed here.

"Saint Joseph !" exclaimed he, and sprung up over-joyed, " is it your Excellency ? It is a long, long time since you were so gracious as to come here !"

I extended to him my hand, which he would kiss.

" Nay, nay, Pietro !" said I ; " it almost seems as if I had forgotten my old friends, but I have not."

" No, the good old mother said so too," cried he ; " Oh, Madonna ! how glad she would have been to have seen you."

" Where is Domenica ? " inquired I.

" Ah !" returned he ; " it is now half a year since she was laid under the earth. She died whilst Excellenza was in Tivoli ! She was only ill for a few days, but through all that time she talked about her dear Antonio. Yes, Ex-cellenza, do not be angry that I call you by that name, but she was so very fond of you. 'Would that my eyes could see him before they are closed !' said she, and longed so very much for it. And when I saw very well that she could not last the night over, I went in the afternoon to Rome ; I knew very well that you would not be angry at my request. I would have prayed of you to have accom-panied me to the old mother, but when I got there you and the gentlefolks were all gone to Tivoli ; so I came home full of trouble ; but when I came to the house she was already gone to sleep."

He held his hands before his face and wept.

Every word which he had said fell heavily upon my heart. I had been her dying thought, and, at the same time, my thoughts had been far away from her. Would

that I had only said farewell to her before I set off for
Tivoli! I was not a good man!

I gave the money to Pietro from Flaminia, and all that
I had also. He sank down upon his knees before me, and
called me his guardian angel. It sounded like a jest in my
heart. With a twofold sense of suffering, cut, as it were,
to the very soul, I left the Campagna. I know not how I
reached home.

For three long days I lay without consciousness in a violent fever. God knows what, during this time, I said;
but Fabiani frequently came to me; he had appointed the
deaf Fenella to be my nurse. No one named Flaminia to
me. I had returned home ill from the Campagna, and had
laid myself immediately on my bed, when the fever took
hold upon me.

I recovered my strength, but very slowly; in vain I endeavoured to compel myself to humour and cheerfulness;
I was possessed of neither.

It was about six weeks after this time, when Flaminia
took the veil, that the physician permitted me to go out.
Almost without knowing whither I directed my steps, I went
to the Porta Pia; my eye gazed down upon the Quattri
Fontane, but I had not courage enough to pass the convent. Some evenings, however, after this, when the new
moon shone in the heavens, the emotions of my heart drew
me thither; I saw the grey convent walls, the grated windows, Flaminia's closed grave. "Wherefore dared I not
to see the burial-place of the dead?" said I to myself, and
felt within me a resolution to do so.

Every evening I took my way past there. "I was very
fond of walking to the Villa Albani," said I to those of my
acquaintance whom I met by chance. "God knows what
will be the end of it!" sighed my heart; "I cannot endure it long!" I was then just at the goal.

It was a dark evening; a ray of light streamed down
the wall of the convent; I leaned myself against the corner
of a house, fixed my eyes upon this bright point, and
thought on Flaminia.

"Antonio!" said a voice close behind me; "Antonio,
what are you doing here?"

It was Fabiani. "Follow me home!" said he.

I accompanied him; we spoke not a word by the way; he knew it all as well as I myself did; I felt that he did so. I was an ingrate; I had not courage to look at him. Presently, and we were alone in my chamber.

"You are yet ill, Antonio," said he, with an unusual solemnity in his voice. "You need occupation, change of scene. It will do you good to mix more in the world. There was a time when you spread out your wings for freedom; perhaps it was unjust in me that I decoyed the bird back to his cage. It is a great deal better for human beings to have their will, then if misfortunes befall them they have only themselves to blame. You are quite old enough to direct your own steps. A little journey will be beneficial to you; the physician is of the same opinion also. You have already seen Naples, visit now the north of Italy. I shall provide the means for it. It is the best thing for you, necessary, and," added he, with a seriousness, a severity, which I had never known in him before, "I am convinced that you will never forget the benefits which we have conferred upon you. Never occasion us mortification, shame, and sorrow, which indiscretion or blind passion might do. A man can do any thing, whatever he will, if he be only a good man."

His words struck me to the earth like a flash of lightning; I bent my knee, and pressed his hand to my lips.

"I know very well," said he, half-jestingly, "that we may have done you injustice; that we have been unreasonable and severe. No persons, however, will intend more uprightly and more kindly towards you than we have done. You will hear more flattering modes of speech, more loving words, but not more true integrity than we have shown you. For a year you shall move about. Let us then see what is your state of mind, and whether we have done you an injustice."

With these words he left me.

Had the world still new suffering for me — still fresh poison-drops? Even the only draught of consolation, freedom to fly about in God's world, fell like gall into my deep wound. Far from Rome, far from the south, where lay all the flowers of my remembrance, over the Apennines, towards the north, where there actually lay snow upon the lofty mountains! Cold blown from the Alps into my warm blood! Toward the north, to the floating Venice, the bride of the sea! God! let me never more return to Rome, to the grave of my cherished memories! Farewell, my home, my native city!

The carriage rolled across the desolate Campagna. The dome of St. Peter's was concealed behind the hills. We drove past Monte Soracte, across the mountains, to the narrow Nepi. It was a bright, moonlight evening. A monk was preaching before the door of the hotel; the crowd repeated his *Viva Santa Maria!* and followed him, singing through the streets. The crowd of people carried me along with them. The old aqueduct, with its thick, twining plants, and the dark olive-groves around, formed a dark picture, which corresponded to my state of mind.

I passed through the gate by which I had entered. Just outside of this lay the vast ruins of a castle or convent, the broad highroad running through its dilapidated halls, a little path turned from the main road, and led into the midst of them; ivy and maiden's hair grew dependingly from the walls of the solitary cells. I entered into a large hall; tall grass grew above the rubbish and the overthrown capitals; enwreathing vine-shoots moved their broad leaves through the great Gothic windows, where now were only small remains of loosely-hanging painted glass. Aloft, upon the walls, grew bushes and hedges; the beams of the moon fell upon a fresco-painting of Saint Sebastian, who stood bleeding, and pierced with an arrow. Deep organ-tones resounded, as it seemed, continuously through the hall; I followed the sounds, and, passing out through a narrow door, found myself among myrtle-hedges and luxuriant vine-leaves, close to a perpendicular descent of great depth, down which a waterfall was precipitated, foamingly white, in the clear moonlight.

The whole romantic scene would have surprised any mind, yet perhaps my distress would have allowed it to slide out of my memory, had not that which I saw further impressed it painfully, deeply into my heart. I followed the narrow, almost overgrown path, close to the abyss, towards the broad highway. Close beside me, from over the lofty, white wall, upon which the moon was shining, stared three pale heads, behind an iron grating, the heads of three executed robbers, which, as in Rome, on the Porta del Angelo, were placed in iron cages, to serve as a terror and a warning to others. There was to me nothing terrible in them. In earlier days, the sight would have driven me away hence ; but suffering makes philosophers. The bold head, which had been occupied by thoughts of death and plunder, the mountain's daring eagle, was now a silent, captive bird, which sat quietly and rationally in its cage, like other imprisoned birds. I stepped up quite close to them ; they had certainly been placed there within these very few days ; every feature was still recognisable. But, as I gazed on the middle one, my pulse beat stronger ; it was the head of an old woman ! The skin was yellow-brown, the eyes half open, the long silver-white air, which hung through the grating, waved in the wind. My eye fell upon the stone tablet in the wall, where, according to old custom, the name and crime of the executed were engraved. Here stood " Fulvia." I saw also the name of her native city, " Frascati ; " and, agitated to the very depths of my soul, I stepped back a few paces.

Fulvia, the singular old woman, who had once saved my life, she who had obtained the means for my going to Naples, my life's inexplicable spirit, did I thus meet with her again ! With these pale, blue lips had she once pressed my forehead ; these lips, which, to the crowd, had spoken prophetic words, had given life and death, were now silent, breathing forth horror from their very silence ! Thou didst prophesy my fortune ! Thy bold eagle lies with clipped wings, and has never reached the sun ! In the combat with his misfortune, he sinks down into the great Nemi-lake of life ! His pinion is broken !

I burst into tears, repeated Fulvia's name, and slowly retraced my steps through the desolate ruins. Never shall I forget that evening in Nepi.

The next morning we journeyed onward, and came to Terni, where is the largest and most beautiful waterfall in

Italy. I rode from the city through the thick, dark olive-groves, the first which I had seen; wet clouds hung around the summits of the mountains, every thing to the north of Rome appeared to me dark, nothing smiling and beautiful, as the Marshes and as the orange-gardens of Terracina, where the green palm-trees grow. Perhaps it was my own heart which gave the whole this dark colouring.

We went through a garden; a luxuriant orange-alley extended itself between the rocky wall and the river, which rushed onward with the speed of an arrow. Between the rocks I saw a cloud of spray ascend high up in the path, upon which a rainbow played. We ascended amid a wilderness of rosemary and myrtle; and, from the very summit of the mountain, above the sloping, rocky wall, was hurled the monstrous mass of waters. A lesser arm of the river moved along, like a broad, silver riband close beside, and united below the rocks to form a broad cascade, which, white as milk, whirled itself down the black chasm. I thought upon the cascades at Tivoli, where I had impro-vised to Flaminia. The lofty, rushing stream sang to me with a penetratingly thrilling organ-tone the remembrance of my loss and my suffering. To be crushed, to die, and vanish, is the lot of Nature!

"Here," said our guide, "was an Englishman shot last year by robbers. It was a band from the Sabine moun-tains, although one may say that they have a home in all the mountains from Rome to Terni. The authorities are now always so much on the alert! They laid their hands on three unfortunates; I saw them driven to the city chained to the cart. At the gate sat the wise Fulvia, as we called her, from the Sabine mountains; she was old, and yet always young; she knew more than many a monk who will get the cardinal's hat; she could tell fortunes in figurative words; and since this people have said that it was a sign that she was in connection with them. Now they have taken her and many of the robbers. Her hour was come, so now her head is placed grinning over the gate at Nepi."

It was as if every thing, man as well as nature, would cast night into my soul; I felt a desire with the speed of

the wind to chase through the country. The dark olive-
groves threw more shadow into my soul; the mountains
oppressed me. Away to the sea, where the wind blew!
to the sea, where one heaven bore us, and another vaulted
itself above us! My blood burned with love, my heart
with longing. I had twice felt the pure, inspiring flame;
I had looked up to Annunciata, and my youthful, increasing
strength clung to her — but she looked another. Flaminia
had slowly grown into my soul; I had not been dazzled,
or transported, but I had learned to value one of the noblest
of human beings. Every time she extended her hand to
me as a sister, and I dared to press it to my lips, every
time she consoled me so kindly, and prayed that the world
might not spoil me, she pressed the arrow deeper into my
heart. I loved her not as a bride, and yet I felt that I
could not have endured to see her in the arms of another.
Now she was dead, dead to the world. No other man
would press her to his heart, or breathe a kiss upon her
lips: this anguish of hell was not allotted to me. I
sought to console myself by drawing this picture, because
I now called my feelings love, the strong passion of the
soul and the heart. If I had had to see her as the bride
of a young noble, daily to have witnessed the happiness of
their love — I, the cast-off herdling of the Campagna,
who had eaten the bread of charity in the rich palace —
would she then have been so gentle, so sisterlike, yet without love! It would have been madness to me! No!
now she belonged to the cloister; no one would raise his
eyes to her — no one saw her! — Yes, it was better, it
was happier! — The world's grief must be great when my
lot was to be envied!

To the sea, the wonderful sea! That is to me a new
world. To Venice, the strangely-floating city, the queen
of the Adriatic! But not through the dark woods, the
together-compressing mountains, quick, in easy flight over
the billows! So dreamed my thoughts.

It had been my plan to go first to Florence, and therefore through Bologna and Ferrara. I altered this, however, left the *vetturino* in Spoleto, took a place in the mail,
and posted over the Apennines in the dark night, through

Loretto, without even visiting its holy house. Madonna, forgive me my sin!

High up, on the mountain-road, I had already discerned the Adriatic Sea as a silver stripe on the horizon; the mountains lay like gigantic waves below me, and now I saw the blue, heaving sea, with its national pennons and flags upon its ships. I thought of Naples as I saw this; but no Vesuvius heaved itself with its black column of smoke, no Capri lay beyond. I slept here one night, and dreamed of Fulvia and Flaminia. " The palm-tree of thy fortune is budding green!" said they both, and smiled. I awoke, and the day was shining into my chamber.

" Signore !" said the waiter ; " a vessel lies here which is about ready to sail for Venice ; but will you not first of all see our city ? "

" To Venice !" cried I, " quick, quick ! that is exactly my wish."

An inexplicable feeling drove me onward. I stepped on board, ordered my light luggage to be sent after me, and looked out over the infinite sea. " Farewell, my fatherland!" Now, for the first time, I seemed rightly to have flown forth into the world, as my feet no longer trod upon the earth. I knew perfectly that the north of Italy would present to me a new style of scenery. Venice itself was really so different to any other Italian city ; a richly adorned bride for the mighty sea. The winged Venetian lion waved on the flag above me: it was a ship from Venice which bore me. The sails swelled in the wind, and concealed the coast from me. I sat upon the right side of the ship, and looked out across the blue billowy sea ; a young lad sat not far from me, and sang a Venetian song about the bliss of love and the shortness of life.

" Kiss the red lips, on the morrow thou art with the dead ; love, whilst thy heart is young, and thy blood is fire and flame ! Grey hairs are the flowers of death : then is the blood ice ; then is the flame extinguished ! Come into the light gondola ! We sit concealed under its roof, we cover the windows, we close the door, nobody sees thee, my love ! Nobody sees how happy we are. We are rocked upon the waves; the waves embrace, and so do we! Love whilst youth is in thy blood. Age kills with frost and with snow!"

As he sung, he smiled and nodded to the others around him; and they sang in chorus, about kissing and loving while the heart was young. It was a merry song, very merry; and yet it sounded like a magical song of death in my heart. Yes, the years sped away, the flames of youth are extinguished. I had poured the holy oil of love out over the earth, which kindled neither light nor warmth: to be sure it does no damage; but it flows into the grave, without brightening or warming. No promise, indeed, binds me—no obligation! Why do not my lips snatch at the refreshing draught of affection which they pine for? I had a feeling; yes—how shall I call it?—a dissatisfaction with myself. Was it the wild fire in my breast, which had scorched up my understanding? I felt a sort of bitterness against myself for having fled from Santa. The holy image of the Madonna fell down! It was the rusted nail which gave way; and the Jesuit school's conventual bashfulness, and the goat's milk in my blood, chased me thence. How beautiful Santa was! I saw her burning affectionate glance, and I grew angry with myself! Wherefore should I not be, like Bernardo, like a thousand others, like all my young friends? None, none of all these would have been a fool as I had been. My heart desired love: God had ordained it, who had implanted this feeling within me. I was still young, however: Venice was a gay city, full of beautiful women. And what does the world give me for my virtue, thought I, for my child-like temper? ridicule and time brings bitterness and grey hairs. Thus thought I, and sang in chorus with the rest, of kissing and loving, whilst the heart was yet young.

It was delirium, the madness of suffering, which excited these thoughts in my soul. He who gave to me my life, my feelings, and directed my whole destiny, will lead me in love. There are combats, thoughts even, which the most mortal dare not to express, because the angel of Innocence in our breast regards them as sinful. They who indulge the longings of their hearts may philosophise beau-

tifully over my speech. Judge not, lest ye be judged! I
felt that in myself—in my own corrupt nature, there
abode no good thing. I could not pray; and yet I slept
whilst the vessel flew onward to the north — to the rich
Venice.

In the morning hour, I discerned the white buildings
and towers of Venice, which seemed like a crowd of ships
with outspread sails. To the left stretched itself the kingdom of Lombardy, with its flat coast: the Alps seemed
like pale blue mist in the horizon. Here was the heaven
wide. Here the half of the hemisphere could mirror itself
in the heart.

In this sweet morning air my thoughts were milder : I
was more cheerful. I thought about the history of Venice,
of the city's wealth and pomp, its independence and supre-
macy: of the magnificent doges, and their marriage with
the city. We advanced nearer and nearer to the sea: I
could already distinguish the individual houses across the
Lagunes; but their yellow-grey walls, neither old nor
new, did not wear a pleasing aspect. St. Mark's Tower I
had also imagined to be much loftier. We sailed in between the mainland and the Lagunes, which, like a crooked
wall of earth, stretched out into the sea. Every where it
was flat. The shore seemed to be scarcely an inch higher
than the surface of the water. A few mean houses they
called the city of Fusina: here and there stood a bush;
and, excepting these, there was nothing at all on the flat
land. I had fancied that we were quite close upon Venice,
which, however, still lay a mile distant; and between us
and it lay an unsightly muddy water, with broad islands
of slime, upon which not a single bird could find footing,
and not a single blade of grass could take root. Through
the whole extent of this lake were dug deep canals, bordered with great piles to indicate their direction. I now
saw the gondola for the first time : long and narrow, quick
as a dart; but all painted coal-black. The little cabin in
the centre, covered over with black cloth: it was a floating
hearse, which shot past us with the speed of an arrow.
The water was no longer blue, as it was out in the open sea,
or close upon the coast of Naples : it was of a dirty green.

We passed by an island where the houses seemed to grow up out of the water, or to have clung to a wreck : aloft upon the walls stood the Madonna and the child, and looked out over this desert. In some places, the surface of the water was like a moving green plain — a sort of duck-pool, between the deep sea and the black islands of soft mud. The sun shone upon Venice : all the bells were ringing; but it looked nevertheless dead and solitary. Only one ship lay in the docks ; and not a single man could I see.

I stepped down into the black gondola, and sailed up into the dead street, where every thing was water, not a foot-breadth upon which to walk. Large buildings stood with open doors, and with steps down to the water ; the water ran into the great door-ways, like a canal ; and the palace-court itself seemed only a four-cornered well, into which people could sail, but scarcely turn the gondola. The water had left its greenish slime upon the walls : the great marble palace seemed as if sinking together : in the broad windows, rough boards were nailed up to the gilded, half-decayed beams. The proud giant-body seemed to be falling away piecemeal ; the whole had an air of depression about it. The ringing of the bells ceased, not a sound, excepting the splash of the oars in the water, was to be heard, and I still saw not a human being. The magnificent Venice lay like a dead swan upon the waves.

We crossed about into the other streets, small narrow bridges of masonry hung over the canals ; and I now saw people who skipped over me, in among the houses, and in among the walls even ; for I saw no other streets than those in which the gondolas glided.

"But where do the people walk ?" inquired I of my gondolier ; and he pointed to small passages by the bridges, between the lofty houses. Neighbour could reach his hand to neighbour, from the sixth story across the street ; three people could hardly pass each other below, where not a sunbeam found its way. Our gondola had passed on, and all was still as death.

" Is this Venice ? — The rich bride of the sea ? — the mistress of the world ?"

I saw the magnificent square of St. Mark. " Here is

life!" people said. · But how very different is it in Naples, nay, even in Rome, upon the animated Corso! And yet the square of St. Mark's is the heart of Venice, where life does exist. Shops of books, pearls, and pictures, adorned the long colonnades, where, however, it was not yet animated enough. A crowd of Greeks and Turks, in bright dresses, and with long pipes in their mouths, sat quietly outside of the coffee-houses. The sun shone upon the golden cupola of St. Mark's church, and upon the glorious bronze horses over the portal. From the red masts of the ships of Cyprus, Candia, and Morea, depended the motionless flags. A flock of pigeons filled the square by thousands, and went daintily upon the broad pavement.

I visited the Ponte Rialto, the pulse-vein which spoke of life ; and I soon comprehended the great picture of Venice — the picture of mourning — the impression of my own soul. I seemed yet to be at sea, only removed from a smaller to a greater ship, a floating ark.

The evening came ; and when the moonbeams cast their uncertain light, and diffused broader shadows, I felt myself more at home ; in the hour of the spirit-world, I could first become familiar with the dead bride. I stood at the open window : the black gondolas glided quickly over the dark, moonlit waters. I thought upon the seaman's song of kissing and of love ; felt a bitterness towards Annunciata, who had preferred the inconstant Bernardo to me ; and why ? — perhaps precisely because of the piquancy which this inconstancy gave him — such are women ! I felt bitterness, even towards the innocent, pious Flaminia : the tranquillity of the convent was more to her than my strong, brotherly love. No, no, I would love neither of them more : there was an emptiness in my heart of all, even of those which had once been dear to it. I would think of neither of them, I resolved ; and, like an uneasy ghost, my thoughts floated between Lara, the image of beauty, and Santa, the daughter of sin.

I entered a gondola, and allowed myself to be taken through the streets in the silent evening. The rowers sung their alternating song, but it was not from the " Gerusalemme Liberata ;" the Venetians had forgotten even the old melodies of the heart, for their doges were dead, and foreign hands had bound the wings of the lion, which was harnessed to their triumphal car.

"I will seize upon life—will enjoy it to the last drop!" said I, as the gondola lay still. We were at the hotel where I lodged. I went to my own room, and lay down to sleep.

That was the first day in Venice.

CHAPTER XI.

THE STORM. — SOIRÉE AT MY BANKER'S. — THE NIECE OF THE PODESTA.

THE letters which I had brought with me obtained for me acquaintances — friends, as they called themselves; and I was the Signore Abbé. Nobody instructed me, but they discovered that every thing which I said was good, excellent, and that I was possessed of talents. From Excellenza and Francesca I had often heard such things said as were very painful to me; I was often told that which was very unpleasant for me to hear; it seemed to me almost as if they sought out for every thing bad against me, that they might tell me that there were a great many people who did not at all mean so kindly by me. But this failed of its object. Of a certainty I had, however, no honest friends, since it was those only who told me disagreeable things. But I, however, felt no longer my subordinate condition, the sense of which not even Flaminia's goodness could remove.

I had now visited the rich palace of the doges, had wandered in the empty, magnificent halls; seen the chamber of the Inquisition, with the frightful picture of the torments of hell. I went through a narrow gallery, over a covered bridge, high upon the roof, above the canals on which the gondolas glided: this is the way from the doge's palace to the prisons of Venice. This bridge is called the Bridge of Sighs. Close beside it lie the wells. The light of the lamp alone from the passage can force its way between the close iron bars into the uppermost dungeon; and yet this was a cheerful, airy hall, in comparison with those which lie lower down, below the swampy cellars, deeper even than the water outside in the canals; and yet in these unhappy captives had sighed, and inscribed their names on the damp walls.

"Air, air!" demanded my heart, rent with the horrors of this place; and, entering the gondola, I flew with the speed of an arrow from the pale-red old palace, and from the columns of St. Theodoret and the Venetian lion, forth over the living, green water to the Lagunes and Lido, that I might breathe the fresh air of the sea — and I found a churchyard.

Here is the stranger, the Protestant, buried, far from his native country, — buried upon a little strip of land among the waves, which day by day seem to rend away more and more of its small remains. White human bones stuck out from the sand; the billows alone wept over them. Here often had sat the fisherman's bride or wife, waiting for the lover or the husband, who had gone out fishing upon the uncertain sea. The storm arose, and rested again upon its strong pinions; and the woman sang her songs out of "*Gerusalemme Liberata*," and listened to hear whether the man replied. But Love gave no return in song; alone she sat there, and looked out over the silent sea. Then, also, her lips became silent; her eye saw only the white bones of the dead in the sand; she heard only the hollow booming of the billows, whilst night ascended over the dead, silent Venice.

The dark picture filled my thoughts, my whole state of mind gave it a strong colouring. Solemn as a church reminding of graves and the invisible saints stood before me the entire scene. Flaminia's words resounded in my ear, that the poet, who was a prophet of God, should endeavour only to express the glorification of God, and that subjects which tended to this were of the highest character. The immortal soul ought to sing of the immortal;

the glitter of the moment changed its play of colour, and vanished with the instant that gave it birth. Kindling strength and inspiration fired my soul, but quickly died away again. I silently entered the gondola, which bore me towards Lido. The great open sea lay before me, and rolled onward to the shore in long billows. I thought of the bay of Amalfi.

Just beside me, among sea-grass and stones, sat a young man, sketching, certainly a foreign painter; it seemed to me that I recognised him, I stepped nearer, he raised his head, and we knew each other. It was Poggio, a young Venetian nobleman. I had been several times in company with him in the families whom I visited.

"Signore," exclaimed he, "you on Lido! Is it the beauty of the scene, or," added he, "some other beauty which has brought you so near to the angry Adriatic?"

We offered each other our hands. I knew something about him, that he had no property, but, on the other hand, great talent as a painter; and yet it had been whispered to me that he, in his solitude, was the greatest of misanthropes. To judge of him by his conversation, he was personified dissipation, and yet he was in reality propriety itself. According to his account of himself, Don Juan might have been his model, and yet, in fact, he combated, like the holy saint Antonius, against every temptation. A deep heart-sorrow was the ground of all this, it was whispered; but what? — whether his small worldly means or an unhappy love-affair? No, nobody knew that rightly. He seemed to speak out every thing, not to conceal the smallest thought; his behaviour seemed simple as that of a child, and yet nobody seemed rightly at all to understand him. All this had interested me, and this meeting with him now was very agreeable to me, it dissipated the clouds from my soul.

"Such a blue, billowy plain," said he, pointing to the sea, "is not to be found in Rome! The sea is the most beautiful thing on the earth! It is, also, the mother of Venus, and," added he, laughing, "is the widow of all the mighty doges of Venice."

"The Venetians must especially love the sea," said I,

U

" regarding it as their grandmother, who carried them and played with them for the sake of her beautiful daughter Venetia."

" She is no longer beautiful now, she bows her head," replied he.

" But yet," said I, " she is still happy under the sway of the Emperor Francis."

" It is a prouder thing to be queen upon the sea than a Caryatide upon land," returned he. " The Venetians have nothing to complain about, and politics are what I do not understand; but beauty, on the contrary, I do; and if you are a patron of it, as I do not doubt but you are, see, here comes my landlady's handsome daughter, and inquires whether you will take part in my frugal dinner!"

We went into the little house close by the shore. The wine was good, and Poggio most charming and entertaining. No one could have believed that his heart secretly bled.

We had sat here certainly a couple of hours, when my gondolier came to inquire whether I would not return, as there was every appearance of a storm coming on; the sea was in great agitation, and between Lido and Venice the waves ran so high that the light gondola might easily be upset.

" A storm!" exclaimed Poggio, " that is what I have wished for many a time. You must not let that escape you," said he to me; " it will abate again towards evening, and, even if it do not, there is convenience here for us to pass the night, and comfortably to let it go over our heads, whilst the dash of the waves sings us to sleep."

" I can at any time take a gondola here from the island," said I to the gondolier, and dismissed him.

The storm beat violently on the window. We went into the open air. The descending sun illumined the dark-green agitated sea, the billows heaved themselves, crested with white foam, and sank down again. Far in the distance, where the clouds stood like cliffs torn by lightning, we perceived several boats—one moment they were in sight, and then gone again. The billows lifted themselves up and struck upon the shore, covering us with their salt drops. The higher the waves flew, the louder Poggio laughed, clapped his hands, and shouted "Bravo!" to the wild element. His example infected me, and my infirm heart felt itself better amid this excitement of nature.

It soon became night. I ordered the hostess to bring us in the best wine, and we drank to the health of the storm and the sea, and Poggio sung the same song about love which I had heard in the ship.

"Health to the Venetian ladies!" said I, and he rang his glass against mine to the beautiful Roman ones. Had a stranger seen us, he would have thought that we were two happy young friends.

"The Roman women," said Poggio, "pass for the handsomest. Tell me, now, honestly, your opinion."

"I consider them as such," said I.

"Well!" said Poggio, "but the Queen of Beauty lives in Venice! You should see the niece of our Podesta! I know nothing more spiritually beautiful than she; such as she is would Canova have represented the youngest of the Graces had he known Maria. I have only seen her at mass and once in the Theatre of Saint Moses. There go all the young Venetians, like me; only they are in love with her to the death, I only adore her; she is too spiritual for my fleshly nature. But one really must adore what is heavenly. Is it not so, Signore Abbé?"

I thought on Flaminia, and my momentarily kindled merriment was at an end.

"You are become grave!" said he, "the wine is really excellent, and the waves sing and dance to our bacchanalia!"

"Does the Podesta see much company?" inquired I, that I might say something.

"Not often," replied Poggio, "what company he has is very select! The beauty is shy as an antelope, fearfully bashful, like no other woman that ever I knew; but," added he, with a jocular smile, "it may be also a way of making herself interesting! Heaven knows how the whole rightly hangs together! You see, our Podesta had two sisters, both of them were away from him a great many years; the youngest was married in Greece, and is the mother of this beautiful girl, the other sister is still unmarried, is an old maid, and she brought the beauty here about four years ago ———— "

A sudden darkness interrupted his speech! it was as if the black night had wrapped us in its mantle, and at the same moment the red lightning illumined all around. A thunder-clap followed, which reminded me of the eruptions of Vesuvius.

Our heads bowed themselves, and involuntarily we made the sign of the cross.

" Jesus Maria!" said the hostess, entering our room, " it is a fear and a horror to think of! Four of our best fishermen are out at sea! Madonna keep her hand over them! The poor Agnese sits with five children — that will be a misery!"

We perceived, through the storm, the singing of a psalm. There stood upon the shore against which the billows broke in lofty surf a troop of women and children with the holy cross: a young woman sat silently among them, with her glance riveted on the sea; one little child lay on her breast, and another, somewhat older, stood by her side, and laid its head on her lap.

With the last fearful flash, the storm seemed to have removed itself to a greater distance; the horizon became brighter, and more clearly shone the white foam upon the boiling sea.

" There they are !" exclaimed the woman, and sprang up and pointed to a black speck, which became more and more distinct.

" Madonna be merciful to them!" said an old fisherman, who, with his thick brown hood drawn over his head, stood with folded hands, and gazed on the dark object. At that same moment it vanished in a foaming whirlpool.

The old man had seen aright. I heard the scream of the despairing little group; it grew all the stronger as the sea became calmer, the heaven clearer, and the certainty greater. The children dropped the holy cross; they let it fall in the sand, and clung, crying, to their mothers. The old fisherman, however, raised it again, impressed a kiss upon the Redeemer's feet, raised it on high, and named the holy name of the Madonna.

Towards midnight the heavens were clear, the sea more tranquil, and the full moon cast her long beams over the calm bay between the island and Venice. Poggio entered the gondola with me, and we left the unfortunates, whom we could neither assist nor comfort.

The next evening we met again at my banker's, one of the richest in Venice. The company was very numerous; of the ladies I knew none, neither had I any interest about them.

They began to speak in the room of the storm the evening before. Poggio took up the word, and told of the death of the fishermen, of the misfortune of the families, and gave it to be very clearly understood how easily a great deal of their distress might be relieved; how a small gift from every person present would amount to a sum which would be of the greatest benefit to the unfortunately bereaved families, but nobody seemed to understand him; they deplored, shrugged their shoulders, and then began talking of something else.

Presently those who were possessed of any company-talent, produced it for public benefit. Poggio sang a merry barcarole; but I seemed to see the while, in his polite smile, bitterness and coldness towards the dignified circle, which would not allow themselves to be guided by his noble eloquence.

" You do not sing ? " asked the lady of the house from me, when he had done.

" I will have the honour to improvise before you," said I, as a thought entered my mind.

" He is an improvisatore," I heard whispered around me. The eyes of the ladies sparkled; the gentlemen bowed. I took a guitar, and begged them to give me a subject.

" Venice ! " cried a lady looking boldly into my eyes.

" Venice ! " repeated the young gentlemen, " because the ladies are handsome ! "

I touched a few chords ; described the pomp and glory of Venice in the days of her greatness, as I had read about it, and as my imagination had dreamed of its being, and all eyes flashed, they fancied that it was so now. I sang about the beauty in the balcony in the moonlight night, thought upon Santa and Lara, and every lady imagined I meant it for her, and clapped her hands in applause. Sgricci * himself could not have had more success.

" She is here ! " whispered Poggio to me, " the niece of the Podesta."

But we were prevented from saying more to each other. I was requested yet again to improvise : a deputation of ladies and an old Excellenza presented the wishes of the company. I was willing, because it was my own wish ; I had anticipated it, and only desired that in some one of the given themes I might find occasion to describe the storm which I had seen, the misery of the unfortunates, and by the might of song to conquer where eloquence could not move.

They gave me the Apotheosis of Titian. If he had only been a seaman, I would have brought him forwards as spokesman on the occasion, but in his praise I could not bring in the idea which I wished to develope. The subject was, nevertheless, a rich one ; my management of it exceeded expectation : I stood like the idol of the company, it was my own Apotheosis !

" No happiness can be greater than yours ! " said the lady of the house ; " it must be an infinitely delightful feeling, that of possessing a talent like yours, that can transport and charm all those around you."

" It is a delightful feeling ! " said I.

" Describe it in a beautiful poem ! " said she, beseechingly ; " it is so easy to you that one forgets how unreasonable one is in making so many demands upon you."

" I know one sentiment," returned I, and my design gave me boldness, — " I know one emotion which is not exceeded by any other, which makes every heart a poet, which awakes the same consciousness of happiness, and I

---

* One of the celebrated improvisatori of our time. — *Author's Note.*

consider myself to be so great a magician as to have the power of exciting it in every heart. But this art has this peculiarity, that it cannot be given, it must be purchased."

"We must become acquainted with it," they all exclaimed.

"Here, upon this table," said I, "I collect the sums, — he who gives the most will be most deeply initiated therein."

"I will give my gold chain," said one lady, immediately, laughing, and laid it in sport upon the table.

"I, all my card-money," cried another, and smiled at my fancy.

"But it is a serious earnestness!" said I, "the pledges must not be reclaimed."

"We will venture it," said the many, who had already laid down money, chains, and rings, still inwardly having doubts of my power.

"But if no emotion whatever takes hold of me," said an officer, "may I not then take back my two ducats?"

"Then, the wagers are forfeited?" cried Poggio. I bowed assentingly.

All laughed, all waited for the result full of expectation; and I began to improvise. A holy flame penetrated me, I sang about the proud sea, — the bridegroom of Venice; about the sons of the sea, — the bold mariners and fishermen in their little boats. I described a storm; the wife's and the bride's longing and anxiety; described that which I myself had seen; the children who had let fall the holy crucifix, and clung to their mothers, and the old fisherman who kissed the feet of the Redeemer. It was as if a God had spoken through me — as if I were the work-tool of His strong word.

A deep silence prevailed through the room, and many an eye wept.

I then conducted them into the huts of poverty, and took help and life through our little gift; and I sang how much more blessed it was to give than to receive, — sang of the delight which filled my breast, which filled every heart, that had contributed its mite. It was a feeling which nothing could outweigh; it was the divine voice in all hearts, which made them holier, and loftier, and elevated them to the poet! And, whilst I spoke, my voice increased in strength and fulness.

I had won every thing. A tumultuous bravo saluted me; and, at the conclusion of my song, I handed the rich gifts to Poggio, that thereby he might take help to the unfortunates.

A young lady sank at my feet — a more beautiful triumph had my talent never obtained for me — seized my hand, and, with tears in her beautiful dark eyes, looked gratefully into my soul. This glance singularly agitated me; it was an expression of beauty which I seemed to have once beheld in a dream.

"The Mother of God reward you!" stammered she, whilst the blood crimsoned her cheek. She concealed her countenance, and withdrew from me, as if in horror at what she had done; and who could have been so cruel as to have made a jest of the pure emotions of innocence? Every one pressed around me; they were inexhaustible in my praise. All talked about the unfortunates of Lido; and I stood there as their benefactor.

"It is more blessed to give than to receive!" This evening had taught me the truth of this. Poggio pressed me in his arms.

"Excellent man," said he, "I esteem and honour you! Beauty brings to you her homage; she, who with a look can make thousands happy, bows herself before you in the dust!"

"Who was she?" inquired I, with a constrained voice.

"The most beautiful in Venice!" replied he. "The niece of the Podesta!"

That remarkable glance, that shape of beauty, stood livingly impressed in my soul; inexplicable remembrances awoke, and I also exclaimed, "She was beautiful!"

"You do not recognise me, then, signore?" said an old lady, who came up to me. "It is a many years since I had the honour of making your acquaintance!" She smiled, offered me her hand, and thanked me for my improvisation.

I bowed politely ; her features seemed familiar to me, but when and where I had seen her was not clear to me. I was obliged to say so.

" Yes, that is natural ! " said she ; " we have only seen each other one single time ! That was in Naples. My brother was physician. You visited him with a gentleman of the Borghese family."

" I remember it," I exclaimed. " Yes, now I recognise you ! Least of all did I expect that we should meet again here in Venice ! "

" My brother," said she, " for whom I kept house, died about four years ago. Now I live with my elder brother. Our servant shall take you our card. My niece is a child — a strange child ; she will go away — away instantly. I must attend her ! "

The old lady again gave me her hand, and left the room.

" Lucky fellow ! " said Poggio, " that was the Podesta's sister ! You know her — have had an invitation from her ! Half of Venice will envy you. Button your coat well about your heart when you go there, that you be not wounded like the rest of us, who approach in the slightest degree towards the enemy's battery."

The beauty was gone. At the moment of emotion, transported by her feelings, she had fallen at my feet ; but in the same moment had awoke her great bashfulness; and maidenly shame, and anxiety, and horror, at her own deed, had driven her away from the great circle, where she had drawn attention to herself ; and yet nothing was said but in her praise and admiration. They united her praises with mine ! The queen of beauty had enchanted every one. Her heart, they said, was as noble as her form.

The consciousness of having done a good work threw a ray of light into my soul ; I felt a noble pride ; felt my own happiness in being possessed of the gift of song. All the praise and love which surrounded me melted away all bitterness from my soul ; it seemed to me as if my spiritual strength had arisen purer and mightier from its swoon. I thought of Flaminia, and thought of her without pain; she would, indeed, have pressed my hand as a sister. Her words, that the poet ought only to sing of that which was holy and for the glorifying of God, cast a clear light into my soul. I felt again strength and courage, a mild tranquillity diffused itself over my whole being; and, for the first time, after many, many months, I again felt happiness. It was a delightful evening.

Poggio rung his glass against mine. We concluded a friendship between us, and sealed it with a brotherly *thou*.

It was late when I returned home, but I felt no want of sleep; the moon shone so brightly upon the water in the canal, the atmosphere was so high and blue. With the pious faith of a child, I folded my hands and prayed, — " Father, forgive me my sins! Give me strength to become a good and noble man, and thus may I still dare to remember Flaminia, to think upon my sister. Strengthen, also, her soul; let her never imagine of my suffering! Be good to us, and merciful, Eternal God! "

And now my heart was wondrously light; the empty canals of Venice and the old palaces seemed to me beautiful, — a sleeping fairy world.

The next morning I was as cheerful as ever; a noble pride had awoke in my breast. I was happy because of my spiritual gifts, and thankful to God. I took a gondola, to go and make my visit at the house of the Podesta, whose sister I knew: to speak candidly, I had also a desire to see the young lady who had paid such living homage to me, and who passed for the queen of beauty.

" Palazzo d'Othello! " said the gondolier, and led me through the great canal to an old building, relating to me the while how the Moor of Venice, who killed his beautiful wife Desdemona, had lived there; and that all the English went to visit this house, as if it were St. Mark's Church, or the arsenal.

They all received me as if I had been a beloved relation. Rosa, the Podesta's old sister, talked of her dear deceased brother; of lively, merry Naples, which she had not now seen for these four years.

" Yes," said she, " Maria longs for it, also ; and we will set off when they least think of it. I must see Vesuvius and the beautiful Capri yet once more before I die ! "

Maria entered and offered me her hand, with a sisterly and yet singularly bashful manner. She was beautiful ; indeed, I thought more beautiful that when last evening .she had bent herself before me. Poggio was right, so must the youngest of the Graces appear ; no female form could have been more exquisitely formed — Lara, perhaps ? Yes, Lara, the blind girl in her poor garments, with the little bouquet of violets in her hair, was as beautiful as Maria in her splendid dress. Her closed eyes had appealed to my heart more touchingly than the singularly dark glance of fire in Maria's eyes ; every feature, how-ever, had a pensive expression like Lara's ; but then, in the open dark eye, was peace and joy, which Lara had never known. There was, nevertheless, so much resemblance as to bring the blind beggar girl to my mind, whom she never had seen, nay, even that strange reverential feeling, as if to some superior being, again into my heart.

My powers of mind exhibited greater flexibility, my eloquence became richer. I felt that I pleased every one of them ; and Maria seemed to bestow upon my talents as much admiration as her beauty won from me.

I looked upon her as a lover looks upon a beautiful female figure, the perfect image of his beloved. In Maria, I found all Lara's beauty almost as in a mirror, and Flaminia's entire sisterly spirit ; one could not but have confidence in her. It was to me as if we had known one another for a long time.

CHAPTER XII.

THE SINGER.

A GREAT event in my life lies so near to me here that it almost dislodges all others from my mind, as the lofty pine-tree of the wood draws away the eye from the low undergrowth; I therefore only passingly describe that which lies in the middle ground.

I was often at the house of the Podesta—I was, they said, its enlivening genius. Rosa talked to me about her beloved Naples, and I read aloud to her and her neice the "Divina Comedia," Alfieri and Nicolini, and I was captivated with Maria's mind and feeling as much as with the works of the poets themselves. Out of this house Poggio was my dearest associate; they knew it, and he, too, was invited by the Podesta. He thanked me for this, and declared that it was my merits and not his, and our friendship, which had introduced him there, for which he was the envy of the whole youth of Venice.

Every where was my talent as improvisatore admired, nay, it was so highly esteemed that no circle would allow me to escape before I had gratified their wish by giving them a proof of my power. The first artists extended to me their hands as brothers, and encouraged me to come forward in public. And in part I did so before the members of the *Academia del Arte* one evening, by improvising on Dandola's procession to Constantinople, and upon the bronze horses on the church of St. Mark, for which I was honoured with a diploma, and received into their Society.

But a much greater pleasure awaited me in the house of the Podesta. One day Maria presented to me a little casket containing a beautiful necklace of lovely, bright-coloured mussel shells, exceedingly small, delicate, and lovely, strung upon a silken thread ; it was a present from the unfortunates of Lido, whose benefactor I was called.

" It is very beautiful," said Maria.

" That you must preserve for your bride," said Rosa ; " it is a lovely gift for her, and with that intention has it been given."

" My bride," repeated I, gravely, " I have not one— really have not one."

" But she will come," said Rosa,— " you will have a bride, and certainly the most beautiful of all."

" Never !" repeated I, and looked on the ground, in the deep sense of how much I had lost.

Maria, also, became silent with my dejection. She had pleased herself so much in the idea of astonishing me by the gift, and had received it from Poggio, to whom it had oeen given, for that purpose ; and I now stood embarrassed, concealing my embarrassment so ill, and holding the necklace in my hand. I would so gladly have given it to Maria, but Rosa's words staggered my determination. Maria certainly divined my thoughts, for, as I fixed my eye upon her, a deep crimson flushed her countenance.

" You come very seldom to us," said my rich banker's wife one day as I paid her a visit— " very seldom come here, but to the Podesta's !— yes, that is more amusing ! Maria is, indeed, the first beauty in Venice, and you are the first improvisatore. It will thus be a very good match ; the girl will have a magnificent estate in Calabria,— it is her own heritage, or has been bought for that purpose. Be bold, and it will succeed. You will be the envy of all Venice."

" How can you think," returned I, " that such a conceited thought should enter my mind ? I am as far from being a lover of Maria's as any body else can be. Her beauty charms me, as all beauty does, but that is not love ; and that she has fortune does not operate with me."

" Ah, well, well ! we shall see for all that !" said the lady ; " love gets on best in life when it stands well in the kitchen— when there is enough to fill the pot. It is out of this that people must live !"

And with this she laughed and gave me her hand.

It provoked me that people should think and should talk in this way. I determined to go less frequently to the house of the Podesta, spite of their all being so dear to me. I had thought of spending this evening with them, but I now altered my determination. My blood was in agitation. Nay, thought I, wherefore vex myself? I will be cheerful. Life is beautiful if people will only let it be so; free I am, and nobody shall influence me!—Have I not strength and will of my own?

In the dusk of the evening I took a ramble alone through the narrow streets, where the houses met one another, where, therefore, the little rooms were brightly lighted up, and the people thronged together. The lights shone in long rays upon the Great Canal, the gondolas flew rapidly along under the single lofty arch which sustained the bridge. I heard the voice of singing; it was that ballad about kissing and love, and, like the serpent around the tree of knowledge, I knew the beautiful face of Sin.

I went onward through the narrow streets and came to a house more lighted up than any of the others, into which a crowd of people were going. It was one of the minor theatres of Venice, Saint Lucas', I believe, it was called. A little company gave the same opera there twice in the day, as in the *Theatro Fenize* in Naples. The first representation of the piece begins about four o'clock in the afternoon and ends at six, and the second begins at eight. The price was very low, but nobody must expect to see any thing extraordinary; yet the desire which the lower classes here have to hear music, and the curiosity of strangers, cause there often to be very good houses, and that even twice in the evening.

I now read in the play-bill, "*Donna Caritea, Regina de Spagna,* the music by Mercadante."

" I can come out again if I get weary of it," said I to myself; " and, at all events, I can go in and look at the pretty women. My blood is warm, my heart beats like Bernardo's and Federigo's; people shall no longer jeer the boy from the Campagna with having goat's milk in his blood. If I had always been devoted to pleasure — as I now am — I should certainly have been much happier! Yes, life is short, age brings cold and ice!"

I went in, received a dirty little ticket, and was conducted to a box near the stage. There were two rows of boxes, one above the other; the places for the spectators were right spacious, but the stage itself seemed to me like a tray; several people could not have turned themselves round upon it, and yet there was going to be exhibited an equestrian opera, with a tournament and a procession. The boxes were internally dirty and defaced, the ceiling seemed to press the whole together. A man in his shirt-sleeves came forward to light the lamps; the people talked aloud in the pit; the musicians came into the orchestra — they could only raise a quartett.

Every thing showed what the whole might be expected to be, yet still I resolved to wait out the first act. I noticed the ladies around me, — none of them pleased me. A young man now entered the box next to mine; I had met him in company. He smiled and offered me his hand, saying, —

"Who would have thought of meeting you here? — But," whispered he, "one can often make very pleasant acquaintances here : in the pale moonlight people easily get acquainted."

He kept talking on, and was hissed, because the overture had begun; it sounded very deplorable, and the curtain rolled up. The whole corps consisted of two ladies and three gentlemen, who looked as if they had been fetched in from field labour, and bedizened in knightly apparel.

"Yes," said my neighbour, "the solo parts are often not badly cast. Here is a comic actor who might figure in any first-rate theatre. Ah, ye good saints!" exclaimed he to himself, as the queen of the piece entered with two ladies; "are we to have her to-night? Yes, then, I would not give a half-zwanziger for the whole thing; Jeanette was much better!"

It was a slight, ordinary figure, with a thin, sharp countenance, and deeply-sunken dark eyes, who now came forward. Her miserable dress hung loosely about her; it was poverty which came forward as the queen; and yet it was with a grace which amazed me, and which accorded so little with the rest, — a grace which would excellently have become a young and beautiful girl. She advanced towards the lamps, — my heart beat violently, I scarcely dared to inquire her name; I believed that my eyes deceived me.

"What is she called?" at length I asked.

"Annunciata," replied my neighbour; "sing she cannot, and that one may see by that little skeleton!"

Every word fell upon my heart like corrosive poison; I sat as if nailed fast; my eyes were fixed immovably upon her.

She sang; no, it was not Annunciata's voice, it sounded feeble, inharmonious, and uncertain.

"There are certainly traces of a good school," said my neighbour; "but there is not power for it."

"She does not resemble," said I tremulously, "a namesake of hers, Annunciata, a young Spaniard, who once made a great figure at Naples and Rome?"

"Ah, yes," answered he; it is she herself! Seven or eight years ago she sat on the high horse. Then she was young, and had a voice like a Malibran; but now all the gilding is gone; that is, in reality, the lot of all such talents! For a few years they shine in their meridian glory, and, dazzled by admiration, they never think that they may decline, and thus rationally retire whilst glory is beaming around them. The public first find out the change, and that is the melancholy part of it; and then, commonly, these good ladies live too expensively, and all their gains are squandered, and then it goes down-hill at a gallop! You have then seen her in Rome, have you?" asked he.

"Yes," replied I, "several times."

"It must be a horrible change! most to be deplored, however, for her," said he; "she is said to have lost her voice in a long, severe sickness, which must be some four or five years since; but with that the public has nothing to do. Will you not clap for old acquaintance sake? I will help; it will please the old lady!"

He clapped loudly; some in the parterre followed his example, but then succeeded a loud hissing, amid which the queen proudly went off the scene. It was Annunciata!"

"*Fuimus Troes!*" whispered my neighbour. Now came forward the heroine of the piece; she was a very pretty young girl, of a luxuriant form, and with a burning glance : she was received with acclamations and the clapping of hands. All the old recollections rushed into my soul ; the transports of the Roman people and their jubilations over Annunciata ; her triumphal procession, and my strong love! Bernardo, then, had also forsaken her : or, had she not loved him ? I saw really how she bent her head down to him, and pressed her lips upon his brow. He had forsaken her — forsaken her, then she became ill, and her beauty had vanished: it was that alone which he had loved !

She again came forward in another scene ; how suffering she looked, and how old ! It was a painted corpse which terrified me. I was embittered against Bernardo, who could forsake her for the loss of her beauty, and yet it was that which had wounded me so deeply; the beauty of Annunciata's soul must have been the same as before.

"Are you not well?" inquired the stranger from me, for I looked deadly pale.

"It is here so oppressively warm," said I, rising, left the box, and went out into the fresh air. I hastened through the narrow streets ; a thousand emotions agitated my breast ; I knew not where to go. I stood again outside the theatre, where a fellow was just taking down the placard to put up the one for the next day.

"Where does Annunciata live?" whispered I in his ear. He turned himself round, looked at me, and repeated, "Annunciata? Signore means, no doubt, Aurelia? she who acted the part of the man within ? I will show you her house ; but she is not yet at liberty."

"No, no," replied I, "Annunciata ; she who sang the part of the queen."

The fellow measured me with his eye.

x

" The little thin woman ? " asked he, " yes, she, I fancy,
is not accustomed to visitors, but there may be good reasons.
I will show the gentleman the house ; you will give me
something for my trouble ? — but you cannot see her yet
for an hour ; the opera will detain her as long as that."

" Wait, then, here for me," said I, entered a gondola,
and bade the man row me about wherever he would.   My
soul was inwardly troubled ; I must yet once more see
Annunciata, — talk to her.   She was unhappy !   But
what could I do for her ?   Anguish and sorrow drove
me on.

An hour was scarcely gone when the gondola again lay
with me before the theatre, where I found the fellow
waiting for me.

He led me through narrow, dirty lanes, to an old desolate house, in the uppermost garret of which a light was
burning : he pointed up. `

" Does she live there ? " I exclaimed.

" I will lead Excellenza in," said he, and pulled at the
bell-cord.

" Who is there ? " inquired a female voice.

" Marco Lugano ! " replied he, and the door opened.

It was dark night within ; the little lamp before the
image of the Madonna was gone out, the glimmering wick
alone shone like a point of blood ; I kept close to him.
A door far above was opened, and we saw a ray of light
shine down towards us.

" Now she comes herself," said the man.

I slipped a few pieces of money into his hand ; he
thanked me a thousand times, and hastened down, whilst
I ascended the last steps.

" Are there any new changes for to-morrow, Marco
Lugano ? " I heard the voice inquire.   It was Annunciata :
she stood at the door ; a little silken net was bound round
her hair, and a large dark wrapping dress was thrown
loosely about her.

" Do not fall, Marco," said she, and went before into
the room, whilst I followed after her.

" Who are you ?   What do you want here ? " exclaimed
she, terrified, as she saw me enter.

" Annunciata!" exclaimed I with painful emotion. She stared at me.

" Jesus Maria!" cried she, and pressed her hands before her face.

" A friend!" stammered I; "an old acquaintance, to whom you once occasioned much joy, much happiness, seeks you out, and ventures to offer you his hand!"

She took her hands from her face, pale as death, and stood like a corpse; and the dark, intellectual eyes flashed wildly. Older Annunciata had become, and bore the marks of suffering; but there were still remains of that wonderful beauty, still that same soul-beaming but melancholy look.

" Antonio!" said she, — and I saw a tear in her eye, — " is it thus we meet? Leave me! our paths lie so wide apart, — yours upwards to happiness, mine down — to happiness also!" sighed she deeply.

" Drive me not from you!" exclaimed I; as a friend — a brother I am come; my heart impelled me to it! You are unhappy, you to whom thousands acclaimed gladness, who made thousands happy!"

" The wheel of fortune turns round," said she. " Fortune follows youth and beauty, and the world harnesses itself to their triumphal car : intellect and heart are the worst dower of nature; they are forgotten for youth and beauty, and the world is always right!"

" You have been ill, Annunciata!" said I; and my lips trembled.

" Ill — very ill, for almost a year; but it was not the death of me," said she, with a bitter smile; " youth died, however; my voice died; and the public became dumb at the sight of these two corpses in one body! The physician said that they were only apparently dead, and the body believed so. But the body required clothing and food, and for two long years gave all its wealth to purchase these; then it must paint itself, and come forward as if the dead were still living; but it came forward as a ghost, and, that people might not be frightened at it, it showed itself again in a little theatre where few lamps were burning, and it was half dark. But, even there they observed that youth and voice were dead, were buried corpses, Annunciata is dead : there hangs her living image !" and she pointed to the wall.

In that miserable chamber hung a picture, a half-length picture, in a rich gilded frame, which made a strange contrast to the other poverty around. It was the picture of Annunciata, painted as Dido. It was her image as it stood in my soul; the intellectually beautiful countenance, with pride on the brow. I looked round upon the actual Annunciata; she held her hands before her face and wept.

"Leave me, — forget my existence, as the world has forgotten it !" besought she, and motioned with her hands.

"I cannot," said I, — "cannot thus leave you ! Madonna is good and merciful ; Madonna will help us all !"

"Antonio," said she, solemnly, "can you make a jest of me in my misfortune ? No, that you cannot, like all the rest of the world. But I do not comprehend you. When all the world acclaimed my praise, and lavished flattery and adoration upon me, you forsook me, forsook me so entirely ! And now, when my glory, which had captivated the world, is gone, when every body regards me as a foreign, indifferent object, you come to me, seek me out !"

"You yourself drove me from you !" exclaimed I ; "drove me out into the world ! My fate, my circumstances," added I, in a milder tone, "drove me out into the world !"

She became silent ; but her eye was riveted with a strangely searching expression upon me. She seemed as if she wished to speak ; the lips moved, but she spoke not. A deep sigh ascended from her breast ; she cast her eyes upwards, and again sunk them to the floor. Her hand was passed over her forehead ; it was as if a thought went through her soul, known only to God and herself.

"I have seen you again !" exclaimed she at length ; "seen you yet once more in this world ! I feel that you are a good, a nob'e man. May you be happier than I have been ! The swan has sung its last ! Beauty has gone out of flower ! I am quite alone in this world ! Of the happy Annunciata there remains only the picture on the wall !

I have now one prayer," said she, " one prayer, which
you will not refuse me ! Annunciata, who once delighted
you, beseeches you to grant it ! "

" All, all, I promise ! " exclaimed I, and pressed her
hand to my lips.

" Regard it as a dream," said she, " that you have seen
me this evening ! If we meet again in the world, we do
not know each other ! Now we part ! " She offered me,
with these words, her hand, and added, " In a better
world we shall meet again ! Here our paths separate !
Farewell, Antonio, farewell ! "

I sank down, overcome by sorrow, before her. I knew
nothing more ; she directed me like a child, and I wept
like one.

" I come ! I come again ! " said I, and left her.

" Farewell ! " I heard her say ; but I saw her no
more.

All was dark below and in the street.

" God, how miserable may Thy creatures be ! " exclaimed I in my anguish, and wept. No sleep visited my
eyes : it was a night of sorrow.

Amid a thousand plans which I devised, and then again
rejected, I went to her house on the day but one following. I felt my poverty ; I was only a poor lad, that had
been taken from the Campagna. My superior freedom of
mind had, in fact, laid me in the fetters of dependence ;
but my talents seemed really to open to me a brilliant
path. Could it be a more brilliant one than Annunciata's ;
and how was this ended ? The rushing river which had
gleamed forth in cascades and amid rainbows had ended
in the Pontine Marsh of misery.

Yet once more I felt impelled to see Annunciata, and to
talk with her. It was the second day after our meeting
that I again mounted up the narrow, dark stairs. The
door was closed ; I knocked on it, and an old woman
opened a side-door, and asked if I wished to see the room,
which was vacant. " But it is quite too little for you,"
said she.

" But the singer ? " inquired I.

" She has flitted," answered the old woman ; " flitted

all away yesterday morning. Has set off on a journey, I
fancy ; it was done in a mighty hurry."

" Do not you know where she is gone ? " I asked.

" No," returned she ; " she did not say a word about
that.   But they are gone to Padua, or Trieste, or Ferrara,
or some such place, as, indeed, there are so many."   And,
with this, she opened the door, that I might see the empty
room.

I went to the theatre. The company had yesterday
given their last representation : it was now closed.

She was gone, the unfortunate Annunciata. A bitter
feeling took possession of my mind. Bernardo, thought I,
is, after all, the cause of her misfortune, of the whole
direction which my life has taken. Had it not been for
him she would have loved me ; and her love would have
given to my mind a great strength and development.
Had I at once followed her, and come forward as improvisatore, my triumph, perhaps, would have united itself
to hers : we should have created ourselves a position ; all
might have been so different then ! Care would not then
have furrowed her brow!

CHAPTER XIII.

POGGIO —— ANNUNCIATA —— MARIA.

POGGIO visited me, and inquired the reason of my depression of mind : but I could not tell him the cause ; I could
tell it to no one.

" Thou lookest really," said he, " as if the bad sirocco
blew upon thee ! Is it from the heart that this hot air
comes ? The little bird within there might be burned ;
and, as it is no phœnix, it may not be benefited thereby.
It must now and then have a flight out, pick the red
berries in the field, and the fine roses in the balcony, to
get itself right. My little bird does so, and finds itself all
the better for it ; has excellent spirits, sings merrily into

my blood and my whole being. And it is that which gives me the good-humour that I have! Thou must do the same also, and shalt do so! A poet must have a sound, healthy bird in his breast — a bird which knows both roses and berries, the sour and the sweet, the cloudy heavens and the clear ether!"

" That is a beautiful idea about a poet," said I.

" Christ became a man like the rest of us," said he, " and descended even down into hell to the damned! The divine must unite itself to the earthly, and there will be produced therefrom a mighty result of —— But it is really a magnificent lecture which I am beginning. I ought, sure enough, to give one, I have promised to do so; but I fancy it was on another subject. What is the meaning of it, when a gentleman all at once forsakes his friends; for three whole days has never been to the Podesta's house? That is abominable — very abominable of him! The family is also very angry. This very day thou must go there, and, kneeling like another Frederick Barbarossa, hold the stirrup. Not to have been for three days at the Podesta's house! I heard that from Signora Rosa. What hast thou been doing with thyself?

" I have not felt well ; have not been out."

" No, dear friend," interrupted he, " one knows better than that! The evening before last thou wentest to the Opera La Regina di Spagna, in which the little Aurelia appears as a knight — that is, a little Orlando Furioso! But the conquest need not bring grey hairs to anybody: it cannot be so difficult. However, be that as it may, thou goest with me to dine at the Podesta's. There are we invited, and I have given my hand to take thee with me."

" Poggio," said I, gravely, " I will tell thee the reasons why I have not been there; why I shall not go there so frequently."

I then told him what the banker's wife had whispered to me; how Venice talked about its being my design to obtain the beautiful Maria, who had a fortune and an estate in Calabria.

" Nay," cried Poggio, " I would be very glad, indeed, if they would say that of me; and so thou wilt not go for

that reason ?   Yes, truly, people do say so, and I believe
it myself, because it is so natural.   But whether we are
right or wrong, that is no reason why thou shouldst be
uncivil to the family.   Maria is handsome, very handsome,
has understanding and feeling, and thou lovest her too,
that I have seen all along plainly enough."

" No, no," exclaimed I, " my thoughts are a very long
way from love !   Maria resembles a blind child whom I
once saw, a child which wonderfully attracted me, as a
child only could.   That resemblance has often agitated me
in Maria, and has rivetted my eye upon her.

" Maria also was once blind !" said Poggio, in a somewhat serious tone ;   " she was blind when she came from
Greece ; her uncle, the physician in Naples, performed an
operation on her eyes which restored her sight."

" My blind child was not Maria," said I.

" Thy blind child !" repeated Poggio, merrily ;   " it
must be a very wonderful person, however, that blind child
of thine, which could set thee a-staring at Maria, and finding out a likeness !   Yes, that is only speaking figuratively ;
it is the little blind Love with whom, once upon a time,
thou madest acquaintance, and he has made thee look at
Maria.   Now confess it thyself !   Before we ourselves are
aware of it, the nuptials will be announced, and you drive
off from Venice."

" No, Poggio," I exclaimed, " you affront me by talking in this way ; I shall never marry.   My love's dream
is over.   I never think of such a thing — never can.   By
the eternal heavens and all the saints, I neither will nor
can !"

" Silence ! silence !" cried Poggio, interrupting me,
" let's have no oath about it.   I will believe thee, and will
contradict everybody that says thou art in love with
Maria, and that you are going to be married.   But don't
go, and swear that you never will marry ; perhaps the
bridal is nearer than you imagine : even within this very
year it is quite possible."

" Thine, perhaps," replied I, " but mine never !"

" Nay, so thou thinkest, then, that I can get married ?"
exclaimed Poggio ; " no, dear friend, I have no means of

keeping a wife ; the pleasure would be much too expensive
for me."

"Thy marriage will take place before mine," replied I ;
"perhaps even the handsome Maria may be thine, and
whilst Venice is saying it is to me that she will give her
hand, it is to thee."

"That would be badly done," replied he, and laughed ;
"no, I have given her a far better husband than myself.
Shall we lay a wager," continued he, "that thou wilt be
married either to Maria or some other lady ; that thou
wilt be a husband, and I an old bachelor ? Two bottles
of champagne we will bet, which we will drink on thy
wedding-day."

"I dare do that," said I, and smiled.

I was obliged to go with him to the Podesta's. Signora Rosa scolded me, and so did the Podesta. Maria
was silent ; my eye rested upon her : Venice said, actually,
that she was my bride ! Rosa and I touched glasses.

"No lady may drink the health of the improvisatore,"
said Poggio ; "he has sworn eternal hatred against the
fair sex ; he never will be married !"

"Eternal hatred ?" returned I ; "and what if I do not
marry, cannot I honour and value still that which is beautiful in woman, that which more than any thing else elevates and softens every relation of life ?"

"Not be married !" cried the Podesta ; "that were the
most miserable thought which your genius ever gave birth
to ! nor either is it handsome behaviour in a friend," said
he, jestingly, turning to Poggio, "to reveal it."

"Only to make him ashamed of it !" returned Poggio ;
"he might otherwise so easily get enamoured of this his
only bad thought, and, because it is so remarkably brilliant, might mistake it for an original one, and regularly
attach himself to it !"

They jested with me, made fun of me : I could not be
other than cheerful. Exquisite dishes and glorious wine
were set before me. I thought upon Annunciata's poverty,
and that, perhaps, she was now famishing.

"You promised to send us Silvio Pellico's works," said
Rosa, when we separated. "Do not forget it, and come, like

a good creature, every day to us : you have accustomed us to
it, and nobody in Venice can be more grateful than we are."

I went—I went right often; for I felt how much they
loved me.

About a month had now passed since my last conversation with Poggio, and I had not been able to speak about
Annunciata : I was, therefore, obliged to trust to chance,
which often knits up the broken thread.

One evening as I was at the Podesta's, Maria seemed to
me singularly thoughtful : a vivid suffering seemed impressed upon her whole being. I had been reading to her
and her aunt, and even during this her mind seemed abstracted. Rosa left the room ; never had I until now been
alone with Maria : a strange, inexplicable presentiment, as
if of approaching evil, filled my breast. I endeavoured to
begin a conversation about Silvio Pellico, about the influence of political life upon the poetical mind.

"Signore Abbé," said she, without appearing to have
heard a word of my remarks, for her whole thoughts seemed
to have been directed to one only subject. "Antonio,"
continued she, with a tremulous voice, whilst the blood
mantled in her cheeks, " I must speak with you. A dying
person has made me give her my hand that I would do so."

She paused, and I stood silent, strangely agitated by her
words.

" We are actually not so very much of strangers to
each other," said she, " and yet this moment is very terrible to me ; " and as she spoke, she became pale as death.

" God in heaven !" exclaimed I, " what has happened ? "

" God's wonderful guidance," said she, " has drawn me
into your life's circumstances, has made me participate in
a secret, in a connection which no stranger ought to know ;
but my lips are silent ; what I have promised to the dead
I have not told, not even to my aunt."

With this she drew forth a little packet, and giving it to
me, continued, " This is destined for you : it will tell you
every thing ; I have promised to deliver it into your hands ;
I have had it in my possession for two whole days ; I
knew not how I should be able to fulfil my promise, — I
have now done it. Be silent, as I shall be."

" From whom does it come ? " inquired I ; " may I not know that ? "

" Eternal God ! " said she, and left the room.

I hastened home, and opened the little packet. It contained many loose papers ; the first I saw was in my own handwriting, a little verse written with pencil ; but underneath it were marked in ink three black crosses, as if they were the writing on a grave. It was the poem which I had thrown to Annunciata's feet the first time I saw her.

" Annunciata ! " sighed I, deeply : " Eternal Mother of God ! it comes then from her ! "

Among the papers lay a sealed note, upon which was inscribed, " To Antonio." I tore it open, — yes, it was from her. Half of it I saw was written during the night of the evening when I had seen her: the latter part appeared fresher ; it was extremely faint, and written with a trembling hand. I read : —

" I have seen thee, Antonio ! seen thee once more. It was my only wish, and I dreaded it for a moment, even as one dreads death, which, however, brings happiness. It is only an hour since I saw thee. When thou readest this it may be months — not longer. It is said that those who see themselves will shortly die. Thou art the half of my soul — thou wast my thought — thee have I seen ! Thou hast seen me in my happiness, in my misery ! Thou wast the only one who now would know the poor forsaken Annunciata ! But I, also, deserved it.

" I dare now speak thus to thee, because when thou readest this I shall be no more. I loved thee — loved thee from the days of my prosperity to my last moment. Madonna willed not that we should be united in this world, and she divided us.

" I knew thy love for me before that unfortunate evening when the shot struck Bernardo, on which thou declared it. My pain at the misfortune which separated us, the great grief which crushed my heart, bound my tongue. I concealed my face on the body of him whom I believed to be dead, and thou wast gone — I saw thee no more !

" Bernardo was not mortally wounded, and I left him not before this was ascertained of a truth. Did this

awaken doubt in your soul of my love for you? I knew
not where you were, nor could I learn. A few days afterwards a singular old woman came to me, and presented to
me a note, in which you had written, 'I journey to Naples!' and to which your name was signed. She said
that you must have a passport and money; I influenced
Bernardo to obtain this from his uncle the senator. At
that time my wish was a command, my word had power.
I obtained that which I desired. Bernardo was also troubled about you.

"He became perfectly well again, and he loved me: I
believe really that he honestly loved me. But you alone
occupied all my thoughts. He left Rome, and I, too, was
obliged to go to Naples. My old friend's illness compelled
me to remain for a month at Mola di Gaeta. When at last
we arrived at Naples, I heard of a young improvisatore,
Cenci, who had made his *début* on the very evening of my
arrival: I had a presentiment that it was you—I obtained
certainty thereof. My old friend wrote immediately to
you, without giving our name, though she mentioned our
residence. But you came not: she wrote again, without
the name, it is true; but you must have known from whom
it was sent. She wrote, 'Come, Antonio, the terror of the
last unfortunate moment in which we were together is now
well over! Come quickly! regard that as a misunderstanding—all can be made right—only do not delay to come.'

"But you came not. I ascertained that you had read
the letter, and that you had immediately set off back to
Rome. What could I believe? That your love was all
over. I, too, was proud, Antonio! the world had made
my soul vain. I did not forget you—I gave you up, and
suffered severely in so doing.

"My old friend died; her brother followed after her:
they had been as parents to me. I stood quite alone in
the world; but I was still its favourite; was young and
beautiful, and brilliant in my powers of song. That was
the last year of my life.

"I fell sick on the journey to Bologna, very sick: my
heart suffered. Antonio, I knew not that you thought
still affectionately on me; that you, at a time when the

happiness of the world deserted me, would press a kiss upon my hand. I lay sick for a year; the property which I had accumulated in the two years in which I was a singer melted away; I was poor, and doubly poor, for my voice was gone: sickness had enfeebled me. Years went on, almost seven years, and then we met—you have seen my poverty! You certainly heard how they hissed off the Annunciata who once was drawn in triumph through the streets of Rome. Bitter as my fate had my thoughts also become!

" You came to me. Like scales, all fell away from my eyes: I felt that you had sincerely loved me. You said to me that it was I who had driven you out into the world,—you knew not how I had loved you, had stretched, as it were, my arms after you! But I have seen you—your lips have glowed upon my hand as in former, better times! We are separated—I sit again alone in the little chamber: to-morrow I must leave it—perhaps Venice! Be not anxious about me, Antonio; Madonna is good and merciful! Think kindly of me: it is the dead which beseeches this from you,—Annunciata, who has loved you, and prays now, and—in heaven for you!"

My tears streamed as I read this: it was as if my heart would dissolve itself in weeping.

The remainder of the letter was written some days later. It was the last parting:—

" My want draws to an end! Madonna be praised for every joy which she has sent me: praised be she also for every woe! In my heart is death! the blood streams from it! only once more and then it is all over.

" The most beautiful and the noblest maid in Venice is your bride, the people have told me. May you be happy is the last wish of the dying! I know no one in the world to whom I could give these lines, my last farewell, except to her. My heart tells me that she will come—tells me that a noble womanly heart will not refuse the last refreshing draught to her who stands on the last step between life and death! She will come to me.

" Farewell, Antonio! my last prayer on earth, my first in heaven, will be for thee — for her who will be to thee what I never could be! There was vanity in my heart — the world's praise had set it there. Perhaps thou wouldst never have been happy with me, else the Madonna would not have divided us!

" Farewell! farewell! I feel peace in my heart — my suffering is over — death is near!

" Pray, also, thou and Maria, for me!

" ANNUNCIATA."

The deepest pain has no words. Stupefied — overwhelmed — I sat and stared at the letter, which was wet with my tears. Annunciata had loved me! She was the invisible spirit which had conducted me to Naples. The letter had been from her, and not from Santa, as I imagined. Annunciata had been ill, sunk in poverty and misery, and now she was dead — certainly dead! The little note which I had given to Fulvia, with the words, " I journey to Naples!" and which she had taken to Annunciata, lay also in the packet of letters, together with an opened letter from Bernardo, in which he sent her his farewell, and announced to her his determination to leave Rome and enter into foreign service, but without saying what.

To Maria had she given the packet of letters for me; she had called Maria my bride. That empty report had also reached Annunciata, and she had believed it, had called Maria to her. What could she have said to her?

I recalled to mind with what anxiety Maria had spoken to me, — thus she also knew what Venice imagined about us both. I had not courage to talk to her about it, and yet I must do it; she was really mine and Annunciata's good angel.

I took a gondola, and was soon in the room where Rosa and Maria sat together at their work. Maria was embarrassed; nor had I courage to say what solely and alone occupied me. I answered at random to every question. Sorrow oppressed my soul; when the kind-hearted Signora Rosa took my hand, and said, —

" There is some great trouble on your mind — have

confidence in us. If we cannot console, we can sorrow with a true friend."

"You really know every thing!" exclaimed I, giving voice to my distress.

"Maria, perhaps!" replied the aunt; "but I know as good as nothing.

"Rosa!" said Maria, beseechingly, and caught her hand.

"No, before you I have no secrets!" said I: "I will tell you every thing."

And I then told them about my poor childhood, about Annunciata, and my flight to Naples; but when I saw Maria sitting with folded hands before me, as Flaminia had sat, and as yet another being beside had sat, I was silent. I had not courage to speak of Lara and of the dream-picture in the cave, in the presence of Maria; besides, it seemed not to belong to the history of Annunciata. I went on, therefore, directly to our meeting in Venice and our last conversation. Maria pressed her hands before her eyes and wept. Rosa was silent.

"Of all this I knew nothing—divined nothing!" said she, at length. "A letter came," continued she, "from the Hospital of the Sisters of Charity to Maria; a dying woman, it said, besought her, by all the saints—by her own heart, to come to her. I accompanied her in the gondola; but as she was to be alone, I remained with the sisters whilst she went to the bed of the dying."

"I saw Annunciata," said Maria. "You have received that which she has commissioned me to convey to you."

"And she said?" I asked.

"'Give that to Antonio, the improvisatore; but, unknown to any one.' She spoke of you, spoke as a sister might—as a good spirit might speak; and I saw blood— blood upon her lips. She cast up her eyes in death, and——" Here Maria burst into tears.

I silently pressed her hand to my lips; thanked her for her pity, for her goodness, in going to Annunciata.

I hurried away, and, entering a church, prayed for the dead.

Never did I meet with such great kindness and friendship as from this moment in the house of the Podesta. I was a beloved brother to Rosa and Maria, who endeavoured to anticipate every wish ; even in the veriest trifles I saw evidences of their solicitude for me.

I visited Annunciata's grave. The churchyard was a floating ark, with high walls—an island garden of the dead. I saw a green plot before me, marked with many black crosses. I found the grave for which I sought. "Annunciata" was its sole inscription. A fresh, beautiful garland of laurels hung on the cross which marked it, unquestionably a gift from Maria and Rosa. I thanked them both for this kind attention.

How lovely was Maria in her gentleness ! What a wonderful resemblance had she to my image of beauty, Lara ! When she cast down her eyes, it seemed to me that they were, spite of the improbability, the same person.

About this time I received a letter from Fabiani. I was now in the fourth month of my residence in Venice. This astonished him. He thought that I should not spend longer time in this city, but visit Milan or Genoa. But he left it quite to me to do whatever seemed the best to myself.

That which detained me thus in Venice was that it was my city of sorrow. As such it had greeted me on my arrival, and here my life's best dream had dissolved itself in tears. Maria and Rosa were to me affectionate sisters, Poggio a love-worthy, faithful friend. I should find nobody like them ; but, nevertheless, we must part. In this my sorrow found its nourishment. Yes, hence—hence ! —that was my resolve !

I wished to prepare Rosa and Maria for it: it was necessary that they should be made acquainted with it. In the evening I was sitting with them in the great hall, where the Balcony goes over the canal. Maria wished that the servant should bring in the lamp, but Rosa thought that it was much more charming in the clear moonlight. The orange trees were so fragrant.

"Sing to us, Maria," said she ; " sing to us that beautiful song which thou learnt about the Troglodite cave. Let Antonio hear it."

Maria sang a singular, quiet cradle-song to a low, strange melody. The words and the air melted one into the other, and revealed to heart and thought the home of beauty under the ethereally clear waves.

" There is something so spiritual, so transparent, in the whole song ! " said Rosa.

" Thus must spirits reveal themselves out of the body ! " exclaimed I.

" Thus floats the world's beauty before the blind ! " sighed Maria.

" But then it is not really so beautiful when the eyes can see it ? " asked Rosa.

" Not so beautiful, and yet more beautiful ! " replied Maria.

Rosa then told me what I had already heard from Poggio, that Maria had been blind, and that her brother had given sight to her eyes. Maria mentioned his name with love and gratitude ; told me how childish her ideas had then been about the world around her—about the warm sun, about human beings, about the broad-leaved cactuses, and the great temples. " In Greece there are many more than there are here," remarked she, suddenly ; and there was a pause in her relation.

" How the strong and the beautiful in sound," continued she, " suggested to me colours. The violets were blue — the sea and heaven were blue also, they told me ; and the fragrance of the violet taught me how beautiful heaven and the sea must be. When the bodily eye is dead, the spiritual eye sees more clearly. The blind learn to believe in a spirit world. Every thing which they behold reveals itself from this ! "

I thought of Lara with the blue violets in her dark hair. The fragrance of the orange-trees led me also to Pæstum, where violets and red gilliflowers grow among the ruins of the Temple. We talked about the great beauty of nature, about the sea and the mountains, and Rosa longed after her beautiful Naples.

I then told them that my departure was near, and that I, in a few days, must leave Venice.

" You will leave us ? " said Rosa, sorrowfully.   " We
had not the slightest idea of that."

" Will you not come again to Venice ? " inquired Maria;
" come again to see your friends."

" Yes, yes, certainly ! " exclaimed I.   And although
that had not been my plan, I assured them that, from
Milan, I would return to Rome by Venice.   But did I
myself believe so ?

I visited Annunciata's grave, took a leaf from the garland which hung there, as if I should never return ; and
that was the last time that I came there !   That which
the grave preserved was dust.   In my heart existed the
impression of its beauty, and the spirit dwelt with Madonna, whose image it was.   Annunciata's grave, and the
little room where Rosa and Maria extended to me their
hands at parting, alone were witness to my tears and my
grief.

" May you find a noble wife who will supply the loss
which your heart has sustained ! " said Rosa at our parting.   " Bring her sometime to my arms.   I know that I
shall love her, as you have taught me to love Annunciata!"

" Come back happy ! " said Maria.

I kissed her hand, and her eyes rested with an expression of deep emotion upon me.   The Podesta stood with
a sparkling glass of champagne, and Poggio struck up a
merry travelling song about the rolling wheels and the
bird's song in the free landscape.   He accompanied me in
the gondola as far as Fusina.   The ladies waved their
white handkerchiefs from the balcony.

How much might happen before we saw each other
again !   Poggio was merry to an excess ; but I felt very
plainly that it was not natural. He pressed me vehemently
to his breast, and said that we would correspond industriously.   " Thou wilt tell me about thy beautiful bride, and
don't forget about our wager ! " said he.

" How canst thou jest at this moment ? " said I.   " Thou
knowest my determination ! "

   We parted.

CHAPTER XIV.

THE REMARKABLE OBJECTS IN VERONA — THE CATHEDRAL OF MILAN
— THE MEETING AT THE TRIUMPHAL ARCH OF NAPOLEON —
DREAM AND REALITY — THE BLUE GROTTO.

THE carriage rolled away. I saw the green Brenta, the weeping willows, and the distant mountains. Towards evening I arrived in Padua. The church of St. Antonius, with its seven proud domes, saluted me in the clear moonlight. All was animation and cheerfulness under the colonnade of the street; but I felt myself a stranger and alone.

In the sunshine all appeared to me still more unpleasing. Onward, yet farther onward! Travelling enlivens and chases away sorrow, thought I, and the carriage rolled forward.

The country was all a great plain, but freshly green, as the Pontine Marshes. The lofty weeping willows hung like great cascades, over the ditches; round about stood altars with the holy image of the Madonna; some of them were bleached by time; the walls even on which they were painted were sunk in ruins, but in other places also stood newly painted pictures of the Mother and Child. I remarked, that the *vetturino* lifted his hat to the new pictures: the old and faded he seemed not to observe. It amused me wonderfully. Perhaps, however, I saw more in it than there really was. Even the holy, pure image of the Madonna herself was overlooked and forgotten because the earthly colours were faded.

I passed through Vicenza, where the art of Palladio could cast no ray of light over my troubled heart, on to Verona, the first of all the cities which attracted me. The amphitheatre led me back to Rome, and reminded me of the Coliseum: it is a pretty little model of that, more distinct, and not laid waste by barbarians. The spacious colonnades are converted into warehouses, and in the middle of the arena was erected a little booth of linen and boards, where a little theatrical company, as I was told,

Y 2

gave representations. I went in the evening. The Vero-
nese sat upon the stone benches of the amphitheatre, where
their fathers had sat before them. In this little theatre
was acted " *La Cenerentola.*" It was the company with
which Annunciata had been. Aurelia performed the principal parts in the opera. The whole was miserable and
melancholy to witness. The old, antique theatre stood
like a giant around the fragile wooden booth. A *contre
bass* completely drowned the few instruments ; the public
applauded, and called for Aurelia. I hastened away. Outside all was still. The great giant-building cast a broad,
dark shadow amid the strong moonlight.

They told me of the families of the Capuleti and Mon-
tecchi, whose strife divided two loving hearts, which death
again united — the history of Romeo and Juliet. I went
up to the Palazzo Capuleti, where Romeo, for the first
time, saw his Juliet, and danced with her. The house is
now an inn. I ascended the steps up which Romeo had
stolen to love and death. The great dancing-hall stood
there yet, with its discoloured pictures on the walls, and
the great windows down to the floor ; but all around lay
hay and straw ; along the walls were ranged lime-barrels,
and in a corner were thrown down horse-furniture and
field-implements. Here had once the proudest race of
Verona floated to the sound of billowy music — here had
Romeo and Juliet dreamed love's short dream. I deeply
felt how empty is all human glory ; felt that Flaminia
had taken hold on the better part, and that Annunciata
had obtained it, and I regarded my dead as happy.

My heart throbbed as with the fire of fever ; I had no
rest. To Milan ! thought I ; there is now my home ;
and I yearned towards it. Towards the end of the month
I was there. No ! there I found that I was much better
at Venice, much more at home ! I felt that I was alone,
and yet would make no acquaintance, would deliver none
of the letters of introduction with which I had been furnished.

The gigantic theatre, with its covered boxes, which range
themselves in six rows, one above another, the whole immense space, which yet is so seldom filled, had in it, to me,

something desolate and oppressive. I once was there, and heard Donizetti's *Torquato Tasso.* To the most honoured singer, who was called for, and called for again, it seemed to me, that, like a gloomy magician, I could prophesy a future full of misery. I wished her rather to die in this her beauty and the moment of her happiness ; then the world would weep over her, and not she over the world. Lovely children danced in the ballet ; my heart bled at their beauty. Never more will I go to La Scala.

Alone, I wandered about the great city, through the shadowy streets ; alone I sat in my chamber, and began to compose a tragedy, " *Leonardo da Vinci.*" Here he had actually lived ; here I had seen his immortal work, " The Last Supper." The legend of his unfortunate love, of his beloved, from whom the convent separated him, was indeed a re-echo of my own life. I thought of Flaminia, of An_nunciata, and wrote that which my heart breathed. But I missed Poggio, missed Maria and Rosa. My sick heart longed for their affectionate attention and friendship. I wrote to them, but received no answer ; neither did Poggio keep his beautiful promise of letters and friendship : he was like all the rest. We call them friends, and, in absence, knit ourselves firmer to them.

I went daily to the cathedral of Milan, that singular mountain which was torn out of the rocks of Carrara. I saw the church for the first time in the clear moonlight ; dazzlingly white stood the upper part of it in the infinitely blue ether. Round about, wherever I looked, from every corner, upon every little tower with which the building was, as it were, overlaid, projected marble figures. Its interior dazzled me more than St. Peter's Church ; the strange gloom, the light which streamed through the painted windows — the wonderful mystical world which revealed itself here — yes, it was a church of God !

I had been a month in Milan before I ascended the roof of the church. The sun blazed upon its shining, white surface ; the towers stood aloft, like churches or chapels upon a mighty marble space. . Milan lay far below ; all around me presented themselves statues of saints and martyrs, which my eye could not see from the street below. I stood up just by the mighty figure of Christ, which terminates the whole gigantic building. Towards the north arose the lofty, dark Alps ; towards the south, the pale blue Apennines ; and between these an immense green plain, as if it were the flat Campagna of Rome changed into a blooming garden. I looked towards the east, where Venice lay. A flock of birds of passage, in a long line, like a waving riband, sped thitherward. I thought of my beloved ones there, — of Poggio, Rosa, and Maria, — and a painful yearning awoke in my breast. I could not but remember the old story which I had heard, as a child, on that evening, when I went with my mother and Mariuccia from Lake Nemi, where we had seen the bird of prey, and where Fulvia had shown herself ; the story which Angelina had told about the poor Therese of Olivano, who wasted away with care and longing after the' slender Giuseppe, and how he was drawn from his northern journey beyond the mountains, and how the old Fulvia had cooked herbs in a copper vessel, which she had made to simmer for many days over the glowing coals, until Giuseppe was seized upon by longing, and was compelled to go home, night and day ; to speed back without stop or stay, to where her vessel was boiling with holy herbs, and a lock of his and Therese's hair.

I felt that magic power within my breast which drew me away, and which is called, by the inhabitants of mountain regions, home-sickness ; but this it was not in me : Venice was really not my home. My mind was strongly affected ; I felt, as it were, ill, and descended from the roof of the church.

I found in my room a letter — it was from Poggio. At length there was a letter ! It appeared from the letter that he had written an earlier one, which, however, I had not received. Every thing was merry and well in Venice ; but Maria had been ill — very ill. They had all been anxious, and in great trouble ; but now all was over : she had left her bed, although she did not venture to go out yet. Hereupon Poggio joked with me, and inquired whether any young Milanese lady had captivated me, and besought me not to forget the champagne and our wager.

The whole letter was full of fun and merriment, very different to my own state of mind, and yet it gladdened me; it was actually as if I saw the happy, fun-loving Poggio. How in the world can we form a true judgment of men and things? It was said of him that he went with a deep, secret sorrow in his breast, and that his gaiety was only a masquerade dress; that is nature. It was said that Maria was my bride, and yet how far from my heart! I longed, it is true, for her, and for Rosa also; but nobody said that I was in love with old Signora Rosa. Oh, that I were but in Venice! Here I could not stay any longer! And again I jested over this strange voice within my breast.

In order to get rid of these thoughts, I went out of the gate above the Piazza d'Armi to the triumphal arch of Napoleon, — the Porta Sempione, as it is called. Here were the workmen in full activity. I went in through a hole in the low wall of boards which enclosed the whole of the unfinished building; two large, new horses of marble stood upon the ground, the grass grew high above the pedestals, and all around lay marble blocks and carved capitals.

A stranger stood there with his guide, and wrote down in a book the details which were given him; he looked like a man in about his thirtieth year. I passed him; he had two Neapolitan orders on his coat: he was looking up at the building — I knew him — it was Bernardo. He also saw me, sprang towards me, clasped me in his arms, and laughed aloud.

"Antonio!" exclaimed he, "thanks for the last parting; it was, indeed, a merry parting, with firing and effect! We are, however, friends now, I imagine?"

An ice-cold sensation passed through my blood.

"Bernardo," exclaimed I, "do we see one another again in the north, and near the Alps?"

"Yes, and I come from the Alps," said he, — "from the glaciers and the avalanches! I have seen the world's end up there in those cold mountains!"

He then told me that he had been the whole summer in

Switzerland. The German officers in Naples had told him so much about the greatness of Switzerland, and it was such a very easy thing to take a flight in the steam-boat from Naples to Genoa, and then one gets so far! He had been to the valley of Chamouni, ascended Mont Blanc, and the Jungfrau, " *La Bella Ragazza,*" as he called it. " She is the coldest that ever I knew," said he.

We went together to the new amphitheatre, and back to the city. He told me that he was now on his way to Genoa, to visit his bride and her parents, that he was just upon the point of becoming a sober, married man ; invited me to accompany him, and whispered, laughing, into my ear, —

" You tell me nothing about my tame bird, about our little singer, and all those histories ! You have now learned yourself that they belong to a young heart's history; my bride might otherwise easily get a headach, and she is quite too dear to me for that ! "

It was impossible for me to mention Annunciata to him, for I felt that he had never loved her as I had done.

" Now, go with me ! " urged he. " There are pretty girls in Genoa, and now you are become old and rational, and have got some taste for these things. Naples has been the making of you ! Is it not so ? In about three days I shall set off. Go with me, Antonio ! "

" But I set off to-morrow morning also," said I, involuntarily. I had not thought of this before, but now the thing was said.

" Where ? " inquired he,

" To Venice ! " replied I.

" But you can change your plan ! " continued he, and pressed his own very much upon me.

I assured him so strongly about the necessity of my journey, that I also began to see myself that I must go.

I had within myself neither peace nor rest, and arranged every thing for my journey, as if it had been for a long time my determination.

It was the invisible guidance of God's wonderful Providence which led me away from Milan. It was impossible for me to sleep at night; I lay for some hours on my bed in a short, wild fever-dream, in a state of waking sickness. " To Venice ! " cried the voice within my breast.

I saw Bernardo for the last time ; bade him to salute his bride for me : and then flew back again whither I had come two months before.

At some moments it seemed to me as if I had taken poison, which thus fomented in my blood. An inexplicable anxiety drove me onwards — what coming evil was at hand ?

I approached Fusina, saw again Venice, with its grey walls, the tower of St. Mark's, and the Lagunes ; and then all at once vanished my strange unrest, my yearning and anxiety, and there arose within me another feeling, — what shall I call it ? — shame of myself, displeasure, dissatisfaction. I could not comprehend what it was that I wanted here, felt how foolishly I had behaved, and it seemed to me that every body must say so, and that every body would ask me, " What art thou doing again in Venice ? "

I went to my old lodgings ; dressed myself in haste, and felt that I must immediately pay a visit to Rosa and Maria, however enfeebled and excited I might feel.

What, however, would they say to my arrival ?

The gondola neared the palace ; what strange thoughts can enter the human breast ! What if thou shouldst now enter at a moment of festivity and rejoicing ? What if Maria be a bride ? But, what then ? I really did not love her ! I had said so a thousand times to myself ; a thousand times had assured Poggio, and every one else who had said so, that I did not !

I saw once more the grey-green walls, the lofty windows, and my heart trembled with yearning. I entered the house. Solemnly and silently the servant opened the door, expressed no surprise at my arrival. It seemed to me that quite another subject occupied him.

" The Podesta is always at home to you, Signore ! " said he.

A stillness, as of death, reigned in the great hall ; the curtains were drawn. Here had Desdemona lived, thought

I ; here, perhaps, suffered ; and yet Othello suffered more
severely than she did.   How came I now to think of this
old history ?

J went to Rosa's apartment ; here also the curtains
were drawn — it was in a half-darkness, and I felt agaiı
that strange anxiety which had accompanied me in th·
whole journey, and had driven me back to Venice.   A
trembling went through all my limbs, and I was obligeċ
to support myself that I did not fall.

The Podesta then came in ; he embraced me, and
seemed glad to see me again.   I inquired after Maria and
Rosa — and it seemed to me that he became very grave.

" They are gone away ! " said he ; " have made a little
journey with another family to Padua.   They will return
either to-morrow or the day after."

I know not wherefore, but I felt as if I doubted his
word ; perhaps it was the fever in my blood, the wild
fever, which my pain of mind had increased, and which
now approached the period of its breaking forth.   This it
was which had operated upon my whole spiritual being,
and had occasioned the journey back.

At the supper-table I missed Rosa and Maria ; nor was
the Podesta as he used to be.   It was, he said, a lawsuit
which had rather put him out of sorts, but it was nothing
of consequence.

" Poggio is not any where to be met with either," said
he,   " All misfortunes come together ; and you are ill !
Yes, it is a merry soirée ! — we must see if the wine cannot cheer us up !   But you are pale as death ! " exclaimed
he, all at once, and I felt that every thing vanished from
my sight.   I had fallen into a state of unconsciousness.

It was a fever, a violent nervous fever.

I only know that I found myself in a comfortable,
darkened chamber ; the Podesta was sitting beside me, and
said that I should remain with him, and that I should soon
be well again.   Rosa, he said, should nurse me ; but he
never mentioned Maria.

I was in a state of consciousness, as it were between
sleep and awake.   After a time I heard it said that the
ladies had arrived, and that I should soon see them ; and

I did see Rosa, but she was much troubled. It seemed to me that she wept, but that, indeed, could not be for me, for I felt myself already much stronger.

It was evening; there prevailed an anxious silence around me, and yet a movement. They did not answer my questions distinctly; my hearing seemed quickened; I heard that many people were moving about in the hall below me; and I heard, too, the strokes of the oars of many gondolas; and the reality was made known to me as I half slumbered: they imagined that I was asleep.

Maria was dead. Poggio had mentioned to me her illness, and had said that now she was recovered, but a relapse had caused her death. She was going to be buried this evening, but all this they had concealed from me. Maria's death, like an invisible power, had weighed upon my life! For her was that strange anxiety which I had felt; but I had come too late; I should behold her no more. She was now in the world of spirits, to which she had always belonged. Rosa had certainly adorned her coffin with violets: the blue, fragrant flowers which she loved so much, now that she slept with the flowers.

I lay immoveably still, as in a death-sleep, and heard Rosa thank God for it: she then went away from me. There was not a single creature in the room; the evening was dark, and I felt my strength wonderfully invigorated. I knew that in the church *de' Frati* was the burial-place of the Podesta's family, and that during the night the dead would be placed before the altar. I must see her — I rose up — my fever was gone — I was strong. I threw my cloak around me — no one saw me, and I entered a gondola.

My whole thought was of the dead. The church-doors were closed, because it was long after the Ave Maria. I knocked at the sexton's door; he knew me, had seen me before in the church with the Podesta's family, and showed me within the graves of Canova and Titian.

" Do you wish to see the dead ?" asked he, guessing my thoughts; " she lies at the altar in the open coffin; to-morrow she will be placed in the chapel."

He lighted candles, took out a bunch of keys, and opened a little side-door; our footsteps re-echoed through the lofty,

silent vault. He ·remained behind, and I went slowly
through the long empty passage ; a lamp burned feebly and
dimly upon the altar before the image of the Madonna. The
white marble statues around the tomb of Canova stood like
the dead in their shrouds, silently and with uncertain outlines. Before the principal altar three lights were burn‗
ing. I felt no anxiety, no pain — it was as if I myself
belonged also to the dead, and that I was now entering into
my own peculiar home. I approached the altar ; the fragrance of violets was diffused around ; the rays of light fell
from the lamp into the open coffin down upon the dead. It
was Maria ; she seemed to sleep ; she lay like a marble
image of beauty scattered over with violets. The dark
hair was bound upon the forehead, and was adorned with a
bouquet of violets ; the closed eyes, the image of perfect
peace and beauty, seized upon my soul. It was Lara whom
I saw, as she sat in the ruins of the temple, when I impressed a kiss upon her brow ; but she was a dead marble
statue, without life and warmth.

" Lara ! " sighed I, and sank down before the coffin,
" in death thy closed eyes, thy silent lips speak to me : I
know thee — have known thee in Maria ! My last thought
in life is death with thee ! "

My heart found relief in tears ; I wept ; my tears fell
upon the countenance of the dead, and I kissed the tears
away.

" All have left me ! " sighed I ; " thou also, the last of
whom my heart dreamed ! Not as for Annunciata, not as
for Flaminia, burned my soul for thee ! — it was the pure,
true love, which angels feel, that my heart cherished for
thee ; and I did not believe that it was love, because it
was more spiritual than my outward thought ! Never have
I understood it — never ventured to express ·it to thee !
Farewell, thou ! the last, my heart's bride ! Blessed be
thy slumber ! "

I pressed a kiss upon her brow.

" My soul's bride ! " continued I, " to no woman will
I give my hand. Farewell ! farewell ! "

I took off my ring, placed it on Lara's finger, and lifted
my eyes to the invisible God above us. At that moment

a horror passed through my blood, for it seemed to me as if the hand of the dead returned the pressure of mine ; it was no mistake. I fixed my eyes upon her ; the lips moved ; every thing around me was in motion : I felt that my hair rose upon my head. Horror, the horror of death, paralyzed my arms and my feet ; I could not escape.

" I am cold," whispered a voice behind me.

" Lara ! Lara ! I cried, and all was night before my eyes ; but it seemed to me that the organ played a soft, touching melody. A hand passed softly over my head ; rays of light forced their way to my eyes ; every thing became so clear, so bright ! ——

" Antonio !" whispered Rosa, and I saw her. The lamp burned upon the table, and beside my bed lay a kneeling figure, and wept. I saw then that I beheld reality before me, that my horror was only that of wild fever-dream.

" Lara ! Lara !" exclaimed I. She pressed her hands before her eyes. But what had I said in my delirium ? This thought stood vividly before my remembrance, and I read in Maria's eyes that she had been witness to my heart's confessions.

" The fever is over," whispered Rosa.

" Yes ; I feel myself much better—much better," exclaimed I, and looked at Maria. She rose up, and was about to leave the róom.

" Do not go from me !" I prayed, and stretched forth my hands after her.

She remained, and stood silently blushing before me.

" I dreamt that you were dead," said I.

' It was a delirious dream !" exclaimed Rosa, and ₂anded to me the medicine which the physician had pre‗ scribed.

" Lara, Maria, hear me !" I cried. " It is no delirious dream ! I feel life returned back to my blood ! My whole life must then have been a strange dream. We have seen one another before ! You have heard my voice before, at Pæstum, at Capri. You know it again, Lara ! I feel it ; life is so short, why, then, not offer to each other our hands in this brief meeting ?"

I extended my hand towards her; she pressed it to her lips.

" I love thee; have always loved thee!" said I; and, without a word, she sank on her knees beside me.

Love, says the Mythe, brought chaos into order, and created the world. Before every loving heart creation renews itself. From Maria's eyes I drank in life and health. She loved me. When a few days were passed, we stood alone in the little room, where the orange-trees breathed forth fragrance from the balcony. Here had she sung to me, but in softer tones, more spiritual and deeper, sounded to my ear the confession of the noblest of hearts. I had made no mistake; Lara and Maria were one and the same person.

" I have always loved thee!" said she. " Thy song awoke longing and pain in my breast, when I was blind and solitary with my dreams, and knew only the fragrance of the violets. And the warm sun! how its beams burned thy kiss into my forehead — into my heart! The blind possess only a spiritual world; and in that I beheld thee! The night after I heard thy improvisation in the Temple of Neptune, at Pæstum, I had a singular dream, which blended itself with reality. A gipsy-woman had told me my fortune — that I should again receive my sight. I dreamed about her, dreamed that she said I must go with Angelo, my old foster-father, and sail across the sea to Capri; that in the Witch's Cave I should receive again the light of my eyes; that the Angel of Life would give me herbs, which, like Tobias's, should enable my eyes again to behold God's world. The dream was repeated again the same night. I told it to Angelo, but he only shook his head.

" The next night, in the morning-hour, he dreamed it himself, on which he said, ' Blessed be the power of Madonna; the bad spirits must even obey her!'

" We arose; he spread the sail, and we flew across the sea. The day passed, evening came, and night, but I was in a strange world, heard how the Angel of Life pronounced my name — and the voice sounded like thine.

He gave us herbs and great riches — treasure collected from the different countries of the world.

" We boiled the herbs ; but no light came to my eyes. One day, however, Rosa's brother came to Pæstum ; he came into our cottage, where I lay, and, affected by the yearning desire which I expressed to see God's beautiful world, he promised me sight to my eyes, took me with him to Naples, and there I saw the great magnificence of life. He and Rosa became very fond of me ; they opened to me another and a more beautiful world — that of the soul. I remained with them ; they called me Maria, after a beloved sister, who was dead in Greece.

" One day Angelo brought to me the rich treasure, and said that it was mine. His death, he said, was at hand ; that he had expended his last strength in bringing me my own inheritance ; and his words were the last of a dying man. I saw him expire, — him, the only protector of my poverty !

" One evening, Rosa's brother inquired from me very seriously about my old foster-father, and the treasure which he had brought. I knew no more than that which he had said, that the spirit in the glittering cave had given him this. I knew that we had always lived in poverty. Angelo could not be a pirate — he was so pious ; every little gift he divided with me."

I then told her how singularly her life's adventure had blended itself with mine ; how I had seen her with the old man in the wonderful grotto. That the old man himself took the heavy vessel I would not tell her, but I told her that I gave her the herbs.

" But," exclaimed she, " the spirit sank into the earth as it reached to me the herbs ! So Angelo told me."

" It appeared so to him," I returned ; " I was debilitated ; my feet could not sustain me ; I sank on my knees, and then fainted among the long green grass."

That wondrously glittering world in which we had met was the indissoluble — the firm knot between the supernatural and the real.

" Our love is of the spiritual world !" exclaimed I ; " all our love tended towards the world of spirits ; towards that we advance in our earthly life; wherefore, then, not believe in it? It is precisely the great reality!" And I pressed Lara to my heart; she was beautiful as she was the first time I saw her.

" I recognised thee by thy voice when I first heard thee in Venice," said she: "my heart impelled me towards thee; I fancy that even in the church, before the face of the Mother of God, I should have fallen at thy feet. I saw thee here; learned to value thee more and more; was conducted, as it were, a second time into thy life's concerns, when Annunciata hailed me as thy bride! But thou repelledst me; said that thou wouldst never love again! —never wouldst give thy hand to any woman!—never mentioned Lara, Pæstum, or Capri, when thou relatedst to us the singular destiny of thy life! Then I believed that thou never hadst loved me; that thou hadst forgotten that which did not lie near to thy heart!"

I impressed a kiss of reconciliation upon her hand, and said how strangely her glance had closed my lips. Not until my body lay bound, as it were, for the grave, and my spirit itself floated into the world of spirits, in which our love was so wonderfully knit together, had I ventured to express the thoughts of my heart.

No stranger, only Rosa and the Podesta knew of the happiness of our love. How gladly would I have told it to Poggio. He had, during my sickness, visited me many times during the day. I saw that he looked extremely pale, when, after I had left my room, I pressed him to my heart in the clear light of the sun.

" Come to us this evening, Poggio," said the Podesta to him; " but come without fail. You will only find here the family, Antonio, and two or three other friends."

All was festally arranged.

" It is really as if it were to be a name's day," said Poggio.

The Podesta conducted him and the other friends to the little chapel, where Lara gave me her hand. A bouquet of blue violets was fastened in her dark hair. The blind girl of Pæstum stood seeing, and doubly beautiful, before me. She was mine.

All congratulated us. The rejoicing was great. Poggio sang merrily, and drank health upon health.

"I have lost my wager," said I, "but I lose it gladly, because my loss is the winning of my happiness," and I impressed a kiss on Lara's lips.

The gladness of the others sounded like tumultuous music; mine and Lara's was silent as the night which embraced us when all were gone.

"Life is no dream," thought I; "and the happiness of love is a reality," exclaimed I, as heart to heart lost all thought in happiness which God only can infuse into a human breast.

Two days after the bridal, Rosa accompanied us from Venice. We went to the estate which had been purchased for Maria. I had not seen Poggio since the bridal evening. I now received a letter from him, which said merely, —

"I won the wager, and yet I lost!"

He was not to be met with in Venice. After some time my conjecture became certainty; he had loved Lara. Poor Poggio! thy lips sang of gladness, but thoughts of death filled thy heart!

Francesca thought Lara very charming; I myself had won infinitely in this journey, and she, Excellenza, and Fabiani, all applauded my choice. Habbas Dahdah even smiled over his whole face as he congratulated me.

Of the old acquaintance there is yet living, in 1837, Uncle Peppo; he sits upon the Spanish steps, where, for many years, certainly he will say his " *bon giorno!* "

On the 6th of March, 1834, a great many strangers were assembled in the Hôtel at Pagani, on the island of Capri. The attention of all was attracted by a young Calabrian lady of extraordinary beauty, whose lovely dark eyes rested on her husband, who gave her his arm. It was I and Lara. We had now been married three happy years, and were visiting, on a journey to Venice, the Island of Capri, where the most wonderful event of our life occurred, and where it would clear itself up.

In one corner of the room stood an elderly lady, and held a little child in her arms. A foreign gentleman, tolerably tall and somewhat pale, with strong features, and dressed in a blue frock-coat, approached the child, laughed with it, and was transported with its loveliness; he spoke French, but to the child a few Italian words; gave merry leaps to make it laugh; and then gave it his mouth to kiss. He asked what was its name? and the old lady, my beloved Rosa, said it was Annunciata.

" A lovely name!" said he, and kissed the little one— mine and Lara's.

I advanced to him; he was Danish: there was still a countryman of his in the room, a grave little man, with an intelligent look, and dressed in a white surtout. I accosted them politely; they were countrymen of Federigo and the great Thorwaldsen. The first, I found, was in Denmark, the latter in Rome; he, indeed, belongs to Italy, and not to the cold, dark north.

We went down to the shore, and took one of those little boats which are calculated to take out strangers to the other side of the island. Each boat held but two persons: one sat at each end, and the rower in the middle.

I saw the clear water below us. It saluted my remembrance with its ethereal clearness. The rower worked his oars rapidly, and the boat in which I and Lara were seated flew forward with the speed of an arrow. We soon lost sight of the amphitheatre-like side of the island, where the green vineyards and orange-trees crown the cliffs; and, now, the rocky wall rose up perpendicularly towards the sky. The water was blue as burning sulphur; the blue billows struck against the cliffs, and over the blood-red sea-apples which grow below.

We were now on the opposite side of the island, and saw only the perpendicular cliffs, and in them, above the surface of the water, a little opening, which seemed not large enough for our boat.

" The Witch's Cave!" exclaimed I, and all the recollections of it awoke in my soul.

" Yes, the Witch's Cave!" said the rower; " it was called so formerly; but now people know what it is!"

He then told us about the two German painters, Fries and Kopisch, who three years before had ventured to swim into it, and thus discovered the extraordinary beauty of the place, which now all strangers visit.

We neared the opening, which raised itself scarcely more than an ell above the blue shining sea. The rower took in his oars ; and we were obliged to stretch ourselves out in the boat, which he guided with his hands, and we glided into a dark depth below the monstrous rocks which were laved by the great Mediterranean. I heard Lara breathe heavily ; there was something strangely fearful in it ; but, in hardly more than a moment, we were in an immensely large vault, where all gleamed like the ether. The water below us was like a blue burning fire, which lighted up the whole. All around was closed ; but, below the water, the little opening by which we had entered prolonged itself almost to the bottom of the sea, to forty fathoms in depth, and expanded itself to about the same width. By this means the strong sunshine outside threw a light within upon the floor of the grotto, and streaming in now like a fire through the blue water, seemed to change it into burning spirit. Every thing gave back the reflection of this ; the rocky arch — all seemed as if formed of consolidated air, and to dissolve away into it. The water-drops which were thrown up by the motion of the oars, dropped red, as if they had been fresh rose-leaves.

It was a fairy world, the strange realm of the mind. Lara folded her hands ; her thoughts were like mine. Here, had we been once before ; — here, had the sea-robbers forgotten their treasure, when no one ventured to approach the spot. Now was every supernatural appearance cleared up in reality, or reality had passed over into the spiritual world, as it does always here in human life, where every thing, from the seed of the flower to our own immortal souls, appears a miracle ; — and yet man will not believe in miracles !

The little opening to the cave which had shone like a clear star was now darkened for a moment, and then the other boats seemed to ascend as if from the deep. They came into the cave. All was contemplation and devotion.

The Protestant, as well as the Catholic, felt here that miracles still exist.

"The water rises!" said one of the seamen. "We must go out, or else the opening will be closed; and then we shall have to remain here till the water falls again!"

We left the singularly beaming cave; the great open sea lay outstretched before us, and behind us the dark opening of the Grotto Azzurra

THE END.

LONDON:
SPOTTISWOODE and SHAW,
New-street-Square.

ImTheStory.com

Personalized Classic Books in many genre's

Unique gift for kids, partners, friends, colleagues

Customize:

- Character Names
- Upload your own front/back cover images (optional)
- Inscribe a personal message/dedication on the
  inside page (optional)

Customize many titles Including
- Alice in Wonderland
- Romeo and Juliet
- The Wizard of Oz
- A Christmas Carol
- Dracula
- Dr. Jekyll & Mr. Hyde
- And more...

CPSIA information can be obtained at www.ICGtesting.com
Printed in the USA
LVOW01s0814300913

354613LV00008B/428/P